Rembrandt paintings

REMBRANDT

Horst Gerson

PROFESSOR OF HISTORY OF ART, UNIVERSITY OF GRONINGEN

PAINTINGS

An Artabras Book

HARRISON HOUSE • PUBLISHERS • NEW YORK

Translated by HEINZ NORDEN
Edited by GARY SCHWARTZ
Around Rembrandt by D.W.BLOEMENA
Designed by FRITS STOEPMAN

The text of this edition is an unchanged reprint
of the 1968 edition. While the selection and order of
the illustrations have remained the same, more than fifty
new color plates have been added to the "Catalogue
Illustration" section from pages 173-455.

ISBN 0.517.254204

© Copyright 1968 by Meulenhoff International, Amsterdam

Library of Congress Card Catalogue Number 78–8193

Printed in Japan

CONTENTS

I wish to express my thanks to my many friends and colleagues in the museum world, the custodians of Rembrandt's work. They have been endlessly generous in helping me to collect the material for this book and enriching my knowledge with their advice and criticism.

A special word of thanks to Gary Schwartz. His constantly devoted collaboration of the past two years, from the preparatory stages of this work until its printing, went far beyond the official obligation of any editor.

Miss M. Korpershoek, Mrs. G. J. A. L. Niemeijer-Dotinga, Miss Yvonne M. Rijdemark, and Miss A. T. Smit have helped me by making extracts from art historical literature. The General Index is by Mrs. M. J. H. Singelenberg. The Catalogue has benefitted from the expert care of Keith Roberts.

Footnotes to the text begin on page 485. Numbers in square brackets [ ] refer alike to the Catalogue, pp. 488–504, and to the Catalogue Illustrations, pp. 169–456.

THE YEAR 1956 witnessed many commemorations of the 350th anniversary of Rembrandt's birth. Great exhibitions were held in the Netherlands, in Stockholm, and in Leningrad and Moscow, where many of Rembrandt's scattered works were brought together. Small national exhibitions were held elsewhere—even in China, which had to make do with photographs. This plethora of shows must have given hundreds of thousands occasion for another look at Rembrandt's paintings, drawings, and etchings—indeed, for many younger people it may well have been the first occasion. Scholars too seized the opportunity to deepen our knowledge of Rembrandt and the history of his reputation—they studied eulogies and appreciations dating from previous "Rembrandt years"; to make this task easier for future scholars, one far-sighted critic recorded the whole story of that Rembrandt year itself.[1] Now, on the eve of another Rembrandt commemoration, the 300th anniversary of the master's death, it may be well to re-examine just what happened in 1956, and what consequences resulted.

Quite unlike the noisy celebrations in 1906, there were virtually no festivities 50 years later. It was the shows that were the real events of the year—the opportunity to stand face to face with Rembrandt's originals. The exhibition catalogues were not notably liberal with their explanatory remarks, while the daily press and popular magazines and books lavished on the public an endless stream of writings on Rembrandt. This is quite typical of the art life of our day, both in respect of the presentation of exhibitions and the way they are received. Those most familiar with works of art through daily contact tend to be reticent and objective. Museum people, moreover, are involved in an unending sequence of shows and simply lack the time to delve and contemplate.[2] On the other hand, the mass media with their sense of timeliness and spontaneity have a much greater hold on the public than ever before.

Of course, matters are not all black-and-white, as may appear from this brief review. For one thing, an admirable kind of teamwork has sprung up among art historians, especially in bringing to the public responsible reports on "esthetic creation in word and picture," to abridge the subtitle of a Dutch radio program on art. Art criticism, moreover, has grown into a separate discipline, and this has profoundly affected our views of Rembrandt—or more accurately, the critical methods by which we arrive at our views.

The mystique of art has begun to be debunked, and surely all of us can breathe a sigh of relief over that. One element, by the way, that has assisted this process is the declining share of German interpretations as against critical work done elsewhere in the world. Aside from demystification, there has been increasing use of iconographic analysis to take a very close look at Rembrandt's work. In this approach themes are studied—the artistic and cultural factors that determine their choice, their changing forms and meanings.[3] Taking a date about halfway between those two Rembrandt anniversaries, 1906 and 1956, and comparing the publications before and after, we at once become aware of how art criticism has changed.

The modern dispassionate approach deprecates the "impressionism" of older generations. How quickly the change came in the case of Rembrandt may be seen by the example of the views of Schmidt-Degener. As recently as 1953, the Dutch art historian J.G. van Gelder called the attention of his British colleagues to the "excellent essays" of that critic, though van Gelder's own method of work was far more advanced than Schmidt-Degener's. Only a few years later van Gelder's pupil J.A. Emmens began his work of unscrambling our falsified Rembrandt image with a biting critique of what he called Schmidt-Degener's irresponsible distortions of history.[4] The grandly conceived work of Emmens may well constitute the definitive chapter in a whole series of studies of the changing image of Rembrandt over the centuries.[5]

Yet the closer we read the works of the older Rembrandt scholars now under fire—whose heirs we must regard ourselves—the more painfully we come to realize that their failings are our own. Limitations in historical perspective, though their boundaries may shift from generation to generation, keep on interfering with our understanding of the past. Van de Waal put it concisely in his Rembrandt study of 1956:

It seems to be a law of history that each ensuing generation is able to perceive but a part of the complex phenomenon we call the past—its own part.

The gist of grasping the meaning of Rembrandt's art in contemporary terms, then, is to apprehend those aspects of it to which we have access. A.B. de Vries has pointed out that this limitation has its positive side. We may, for example, be coming much closer to Rembrandt's Bible pictures than earlier generations whose greater orthodoxy in religious matters circumscribed the way they looked at works of religious art.[6] Emmens, by contrast, draws a more depressing conclusion. Looking at Rembrandt's art in terms of our own age, he insists, cannot but blind us to his significance to his own age, the presumed aim of our study. Emmens seeks to break this deadlock by analyzing the art concepts that were dominant in Rembrandt's time and thus helped determine Rembrandt's own art concepts. This is not the place to argue the merits and limitations of that "analytical" method. In Holland the debate between those who defend the propriety of an approach in terms of today and those who favor a more uncompromising scholarship rid of all anachronisms flares up anew whenever an important publication or exhibition brings the problem to the fore.[7] It goes without saying that elsewhere, too, scholars have delighted in debunking the myths perpetuated by slavish adherence to traditional views of art and artists.

When one puts this controversy in the total context of present-day art criticism, it seems to reflect a certain reluctance to deal with works of art in terms of their esthetic—or even historical—essence, and a preference for investigating only the older opinions about the works. Many scholars seem to wish to avoid the embarrassingly untheoretical element of art study—connoisseurship. There is an attempt to escape from the realm of art itself with its many contradictions into a neighboring realm more scientific in appearance—the history of art interpretation. The skepticism of this approach is all to the good, encouraging a praiseworthy sobriety in evaluating our progress in understanding the history of art. But while this may foster caution and modesty, it contrib-

utes nothing to advancing our knowledge of style. No matter how distorted the Rembrandt image of the art historians who preceded us may have been, our mere knowledge that this is so is not particularly productive. We must take up their work—to enter into Rembrandt's work and to test, cleanse, and enrich our knowledge of it. Connoisseurship must play an important role here; and although it is often belittled, it is at least as important in clarifying our picture of Rembrandt and deepening our insight as is the analytical approach to the views of art historians, living and dead.

On the eve of the Rembrandt commemorations of 1969 it may be well to temper our sense of joyous anticipation. Aware that our insight is limited, we must display a seemly modesty—listen attentively rather than make brash claims. Yet while we would avoid the errors of those who came before us, while we would espouse objectivity, we shall in no way relinquish the living experience of steeping ourselves in Rembrandt's works. The recognition of human limitations—our own as well as our predecessors'—should not seem a counsel of despair. With all the diligence of which we are capable, we shall carry on the task of studying the surviving records and works of art in order to formulate our own picture of Rembrandt. Surely this is a more vital expression of our real concern with Rembrandt than the erection of a public statue, an instinctive gesture (carried out in 1852) doomed to earn the scorn of the next generation.[8]

Dutch Painting in the Early 17th Century

It is part and parcel of the human mind to seek to bring order into the past, to gain insight into history. To that end we always strive to arrange the sweep of events by neat time segments. Historians are fond of using centuries as their measuring rods, and art historians follow in their footsteps. Even the style periods the art historians have adopted—tags like the Renaissance or the Baroque—are fitted into these hundred-year divisions, not without some difficulty; and the turn of a century, then, always seems to present itself as a period of transition.

We know quite well, of course, that this way of chopping up history is capricious; and we keep on hoping that as we subdivide time into smaller and smaller units, we somehow come closer to historical truth and thus refine our originally crude conceptions. But we do so only at the cost of losing the larger view. The meaningful texture of time goes by the board. Ultimately, we discover that every instant in history—and, of course, in the history of art as well—is incredibly complex, whether we place it in the middle of an era or at a time of transition.

Art history resists order just as stubbornly as history in general; and thus we find ourselves in the end reduced to the familiar expedient of sticking to the centuries. In recording the story of Dutch art, a starting date of "around 1600" exerts a special fascination, particularly on anyone who seeks to outline the antecedents of Rembrandt's art; for how can one comprehend the art of a painter who began his work around 1625 without studying his teachers and precursors? One is almost bound to wind up with an introductory inquiry that begins with the century. Indeed, the Dutch victory over the Spaniards at Nieuwpoort in 1600 may well serve as our opening gun; and the Twelve Years' Truce, which began in 1609, is a kind of historical landmark, signaling the incipient independence of the northern Low Countries, the birth of a new state.

To the art historian, the turn of the century reveals itself as a time of transition from Mannerism to—well, something else. Unfortunately, this new element cannot conveniently be put under a single, simple term. As far as Mannerism itself is concerned, art scholars have told us quite clearly within the last decades what it is. Dutch Mannerism as such or, to be more specific, late Dutch Mannerism, which reached its pinnacle of refinement just before 1600, is a style of extreme agitation and complexity, with the

spatial elements kept deliberately unresolved (Illustration a, p. 14). Its outstanding characteristic is tension—a tension instinct in every figure, from head to toe. What we have here is Mannerism as the art of *Formauferlegung*, "imposition of form," to use Pinder's locution. Everything seems frozen at a moment of supreme tension. Neither mood nor motion is resolved. All too often there is a kind of gelid surface smoothness from which not a trace of emotional warmth emanates. Karel van Mander, Abraham Bloemaert, Cornelis Cornelisz. van Haarlem, Hendrick Goltzius—all these were closely related in style, expression, and power during these years. What ties this group even more closely together stylistically is a common derivation from the art of Bartholomeus Spranger, to whom lesser artists also owed allegiance. Spranger came from Antwerp but studied art in Italy. It was by virtue of his influence that Dutch Mannerism took on certain international pretensions.

Soon after 1600 the element of tension vanished. What was left was a certain lame and expansive classicism informed with the forthright naïveté that seems to be inherent in the Dutch character. Whether one compares the various similar pictures of Cornelis Cornelisz. van Haarlem with one another or with related hands, the overall impression is much the same (Illustration b, p. 14). The trend is invariably away from agitation and in the direction of tranquillity, from tension to relaxation, from mannered calligraphy toward clear lettering. There are, of course, nuances—Mannerists like Joachim Wttewael clung to their labored style for some time after 1600; others, like Abraham Bloemaert, passed through several phases and ultimately projected a more vital vision of classicism; or like Hendrick Goltzius, an arch-Manneristic graphic artist before 1600 who began painting only after that date, and whose work as a painter goes beyond Mannerism.

Yet this was not the generation that shaped the art of the new century, even though Abraham Bloemaert, for one, lived past the century's halfway mark to 1656, enjoying great success and productivity. It was the classicists, both old and young, who invested the Dutch art scene at this time with greater richness and complexity. One member of the younger generation was Rembrandt's teacher Pieter Lastman (1583–1633). His career is typical of the group of painters who have been lumbered with the hapless desig-

ANNA ACCUSED BY TOBIT OF STEALING THE KID [4▶

Pieter Lastman CORIOLANUS
Dublin, Trinity College

nation of "Pre-Rembrandtists." Only his very earliest works, a few drawings dating from 1602, still show Mannerist features. His style actually took form in Italy, around 1605, under the influence of Adam Elsheimer. Caravaggio meant nothing to him; but he developed Elsheimer's style with its minisculé figures into a dramatic form of classicism marked by sweeping, expressive, and harmonious movement. A fine sense of sinuous line, figures modeled in depth, robes that almost seem to rustle, boldly conceived landscape backgrounds—all these elements are authoritatively blended into an impressive narrative style (see Illustration). What Lastman did was, in effect, to introduce into Dutch art a distinctive version of the new classicistic style that was also making its appearance in Flemish art in those years in the work of Abraham Janssens and Peter Paul Rubens.[1]

There were other groupings that played a part in the years spanned by Rembrandt's youth. One of them was the movement that modeled itself on Caravaggio. It actually took root only in Utrecht, though its influence was felt in Haarlem and Amsterdam as well. The year 1620 is the earliest date we can assign to any Dutch painting in this style—a puzzling phenomenon, for the member of this group who seems to our eyes the most talented and sensitive, Hendrick Terbrugghen (1588?–1629), had returned from Rome as early as 1615. We do not have even a single example of his work done in Italy. The most successful painter of the group in question, at least to his contemporaries, was surely Gerard Honthorst (1590–1656). During the twenties, Honthorst and Terbrugghen served almost as missionaries of the Italian visual and technical approach, though their art lacked the sheer inspiration of Caravaggio's revolutionary realism and all but ecstatic expressive power (Illustrations, p. 16; a, p. 20). They did take over his lighting effects, for the sake of their glitter and glamour. Of Caravaggio's deeply molded limbs and sweeping gestures, all they found congenial to the Dutch taste was the sensitive and sensuous surface treatment. Honthorst invested his representations of everyday life with a touch of splendor and elegance that lifted them beyond crude realism. As for Terbrugghen, he also painted sentimental religious scenes, probably in an attempt to appeal to Dutch Roman Catholics. During his lifetime, however, Terbrugghen's work never exerted a particularly widespread influence. His early death, together with the rise of Rembrandt's art in Am-

sterdam and Frans Hals' popular style in Haarlem, kept his work rather closely confined to the immediate environs of Utrecht —and even there he was overshadowed by Honthorst.[2]

The dying spasms of Mannerism, the passing fad for Caravaggio, the growing impact of classicism—these were the stylistic currents that set the tone of Dutch painting at the outset of the new century, at least for painting in the grand style, history painting. This was the term used for all paintings with themes from religious or secular history, and we shall use it here in this sense. It is a good deal harder to elucidate the stylistic growth of the more unassuming genres—landscape, portraiture, still life— with the help of the same phases and concepts. Yet this does not mean that the emergence of the genres into full autonomy failed to put its mark on the art situation in Holland in the early years of the century.

The various genres bred their own specialists and styles, swept in varying degree by the impact of Mannerism, "Caravaggism," and classicism. In portraiture, for example, there never was a Caravaggesque style or, at least in the Netherlands, a developed late Mannerist school. Portraiture was dominated rather by a robust naturalism of classicist stamp, along lines pioneered by Rubens; and here, too, it was the "universal" Rembrandt rather than the "Dutch" Frans Hals who modified and deepened the character of portraiture later in the century.

It is perhaps in the burgeoning sphere of landscape painting that we can best follow the rise of a peculiarly Dutch approach. As described by Kenneth Clark, there are landscapes of fantasy, stemming from Italo-Flemish tradition (Illustration, p. 60); and (particularly in drawings) landscapes of fact, transcribing with spontaneous visual pleasure what the eye has seen; while still other landscapes are romantic in conception, Italianate views charged with imaginative meaning.[3]

Nor can still life be captured in purely stylistic terms. It often blends hidden symbolism with simple joy in realistic depiction and with reverence of God's wisdom, manifested even in the minor and unassuming works of his creation. What then are the aspects that truly comprise the character of Dutch painting? Is it the naïve joy in observation, a more thoughtful contemplation of the misleading appearances of the natural world, or the sentimental simplicity of Lastman and his circle? Is it the fondness for

a Cornelis Cornelisz. van Haarlem THE FALL OF MAN. 1592
Amsterdam, Rijksmuseum

b Cornelis Cornelisz. van Haarlem THE FALL OF MAN. 1622
Hamburg, Kunsthalle

minutiae or the picturesque overall mood? Both the propensity
for minute observation and the wealth of realistic interpretation
seem to reflect the particularism of Dutch urban culture. The
consensus in formal values that resulted from the patronage of
church and nobility had vanished. To Calvinism, the state religion, all that was sensuous was suspect. Indeed, all Dutch art of
this period may be said to bear a Calvinist tinge in one respect,
in that it shunned excessive ostentation and pathos—until Rembrandt, during the thirties, gave these elements a positive function in his art.

It is not hard, in retrospect, to understand why we concede to
Rembrandt a focal position in Dutch art; but there is little excuse
for allowing our judgment of what happened before his time to be
colored by his subsequent emergence. How did Rembrandt's own
contemporaries view his position as an artist? What did they
think of the whole art situation in Holland early in the 17th century? We are fortunate in being able to call on the testimony of an
extraordinary man who in the late twenties happened to write his
autobiography, of which even the original manuscript has come
down to us. He was Constantijn Huygens (1596–1687), secretary to
the Stadholder, Prince Frederick Henry, and a poet, scholar, connoisseur, collector, and architect (Illustrations a, p. 28; a, p. 52).
Rembrandt's senior by ten years, Huygens was in his mid-thirties
when he noted his impressions of the artists of his time in an autobiographical sketch of around 1629. He brought unusual qualifica-
tions to the task, for he had enjoyed a well-rounded education in
the arts and the humanities. He had played musical instruments
and written poems while he was still a boy. He was versed in
several languages and especially familiar with Latin language and
literature. It is in Huygens' autobiography that we find the
earliest known evaluation of Rembrandt's art, and we shall have
occasion to refer to him more than once in the following pages.[4]

How did Huygens view the art of his time? To him the outstanding works were the Mannerist etchings, drawings, and
paintings of Goltzius and—in particular—Jacob de Gheyn II,
whom he admired and held in awe as great masters. He had
known them both in person, and to him they were the bearers of
the new truths. He found words of praise not only for de Gheyn's
Mannerist figure compositions but even more for his realistic
flower pieces. We ourselves tend to date the new age from a

younger generation, whose members are but briefly mentioned
by Huygens—Lastman, Terbrugghen, Jan van Goyen, and (with
impressive perceptiveness) Jan Porcellis. Oddly enough, Huygens
admired the realistic portraits of van Ravesteyn and van Mierevelt, while devoting not a single word to Frans Hals, then in his
forties, with the first large group portraits of the Haarlem civic
guard already to his credit.

The prototype of the history painter, Huygens added, was none
other than Peter Paul Rubens, the Apelles of the age, a veritable
prodigy. "I have ever been convinced that even beyond the
Netherlands there is not now or in the offing anyone who can
compare with him in abundance of creative ideas, in venture-
someness and grace of form, and in range of themes, encompass-
ing every sphere of painting."[5] It is noteworthy and instructive
that this discriminating 17th-century connoisseur made no distinction between Dutch and Flemish painting. The Netherlandish
cultural ambience embraced both Rubens and Rembrandt, both
the Fleming van Dyck and the Dutch portrait painters. In enu-
merating the best-known landscape painters, Huygens brackets
the names of Bril and Wildens of Flanders with those of Esaias
van de Velde and Jan van Goyen of Holland. Abraham Janssens
and Frans Snyders of Antwerp are mentioned in the same breath
with the Dutchmen Lastman, Honthorst, and Baburen. The tribute to Rubens already cited is followed by an amusing discourse
on illusionism and its hazards (as exemplified by the portraitists
van Ravesteyn and van Mierevelt), and then by an ardent and
detailed estimate of those "two young Leyden painters, Rembrandt and Lievens" to which we shall have occasion to revert.
Huygens concludes his discussion of contemporary painters with
that seductive prestidigitator, Jacobus Torrentius.

The art scene outlined by Huygens does not altogether coincide
with the views modern historians have formed of that period. We
have profounder insight today than contemporary witnesses—or
at least we think we have—into the strengths and weaknesses of
the various painters and movements, their zeniths and nadirs, the
way they were related, one to the other. On the other hand, we,
too, labor under certain limitations. Our perspective and judgment, for example, are restricted by our own artistic and historical prejudices, to say nothing of those of our immediate predecessors, whose grip we have not entirely escaped. We may cite the

Gerard Honthorst THE PRODIGAL SON IN THE TAVERN. 1623
Munich, Alte Pinakothek

historian Pieter Geyl, who died a few years ago. He drew particular attention to our ingrained habit of considering the history of Holland and Flanders in the 17th century as two separate streams, which is nothing but a fallacious backward projection of the much later division of these territories into two countries, the Netherlands and Belgium. This division simply did not exist for Huygens, nor for the artists and scholars of his time. From the vantage point of Italy, all the people of the Low Countries were *ultramontani* or *fiamenghi*, whether they came from Amsterdam or Antwerp.[6] In some respects, then, Huygens' judgment may be more sound historically than ours. Certainly his opinions on art, whether or not we quite agree with them, always make sense; and modern art critics may take comfort from the fact that their historical judgments are not, after all, so remote from the values of this 17th-century connoisseur.

The Leyden Years

Rembrandt van Rijn was born on July 15, 1606, in Leyden, the eighth child in a family of nine. His father was a Leyden miller, Harmen Gerritsz. (i.e. Harmen Gerritszoon—Harmen, Gerrit's son; it was Harmen who first added to his name the designation van Rijn, after his mill, which was located on the Old Rhine). Harmen followed the family trade—for at least four generations his forebears had been millers—but he seems to have deserted the family faith; there is evidence that he alone among his brothers and sisters converted from Catholicism to Calvinism. In 1589 Harmen was married, in a Reformed church, to Neeltje van Suydtbroeck, daughter of a Leyden baker. Neeltje's mother belonged to a prominent Leyden family, which had clung to the Catholic faith even after the town went over to the Calvinist party of Prince William of Orange. Harmen and Neeltje named their next-to-last child after Neeltje's grandmother, Remigia or Reijmptge Cornelisdochter van Banchem.[1]

People have always been curious about Rembrandt's family. Did he ever paint his parents and his brothers and sisters? There is a single drawing of an old man inscribed in a 17th-century hand: *Harman Gerrits van de Rhijn* (Illustration c, p. 188). Three paintings around 1630 may justly be called REMBRANDT'S FATHER on the basis of the sitter's resemblance to the old man in the drawing [23, 24, 29; Colorplates, pp. 19, 23], while a host of other paintings often given that title [e.g. 19, 36, 42, 43, 46, 47, 48, 49] must be regarded as studies after other models. Rembrandt's father died in 1630, his mother in 1640. She is traditionally identified—no doubt rightly—as the aged woman Rembrandt etched (Illustrations a, p. 192; b, p. 197) and painted [27, 34, 35, 37, 190] so often in his youth. Two other faces that occur with some frequency in Rembrandt's paintings have been called Liesbeth, Rembrandt's sister, and Adriaen, his brother. These identifications are not at all likely. Sister Liesbeth stayed in Leyden when Rembrandt went to Amsterdam, where her "portraits" were painted. And one of the so-called Adriaen portraits is dated 1654, two years after the death of Adriaen van Rijn. Evidently there is a large element of wishful thinking in these identifications, which do nothing to help us understand Rembrandt's art or give us insight into his character.[2]

Rembrandt's parents, his mother in particular, were not without means, and they gave him the best education Leyden had to offer. They sent him to Latin School for seven years and then had him enrolled in the University of Leyden, at the age of fourteen. In the *Album Studiosorum* he is entered as *Rembrandus Hermanni Leydensis studiosus Litterarum, annorum 14* (Rembrandt Harmensz. of Leyden, student of letters, 14 years old).[3] Clearly his family wished to give the young man an education that would prepare him for a more genteel profession than his father's. However that may have been, after only a few months Rembrandt left the University to study painting.

For three years he served as apprentice to Jacob van Swanenburgh, a Leyden painter about whose work we know very little. Van Swanenburgh must have spent a good many years in Italy, which attracted so many Dutch artists, and he brought back with him a wife who was a native of Naples. Some 17th-century sources also name the Leyden portraitist Joris van Schoten and Jacob Pynas of Amsterdam as Rembrandt's teachers.[4]

The only one of Rembrandt's teachers to make a lasting impression on his art was Pieter Lastman, with whom Rembrandt spent his final half-year of study, in Amsterdam, in 1624. In that decade—indeed, ever since his return from Italy in 1610—Lastman was Holland's leading history painter. Everything we know of young Rembrandt's work points to his fascination with Lastman's history paintings.

More than the painters of landscapes and scenes from everyday life, Lastman was involved with a branch of painting firmly linked with 16th-century Netherlandish and Italian art. In Lastman's studio Rembrandt's attention would have been turned not to the work of the craftsman-like specialists of Dutch painting but to the grand aristocratic productions of the Fleming Peter Paul Rubens.

The style and technique of Rembrandt's earliest paintings derive their basic elements from the art of Lastman. In one of Rembrandt's very early paintings [1], a fluid, vivacious group of figures in the background could be taken for the work of Lastman himself. This picture—whose subject has never been convincingly identified—is signed and dated, though not altogether legibly. In artistic quality the work is distinctly uneven. When we place it beside Lastman's CORIOLANUS of 1622 (Illustration, p. 12), we are struck with the far greater harmony and rhythm the teacher was able to impart to his own composition. Lastman brings the figures into the clearest possible relation to each other.

THE PROPHET JEREMIAH LAMENTING THE DESTRUCTION OF JERUSALEM (REMBRANDT'S FATHER) [24]

a Hendrick Terbrugghen SAINT SEBASTIAN ATTENDED BY SAINT IRENE. 1625. Oberlin, Allen Memorial Art Museum

b Peter Paul Rubens THE STONING OF SAINT STEPHEN. 1625 Valenciennes, Musée des Beaux-Arts

Drapery and gesture perform their expressive function with attractive directness, and details and anecdotal embellishments are allowed to entertain and divert us.

By contrast, Rembrandt's rendering of an oration (whatever its content) in the Leyden painting [1] is awkward—one is forced to say wooden. Rembrandt's stylistic development was still at an early stage, but if we simply excuse him on account of his youth, we shall never learn the deeper lesson that the difference between the two works teaches us. Rembrandt replaced Lastman's flowing narrative with a compelling gravity inherent in the scene itself. We are made uneasy by such an emphatic presentation of emotion. Lastman on his part tells his story with a pathos that is far too amiable; indeed, the flow of his line and his rhythmic movement are out of character with the spirit of his scene—one of condemnation and mortal fear.

Only later, in Amsterdam, did Rembrandt achieve a proper appreciation for the fine flow of Lastman's relief-like compositions. Here in Leyden he was still intent upon demonstrating how very much different he was from his teacher's pleasing manner—though Lastman's masterly technique seems to have deeply impressed the youthful student.

Rembrandt's approach to history painting is intense and impressionable. Anger and personal involvement stamp the disturbing STONING OF SAINT STEPHEN [2; Colorplate, p. 9], plainly dated 1625 and marked with young Rembrandt's monogram. The painting's roughness is a direct expression of its fearsome theme. The saint is hemmed in by a frighteningly aggressive throng, among them Rembrandt himself. His child's face, staring out at us in an ugly grimace, adds horror to the painting's evocation of cruelty and the living presence of evil in man. We look in upon the scene over the shoulders of the mounted officers in the foreground, while other witnesses deep within the painting's space face us to watch the event, a confrontation that heightens dramatic tension even more. Rembrandt rejects the glibness of Lastman's depiction of emotions in favor of a more unconventional treatment of states of mind. Even his colors outshine Lastman's, evoking more vehement sensations. His subdued tones sometimes remind us of Terbrugghen's, especially the shimmering bluish-purple glow in the shadows. But it is only when we compare THE STONING OF SAINT STEPHEN with Terbrugghen's

tranquil and poetic SAINT SEBASTIAN (Illustration a) that we begin to appreciate how thoroughly Rembrandt rejected the older generation of Dutch painters, even the most gifted of them. Terbrugghen's lyricism seems sentimental next to Rembrandt, who preferred forthright, even harshly expressive, realism.

THE STONING OF SAINT STEPHEN is the same size as the puzzling oration scene [1], suggesting that the two paintings were designed as a pair, or as part of a still larger series. We do not know who commissioned these early works, nor to what purpose they were put. But it is probable that in his expressive depiction of religious oppression (and political, in the Leyden painting?) Rembrandt was reacting to the murderous civil and religious disturbances that divided Holland in his student years. We have no written evidence to support such a conjecture, but if we compare Rembrandt's STONING OF SAINT STEPHEN with a martyrdom painted by Rubens in the same year (Illustration b), we see that Rembrandt's vision is anything but institutional and impersonal, as is Rubens'. Naturally, THE STONING OF SAINT STEPHEN could not have been painted for a church—the Calvinist faith forbade such images. Nor was the picture designed for religious veneration by Dutch Catholics, for it omits the external symbols of the martyr's beatification, such as the wreath and reception by angels. Rubens envisions the martyrdom as a sacramental apotheosis. The composition and the glorious colors of his Valenciennes altar contribute to this central concept. They work to transform, as if by enchantment, man's hatred into God's harmonious love. Rembrandt does not pretend to resolve the problem of evil. His figures are each caught up in the grip of his personal moral dilemma.

For one reason or another, then, Rembrandt was out of sympathy with the best Netherlandish art of the new century. The pathos of Lastman, the cultured traditionalism of Terbrugghen, the consummate showmanship of Rubens—this was Rembrandt's rightful artistic heritage, and he began his career by rejecting it. As soon as he achieved independence at the age of 19, Rembrandt bent every effort to forging an original style that would unequivocally express his vision of life in art.

The power of Rembrandt's gift of expression during this earliest period may be gauged by comparison with a Leyden painting

A SCHOLAR IN A LOFTY ROOM ("SAINT ANASTASIUS") [26]

a Jan Lievens THE WRATH OF AHASUERUS
Raleigh, North Carolina, Museum of Art

b Pieter Lastman THE ASS OF BALAAM BALKING BEFORE
THE ANGEL. 1622. Great Britain, Private Collection

from Rembrandt's own circle, THE WRATH OF AHASUERUS (Illustration a), a painting of even greater dimensions than the two Rembrandt history paintings already discussed [1, 2]. Several scholars give THE WRATH OF AHASUERUS, which is neither signed nor dated, to the youthful Rembrandt himself.[5] One can understand why: the splendor of the painting's palette is overpowering. Wild expressiveness, rough brushwork, and exaggerated contrast of light and dark are further elements suggesting an attribution to Rembrandt. Yet the pathos of these oversized figures betrays a rather different artistic temperament. In a certain sense Ahasuerus is less ambiguous than a Rembrandt figure would have been, on a more lavish scale, his gestures more restrained. I see this work as a precursor of Jan Lievens' SAMSON BETRAYED BY DELILAH (Illustration b, p. 26). This later painting offers an appropriate counterpart to Rembrandt's own SAMSON BETRAYED BY DELILAH [9], differing from it in the same way as THE WRATH OF AHASUERUS differs from THE STONING OF SAINT STEPHEN. The tension, in the Lievens paintings, is kept under control by the constricting compactness of the composition. Emotion is pent up within, while Rembrandt, in this period, tries to express emotions with explosive force, both in the gestures of the figures and the lines of the composition. The differences between Rembrandt and Lievens, however, are limited to these personal turns of understanding. In technique and general outlook—in their rejection of the refinements of traditional painting—they are very close, and they founded together, in the years between 1625 and 1631, what may be called the new Leyden school of history painting.

Lievens, wrote Huygens in 1629, *in the spirit of youth, aims only for vastness and splendor, painting his subjects in life size or even larger. Rembrandt is utterly absorbed in his work; he likes to pack into the limited scope of small paintings effects one can look for in vain in even the hugest works of other artists.*[6]

When he wrote this, Huygens must have been thinking of Rembrandt's small paintings of 1626, paintings in which Rembrandt deliberately insisted on dramatic effects. But Huygens was equally pleased by Lievens' less frenetic style. We readily concede that the precocious Lievens, who was a year younger than Rembrandt, was superior to him during these years in terms of his monumental approach to composition and the human figure. It was Lievens who painted Huygens' portrait during these years (Illustration a, p. 52), and apparently it was Lievens who first got on close terms with the influential diplomat. The fact that Lievens' talent later faded should not affect our acknowledgment of his eminence in the Dutch art of this period.

Rembrandt's small panels of 1626 are doubly interesting to the student. They contain the germs of his first independent style, which asserted itself around 1630, but they themselves hold many unresolved elements: undigested borrowings of some of his masters' teachings, impulsive rejection of others, premature aspiration to the high goals of mature artists. THE ASS OF BALAAM BALKING BEFORE THE ANGEL [6] takes off from Lastman's version of this theme done three years before (Illustration b), which may still have been in Lastman's studio at the time Rembrandt worked there. Both painters, to be sure, built their scenes around the emotional side of the situation; but it is Rembrandt who best projects the dramatic and psychological climax of the story in visual terms. In Rembrandt's version, figures and animals are interlocked into a single group, generating immense tension. Even the escort moving up from behind is swept into the happening, in the same way as are the spectators in THE STONING OF SAINT STEPHEN [2]. Lastman's angel with his classic profile, rustling robe, and proud gesture is cast in the heroic mold, carrying out God's commandment with dignity. But Rembrandt's personal involvement once again defeats good manners and mere pleasantness, disrupting the stately beauty of the formal idiom Lastman and his generation had projected with such demonstrative pathos. On occasion—as in the present instance—Rembrandt, in creating his new style, was influenced by the art of the 16th century, which tended to be less smooth and polished than that of his teachers.

Another of the small-scale biblical subjects of that year is DAVID PRESENTING THE HEAD OF GOLIATH TO SAUL [3], which may be a study for a larger painting that has not come down to us or was never executed. Doing an oil sketch for a projected painting was a method often used by Rubens, and it is noteworthy that this sketch bears, in its details, a certain resemblance to Rubens' style. Rembrandt's deep admiration for Rubens remained a constant element in his art for many years. But even here, at its first appearance, this admiration never becomes a subservient

REMBRANDT'S FATHER [29]

a Frans Hals MERRY COMPANY
New York, Metropolitan Museum of Art

b Hendrick Terbrugghen MUSIC-MAKERS
Great Britain, Private Collection

attempt to ape Rubens. The deeper ties between the two great masters emerge only later in Rembrandt's career, as we shall see.

The subject of CHRIST DRIVING THE MONEY-CHANGERS FROM THE TEMPLE [5] always calls for highly dramatic treatment. Rembrandt's half-length figures threaten to burst out of the confined space into which they have been crowded. This jumble of shrieking visages and grasping hands, contrasted with the single controlled gesture of Christ, casts a powerful spell of almost physical menace upon the beholder. The rough brushwork, the strong tints, the unrestrained movement all proclaim Rembrandt's break with the classicist trend that still survived throughout Holland, especially in the noble rhetoric of Lastman, Rembrandt's teacher.

We may speculate that Rembrandt's new versions of old themes were the outgrowth of an intellectual process, a conscious reassessment of the function of history painting. He would start by studying the iconography of his subject in older prints and paintings, but also with a fresh, deep reading of the historical or biblical text he was illustrating. His primary aim would then be the dramatization of the text in the most powerful possible terms. When he used older models to achieve this end it was always done quite consciously, not from mere respect for convention. Van de Waal once said in another context that with due appreciation for Rembrandt's powers of imagination and sense of realism, one should never overlook his ingrained "studious zeal"—to use Rembrandt's own words.[7] Zeal of this kind does not mean merely carrying out a commission with the greatest care. It means thorough immersion in the theme and its past tradition in art. Even in the 17th century Rembrandt was recognized as a conscientious "illustrator." In 1641 the artist and art critic Philips Angel praised Rembrandt specifically for his respect for the text, for his concern for archaeological as well as dramatic-emotional veracity in his characterizations.[8]

This approach does have drawbacks. In his concern to get the setting and the mood of his personages just right, Rembrandt often fails to be very explicit about the "story line." In this way he is very much like an illustrator, whose audience never needs be told what story is being illustrated—they have the text at hand. Rembrandt's audience all "had the text" because they "had the Bible." Even in so successful a depiction of character as ANNA

ACCUSED BY TOBIT OF STEALING THE KID [4; Colorplate, p. 11], the narrative thread is difficult to grasp without a knowledge of the Bible story. As a composition, ANNA ACCUSED BY TOBIT is no more than a simple juxtaposition of two figures. It is their poignant gestures and features, delineated so sharply in vigorous, thickly applied brushwork, that turn them into a quarreling couple—the wife indignantly rejecting her husband's accusation that she has stolen the kid.

Rembrandt's earliest non-historical composition is THE MUSIC-MAKERS [18], which is not, despite its theme, the kind of genre painting practiced by Frans Hals and his circle (Illustration a). Indeed, the comparison with Frans Hals shows how different was Rembrandt's aim: he lifts his people out of their everyday sphere of life by giving their secular actions an air of sanctity. Music is itself part of the subject, and the still-life details, such as the lute and books in the foreground, also contribute meaning to the central theme. The figures look out of the picture with grave expressions. We should do Rembrandt an injustice were we to take the painting merely at face value, though in truth we do not comprehend its deeper meaning. For that matter, neither are the genre pictures of Frans Hals simple representations of everyday life—they are often charged with allegorical allusions. Yet in Rembrandt the deeper layers of meaning are given stronger, if not more lucid visual expression.

Terbrugghen gives a still different note to the concert theme (Illustration b). In his tranquil and dignified style, the gravity of the occasion is implied by the subdued color range. The pigments are applied with care and with a feeling for subtle nuances. Rembrandt's concert is rough, compared with Terbrugghen's. His obsession with truth inevitably brings about blemishes on the smooth surface of beauty.

In 1627 and 1628 Rembrandt sought to impart to his pictures a deeper mood, at the cost of those striking effects of color and technique of his earlier works, with their exciting and disorderly brushwork. For that matter, everywhere in Holland the naïve and indiscriminate joy in color was giving way to a more straightforward, descriptive approach, favoring a more restricted palette and concentration on only a few Baroque compositional elements.

The small MONEY-CHANGER [19] of 1627 is more intimate in mood than THE MUSIC-MAKERS. With the fastidiousness of a

a Jan Lievens THE RAISING OF LAZARUS. Etching
Amsterdam, Rijksprentenkabinet

b Jan Lievens SAMSON BETRAYED BY DELILAH
Amsterdam, Rijksmuseum

miniaturist, Rembrandt painted in minute details: the old man's wrinkles, the stitching in his garments, the books and coins that litter his desk. A single light source unifies all the disparate elements, a device that Rembrandt learned from the Utrecht artists of the school of Caravaggio. AN ARTIST IN THE STUDIO [20] is striking in its contrast of light and dark and its painstaking surface modeling. An emphatically scrupulous technique underlines the mood of solemnity and makes us aware that the peace of the studio is attained only by suppressing a certain inward agitation. A more harmonious balance of form, light, and unitary pictorial effect is struck in A SCHOLAR IN A LOFTY ROOM [21]. Interior space and still-life objects have obtrusive importance in these paintings; the human figures adapt themselves to the coloration of their environment. The chambers and the single human beings they contain merge into one character.

A series of biblical figures, grander in original conception, is opened by THE APOSTLE PAUL IN PRISON [22], who might be described as a more monumental version of the blind Tobit [4]. The apostle is seen within the narrow confines of his prison cell, his personality dominating the scene. The sword and books displayed so conspicuously are tokens of the active and contemplative sides of Paul's faith. As in A SCHOLAR IN A LOFTY ROOM [21], the main figure is silhouetted against a wall illuminated by an oblique beam of light from above. In a slightly later APOSTLE PAUL [23], the brightness that pervades the space engulfs the meditating figure even more strongly. The note of heroic pathos is superseded as the divine light dissolves the prison walls and pours its own life into the passive saint.

Some paintings of the early years have a stability and sense of reserve that link them rather closely to Lievens. Among these are TWO SCHOLARS DISPUTING [11] and THE PRESENTATION OF CHRIST IN THE TEMPLE [10], with its steep pyramid of figures. Both compositions are monumental in conception yet restrained in the language of gesture they employ. Once again light widens the space, casting its bright glow on faces, dress, books, the pale gray walls. The sinuous diagonal lines arising where light meets shadow have an agreeable rhythm in keeping with the dignity of the scene. The great care with which Rembrandt planned the exact pose of his figures is shown in a fine preliminary sketch of the seated scholar in TWO SCHOLARS DISPUTING (Illustration

b, p. 178). Such drawings from life in red and black chalk remind us of Rubens' working procedure during his first Antwerp period. It was precisely during these early years that Rembrandt worked so hard to perfect his compositional technique, by means of large drawings full of sweeping pathos, unique in the clarity and pureness of their line (Illustrations a, p. 182; b, p. 191). The great qualities of Rubens' art made rather a strong impact on Rembrandt's drawings of this period. His paintings, on the other hand, with their heavy brushwork, sharp light contrasts, and realistic detail, are utterly unlike Rubens. They have an emphatic quality that is typically Dutch and that is alien to the verve of the Flemish spirit. In their dead earnest solemnity, Rembrandt's early history paintings forfeit the pathos and grand sweep that are an inherent part of the Flemish tradition—the decorative balance, the easy sense of roundness in space. Lastman had greater sympathy for these elements and so, in particular, did Jan Lievens who, "in the spirit of youth, aimed only for vastness and splendor."[9]

Lievens' taste for grandeur is saved from bombast by his sense of humor, as we see in his SAMSON BETRAYED BY DELILAH (Illustration b). The figures have an exaggerated physical presence, like actors, and each one plays his role with good-natured willingness. Quite different is Rembrandt's treatment of the same theme [9], which evokes an atmosphere of deadly terror through its deep thrust into space, the discontinuous diagonal, the glancing highlights reflected from parts of the figures. These, along with the gestures and expressions of the figures, make us sense the threat of mortal violence. Rembrandt has succeeded so completely in integrating imagery with meaning that here, for the first time in art, menacing doom and treachery can take form as glittering light piercing a thick gloom to fall on rich fabrics.

This new approach to lighting effects was heralded in some small paintings done only a short time before, such as THE APOSTLE PETER DENYING CHRIST [7] and THE FLIGHT OF THE HOLY FAMILY INTO EGYPT [8]. Initially, these night scenes tended to be literal-minded adaptations of the delicate narratives of Elsheimer, preserving their sense of quiet but not their rich atmosphere. Rembrandt did not begin to exploit the dramatic potential of chiaroscuro until 1628–9, in impassioned scenes from the life of Christ, such as THE TRIBUTE MONEY [15] and THE RAISING OF LAZARUS [16]. Only in later life did he return to

a Thomas de Keyser CONSTANTIJN HUYGENS AND HIS CLERK. London, National Gallery

b Jan Anthonisz. van Ravesteyn PIETER VAN VEEN AND HIS CLERK. Geneva, Musée d'art et d'histoire

Elsheimer, to do him full justice in a series of breathtaking masterpieces [278, 348, 350].

To Huygens, JUDAS RETURNING THE THIRTY PIECES OF SILVER [12] represented the pinnacle of Rembrandt's dramatic power. This painting must have been only just completed when Huygens saw it; its imagery still fresh in his mind's eye when he wrote this perfervid description:

As an example of his works let me cite the painting of the repentant Judas returning to the high priest the silver pieces, the price of our innocent Lord. All of Italy can be placed beside it, and the most imposing and admirable remains of the first ancients. The gesture of this desperate Judas alone— not to mention all the many impressive figures in this one work—this Judas, I say, raging, whining, groveling for mercy without expecting it; the hope written on his face, the dreadful visage, torn-out hair, rent garment, twisted arms, hands clenched to the point of bleeding—fallen to his knees in a heedless outburst, his whole body contorted in raging despair, this whole figure I set against the elegance of centuries.[10]

Huygens' report is priceless—it tells us exactly how a sensitive connoisseur and sophisticated collector, respected by Rembrandt, reacted to one of the artist's first major works. We see how far Rembrandt could expect his audience to go in reading the expressive details of his works. And we have a hint as to how far we should go in interpreting them—if we trust ourselves to understand Rembrandt's intentions as well as Huygens did. Huygens was not alone in his admiration for JUDAS RETURNING THE THIRTY PIECES OF SILVER. The large number of old copies of this painting (Illustration, p. 166) testify to its popularity in the 17th century.

The Leyden paintings we most admire today are the small but exceedingly dramatic works such as THE RISEN CHRIST AT EMMAUS [14; Colorplate, p. 15]. The conception of the subject is new and daring. Christ leans back at an oblique angle, his figure merging with that of a startled disciple. The second disciple dodges toward the other side, while the line of the paneling on the brightly lit wall of the narrow chamber echoes the first diagonal. Utterly heedless of what is happening in the foreground, a maid goes about her business in the kitchen, her silhouette echoing the shadow of Christ in delicate diminution. The quiet light we know from Elsheimer glows deep in the background, while at the front light and dark clash with a power worthy of Caravaggio.

The Leyden style reaches its dramatic climax in THE PRESENTATION OF CHRIST IN THE TEMPLE of 1631 [17; Colorplate, p. 17]. The shadowy cavern of the temple works with and against the brilliantly lit main group of Hannah, the High Priest, and Simeon kneeling with the Christ Child in his arms. The temple surrounds the figures with its velvety darkness, as if to draw them into its bosom, but it also thrusts them out at us; they are impelled by the very strength of the contrast between their light and its blackness. The insistent and painstaking draftsmanship is saved from dryness by the supernatural light and the disquieting gloom, which change the character of the seemingly realistic detail. Architectural diagonals fade into gray and violet depths. The eye sweeps from the illuminated main group into the soaring vaults and flight of stairs shaded by a canopy. The voice of Hannah giving the blessing seems to reverberate in the vast temple.

By the end of the Leyden period Rembrandt had evolved a successful formula for depicting individual figures from the Old and New Testament, a type of painting much in demand in those days. The characters now come across as old men and women of great dignity and humanity. In a notable series of such figures dating from 1630–1, Rembrandt presents his personages encased in warm robes of purple [27]; or dwelling in the fitful light of quiet vaulted chambers [26] and prison cells [25]; or, like the Rijksmuseum JEREMIAH [24; Colorplate, p. 19], tarrying on the dividing line between light and shadow. Precious vessels of gold and oriental rugs send up their gleam from the dark foreground. The light pierces beard and hair, lingers on the fabric of the robe, picks out highlights in the gilt trimming. It gives resolute form to the prophet, but here, too, it veils the overemphatic realism of conscientious execution. This time the second light in the background represents the torch of destruction, while the gloom in the foreground is the symbol of sorrow.

History painting was Rembrandt's great concern in Leyden. His "portraiture" of those years was experimental and unpretentious, consisting mainly of studies of himself and of his parents. To a large extent a painter's seriousness was then judged by the ambitiousness of his subjects, with history painting ranking highest; and Rembrandt seems to have taken his career with great seriousness. With the benefit of Impressionism to enlighten them, 20th-

AN OLD MAN IN A CAP [36]

Isaak Nicolai van Swanenburgh THE PREPARATION OF WOOL
Leyden, Stedelijk Museum "De Lakenhal"

century critics are prone to smile at such prejudices. To set the value of a work by its theme seems particularly pointless in respect to Dutch art, which performed such prodigies in the "vulgar" genres of landscape and portraiture, still life and everyday life. Yet this hierarchy of genres was still very much alive in the art theories of Mannerism, and it had been by no means superseded in the 17th century. Huygens—to name only one of our witnesses—still had to protest against the contempt for portraiture among his contemporaries—including Rembrandt, it seems. In the early Amsterdam years Rembrandt turned out dozens of society portraits, many of them routine productions, others original and interesting paintings. This was a type of painting he never practiced in Leyden, so far as we know, and he may very well have adopted features of Jan Lievens' portrait style when he was suddenly called upon to practice as a portrait painter. His own studies of heads and individual figures, in the Leyden period, were altogether personal. Even when they were character studies, intended to serve as figures in a history painting, the personality of the sitter makes itself felt strongly and boldly. On the other hand, self-portraits and studies of his parents always seem to take on a meaning above and beyond their meaning as portraits. Rembrandt's mother appears to us as a biblical prophetess [27]— some scholars are so impressed by her gravity that they call her a prophetess even when she is shown without attributes [35]. The self-portraits, too, are so much more than records of Rembrandt's own features that scholars see in them exercises in "emoting," like an actor's gestures before the mirror. In one sense this is proved by the occurrence in some history paintings of the head of Rembrandt as a participant in the events [2, 64]. These images of the painter involved in scenes of his own creation serve to make the biblical pictures even more immediate, almost in the sense of a Passion play: here before our eyes unfolds the suffering of Christ and the saints. This admirably suited the dramatic Baroque style of Rembrandt's early years. The Passion and apostle pictures of his late period carry an altogether different mood and significance.

SOLDIER IN A PLUMED CAP [28], the "scratched" self-portraits of the earliest period [30, 32], and an etched self-portrait equally raw in technique (Illustration b, p. 195) overwhelm us with their wild, impulsive power. Just as some of the self-portraits were meant to serve as extra figures in some religious tableau,

SOLDIER IN A PLUMED CAP may well be a discarded study for some soldier's head in that early historical painting in Leyden [1].

It is noteworthy that in the early self-portrait drawings (Illustration a, p. 195) Rembrandt presented himself in a more reserved attitude than in the painted sketches [30, 32]. The drawings give the impression of more space about the figures, while the oil sketches show a head crowded onto a small panel that often looks like a fragment. It is quite understandable that a study like the one in Munich [32] should have been enlarged by a restorer. (The additions are now covered by the frame.) The etchings range from quick sketches of Rembrandt "making a face" (Illustration a, p. 191) to very distinguished presentations of the artist as a successful and cultured young man (Illustration a, p. 255). The portraits of his mother share this protean range of possibilities. Sometimes we think we can trace a pictorial idea in its growth through various steps: an oil sketch [35] is carefully elaborated into an etching (Illustration b, p. 197), only to appear before us ultimately as a finished portrait [37] done with loving care and penetration and no longer bearing the slightest trace of a sketch. Yet its portrait aspect is fully preserved, just as in THE PROPHETESS HANNAH [27]. At the same time the etching could be developed into a totally different Hannah, that in THE PRESENTATION OF CHRIST IN THE TEMPLE [10].

In the self-portraits around 1630 we can trace a development toward painterly enhancement of the image by flooding the surrounding space with light [38, 41]. Another feature of this group of self-portraits is a fascination with perfect technique, in strong contrast to the first self-portraits. The face is explored and reproduced with almost the solicitude of the miniaturist [39, 44]. The emotional quality of Rembrandt's confrontation with life is sometimes expressed in the gentle play of light on the surfaces of his face, the mood of the background [45; Colorplate, p. 31].

An old man who was once regarded as Rembrandt's father posed for a number of exercises in character portrayal. He appears as "THE REPENTANT SAINT PETER" [43] and as an officer [46, 47, 49]. The best of the series, OFFICER WITH A GOLD CHAIN [49], has the same authority that marks the first full-fledged portraits of this period, probably done in Amsterdam [53, 54]. A sense of movement is conveyed in these portraits in that the sitter seems only just to have turned toward the beholder.

Joris van Schooten TABULA CEBETIS. 1624
Leyden, Stedelijk Museum "De Lakenhal"

Alertness and attention are similarly conveyed, in that the sitter peers at us with the intent look of a man at his work. These devices keep Rembrandt's portraits from lapsing into the static rigidity that lends an air of uniformity to the run-of-the-mill portrait commissions executed by Dutch painters of this period. The books and papers in the portraits are not merely clues to the sitter's profession or identity. They enhance his social rank—the schoolmasters, theologians, and merchants become men of culture, Amsterdam patricians. Rembrandt never managed to depict his sitters in the perfectly accomplished pose, the majestic assurance that Rubens could offer his patrons (Illustration, p. 54). Yet Rembrandt's experience in returning to Amsterdam in 1631—which meant renewed exposure to Flemish portrait painting and contact with a new class of patrons—did give rise to a new respect for portraiture and for patrons. The resulting works combine monumentality with an exciting sense of living presence.

At the same time Rembrandt continued to paint those much more personal, picturesque studies of old men. The turbulent, daring brushwork of the early examples [31] gave way to a technique that allows complete visual comprehension of the sitter [109]. What was once a mere sketch has now become a full-fledged picture, challenging the beholder by its suggestion of meaningfulness.

This constant changing of the purpose to which Rembrandt put portraits and studies—even of himself—cannot but puzzle us. Why did Rembrandt paint Orientals or dress up his Dutch models in turbans, plumed hats, gold chains, and cuirasses? Was it mere curiosity, mere pleasure in the exotic? Or did he deliberately use disguise and masquerade to undermine the pretentious claims of portraiture, to isolate his sitters from a conventional setting that blocked access to the deeper layers of the personality? Huizinga once said of Rembrandt that "all his life he pursued the idea of rendering another world, a form of life different from that of his own daily environment: the bourgeois society of the Dutch Republic."[11] During his years in Amsterdam this discrepancy between Rembrandt's creative vision and the world of appearances deepened still further. Yet, even in his early career in Leyden we can see the inner conflict that tore at him whenever he depicted the human countenance.

The Leyden School of Painting

Now that we have examined the art scene in the Netherlands during the first quarter of the 17th century, as well as the works of Rembrandt's earliest period, it may be useful to take a closer look at the state of painting in Leyden, to enable us to judge Rembrandt's borrowings from and influence on his immediate environment. In Orlers' *Beschrijving der Stad Leyden*, first published in 1614, we find that the oldest painter whom Orlers knew personally was Isaak Nicolai van Swanenburgh (1538–1614). Van Swanenburgh very probably got his art training in Antwerp. After moving to Leyden he was commissioned by the municipality to paint a series of pictures showing the processing of wool. He supplemented these with two or three allegories in which a prominent place was assigned to the *Stedemaagd*, the female personification of the town, who welcomes and protects trade and commerce.

The wool sequence, painted between 1595 and 1612, succinctly reviews all the major stages in the preparation of that fiber. It is an informative documentation, translated into visual terms in a rather heavy-handed Mannerist style, even though one main group, consisting of two women spinners and a man holding wool hanks, has an almost elegant touch (Illustration, p. 30). The sense of tension originally characteristic of Dutch Mannerism has become transformed, in van Swanenburgh's style, into a kind of provincial prose. The street backgrounds form a particularly attractive feature, for here no preconceived stylistic attitudes intrude on the unselfconscious effort to depict nature faithfully. The painter himself served more than once as a town magistrate, and his name and reputation almost certainly gained a certain acceptance for his conservative style. We may assume, further, that this prestige was handed down to his son, to whom Rembrandt was apprenticed about 1621, at the age of 15.

This Jacob van Swanenburgh, who died in 1638, spent many years in Venice and Naples where he managed to get into trouble with the Inquisition as the result of trying to sell a painting of a witches' dance. A hell scene by van Swanenburgh with a generous sprinkling of witches in it has come down to us—at least if the monogram J V S correctly identifies the artist. We find here all the ingredients that go to make up the late Mannerist style—torn and tattered shapes, a disjointed composition, unresolved spatial elements, architecture blending into ornament. Van Swanenburgh was undoubtedly a man of considerable imagination, and his hell scenes evoke the great Jerome Bosch. Actually his vision is closer to that of his French contemporary, Jacques Callot. The styles of van Swanenburgh and Callot must be viewed as peculiarly personal forms of provincial Mannerism within the broader European trend. In Rembrandt's earliest mythological compositions [61, 62] we think we can still discern some part of van Swanenburgh's active imagination.

When Rembrandt joined Lastman in his Amsterdam studio in 1624, Mannerism had already run its course in Leyden. An air of classicist serenity overlies even the luxuriant TABULA CEBETIS (Illustration, p. 32) by Joris van Schooten (1587–1651), a painting of 1624 commissioned by the city of Leyden for the Latin school Rembrandt had attended only four years before. In it, man's follies are carefully documented, according to the teachings of the philosopher Cebes of Miletus. A nude and seductive goddess of Fortune exemplifies the error of worshipping the glitter of gold. A ruined building represents the abode of misery from which man is freed only by repentance. Some figures disport themselves beneath a precious baldachin. Only a handful have escaped the encircling walls to reach the mountain of true happiness.

Orlers mentions Joris van Schooten but briefly, though this painter was a figure of some importance in the Leyden school. While he cannot be compared to Lastman in Amsterdam, he has considerable merit as a portrait painter. His group portrait showing seven officers of the company of Captain Harman van Brosterhuyzen (Illustration, p. 36) is a sturdy example of finished craftsmanship. Of course it is old-fashioned in effect when one compares its artless arrangement and heavy-handed gestures with Frans Hals' contemporary civic guardsmen (Illustration, p. 78). Yet van Schooten's carefully molded countenances are full of character and eloquent in their gravity. The bareheaded young man in the painting is the company's ensign, David Bailly (1584–1657), in civilian life himself a painter. There is a theory that he painted his own likeness, as well as that of the captain, in this portrait.[1] In any event, both artists were competent portraitists, and young Rembrandt must have known them both.

The great 16th-century tradition of Leyden painting had dried up with Cornelis Engebrechtsz., Lucas van Leyden, and their

Joris van Schooten THE COMPANY OF CAPTAIN HARMAN VAN BROSTERHUYZEN. 1626
Leyden, Stedelijk Museum "De Lakenhal"

sons. Mannerism was far more alive in Haarlem and Utrecht; the classicism of Amsterdam was more heroic and dramatic. Jan van Goyen and Pieter de Neyn might have laid the groundwork for a new school of landscape painting in Leyden, but Jan van Goyen left town, as had Rembrandt and Lievens before him, and after 1632 Pieter de Neyn found the office of town mason more congenial and lucrative.

There was one child prodigy in Leyden, Jan Lievens, already mentioned more than once. Apprenticed to Joris van Schooten and Pieter Lastman—this must have been before 1620—he is said to have painted his own compositions and inventions "from life" at the age of twelve, with no further master to instruct him. At fourteen he painted his mother's portrait, and he also did copies of works by other artists which were so perfect that they could not be told from the originals—but this, of course, is a tribute paid to many talented neophytes. His biography in the second edition (1641) of Orlers' book runs to more than twice the length of Rembrandt's![2]

We have already noted that as early as the late twenties Constantijn Huygens had recognized the stature of Lievens and Rembrandt, not just as exponents of the Leyden school but within the total framework of Netherlandish art. Huygens had visited Lievens in Leyden with his brother, on what errand we do not know. The painter had never met Huygens before but conceived so strong a desire to paint his likeness that Huygens agreed to sit for him. This painting has come down to us (Illustration a, p. 52). So overwhelmingly modern is it in conception that some scholars believe it should be assigned to a later stage in Lievens' career. I see no reason to doubt Lievens' precocity, as documented by Orlers; but this is hard to prove, since few of Lievens' early works are dated. We have no idea at all of how he painted at the age of fifteen; but neither do we have reason to believe that the stories about him were solely a matter of local pride and that his youthful paintings did not deserve to be taken seriously. The vigorous treatment of the hands in the Huygens portrait, at any rate, fits in well with his early rough sketches. The features are projected with singular penetration and warmth. Rembrandt achieved such power only at the very end of his Leyden period.[3]

An etching of THE RAISING OF LAZARUS (Illustration a, p. 184) that Rembrandt did just around the time he moved to Am-

sterdam demonstrates how important Lievens was for Rembrandt—and how different in temperament they were. In a Lievens etching of the same subject (Illustration a, p. 26), the backdrop is a brightly lit wall whose broad expanse serves to carry the whole composition. The spectators hug the margins, leaving ample scope for the luminous spirituality that emanates from Christ as he raises Lazarus from the dead. In point of fact, the dimensions of the etching are not overgenerous, yet the wide, bleached surface suggests a feeling for the monumental that was Lievens' hallmark. Rembrandt's etching, which may have been based on a pictorial idea by Lievens, speaks a different idiom. The raising takes place in a setting of dramatic gestures and sharp contrasts of light and dark. There is a sense of counterpoint between Christ's imperiously upraised hand, pointing obliquely away, and the response by Lazarus and the deeply involved witnesses. The story is told in terms of the play of light and shadow, with their evocation of depth. More than Lievens, Rembrandt understood and responded to Caravaggio's challenge to Mannerism and its artificiality. Rembrandt completely captured the meaning of Caravaggio's anti-Mannerist message in its dramatic power. In Lievens' Christ type, on the other hand, the example of Guido Reni is discernible, a borrowing highly significant for Lievens' character. Reni, and indeed Bolognese classicism as a whole, accorded far better with Lievens' ideal of decorative grandeur than Caravaggio's acerbity, which Rembrandt unquestionably must have admired.[4]

In Holland, except for Leyden, "Caravaggism" meant, as we have seen, an elegant toying with light and shade, painstaking attention to surfaces and occasionally exaggerated lighting effects. Lievens and Rembrandt stood shoulder to shoulder in rejecting Hendrick Terbrugghen's sensitive painterliness. Despite its external similarity, Lievens' SMOKER (Illustration a, p. 38) is as different from Terbrugghen's version of the same theme (Illustration b, p. 38) as is Rembrandt's STONING OF SAINT STEPHEN [2] from Terbrugghen's SAINT SEBASTIAN (Illustration a, p. 20). Every trace of glamour, of surface delicacy, of reflected highlights, is here foregone. Pigment is dabbed on thickly in loud shades and with exaggerated accents, and all the revered artistic standards an older generation, fed from Italian sources, had introduced and elaborated in Holland are ruthlessly demolished.

a Jan Lievens SMOKER
Warsaw, Muzeum Narodowe

b Hendrik Terbrugghen SMOKER 1623
Eger, Hungary, Dobó István Múzeum

Huygens reproached young Rembrandt and young Lievens for refusing to journey to Italy. They protested that there were enough Italian paintings in Holland for study purposes, a view for which there is indeed good evidence. Another factor may have been that what the Utrecht disciples of Caravaggio had brought back to the Netherlands was not exactly in accord with their own ideals. Besides, both Lievens and Rembrandt were making extensive use of engravings that conveyed all manner of Flemish and Italian pictorial ideas to them. Huygens' reprimand may have been provoked in part by their rejection of the cultivated formal idiom of Mannerism and the tasteful palette of the Caravaggists, artistic currents he himself admired.

Perhaps the oddest element of all is the close collaboration between the two painters during the early years in Leyden. Rembrandt and Lievens used the same aged men and women as models, and each of them owned (and went over!) paintings by the other. They did several works together, leaving us unable to tell which hand did what. Indeed, even their contemporaries were baffled on this point. In 1632 an inventory of paintings in the possession of Frederick Henry was compiled; and No. 64, a PRESENTATION IN THE TEMPLE in the gallery at Noordeinde, is listed as "by Rembrandt or Lievens"! Although the painting had been done only a few years before, none could tell who was the actual painter. Similar confusion apparently surrounded another painting, described as showing "a youthful student seated by a peat fire, reading." Frederick Henry bought such a painting from Lievens and presented it to the English ambassador at The Hague, who turned it over to his king; but in an inventory of the English royal collection dating from 1639, it is ascribed to Rembrandt. Both of these paintings, by the way, are lost or at least have not been identified.[5]

No wonder the confusion was to become even greater with time. We have already expressed our reservations on the attribution of the large WRATH OF AHASUERUS (Illustration a, p. 22). There are in existence portrait studies on which both artists worked, like the picture in Schwerin with its odd monogram. There are paintings plainly signed by Rembrandt, yet actually done by Lievens; and there are portraits now listed as by Rembrandt which, nevertheless, were painted by Lievens.[6] The Rijksmuseum, lastly, owns a portrait of a curly-haired child, legibly signed *Rembrandt geretoceer*

Liev (Rembrandt retouched Lievens), followed by traces of a date (Illustration b, p. 64).

We can draw two lessons from these examples: Rembrandt and Lievens played an important part in the Leyden school during these years. They, rather than the old-established artists, got the commissions for portraits and history paintings from the court at The Hague. And their collaboration must have been extremely close, with neither playing second fiddle. There is no other known instance of such a symbiosis in 17th-century Dutch art. Rembrandt, by the way, seems to have taken along a number of works by Lievens when he settled in Amsterdam in 1631.

Rembrandt must have had several pupils and assistants during his years in Leyden, a further token of the prestige he enjoyed even then. We have explicit testimony concerning one of them, young Gerard Dou. At the age of 15, following an apprenticeship with a stained-glass artist, he was on February 14, 1628 entrusted to the "artful and renowned Mijnheer Rembrandt," under whom, at the end of another apprenticeship of three years, he "had grown into an eminent master, particularly skilled in small, subtle, and curious things." This at least was the view taken in 1641 by Orlers, in the second edition of his description of Leyden. Rembrandt, now in Amsterdam, was "one of the most famous painters of our century," while Dou did works of small size that were held in awe by connoisseurs because of their singular style and skillfulness—and that brought high prices.[7]

Dou himself was held in extraordinary esteem in the 17th century. The perfection of his technique was extolled to the skies, and people could scarcely believe that a painter's brush could achieve such polish. He was the prodigy of his age whom none could ignore when discussing Dutch painting—but, alas, his approach had little to do with Rembrandt's. As Joachim von Sandrart, a German painter and art commentator, put it in 1675 with some wit: *It is true that Gerard Dou of Leyden was planted in our garden of art by Rembrandt, but the flower turned out rather different from what the gardener had thought it would be.*[8]

Roger de Piles in 1699 was more sweeping in his judgment: *Dou's paintings are altogether marvelous, but I doubt they merit emulation. The art of painting feeds on fire, and that spark ill accords with Dou's extraordinary patience, with the painstaking care he lavishes on every detail.*[9]

Gerard Dou THE RETURN OF TOBIAS
Rotterdam, Museum Boymans-van Beuningen (on loan)

What, in fact, happened? In the studio Dou had occasion to study how Rembrandt crowded his powerful historical compositions into a small space, and he must have admired the painstaking care with which Rembrandt characterized his portrait-like biblical figures. But under Dou's brush the narrative simply tended to drift away into the humdrum. The tension engendered by a slanting element in the composition, or by the contrast of light and dark, vanished—the disciple was never able to grasp Rembrandt's art in all its integrity. Technique became an end in itself, going into infinite detail, dwelling on every trifle with the most extreme subtlety and glossiness. Dou was at heart no more than an excellent craftsman who was never carried away by his creative imagination. His ideal was a painting of shining serenity, without the slightest trace of individuality or personal involvement.

With such a gulf between the character of master and pupil, it should not be hard to identify Dou's work, even the pictures done during his apprenticeship. But the fact is there are pictures that do pose problems—some that Rembrandt went over and others that Dou copied after Rembrandt. We must bear in mind, further, that Dou's earliest works were painted under Rembrandt's direction, allowing the pupil's own propensities to shine through only in subsidiary details. In my view, THE RETURN OF TOBIAS presently displayed in the Boymans-van Beuningen Museum in Rotterdam belongs to this group (see Illustration). THE RETURN OF TOBIAS has certain obvious affinities to Rembrandt's large compositions of the mid-twenties, but although it is occasionally as-

cribed to Rembrandt, the gentle gestures and the fussy detail work in the faces, hands, and dress point to a temperament very much different from Rembrandt's.

Of course, it is still a long way from pictures in this style to such typical Dous as THE APOSTLE PETER (Dresden, Gemaeldegalerie); but it should be remembered that this earliest group of Dou's authentic works came into being only in the mid-thirties, when the painter had put his apprenticeship under Rembrandt (1628–31) behind him.

Rembrandt had two other pupils besides Dou during his Leyden years—a certain Isaak de Jouderville and a Jaques des Rousseaux. They are rather different from Dou, but no better. So perfectly did they repeat Rembrandt's character heads of old men that these imperceptibly turn into caricatures. One cannot really concede true individuality and character to their output. It falls into the group of Rembrandt imitations that may deceive the casual observer with his guard down.[10] Here we have the starting point for the cult of Rembrandt as the painter of the bizarre and fantastic, a tradition taken up once again in the 18th and 19th centuries with their anti-classical orientation and veneration of the picturesque. It is a matter of considerable interest that Rembrandt's work during the Leyden years served both as the point of departure for Dou's prosaic misapprehension of Rembrandt's art and the inspiration for the revival of a romantic and over-dramatized Rembrandt cult in later centuries.

Rembrandt in Amsterdam

When he was about 23 years old, Rembrandt's career got under way with a jolt. Arnold van Houbraken tells us how it happened: *Rembrandt was on fire with enthusiasm while he was living in his parents' home, making daily progress in art all by himself. Every now and then he would be visited by connoisseurs; eventually they recommended that he visit a certain gentleman in The Hague to show him and offer him a newly finished painting. Rembrandt carried the painting to The Hague on foot, and sold it for 100 guilders. Bursting with delight, and unused to having so much money in his purse, Rembrandt was anxious to get home as quickly as possible, to let his parents share his joy....Since he was often called upon thereafter to come to Amsterdam to paint portraits and other pictures, he decided (considering that the place particularly appealed to him as a city most favorable to his rise) to move there. This was about 1630.*[1]

Houbraken did not write his lives of the Netherlandish painters until about 50 years after Rembrandt's death; and he was in the habit of mingling firsthand observations and serious reporting with gossipy, sometimes pointed anecdotes. But his account of Rembrandt breaking into the big-time art world coincides with the facts as we know them, and may very well be literally true. It was toward the end of the twenties that Rembrandt first came to the attention of influential collectors, and the first of them to take serious notice of him was indeed "a certain gentleman in The Hague"—Constantijn Huygens. As secretary to Frederick Henry, Huygens was well connected. As we shall presently see, he had a hand in Rembrandt's commission from the Stadholder that may go back to the Leyden period. In all likelihood, it was Huygens, too, through whom the English ambassador at The Hague, even prior to 1630, procured certain paintings by Lievens and Rembrandt that soon afterward passed into the possession of King Charles I.[2]

Very quickly Rembrandt discovered that his art would find a readier market in Amsterdam than in The Hague. Houbraken notes that Rembrandt received portrait commissions in Amsterdam before he settled there. It is easy to understand why Rembrandt gravitated toward the great commercial center, where he could be his own master, while Lievens was always attracted to the courtly cities. The appeal of getting rich quick seems to have moved Rembrandt at the beginning of his career. He began to invest in the Amsterdam art market as soon as he was able to raise a stake. On June 20, 1631 he took a 1,000-florin share in the shop of the Amsterdam art dealer Hendrick van Uylenburgh. It must have been very soon after this date that he went to Amsterdam to live. He made his home with van Uylenburgh, in whose art business many Amsterdam painters had a financial interest. Everything points to the conclusion that the shrewd art dealer sensed a promising talent in Rembrandt and was eager to sponsor him in Amsterdam. However that may have been, Rembrandt not only had room and board in van Uylenburgh's home, but a studio as well.

He was certainly living there by July 26, 1632, for a notary looked him up there on that date, to establish whether the painter was "well and in good health." According to the record, Mijnheer Rembrandt Harmensz. van Rijn, painter, replied: "I am indeed well and in good health, thank God!" The occasion for this formal colloquy was a bet, entered into the year before by two persons who had wagered that 100 people, identified by name, would still be alive one year thence. By the merest chance Rembrandt was one of the 100 whose existence had to be documented.[3]

It was probably on van Uylenburgh's recommendation that Rembrandt now received new portrait commissions. His sitters included relatives of van Uylenburgh, clerics, respected merchants, simple artisans, and Jewish scholars. Above all, it was in van Uylenburgh's house that he made the acquaintance of his host's niece, Saskia van Uylenburgh, whom he married in 1634. The couple continued to live with van Uylenburgh for some time before moving to the Nieuwe Doelenstraat and then to temporary quarters in a house on the bank of the Amstel until May 1, 1639, when they took possession of a large house Rembrandt had bought in the St. Anthonisbreestraat.

Rembrandt had become a successful and prosperous young artist. He was now married to a woman from a well-known Frisian family. Saskia's father, who had died in 1624, had once been Burgomaster of Leeuwarden and a member of the Frisian high court and other public bodies. Saskia's elder sister was married to Gerrit van Loo, who was very wealthy—their wedding was celebrated for a solid week! As for Leyden, Rembrandt seems to have lost touch with his old circles now that he had grown away from his background in terms of social position. It was his in-laws rather than his own family who attended christenings in his

a Jan Lievens CHRIST ON THE CROSS
Nancy, Musée des Beaux-Arts

b Peter Paul Rubens CHRIST ON THE CROSS. Drawing
Rotterdam, Museum Boymans-van Beuningen

home, were drawn and painted by him—and quarreled with him.

The surviving paintings confirm the traditional account, according to which Rembrandt first became known to the public in Amsterdam as a portrait painter. We shall, nevertheless, postpone a discussion of his portraits from this period and first deal with the history paintings, since they more than any of the other works carry on the Leyden tradition in some measure.

Recently a CHRIST ON THE CROSS [56] by Rembrandt was discovered in France, a painting dated 1631. In the arrangement of its elements and in its whole approach, this picture belongs with the Passion series now in Munich [64, 65, 80, 87, 88]. It is also clearly related to Lievens (Illustration a). CHRIST ON THE CROSS may have been a sort of trial piece for the Stadholder's commission for a series of paintings of the Passion; it was very likely painted in Leyden, where Rembrandt still had connections with The Hague through Lievens. The painting seems almost an attempt on Rembrandt's part to accommodate his intense style of history painting to the more monumental approach of Lievens, though here too, as in the two etchings of THE RAISING OF LAZARUS (Illustrations a, p. 26; a, p. 184), there are notable differences in creative interpretation. Lievens' Christ hangs limply, pathetically defenseless. Rembrandt gives a slight arch to Christ's body, at once investing the image with dramatic tension. Yet it is surely no accident that Lievens gives greater stress to the horizontal accents—the feet put down side by side for support, the wide, sweeping banderole, the gentle arch of the painting's top border.

Rembrandt's treatment of these elements follows the example of Rubens (Illustration b). His Christ, moreover, is closer to the top of the picture, as with Rubens. The reason for the semicircular termination at the top now becomes evident—it is the style of framing customary in Flemish altarpieces since the 16th century. Rembrandt and Lievens both turned toward Flemish art for inspiration in painting CHRIST ON THE CROSS. Lievens shows himself at this point to be the weaker personality—he is quicker to pick up the knack of the style, but he fails to develop it further. From 1631 on, he becomes increasingly passive in the grip of a mild Flemish classicism. Rembrandt, while in CHRIST ON THE CROSS he comes closer to Rubens than ever before or

after, is much tougher in his attitude toward Flemish art. He makes more penetrating use of Rubens' classicism than does Lievens, but he rejects more of it too. An inner pressure to impose his own emotional interpretation on the theme marks Rembrandt's version. By infusing dramatic expression into every individual element of his picture Rembrandt deliberately sacrificed Rubens' broad sweep and powerful molding. There is one element of Rembrandt's style, moreover, that always remains incompatible with the outgoing style of Rubens—color. The all but enameled luminosity of Christ's body in the Rubens becomes a pale gleam under Rembrandt's brush, a barely lighted surface harboring the shadows that threaten it.

CHRIST ON THE CROSS must have originally formed the central scene in a series that included THE RAISING OF THE CROSS [64] and THE DESCENT FROM THE CROSS [65; Colorplate, p. 47]. The two latter paintings were acquired by Frederick Henry, but the former did not remain in his collection, if indeed he ever purchased it. Rembrandt wrote Constantijn Huygens, probably in February 1636, asking him to tell the Stadholder that he was busy on three paintings of scenes from the Passion of Christ, an ENTOMBMENT [87], a RESURRECTION [88], and an ASCENSION [80], which "accorded" with a RAISING OF THE CROSS and a DESCENT FROM THE CROSS [65]. All we learn from this first letter written by Rembrandt to Huygens is that the two earliest pictures in the Passion series were painted before 1636.[4] The information is not very valuable, however, since we have an earlier date before which THE DESCENT FROM THE CROSS [65] must have been done: Rembrandt made an etching of his own composition, dated 1633 and bearing his personal proscription of unauthorized reprinting (Illustration a, p. 46). THE DESCENT FROM THE CROSS [65] must have been finished, then, by 1633; THE RAISING OF THE CROSS can be dated, on stylistic grounds, a bit earlier, placing both pictures in the very first Amsterdam years.

Rembrandt was following Rubens' example in more ways than one by publishing this etching. The custom of giving greater circulation to compositions by means of prints was introduced in the Netherlands by Rubens, who also used a kind of copyright formula (Illustration b).

The affinities in style and detail between the Passion compo-

a Rembrandt THE DESCENT FROM THE CROSS. Etching. 1633 Amsterdam, Rijksmuseum

b L. Vorsterman after P. P. Rubens THE DESCENT FROM THE CROSS Engraving. 1620. Amsterdam, Rijksmuseum

sitions of the two masters were anything but accidental. The heaving and hauling in THE RAISING OF THE CROSS, the similar arch (in reverse) of Christ's body, even details like the escort of one Thief all point to Rembrandt having known engravings after Rubens' RAISING OF THE CROSS in Antwerp Cathedral. Nor could he have failed to realize that to the Stadholder—and, indeed, to every cultivated connoisseur of the day—the art of Rubens represented the ideal when it came to history painting in the grand style. Rembrandt must have anticipated that his patrons would measure his interpretation against Rubens.

But the comparison with Rubens must not be carried too far. Rembrandt's style of pictorial narration was different in many essentials from Rubens' showy and almost brazen manner. Rembrandt's Passion pictures are not very much larger than THE PRESENTATION OF CHRIST IN THE TEMPLE [17] and are still closely related to that painting from the Leyden period in terms of precision and detail. Lighting effects first pioneered in Leyden are now brought to full development—the main scene seems almost to soak up all the light there is, while the subsidiary figures are caught in a kind of shimmering gloom.

THE ASCENSION OF CHRIST [80] was completed in 1636, according to the letters and the date on the painting itself. X-ray studies have shown that Rembrandt made changes in the composition as he worked on it, indicating that he must have spent a considerable time painting it. God the Father originally appeared above the head of Christ, a compositional element more in keeping with the iconography of the Assumption of the Virgin, as are the angels supporting the cloud on which Christ ascends. These details and the whole conception of the scene suggest that Rembrandt had been studying a print or copy of Titian's ASSUMPTION OF THE VIRGIN in the Frari church in Venice. The shift of models from Rubens to Titian parallels Rembrandt's own progression from dramatic narrative to poetic spectacle. The cluster of agitated shepherds forms but a muted echo of the dramatic gesture with which Christ greets heaven's radiance, a pose of grandeur that dominates all else in the picture.

Every one of the seven letters from Rembrandt's hand that have come down to us deals with this commission—its delivery, payment for it, pleas for settlement. Only once in the letters does Rembrandt speak of what we might call his art as such. On

January 12, 1639, he reports that two pieces [87, 88] are finished, owing to "studious zeal."

I have observed the greatest and most natural mobility in these two, and that is one reason why they have been so long in the making.

There has been much puzzlement over the proper rendering of the Dutch phrase "die meeste ende die naetuereelste beweechgelickheijt." Does it mean movement in the ordinary sense? Or did Rembrandt use the term to imply inner agitation, a usage for which there is authority going back to the 17th century? THE RESURRECTION OF CHRIST [88], in Rembrandt's own words, shows "Christ rising from death to the utter consternation of the guards." The scene is plainly one of extreme turbulence and confusion—the small figures of the soldiers scatter helter-skelter, their weapons dropping from numbed hands. Here is movement with a vengeance.[5]

THE ENTOMBMENT OF CHRIST [87; Colorplate p. 69], on the other hand, presents a subdued air. Even the gestures of grief are muted. A pyramid of figures rising on the right is balanced on the opposite side by a broken group in which the man lowering Christ into the grave by his shroud forms a steep accent. Here the very postures speak of contained inward agitation.

Emmens, for one, contends that the contrast between outward movement and inward agitation we see in these paintings is quite foreign to the spirit of the 17th century, which did not conceive of it as a contrast at all. Rembrandt's goal, following the rules of ancient rhetoric, was to stir his audience in each case, by expressing feelings as emphatically and naturally as possible through posture and movement.[6]

These were the final pictures in the series—final, at least, for the time being. During the forties Rembrandt added two further paintings; one of them has come down to us [215], while the other is known only through an old copy (Illustration a, p. 92). The Passion series proper—which was not a complete series in the traditional sense—really belongs to the thirties and should enable us to follow the growth of Rembrandt's art during that decade. In some measure, this turns out to be true: the road leads from a dramatically crowded RAISING OF THE CROSS [64] to a serenely muted ENTOMBMENT [87]. At the outset Rubens was the exemplar; at the end Titian. But the series as a whole follows, to a certain degree, the logic of its original conception in the

THE DESCENT FROM THE CROSS [65]

Peter Paul Rubens THE ABDUCTION OF PROSERPINA
Paris, Petit Palais

early years of the decade; thus, not every aspect of Rembrandt's art during this period finds a proper expression in it.

There is a replica of THE DESCENT FROM THE CROSS [66] almost certainly executed by Rembrandt himself. It contains many more figures, and it is grander and richer than the Munich DESCENT [65]—in the main motif, in the scene about the swooning Virgin, in the group preparing the shroud. No longer are the people mere spectators—they take part in the painful event. Note how the body of Christ droops from the cross, how light and shadow from a candle, shielded from our view, divide up the space. The main group is reversed from the original composition, one aspect, albeit not the only one, that moves it closer to Rubens (Illustration b, p. 46).

Until about 1633 Rembrandt's narrative paintings were still related to the small-scale works of the Leyden period, in which, to quote Huygens, "he crowds the scene and achieves, in concentrated composition, an effect for which one looks in vain in large paintings by others." [7] We may note that this limitation does not apply to Rembrandt's own works on a larger scale. For that matter, large and small are relative terms. CHRIST IN THE STORM ON THE SEA OF GALILEE [60] is certainly not small in format, yet the powerful diagonals that organize it are broken up and subdivided by the tense and busy ministrations of the twelve apostles to the shrouds and sails amid the roaring sea, by the rigging itself, and by the gray highlights and deep violet shadows. Peril at sea is documented with the sailor's realistic eye. A line has parted and the loose ends flutter in the wind. Some of the crew anxiously test the remaining stays, while others reef foresail and mainsail to save the mast. Houbraken comments:

I have noticed that in his youth he had much more patience than later to execute his pictures in all fullness of detail. This is particularly noticeable in a picture which is known under the name of ST. PETER'S BOAT, *which long hung in the cabinet of the late alderman and burgomaster Jan Jacobsz. Hinloopen at Amsterdam. The attitudes of the figures and their features are expressed as much in conformity with the events as can be imagined, and at the same time the whole is executed in much greater detail than one is accustomed to see anything done by him.* [8]

We see realistic detail and expressive power were qualities still held in high esteem in Houbraken's day.

The same blend of robust and explicit narrative, sparkling and

picturesque detail, and joy in the bizarre flashes from the mythological pictures of this period [55; Colorplate, p. 33; 57, 61, 62]. Huygens would have taken sheer delight in the struggling Proserpina, the startled gestures of Europa's companions, and the lusty story of Callisto's escapade (combined in the picture with the story of Actaeon's death). THE ABDUCTION OF PROSERPINA [57] was certainly the kind of painting the classical-minded Huygens admired—it is plainly in the spirit of a Rubens composition that, in turn, goes back to a relief from late antiquity (see Illustration). The close connection between this group of pictures and the works from the Leyden period is shown in the background composition of THE ABDUCTION OF EUROPA [62], which agrees in structure with THE BAPTISM OF THE EUNUCH, an early Rembrandt now lost, though known through many copies and an engraving. The ties to Rubens are characteristic: the small nude figures playing in the water are borrowed from Rubens' DEATH OF LEANDER, a painting (or a replica of which) Rembrandt owned, though we cannot know if he had it as early as 1632. [9]

Looking at the "little histories" we do not feel that an abrupt change of style had been brought about by the move to Amsterdam. The portraits, however, give quite another impression. In Leyden Rembrandt was not a portraitist. It was he who received the commission for the Passion series, while it was Lievens who painted the portrait of Huygens. Rembrandt's excursions into portraiture were limited to self-portraits, studies of his parents, and other character sketches. The many paintings in which models are depicted in the guise of biblical figures are even more removed from the sphere of portraiture proper. All the same, Rembrandt must have made his bow in Amsterdam as a portrait painter. The portrait of NICOLAES RUTS of Amsterdam [53] provides evidence to that effect, as do numerous other likenesses from the years 1632–3, such as those of MARTEN LOOTEN [110; Colorplate, p. 53], JORIS DE CAULLERY [124], and JOHANNES UYTTENBOGAERT [137]. In addition to such grand representative portraits, Rembrandt was called upon to do more modest and intimate portraits, tokens of the friendship between two men [104, 105].

If any one picture was calculated to make Rembrandt's reputation with the Amsterdam public, it should have been DOCTOR

THE BLINDING OF SAMSON BY THE PHILISTINES [76] Detail

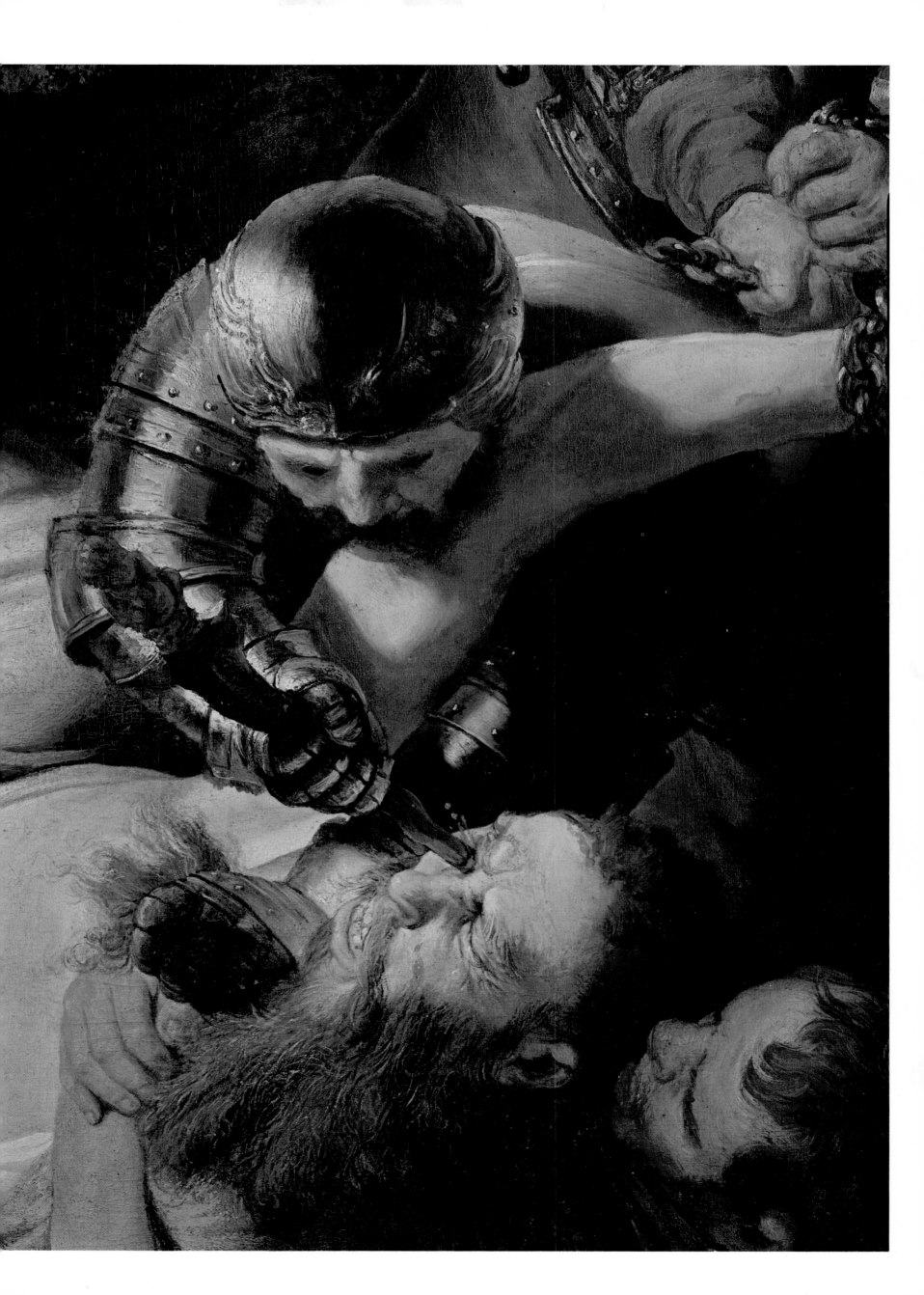

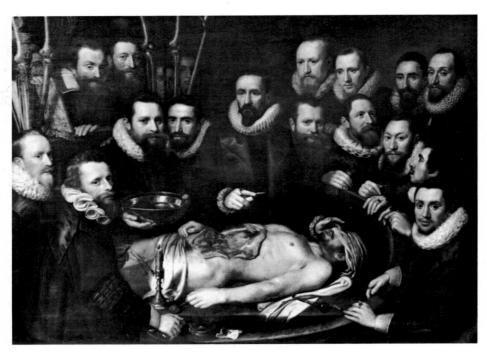

Pieter and Michiel van Mierevelt THE ANATOMY LESSON OF DOCTOR W. VAN DER MEER. 1617
Delft, Oude en Nieuwe Gasthuis

NICOLAAS TULP DEMONSTRATING THE ANATOMY OF THE
ARM [100; Colorplate, p. 51]; but oddly enough it is not singled
out in any of the Rembrandt biographies of the 17th or 18th centuries as the epitome of his precocious skill as a portrait painter.
Only Caspar Commelius, in his *Beschrijving der Stadt Amsterdam*
(1693), mentions two anatomy pictures done by the famous Rembrandt and said to excel all others. When the much-traveled
Zacharias Conrad Uffenbach visited Amsterdam in 1711, he also
saw Rembrandt's two anatomies, but while he gives the names of
the anatomists shown, Rembrandt is not mentioned.[10] Modern
art criticism, on its part, has showered much zeal and scholarship
on the interpretation of precisely this painting. What, in fact, is
the novel element in the TULP, compared, say, to an anatomy by
Pieter van Mierevelt (see Illustration)? Next to the van Mierevelt, the TULP looks more like a history painting than a portrait.
Does it have some hidden meaning, some symbolic association
with death? Does it represent the triumph of science over life
and death? What seems plain is that for the first time in Rembrandt's career a patron had a voice in determining what was
to be painted, and how it was to be done.

Nicolaas Tulp was a disciple of the well-known anatomist Pieter Paauw, follower of Andreas Vesalius, a Fleming who revo-
lutionized Renaissance anatomy in Padua in the 16th century.
The Anatomy Theater in Amsterdam had been built at Tulp's
behest—he was the foremost promoter of the art in Holland. In
Rembrandt's painting he is demonstrating the function of the
muscles of the left arm. It was not an anatomy session in the conventional sense, for such public demonstrations usually began
with the dissection of the abdominal viscera, and people were
prepared to pay to attend the gruesomely titillating spectacle.
Rembrandt's anatomy is more in the nature of a private affair,
an occasion for a group of friends to honor a great anatomist.
Only two of the men shown were members of the physicians'
guild. Tulp has done the difficult job of dissecting the brachial
musculature himself and is demonstrating the delicate adductive
mechanism of the extremity, his own left hand performing the
movements worked by the muscles demonstrated. The suggested
meaning is that man's body serves as an example of God's wisdom and providence and that doctors are chosen to gain insight
into that wisdom and thus heal the sick. Rembrandt, by the way,

did not paint the dissected member from life—or rather in this
case death—but from an anatomical illustration in the *Humani
Corporis Fabrica* of Adriaen van den Spiegel. The tome at the feet
of the cadaver is probably the anatomical text in question.

At first view the realistic staging is so compelling that one is
hard put to abandon the notion of an actual event being shown
here. Indeed, some observers believe they can recognize the very
dissecting theater in Amsterdam—Tulp is seen as lecturing to a
group of attentive listeners beyond the bounds of the painting,
on the occasion of his honorific public anatomy lesson in January,
1632. But this view flies in the face of the visual as well as historical evidence. Tulp's rhetorical and demonstrative gesture
does not seem to demand any greater audience or more fitting
occasion than the one before our eyes: an intimate, not an institutional, confrontation of death and life by a small group of
doctors.

The crowded compactness of the Leyden period, so much admired by Huygens, is here for the first time projected in monumental terms. Theme and likenesses have become one. Even the
locale, sketchy as it is, is more concrete than the temple in the
PRESENTATION [17] painted only the year before. The light is
meant to give a realistic feeling of depth to the figures and the
cadaver as well, and at the same time to gather into its wide cone
the multiplicity of gazes and postures. All the delicate profuseness
of the Leyden period is here projected on a large scale, at the
cost, alas, of sacrificing some of the miniature-like subtlety. Tulp's
left hand, for example, despite its eloquent gesture, is almost
wooden in effect when compared with the sensitively textured skin
of Rembrandt's mother as THE PROPHETESS HANNAH [27].

We must take into account that a commission of this character
scarcely lent itself to straightforward execution under a fixed plan
formulated at the outset. When the picture was last cleaned, it
was found that Rembrandt himself had overpainted and corrected many places. It suffered further at the hands of restorers
in the 18th and 19th centuries—the two figures at the left have
fused into a single black mass, and an added coat of yellow varnish has robbed the corpse of much of its original deathly pallor.
The illusion of diagonal depth has also been impaired.

Perhaps as a result of his work on the TULP, Rembrandt grew
fascinated with the notion of something "happening" in his por-

DOCTOR NICOLAAS TULP DEMONSTRATING THE ANATOMY OF THE ARM [100] Detail

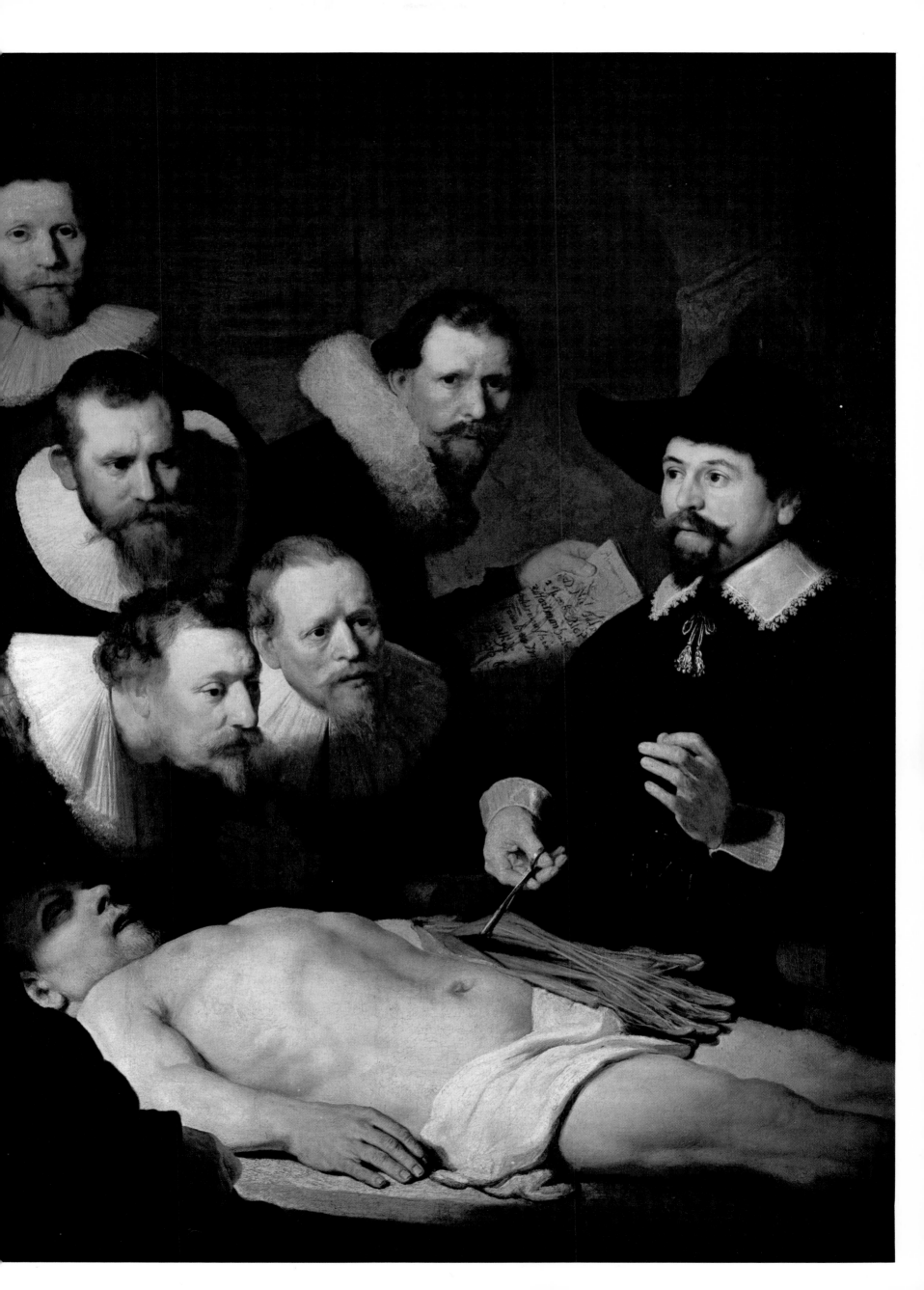

a Jan Lievens CONSTANTIJN HUYGENS
Amsterdam, Rijksmuseum (on loan)

b Bartholomeus van der Helst PORTRAIT OF A PREACHER
1638. Rotterdam, Museum Boymans-van Beuningen

traits. The FASHIONABLE COUPLE [130] are themselves motion-less, but the contours of their black dress are extremely lively, and their intersection of the architectural lines introduces a further sense of movement. In "THE SHIPBUILDER AND HIS WIFE" [139] the woman's wide reach dominates the grave figure of the man. Particularly impressive are the paired lifesize portrait heads of couples, each spouse perfectly attuned to the other in gaze and gesture. They are indeed group portraits, properly speaking, made for each other. There are some at bust length, and in them the man usually wears a broad-brimmed hat, giving him an emphatic accent. Rembrandt's female portraits generally tend to be somewhat more reserved in expression, pose, and gesture.[11]

Double portraits and paired portraits have a tradition in the Netherlands going back to the 15th century—in panel painting, miniatures, and the graphic arts. Mannerism had taken up the motif in its own spirit of playful elegance. In the first quarter of the 17th century portraitists tended to deemphasize elements that integrated matched portraits, and it was surely no accident that a "history painter" enlivened these rather stiff and starchy set-pieces with his narrative power, running the full gamut from small bust-length pictures that have barely outgrown miniature format to proud lifesize portraits.

In Haarlem, the painter who enriched the art of portraiture was Frans Hals—along rather different lines but from the same desire for a livelier style. To The Hague, somewhat later, van Dyck's students brought back a certain sense of courtly elegance from England. There was little creative contact among the various centers. The intensity of Rembrandt's style—the rooms flooded with light in which he placed his figures—gave his art a character all its own. Although Rembrandt and Frans Hals were very different in temperament, and seem seldom to have taken sympathetic notice of each other's work, there is at least one Rembrandt portrait [264] that reminds us of Frans Hals works of the same years.

In portraiture as in history painting, Rembrandt meant to rival Rubens in the early Amsterdam years. He sought to give his portraits monumental three-dimensionality, contained movement, and—especially in lifesize portrait heads—picturesque elaboration [119; Colorplate, p. 39]. In the shaded portions, Rembrandt deliberately allows the ground over the wood to shine through as a background color element. Combined with the rich glow of the painting, this gives rise to a firm pigment tissue of piercing luminosity. Under the X-ray Rubens' portraits of the early Antwerp years show, in their sense and use of pigment structure, more agreement with portraits by Rembrandt from the early Amsterdam years than can be discerned by the naked eye.

On January 12, 1639 Rembrandt wrote Huygens that he wished to show his appreciation by presenting the diplomat with a painting worthy of hanging in Huygens' home. Huygens seems to have resisted such a gift, for a few days later Rembrandt returned to the matter:

I now send this canvas, against your express wishes, in the hope that you will not hold it against me; it is the first time that I have given any token of my gratitude. He added a postscript: *My Lord, hang this piece in a strong light and so that one can stand at a distance from it, then it will sparkle at its best.*[12]

In the light of the measurements, which Rembrandt also gave, this must have been the huge painting of THE BLINDING OF SAMSON BY THE PHILISTINES [76; Colorplate, p. 49], done a few years before, apparently not on commission. Did it find favor in Huygens' eyes? His new home in The Hague had just been finished, a house of fine classical proportions and a fit setting for this cultivated diplomat and loyal servant of the state. But was it a fit setting for Rembrandt's savagely realistic painting? As a matter of fact, Huygens did admire scenes of horror in art. He once described with relish the terrible sight of Rubens' HEAD OF MEDUSA:

Rubens displays the face of a wonderfully beautiful woman... just struck dead, repulsive serpents hanging about her temples, yet composed with such unimaginable discretion that although the viewer is startled by it—the painting is usually covered by a curtain—he nonetheless enjoys it, so vivid and lovely is the face, despite its gruesomeness. Yet I should prefer to see such a thing in the homes of my friends rather than my own.[13]

Rembrandt, nevertheless, sent Huygens his fearsome SAMSON for the diplomat's own collection.

Scarcely another picture illuminates Rembrandt's art during this period so thoroughly, even with all its flaws, as this Dutch "martyrdom." As it happens, martyrdom was no longer envisaged in Dutch art as the divine reward for human suffering for

THE AMSTERDAM MERCHANT MARTEN LOOTEN [110]

Peter Paul Rubens PHILIP RUBENS
Whereabouts unknown

the sake of faith. There was, however, a continuing demand for horror pictures. Rembrandt submitted to this limitation. His version of the blinding is unrelieved by even a trace of solace. A glaring light bursts upon the scene with the utmost harshness. Nowhere is there a gentle glow that might presage deliverance. The robust figure of a soldier, striking an almost clumsy attitude, ruthlessly breaks up the bright back screen. Almost everything that manages to emerge from the half-shadows betokens cruelty and pain and fear—fists smashing the victim, chains, knives, armor glittering in the light. Even the fateful shears and locks are held against the light by Delilah as she hastens away. If it be the goal of painting to move and shake the beholder, as one 17th-century school of criticism contended, that end is here attained. Looking from a proper distance into the depths of this overwhelming scene, one can all but sense the esthetic satisfaction the sophisticated recipient of this princely gift must have felt at his great good fortune.

Once again the Rubens parallel is noteworthy, much more telling than the ties with the older Dutch art of the time. During his first Antwerp period, the young Rubens, too, painted a series of pictures that have been collectively called "The Deeds of Violence," and they included a CAPTURE OF SAMSON.[14] Among Rembrandt's paintings that deserve comparison with Rubens on this score are THE ANGEL STOPPING ABRAHAM FROM SACRIFICING ISAAC [74] and BELSHAZZAR SEES THE WRITING ON THE WALL [77; Colorplate, p. 41], scenes in which action is frozen at the moment of supreme fear and horror, the moment of sudden intervention, a favorite dramatic device in this form of art.

Aside from the Passion of Christ, the New Testament offers little occasion for drama. Rembrandt's new approach to life and art, however, was quite equal to themes of tranquillity and grandeur. THE HOLY FAMILY [63] serves as a good example of this new monumental art with its compact, diamond-shaped compositions. The deep modeling is surely a sign that the study of Rubens' art has been resumed, while the use of strong light to organize and emphasize form eloquently suggests a consistent application of Caravaggesque ideas. The boy's body in THE ABDUCTION OF GANYMEDE [73] is reproduced with great realism. Zestful nudity was not uncommon in earlier scenes from mythology, but only now did it achieve an appropriate ruggedness.

The years 1635–6 mark the high point of this heroic and barbarous style. The second half of the decade saw the thirst for grandeur ebb away. Nor can it be an accident that Rembrandt painted so many monochrome sketches in oil, partly as preliminary studies for etchings, partly for their own sake. What happened is that the grand, heroic, and deeply modeled scenes gave way to a less heroic and more painterly rendering of narrative, even in paintings of substantial size such as THE ANGEL LEAVING TOBIAS AND HIS FAMILY [81]. Despite the angel with his rather frantic flapping movements, the scene remains one of cozy intimacy. The startled family group is shown huddled at the entrance to its home, lending it an air of dignity and solidarity. The angel soars toward the bright light, a shimmer of which brushes the bowed head of the father. Warm browns and greens blend figures, architecture, and background landscape into one. THE ENTOMBMENT OF CHRIST [87], SAINT JOHN THE BAPTIST PREACHING [71], THE PARABLE OF THE WORKERS IN THE VINEYARD [83], the marvelous vision of THE RISEN CHRIST APPEARING TO MARY MAGDALENE [82]—all are delicate and sensitive translations of stories to a painting technique in which the pigment is carefully dabbed on, creating a complex pattern of small overlapping forms.

Paintings from these years often look like drawings done with the brush, while drawings have the character of paintings (Illustration a, p. 224). Whatever the medium, the works of this period often possess a more immediate unity of creative idiom than in almost any other period. The figures seem to be bathed in a mild radiance. At the same time, the brushwork of the foreground zone is done with such loving care and quiet emphasis that the beholder's eye is made to dwell on it. The etchings share this creative power and with their rich play of light and their thickets of fine lines they have an even more fantastic and unreal air than the more conventional paintings and drawings (Illustration b, p. 224).

Een vroom gemoet
Acht eer voor goet.
"A devout soul puts honor before gain"—Rembrandt wrote in the album of the German merchant Burchard Grossmann, who visited Hendrick van Uylenburgh in June 1634. On the other side

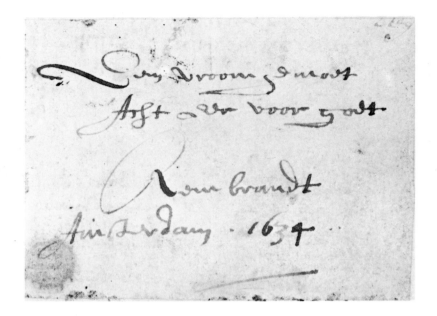

Rembrandt's inscription in the friendship album of Burchard Grossmann. 1634
The Hague, Royal Library

of the sheet he drew the head of an old man (see Illustration), a type we encounter in the pictures done during the thirties in many guises and roles. These studies are sometimes described as "rabbis," sometimes as "Orientals," and often simply as "Jews." But might not Rembrandt's saying mean that these old men symbolize devoutness, a certain attitude and cast of mind, rather than being studies done purely for their own pictorial value? They certainly belong to another world than the works plainly done on commission. It is not easy for us to fathom the large figures that belong to this group—the SCHOLAR in Prague [93], the MAN IN POLISH COSTUME [186], the Levantines [170, 182]. To say that they are casual workaday studies is not good enough, in view of their finished quality. Sometimes a new observation points the way to deeper understanding—the "Oriental" in the Devonshire Collection [70; Colorplate, p. 45] has now been identified by a scholar who took the care to ponder the meaning of all the details in the painting as KING UZZIAH STRICKEN WITH LEPROSY.

Women of dignity or heroic cast appear more rarely. Delilah, so far as we know, was never depicted separately from the dramatic event in which she was involved. Bathsheba is readily recognized, as is Susanna, even when the two lecherous elders are hidden in the thickets [84]. Esther is another matter—she is shown to us at a time prior to her act of valor [58]. It is no one else but Saskia at her morning toilet, presented to us in the guise of Queen Esther; but a comparison with the preliminary drawing (Illustration a, p. 249), which is far more domestic in character, shows us how significant and remote from everyday life the toilet scene has become in the painting. Here indeed is Queen Esther beautifying herself before entering the chamber of King Ahasuerus on her mission to see that her people are spared.

Nearly all the painted portraits of Saskia have a character distinct from traditional portraiture.[15] Dutch portraiture was essentially straightforward and direct, and so were Rembrandt's formal portraits during his early years in Amsterdam. If the sitters have any attributes of special significance, these take the form of hidden allusions that do not compromise the outright portrait character of their likenesses.

Saskia commands a genre of her own in Rembrandt's work. She comes to meet us from a glamorous and intriguing world. She

dwells in a picturesque, shadowy sphere different from our own familiar four walls, emerging only as the light picks her out [132; Colorplate, p. 55]. Even in the strikingly lifelike study in Dresden [134] she cuts an extraordinary figure by virtue of the poise and glamour with which Rembrandt has invested her—not to mention the colorful jewelry. This becomes especially evident when the Dresden painting is placed beside Rembrandt's unpretentious drawing of his fiancée in Berlin (Illustration a, p. 270). A rather wordy caption was added to this drawing, probably a bit later: "This is drawn after my wife, when she was 21 years old, the third day after our betrothal—the 8th of June 1633." Hence the sheet must have become something more than a swift sketch drawn in an hour of happiness, indeed a kind of engagement record.

Can Rembrandt's Flora pictures be regarded as portraits of Saskia [92; Colorplate, p. 43; 96]? Are they not rather personifications of that goddess, given a sense of immediacy in that Saskia served as the model? The tendency to give Bible stories and myths a touch of the present is seen in some of Rembrandt's earliest works. Recall his self-portrait among the assailants of Saint Stephen [2].

He appears to us again, this time with Saskia, in biblical guise as THE PRODIGAL SON IN THE TAVERN [79]. We are left wondering whether this picture is a Bible story in which Rembrandt and Saskia serve as models, or a double portrait as biblical masqueraders. In calling the picture THE PRODIGAL SON IN THE TAVERN we must bear in mind that there is no other representation of this theme with so sharply marked a portrait character. Other painters were given to telling the story in contemporary terms, as an everyday occurrence, an occasion for jollity. Their genre-like interpretation of the Bible message was at odds with Rembrandt's predilection for a sincere and direct reading of the Bible.

But for the double portrait described, Rembrandt's self-portraits during the thirties are never very far from reality. They have a certain flair, occasionally verging on the bombastic. The eyes, shaded by a beret that may be plumed, often seem to be engaged in searching scrutiny. The earliest painting in this series [99; Colorplate, p. 35] is done with painstaking care, in the Leyden tradition. A new Baroque touch is the boldly cocked hat

THE POET JAN HERMANSZ. KRUL [138]

56

a Adam Elsheimer TOBIAS AND THE ANGEL
  London, National Gallery

b Hercules Seghers and Rembrandt LANDSCAPE
  Florence, Uffizi

brim, lending an air of urbanity. This was how Rembrandt was still painting his patrons some years later [159, 166]. The change in his own expression and pose within a single year is startling. He has not only become graver—he has visibly aged [129]. Henceforth his favorite pose before the mirror is with his eyes glancing across his right shoulder, a pose that may express thoughtful reserve [142] or aggressiveness [144]. In the latter version the arrhythmic outline of the shoulder and beret lends a decidedly restless note.

Late in the thirties sheer fine painting crowded out the Baroque pathos—Rembrandt the hunter is shown holding up a dead bittern, her purple pinions spread out before him like a fan [191]. The man retreats behind a splendid still life. The loose composition is given support by a gallows-like post on the left, bearing Rembrandt's proud signature, and less strongly by a board fence in the background.

During the Leyden period Rembrandt, Lastman's star pupil, was mainly a history painter. In the Amsterdam years portraiture was added as a major activity—and so was landscape painting, to which we must now devote our attention. Yet, in considering Rembrandt's art by themes or genres we must not be misled into viewing it as nothing more than an aggregation of carefully developed specialties. In terms of the specialization to which the relatively young Dutch school of painting was given, Rembrandt was distinctly old-fashioned. He was the heir of 16th-century history painting, into which he breathed new life. More than any of his contemporaries, he aspired to the universality in art that was the ideal of the century before his own. In the years we are discussing, he dwelt on the heroic element in his art; and here Rubens the Fleming served as his inspiration and challenge in far greater measure than the Dutch realists with their eager eyes for the beauty of everyday life and Sunday landscape. In Holland, the new landscape style was developed above all by the draftsmen, artists like Jan and Esaias van de Velde, the youthful Jan van Goyen, Poelenburgh, and Breenbergh who, with the joy of discoverers, put down on paper the countryside as they saw it, at home and in Italy.

Rembrandt's landscapes dating from the thirties are of an altogether different order. There are only a few drawings from these years. Apparently his paintings were not based on landscape sketches. His early use of landscape is as a background and setting for his small mythology paintings [61, 62]. The countryside lends these works an unpretentious framework, a homeliness from which the narrative benefits. It must have been Adam Elsheimer who gave Rembrandt this classic outlook on landscape (Illustration a). In the LANDSCAPE WITH THE BAPTISM OF THE EUNUCH [195] the very story yields to the large forms of a fanciful landscape. Compared with the landscape style then dominant, Rembrandt's approach was old-fashioned and heavy-handed. His landscape is not an "inventory" of nature, but rather a series of compositional notions that happen to have taken on landscape form—light, air, and water impinging upon and permeating one another.

This fanciful approach to landscape has a tradition of its own. Links in the chain are, in retrospect, Hercules Seghers, Joos de Momper, Gillis van Coninxloo, Paolo Fiamingo, and in one aspect of his art Pieter Brueghel. That Rembrandt knew Seghers' landscapes is seen from the 1656 inventory of his possessions that lists several paintings by this artist.[16] Another point is that much later, probably after Seghers' death, Rembrandt acquired one of Seghers' copperplates, which he worked over and reprinted (Illustration, p. 108). One fascinating aspect of this revision is that Seghers' original etching copied a composition by Adam Elsheimer, which shines through even Rembrandt's retouching. We have, lastly, still another major document, Seghers' large landscape in the Uffizi, which may well have been the picture that hung in Rembrandt's salon—"a large landscape by Hercules Seghers" (Illustration b). Not without good reason it is thought that Rembrandt himself put the figures into the painting, also revising, adding, and retouching here and there in order to impart to the composition a degree of tonal unity still unattainable to Seghers and his generation.[17]

So far as we know today, Rembrandt never again painted a landscape as large as the early LANDSCAPE WITH THE BAPTISM OF THE EUNUCH of 1636. All the other landscapes of the thirties were really no more than oil sketches on panel, enjoying the special charm of fanciful brushwork that ties together both the reddish-brown ground of the wood in the shadows with the juicy yellow-white highlights. These swirling lines of light, shade, and

STORMY LANDSCAPE [200]

58

Roelant Savery FANTASY LANDSCAPE
Glimmen, Holland, Collection of Mr. T. E. Niemeyer

movement strengthen and dramatize even the most familiar motifs into landscapes of fantasy [198, 199]. We may call them sketches—works created on the impulse of strong inward feeling—but this does not mean that they were preliminary studies, laying the groundwork for more elaborate and finished paintings. Pictures like those in Cracow and Boston are marked by a degree of conviction, assurance, and definitive validity of creative form that precludes any thought that they were done for some ulterior purpose.

The dramatic element fades in the early forties. Large structures are given greater prominence in the overall picture [265, 266]; but the churches, portals, ruins, towers, and walls that now dominate the landscape are weird and unreal. The last landscapes, probably done in the fifties, are constructed with marked emphasis and severe organization. They are the true Dutch counterparts to the classical landscapes of Claude and Poussin.

On two occasions Rembrandt did paint landscape sketches that seem to depict a locale he had actually seen [267, 345]. Vivid and vigorous as his brush is, these works lack the soaring, airy delicacy of true sketches. The colors are heavier, the brushwork more emphatic, the composition graver. It is indeed the landscape drawings of this period, which we shall treat in a later chapter, that capture nature with freshness and intimacy.

Rembrandt as a Teacher

We have already noted with some surprise that Rembrandt had pupils even as a very young artist in Leyden. One of them, Gerard Dou, attained a measure of fame, though with a style of painting that had by then ceased to bear any relation to Rembrandt. The other disciples are of small importance. Yet there are some works from the Leyden circle that resemble Rembrandt's early paintings so closely that they still puzzle us today.

In Amsterdam Rembrandt resumed his teaching almost at once, and we have rather precise documentary evidence on who his students were. A highly controversial group of pictures are given by some scholars to Rembrandt himself, by others to various disciples. It seems to have been the custom then for a master to sell the work of his students and assistants under his own name and even to sign such paintings after touching them up. On the back of one Rembrandt drawing we find a note in his own hand, recording that he had sold works by "Fardynandus" (Ferdinand Bol) and "Leenderts" (Leendert Cornelisz. van Beyeren); these works were probably copies of paintings by Rembrandt himself.[1] On the other hand, there are virtually no signed works by Rembrandt pupils dating from the time of their apprenticeship.

The German painter and art historian Joachim von Sandrart reports that Rembrandt's "home in Amsterdam was crowded with countless young people from leading families who came there for instruction and tuition, each paying him an annual fee of 100 guilders."[2] Added to this were the profits Rembrandt realized from the sale of his students' works. Sandrart was in Amsterdam in the years 1637–42, and his testimony inspires confidence, for as a noted painter he had entrée to the best circles. That Sandrart should call Rembrandt's pupils "aristocrats" is a reflection of his own preoccupation, as a court painter, with social class. Indeed, some of Rembrandt's former pupils, such as Govaert Flinck and Ferdinand Bol, were by the time Sandrart published his work (1675) as well-placed in Dutch society as Sandrart was in Germany. Most painters' apprentices, however—Rembrandt's included—came from the lower middle class.

A few drawings from the school of Rembrandt actually show the master with his students (Illustration a, p. 64). Rembrandt does not seem to have run the usual kind of studio, with only a handful of apprentices. His included older men as well as well-dressed young men, neither of whom can have been apprentices, but who came for a less formal kind of instruction in art, attracted by Rembrandt's personality and art. Thus, there is nothing implausible in Sandrart's report that well-to-do Amsterdam citizens were given to sending their children to Rembrandt for drawing lessons at fancy rates. By the thirties he had become quite a famous artist, with commissions from the Stadholder himself, and he was able to spend large sums on works of art at Amsterdam auctions. Indeed, his own works had already become so well known that even copies of them commanded a certain market value!

The drawing of Rembrandt's studio shows his students in a life class. Some of these student drawings of nudes have come down to us, and we can actually make out the same model in the same pose, drawn from different aspects and distances. We know from van Mander that drawing after life was an important part of the training in painters' studios. We also know from inspecting students' drawings that Rembrandt often took the trouble of correcting their work in his own hand.[3] What is striking in the surviving drawings and paintings made by Rembrandt pupils during their apprenticeship is the large number of copies after other works of art—paintings and etchings by Rembrandt himself and the Italian drawings and prints he collected so eagerly.[4]

That drawing from life was part of Rembrandt's teaching technique is confirmed by an anecdote which Houbraken relates. Rembrandt had rented a warehouse on the Bloemgracht to accommodate his large enrolment of students, and the working space had been divided into small compartments with paper and canvas partitions, so that the students could work undisturbed. But on one occasion Rembrandt overheard a student telling a model: "Now we are both naked, as in the Garden of Eden." The master knocked on the door with his maulstick and said: "Since you are both naked, you are expelled from the Garden of Eden!"[5]

When Rembrandt left Leyden, and Lievens, to move to Amsterdam, he apparently took along several works by Lievens, which is not surprising in the light of their long friendship and close collaboration. He put these works to different purposes in his studio. The Lievens paintings and etchings were used as study material by Rembrandt's new pupils. Some Lievens heads of old men were etched by Rembrandt himself as well as his pupils, and

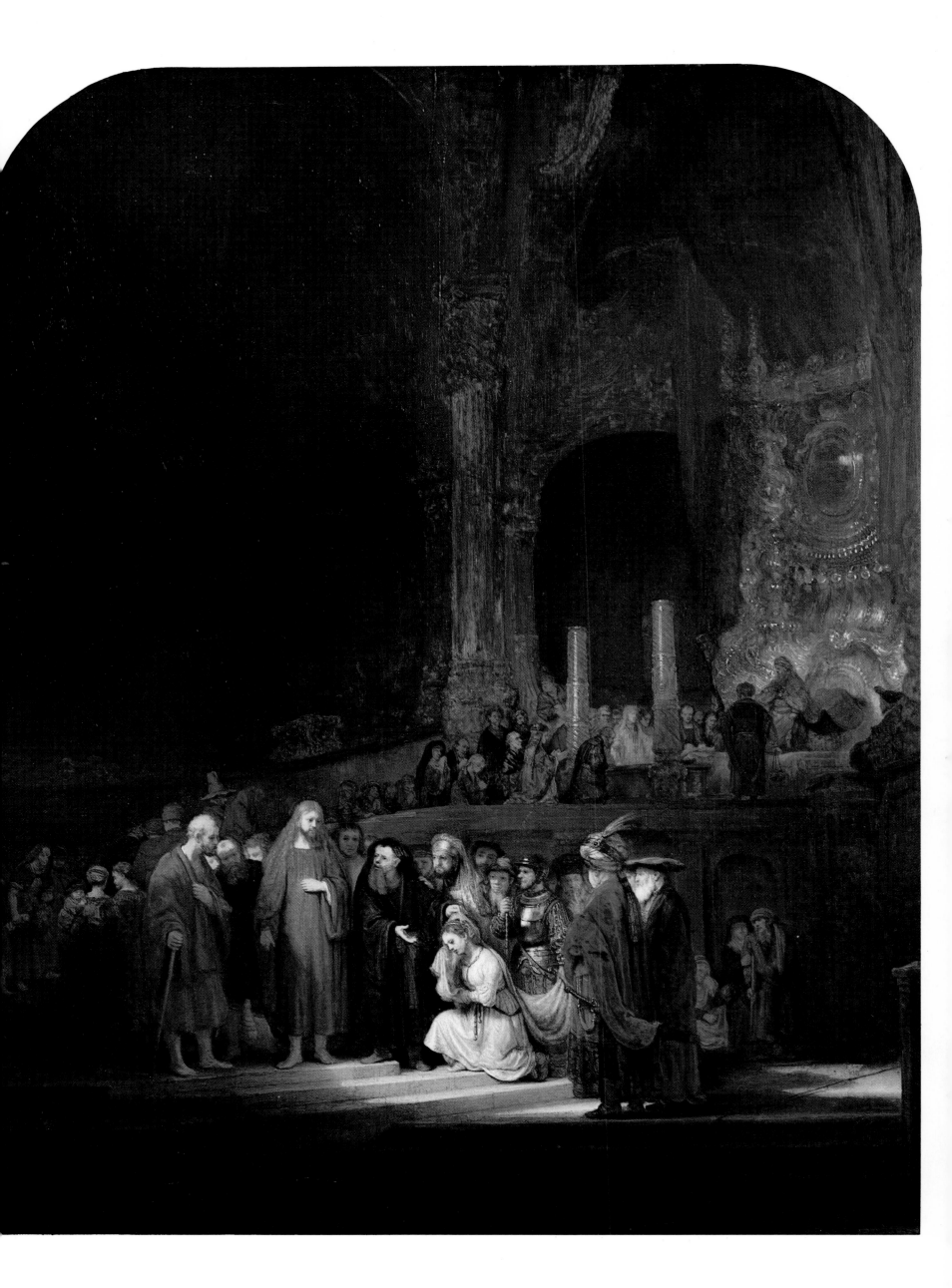

a School of Rembrandt THE STUDIO OF REMBRANDT
Drawing. Darmstadt, Landesmuseum

b Jan Lievens and Rembrandt HEAD OF A CHILD
Amsterdam, Rijksmuseum

then signed "worked over by Rembrandt". We have already mentioned a Lievens painting of a child (Illustration b) signed *Rembrandt geretuceer Liev*, which was probably worked over by Rembrandt without the help of pupils, around the time of his move to Amsterdam. Lievens' influence on Rembrandt's portrait style remained rather strong—we often suspect that Rembrandt is dealing with concepts of portraiture first formulated by Lievens.

Among the first Rembrandt pupils of the Amsterdam period was Jacob Backer. Backer came to Amsterdam around 1632 from Leeuwarden, where he had studied under a local painter whose work is not unlike Lastman's. While there is no documentary evidence that he studied under Rembrandt, Backer's portraits dating from his early years in Amsterdam bear the strong impress of Rembrandt's style (Illustration b, p. 66); and whether or not he was actually Rembrandt's student, he clearly modeled his portrait style after Rembrandt's, rather than the distinctive Amsterdam manner best seen in the works of Thomas de Keyser and Nicolaes Elias (Illustration a, p. 28). The deep and powerful modeling that Rembrandt adopted in deliberate emulation of Rubens is found in Backer as well. Moreover, we can discern a strong creative kinship with Lievens in Backer's work, which he could only have developed, in Amsterdam, in Rembrandt's studio.[6]

A large version of THE ANGEL STOPPING ABRAHAM FROM SACRIFICING ISAAC TO GOD in Munich bears the explicit legend: "Modified and overpainted by Rembrandt. 1636." It is indeed a copy, with some changes, of the painting now in Leningrad [74], which Rembrandt had finished the year before. The copy has been ascribed to Govaert Flinck who, during the year in question, had first begun to sign his own paintings. It must have been done in Rembrandt's studio, for apparently Flinck had been required to study and copy not only Rembrandt's original but also a drawing from it (Illustration a, p. 226). Rembrandt probably went over the entire copy and signed it with unusually scrupulous exactness.

Other accomplished copies after Rembrandt have been attributed to Flinck, but the disciple's own history paintings of the later thirties lag far behind the master. Flinck's dramatic invention seems rather vacuous and superficial. During the forties,

however, Flinck cast off the strong Rembrandtesque elements of his style, a step eventually taken by nearly all the master's pupils. Flinck's portraits and studies dating back to the thirties, together with his scenes of daily life, are much closer to Rembrandt's approach. His charming portraits of Rembrandt and Saskia show them as shepherds (Illustrations a, b, p. 134), in a free approach to portraiture that bears the mark of Rembrandt's influence. His portrait of the Jewish scholar Manasseh ben Israel, done in 1637, is worthy of Rembrandt himself (Illustrations a, b, p. 156). The original Flinck signature has, in fact, been scraped away and replaced with a spurious Rembrandt signature. It is not at all unlikely that some other signed "Rembrandts" have suffered the same treatment, which can be ascertained only when the paintings are cleaned.[7]

Arnold Houbraken, whose artists' biographies, published in 1718, form our most important source for the art of Rembrandt and his disciples, tells us in considerable detail how Jacob Backer and Govaert Flinck (who were friends) came to Amsterdam, where Flinck had wealthy relations. Although both men were already full-fledged painters, Flinck found it expedient to take instruction under Rembrandt for another year, "for at this time Rembrandt's style was so universally admired that everything had to fit its mold in order to please the world." Within a short time Flinck had learned to follow Rembrandt's style so closely that many of his paintings were considered genuine Rembrandts and sold as such.

Yet later on, at the cost of much effort, he managed to cast off Rembrandt's style. Rembrandt was still alive, but the scales were struck from the eyes of the world when Italian paintings began to be imported by the true connoisseurs; from then on lucidity in painting was once more appreciated.[8]

So characteristic is this sequence of phases that one might conclude Houbraken was simply repeating a familiar stereotype: the student whose work can scarcely be distinguished from the famous master's, and who then turns in a new direction when the master falls out of fashion. Rembrandt's pupils did tend to follow this pattern, although most of them adapted themselves to the "Italian manner" with greater ease than did Flinck.

Of course we would expect Rembrandt to go his own way, creating, within the period style, a personal style of great originality, and this is what he did. Yet to suggest that this put him

a Adriaen van Ostade LANDSCAPE. 1639
Rotterdam, Willem van der Vorm Foundation

b Jacob Backer JOHANNES UYTTENBOGAERT. 1635
Amsterdam, Rijksmuseum (on loan)

seriously at odds with the newer generation is a fiction of later times. Houbraken was basing himself on late 17th-century classicistic theory when he drew a sharp line between Rembrandt, the "son of darkness," and the radiant new style of his classicist followers.

In the course of the years Flinck amassed a large art collection. Among the drawings he owned were magnificent late landscapes by Rembrandt; together with some Italian drawings, these were bequeathed to his son, who ultimately sold them to the Duke of Devonshire—they are still preserved in the Devonshire Collection at Chatsworth. They give a small but significant indication that Flinck continued to hold the late art of Rembrandt in high esteem, despite current changes in taste.

Ferdinand Bol, a wealthy young aristocrat (as seen by Sandrart), must have entered Rembrandt's workshop a few years later than Backer. Stylistic analysis of his early works, dating from the early forties, indicates that he admired above all the warm glow of Rembrandt's mood paintings from the late thirties, unlike Flinck, who was captured by the master's vehement pathos. Bol's portraits, in particular, continue to echo the warmth of Rembrandt's palette. He displays an extraordinary empathy with Rembrandt's portrait style of the forties. A few portraits with spurious Rembrandt signatures may actually be by Bol.[9]

We need not follow the story of every one of Rembrandt's more than 30 disciples. Rembrandt's own growth is reflected in successive student generations, sometimes with a certain time lag and some curious distortions—all this will be discussed when we consider the fourth decade. A much more disquieting question concerns the early works by these pupils and still others that must have been painted in Rembrandt's studio but still remain unidentified. Leendert Cornelisz. van Beyeren, a shadowy figure, is known to have done a series of copies after Rembrandts as early as 1638, chiefly copies of heads of a kind that occur in Dutch inventories of the time with some frequency. But where have these particular copies gone? And what about the six still lifes, the night scene, and the Good Samaritan, student pictures that were touched up by Rembrandt and listed in his own 1656 inventory?[10] Could the "lost" heads be identical with certain "Rembrandts" of which there are several replicas of equal but not particularly outstanding merit? It seems quite probable that some of the

young men in Rembrandt's shop made these mediocre copies, while Rembrandt's original may not have been preserved.[11] And since we know portraits of Rembrandt by Flinck, we must surely reckon it plausible that other students painted his likeness. They probably copied self-portraits, which would have been the most readily available of all Rembrandt's paintings—and the likeliest starting points for experimentation.

Rembrandt's dramatically effective lighting, his picturesque old men, his emotion-charged Bible stories became valued creative coin even beyond the circle of his students—indeed, even beyond the walls of Amsterdam. Many of his contemporaries regarded Rembrandt's early Amsterdam style as his greatest contribution to the art of his age. It was a style that painters like Salomon Koninck, only a little younger than Rembrandt, modified to suit a more popular taste. The sheer technical side of Rembrandt's art in the thirties—mainly his eminently dramatic use of chiaroscuro—inspired still other artists to try out new possibilities. Some minor Amsterdam painters adopted a Rembrandtesque chiaroscuro, but the only chiaroscuro painting of real artistic importance, apart from Rembrandt himself, was being done elsewhere. There were Leonard Bramer in Delft, Simon de Vlieger in Rotterdam, Adriaen van Ostade in Haarlem —though for the last two the flirtation with Rembrandt's art lasted but a short while. In Haarlem, particularly, its echo took on many forms. Ostade's early landscapes and his studies for heads—perhaps to be dated even earlier—are truly splendid works that express the spirit of Rembrandt (Illustration a); and the brown palette of Rembrandt became almost second nature to Jacob de Wet, an early work by whom was but a short while ago mistakenly ascribed to Rembrandt.[12]

The history painters Salomon de Bray, Pieter de Grebber, and Willem de Poorter for a time created pictures with a dramatic pointedness altogether unknown to their Haarlem colleagues, Frans Hals and his circle. And around 1635 even still lifes—such as those by Pieter Claesz.—are wrapped in a warm golden-green light borrowed from Rembrandt's work of the early thirties. By 1640, however, the passion for concentrated dramatic narrative on the model of Rembrandt had given way to other preferences. As has already been emphasized, this was no more than a natural development. Houbraken may have found the artistic career of

PHILIPS LUCASZ. [178]

a Carel Fabritius THE RAISING OF LAZARUS
Warsaw, Muzeum Narodowe

b Rembrandt THE RAISING OF LAZARUS. Etching. 1642
Amsterdam, Rijksmuseum

Govaert Flinck a noteworthy phenomenon, but for us it merely confirms the historical rule. In the thirties the fascination that issued from Rembrandt's art was all but irresistible. For the painters born after 1615 its grip became progressively looser.

More surprising is the observation that even painters whom art historians are fond of labeling as the complete antithesis to Rembrandt are indebted to him at earlier stages of their development. The dazzling figures of Bartholomeus van der Helst, whose brilliant civic guard pieces outshine even Rembrandt's NIGHT WATCH, owe much more to Rembrandt than to Nicolaes Elias, van der Helst's teacher. His PORTRAIT OF A PREACHER, done in 1638 (Illustration b, p. 52), is indeed worthy of Rembrandt himself.

Yet to art lovers of the 17th and 18th centuries the contrast between Rembrandt and van der Helst represented the ultimate opposition of 17th-century Dutch painting.[13] More recent generations have tended to apply such a polarity rather to Rembrandt and Vermeer, with Carel Fabritius forming the link between them. Fabritius studied with Rembrandt—and he may have been Vermeer's teacher. His ties with the school of Delft are clearly seen in his paintings dating from 1654, the year he died. The lucid construction of his interiors, his bright palette, his neat and tranquil world—all these qualities mark the essence of Vermeer as well. The connection between Fabritius and Rembrandt was less obvious, at least until the discovery of Fabritius' RAISING OF LAZARUS (Illustration a) dated 1642, in which he adapted Rembrandt's etching, done ten years earlier (Illustration a, p. 184), to the spirit of his own generation. The cool new taste preferred to see even so dramatic a theme stripped of the accentuated pathos of earlier years. In Fabritius' version, Jesus still dominates the scene, but Lazarus no longer serves as a counterpoise. The agitated witnesses encircle the risen man's tomb, and in this way the picture area is more evenly filled than in Rembrandt's earlier composition. Further, the horizontal element of the stone sarcophagus is shifted to become an emphatic division between light and shadow.

In that same year of 1642 Rembrandt himself did another etching of THE RAISING OF LAZARUS, which also reflects the new style (Illustration b). If Fabritius was familiar with the new etching, he did not draw on it for his composition. It is entirely in

keeping with our high estimate of Fabritius' talent that he should have been capable of autonomous creative achievement even while he still served in Rembrandt's workshop. We are quite prepared to entertain the idea that master and student worked side by side in recasting the same theme.

During the forties Fabritius developed a new type of portraiture in which heads of great expressiveness are shown against a bright wall. The broad, flat brush strokes that speak of quick, rapt execution are not unlike the Rembrandt technique of those years, but Rembrandt worked with such ardent intensity only on his small Bible paintings, not on his portraits. All the same, he did pose some of his sitters against a lighted wall in those years [230, 232, 245], possibly as a deliberate tribute to his disciple. One of these studies—a reading man—survives in a confusing abundance of replicas, and once again we are brought face to face with the likelihood that Rembrandt's pupils frequently made copies after the same original work by the master, perhaps as an exercise. Is it possible that in this case, Rembrandt's original was inspired by Fabritius?[14]

We have already noted that in the forties Rembrandt began to avoid dramatic postures used purely for effect, just as he now stopped overdramatizing his themes as a whole. The typical "grandstand play" of the sharply foreshortened hand reaching out toward the viewer, for example, went into limbo. It still occurs in THE NIGHT WATCH and—very conspicuously—in the etched portrait of JAN CORNELISZ. SYLVIUS of 1646 (Illustration b, p. 349).

Rembrandt was fond of the motif of the painted frame, not so much to lend his portraits and themes a greater semblance of reality, "as though they were stepping into our own world," but rather to give support to his delicate, floating figures, to circumscribe the world in which they dwell. The pendant portraits of 1641 [232, 233; Colorplates, pp. 82, 83] are the finest examples from this period. Rembrandt's disciples—both those who are known to us by name and some others—misused this motif purely for the traditional purpose of enhanced realism. Govaert Flinck, in that very same year of 1641, takes over his master's original motif by allowing a shepherd's crook to project and overlap the painted frame.[15] Jan Victors and Ferdinand Bol employed the device with much emphasis and elegance (Illustration a, p. 70).

THE ENTOMBMENT OF CHRIST [217]

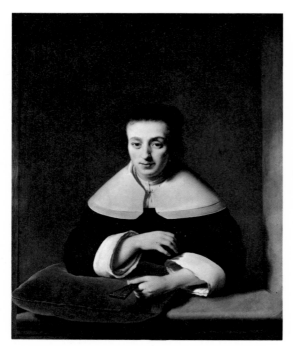

a Ferdinand Bol WOMAN IN A WINDOW. 1652
Scotland, Private Collection

b Bartholomeus van der Helst WOMAN BEHIND A CURTAIN. 1652
Dresden, Gemaeldegalerie

Van der Helst, finally, elaborates it with all the craft of which he was master (Illustration b). Rembrandt himself took up the motif once again in his later years [285]; but a greater contrast than that between his approach and van der Helst's can scarcely be imagined.

Rembrandt's contemporaries, however, did not seem to appreciate that he possessed greater subtlety than his pupils. Roger de Piles, whose ideas about Rembrandt were less distorted by classicistic bias than those of Houbraken and other later commentators, tells us that he bought "LA SERVANTE de Rembrandt, un véritable trompe l'œil" when he was in Holland. He insists that the artist had hung the finished painting in a window frame that fitted it exactly, and that all passers-by "furent trompés." Dutch art, to Roger de Piles, exemplified what he considered the ultimate mission of all painting—to reproduce the visible world with such perfection as to fool the eye. He praised Rembrandt's sovereign grasp of chiaroscuro; and, indeed, in his *Balance des Peintres* Rembrandt took pride of place beside Rubens, Duerer, the Italians, and the French.[16] To our delight—and his exculpation—it turns out that de Piles was fooled in more ways than one. What he bought was no more than a school picture. It hangs today in Woburn Abbey, having been acquired in 1742, at the de Piles

auction, by an ancestor of the present Duke of Bedford. It was once thought that de Piles had bought the picture now in Stockholm [285]; one cannot really see why, for that painting is of such a character as to rule out any thought of illusionism.

In sum, Rembrandt's activity as a teacher was important in a number of respects. It was an important source of income and, no doubt, of gratification. It served to broadcast the new elements of his style and technique all over Europe. Further, as a teacher Rembrandt came to form the early careers and styles of more than 30 young men. Alas, not one of the young men who studied with him in the thirties and forties carried Rembrandt's style of those decades forward to the following generations. His weaker students responded to the demands of the market and of changing fashion; while the only one to bear the mark of greatness, Carel Fabritius, evolved a highly personal style and paid his teacher the ultimate compliment of achieving a stature entirely his own. Yet the bond between Rembrandt and Fabritius and Vermeer is no less real for the lack of superficial similarity between the works of the three. The example of uncompromising integrity set by Rembrandt was equally capable of inspiring a romantic genius like Fabritius and a creator like Jan Vermeer who rivaled nature in all her richness.

The Night Watch

Rembrandt's great painting, done in 1642 and perhaps the best-known among Dutch works of art, still poses a great many puzzles. True, it is unambiguously signed and dated, and its original location in the great hall of the civic guard headquarters in Amsterdam is well documented, as are its subsequent vicissitudes down to the time it was installed in the Rijksmuseum. Its provenance is thus known without a break, a record equaled by only a few other Rembrandts. The difficulties begin when it comes to interpreting its meaning, indeed the very title, THE NIGHT WATCH, which the painting has borne for something like 150 years [239; Illustration a, p. 339; Colorplate, p. 73].

THE NIGHT WATCH certainly does not depict what the title says it does; nor is it a "night patrol," to use a descriptive term from the year 1808. No, the title is wrong and misleading; indeed it came to be applied to the painting only in the 19th century. The current catalogue of the Rijksmuseum entitles the picture THE COMPANY OF CAPTAIN FRANS BANNING COCQ AND LIEUTENANT WILLEM VAN RUYTENBURCH, POPULARLY KNOWN AS THE "NIGHTWATCH."

Is it a mere accident that we cling to this improper designation? Surely it is not without significance that for many people the title has become the epitome of Rembrandt's art, a symbol—possibly outmoded today—of what his style is conceived to be, a blend of darkness and gloom broken by sudden glows and flashes. Much in it is dark and hidden. Even at first glance it leaves an oddly unsatisfactory impression when compared with other civic guard pieces. Yet we know a good deal about how it came to be painted and at whose behest, though the story is by no means complete. A glass cabinet in the room in the Rijksmuseum where THE NIGHT WATCH is displayed holds a family album once owned by Captain Frans Banning Cocq, who had a copy of the picture drawn in it (Illustration, p. 74) with the following explanatory text:

This is a sketch of the painting in the great hall of the Kloveniersdoelen [civic guard headquarters], *showing the young Squire of Purmerlandt* [Banning Cocq's title], *as captain, ordering his lieutenant, the Squire of Vlaardingen, to move off with his civic guard company.*

Two facts emerge: the painting was destined from the beginning for the civic guard hall and Rembrandt had to take this assigned location into account; and Frans Banning Cocq saw himself as the central figure, allowing the inference that he and he alone commissioned the painting. The question remains whether he had particular occasion to have his company with its officers portrayed in this particular year of 1642.

Had Banning Cocq been the sole patron, he would surely have paid the full fee himself. Yet two of the civic guardsmen were later to testify, in identical notarized statements, that "16 of them had each paid 100 guilders, some a little more, others a little less, according to the place they occupied in the painting."[1] For the guardsmen who each paid their 100-odd guilders, then, the painting was simply a group portrait; but to the captain it commemorated his tenure as commander of the company. There are, by the way, many more people in the picture than the 16 paying guardsmen and their two officers. It is possible, though unlikely, that Rembrandt's civic guard picture was painted to commemorate the festive procession in which Maria de Medici entered the city of Amsterdam.[2] This event occurred in 1638. A printed description records in words and engravings the splendor, merriment, and popular entertainments that attended this event. A mounted detachment of militiamen rode out to receive the party, while others lined the streets, canals, and bridges. The civic guard, by the way, had long ceased to be a proper military force by then. The companies were little more than clubs that served social purposes.

Other painters commemorated other guards groups on this occasion and all of these pictures were at one time on display in the Amsterdam guildhall. Today they are all assembled in the Night Watch Hall of the Rijksmuseum, and in their company the unusual approach of Rembrandt's group picture makes itself felt even more strongly. Rembrandt had set himself the task of painting not merely the portrait of a group of men, but the portrait of a group performing a common action—falling in for the march, as it is described in Banning Cocq's album. Even the manner in which the men are deploying may reflect Banning Cocq's feeling about how he would have liked to see his order carried out, for we certainly cannot exclude the possibility that the unusual suggestion of a "group portrait in action" stemmed from him.

The first impression is one of sheer movement. The captain is in black, the lieutenant in yellow—he is struck by the full light—and the ensign completes the officer group. Rembrandt shows the

Sketch after THE NIGHT WATCH, in album of Capt. Banning Cocq. Amsterdam, Rijksmuseum (on loan)

ensign waving the big flag with the arms of Amsterdam underneath the archway. By tradition the Amsterdam school included the ensign along with the captain and lieutenant in a compact central group (Illustration, p. 76); the sergeants, too, are usually easy to identify, as are the ranks with their swords, bucklers, and muskets. In THE NIGHT WATCH the arrangement of the red musketeers, at least, is readily understood. The one on the left is loading his reversed weapon. Another, almost hidden behind the captain, is firing off a shot, while a third, to the right of the lieutenant, is blowing the powder from his lock. Three exercises from the manual of arms are thus shown here. The drummer can also be seen on the right—his doublet is of a rich-hued green that seems to be borrowed from a Titian.

By comparison with other guards pictures, by such as Flinck, Sandrart, and Jacob Backer, Rembrandt's men do not seem to be in proper uniform at all. Was it Rembrandt himself who dressed up his characters in such picturesque garb, or did other painters simply tidy up their portraits, improving on reality? We are always strongly tempted to look to Rembrandt for the kind of freedom and imagination realistic Dutch portraiture in general seems to lack. On the other hand, we prick up our ears when we hear Caspar van Baerle, in his description of Maria de Medici's entry into Amsterdam, complaining that "some guardsmen dressed up to suit themselves, while others donned armor from head to toe."[3] Perhaps the realities of Dutch life were after all more picturesque than the neat and tidy pictures of the custom painters would have us believe—though not as sweepingly and ardently dramatic as they appear in the art of Rembrandt.

An escutcheon on the archway lists the names of the 18 guardsmen portrayed in THE NIGHT WATCH. When captain and lieutenant are excluded, the number agrees precisely with the 16 guardsmen who paid an average fee of 100 guilders for their portraits. A full count, however, runs to no less than 28 people and three children on the huge picture—and originally there were still three more. Clearly Rembrandt added many figures in order to round out the dramatis personae, and who is to say which of these are portraits and which creatures of the imagination? What business have the children there? The lad hastening ahead is probably the "powder boy" bent on having his horn refilled. But what about the two girls? Are they added merely for their pic-turesque dress, to provide a bright patch of color amid the dark tones?

Yet it is not merely by the addition of these fanciful and unmotivated supernumeraries and children that Rembrandt broke with the tradition of the Amsterdam guards piece and its fixed scheme. Whether by the terms of Banning Cocq's commission or on his own, what Rembrandt wanted to show was a group of soldiers on the point of moving off. He wished to represent movement—movement in depth, coming toward us and involving us in the event. Under this aspect, THE NIGHT WATCH represents a landmark in the art of the Baroque during the 1630's, outdistancing in sweep and power even Rembrandt's deeds of Old Testament violence with their sharp light and shadow effects. The captain and lieutenant stand almost literally in the limelight, as though on a stage. The officer's hand and his companion's weapon thrust forward from the picture surface—the illusion is complete. The shadow of the extended hand is plainly projected on the lieutenant's uniform, enhancing the sense of striding forward, a movement that brings the group closer to the center. Behind them the platoon is falling in, but on either side the eye is drawn into vague depths, while at the edges of the picture people loom up once more. This movement of the figures in and out of depth is organized within the picture area by a system of diagonal lines. On the right side the lieutenant's spear, the powder-blowing musketeer's weapon, and another single long lance strike a gentle falling note, in contrast to the noticeable rise on the left created by the red guardsman's musket and the ensign's flagstaff. Our eyes, accustomed to scanning a picture from left to right, resist the dynamic trend in this composition and its figures, and this counterpressure enhances the picture's air of imminent departure.

As yet we have not mentioned an element of considerable importance to the structure of the picture, the architecture. The heavy horizontal cornice and the large arch are classic forms of repose and detachment. Kenneth Clark sees in all this hints of Raphael's *Stanze*, known to Rembrandt from engravings.[4] The harmony of figures and architecture was even more eloquent—especially on the left—before the canvas was cropped. There was more "stage" on the left and to the front, drawing the two main figures toward the center, accented by the arch in the back wall. A copy attributed to Gerrit Lundens reproduces the original

Cornelis Ketel THE COMPANY OF CAPTAIN DIRCK JACOBSZ. ROSECRANS. 1588
Amsterdam, Rijksmuseum

state (on loan to the Rijksmuseum). In any event, so emphatic an architectural framework is something new in Rembrandt's art, an element tempering the Baroque hustle and bustle. In this respect, THE NIGHT WATCH has grown far beyond the "violence" pictures.

Though THE NIGHT WATCH represents an unusually dynamic formal solution to the problem posed by the group portrait at mid-17th century, it is by no means the only such solution possible. Frans Hals had already developed an equally dynamic type of civic guard painting much different in character. He achieved pictorial unity and liveliness not by bold effects of chiaroscuro and deep space above and about the figures, but by an ingenious arrangement of the figures themselves and of compositional lines in the traditional horizontal format. His paintings of the thirties (Illustration, p. 78) may seem conventional beside THE NIGHT WATCH, but they are planned with the same consistency and concentration. In any case, they show us that there were alternative solutions to the Baroque group portrait—and enormously successful ones at that—quite different from Rembrandt's solution in THE NIGHT WATCH.

So far we have been considering THE NIGHT WATCH merely as a commissioned guards piece—true, a rather unusual one. Scholars have lately sought to give it deeper allegorical meaning, however, quite apart from its immediate theme and the circumstances in which it was commissioned. According to one interpretation, it symbolizes the stalwart militancy of Amsterdam's glorious past, as exemplified by the city's hero, Gysbrecht van Amstel, whose personality and career were brought vividly to life in the 17th century by the great Dutch poet, Joost van den Vondel, in his play of 1636. In this reading of the painting, obscure details become more comprehensible when they are viewed as allegories—the girl in the light dress, for example, symbolizes the goddess of victory, Banning Cocq's gesture drives home the point of an irrefutable argument. The captain himself personifies Gysbrecht van Amstel, in this interpretation.[5]

Such theories are of never-ending interest to the art historian. They hint that 17th-century Dutch realism masked a picture language using veiled symbols and allegories; but Rosenberg-Slive and Knuttel argue, against the view of Hellinga, that the

many portrait and documentary elements in THE NIGHT WATCH should not take second place to any hypothetical disguised meaning.[6] The allegorical readings that have been proposed so far, moreover, are far less plausible than in some other Dutch portraits; for example, the very consistent interpretation of Frans Hals' dual portrait of Isaac Massa and his wife proposed by de Jongh and Vinken.[7] All the same, the notion is intriguing that this queer group portrait might carry a second reality, a deeper layer of meaning, just as Rembrandt's portrait sitters in fanciful dress, his Orientals and biblical patriarchs all point in the direction of a deeper reality. It is no accident that we are so often uncertain whether a given Rembrandt represents a portrait, a piece of history, or an allegorical concept. This ambiguity seems to be rooted in his unconventional outlook, which grew more and more personal with age. Rembrandt simply did not share the Dutch contentment with everyday visual impressions.[8]

The ambiguity that envelops THE NIGHT WATCH is deepened when we regard the veiled visual idiom of an outright allegory that Rembrandt painted about the same time and that has often been linked to THE NIGHT WATCH. It was listed in his 1656 inventory under the title of THE CONCORD OF THE STATE [206; Colorplate, p. 75], which must have been Rembrandt's own name for the composition. The painting was evidently never sold. It is painted in grisaille, and may represent an oil sketch for an etching that was never done. However the various motifs may be interpreted in detail, the basic meaning is plain—the union of the Dutch provinces to meet the common foe. Confederation (the column with arms), religion, armed force, and justice—these are the pillars of concord. The armorial bearings of the Netherlandish towns are strung out behind the escutcheon of Amsterdam; and it is the emphasis on Amsterdam within the union, together with the mobilization of the militia to defend city and country, that are elements potentially linking this allegory with THE NIGHT WATCH. One scholar even goes so far as to suggest that the guardsmen at the rear of THE NIGHT WATCH may have been mounted originally, like the horsemen in THE CONCORD OF THE STATE. Both works certainly share ostentation in dress. Still, THE CONCORD OF THE STATE flaunts its allegorical message, while the portrait character of THE NIGHT WATCH remains very strong.[9]

Frans Hals THE COMPANY OF CAPTAIN REYNIER REAEL
Amsterdam, Rijksmuseum

We owe much to Hellinga for his detailed interpretation of the puzzling visual idiom in which these two works are done. His basic premise is that in the structure and grouping of THE NIGHT WATCH Rembrandt drew on impressions of a performance of Vondel's *Gysbrecht van Amstel*, which he may have seen in 1638. This view finds support in van de Waal's observation that Rembrandt did at this time make drawings of other characters in Vondel's drama.[10]

This wonderful transmutation of the conventional, static group portrait into a dramatic incident in which the figures happen to be portraits may, of course, have been part and parcel of Banning Cocq's commission. Van Ravesteyn too, after all, had been required to show the officers of the St. Sebastian Company taking part in a reception for the magistrate, thus painting something more than a group portrait. At the same time, there is no reason to doubt that Rembrandt's imagination may have been stimulated by a stage performance—a supremely visual experience with the power of transporting him from the bourgeois world around him to a world of glamour, fancy dress, and exotic architecture. It may be no accident that the two main figures in THE NIGHT WATCH seem, as we have already noted, to be standing and gesticulating just behind the footlights.

How Rembrandt's extraordinary group portrait was regarded in the 17th century, whether it was admired or disliked—on these points we have very little evidence. Apart from the notarized statement by two of the sitters—who are not likely to have said anything unfavorable—we have only the testimony of Rembrandt's pupil, Samuel van Hoogstraten, who deals with certain questions of art theory in his *Inleyding tot de Hooge Schole der Schilderkonst*, published in 1678. Van Hoogstraten says nothing on such subjects as allegory and symbolism, but he does discuss the composition as such, and as we do even today he puzzles over the relationship between portraiture and the imagination. Since his is a defense of Rembrandt, there must have been some contemporary criticism, which should scarcely surprise us. Van Hoogstraten begins by attacking the traditional manner of lining up portraits side by side, as was the custom in Dutch militia pieces. What was important was to integrate the work of art as a whole.

Rembrandt observed this quite correctly in his painting in the guards hall—too much so, in the view of many—paying greater heed to the sweep of his imagination than to the individual portraits he was required to do. There may be some fault in this, yet as far as I am concerned his picture outdistances all the others. So painterly in invention is his work, so skillful in composition, so full of power, that beside it the other paintings are said to look more like mere playing cards. I must admit, however, that I could have wished he had brought more light into it.

Criticism van Hoogstraten voiced, but he remained full of admiration for the unique grandeur of Rembrandt's group portrait.[11]

In the course of the years THE NIGHT WATCH suffered the kind of vicissitudes to which many other Rembrandt paintings were exposed. It was mutilated, disfigured, cleaned, and then buried in yellow varnish again. With the expenditure of much effort it has now been expertly restored and installed in good light conditions in the Rijksmuseum. Viewers are kept at a respectful distance, as before a sacred shrine. Sad to say, during the 17th century the civic guardsmen were less scrupulous in cherishing the pride of their hall. Traces of scars and scratches can be made out on the canvas even today—the guardsmen, brandishing their formidable lances and halberds, were much closer to the painting than we are allowed to come.

In 1715 it was taken down from the great hall of the guard headquarters and removed to the small war council chamber of the Town Hall. It was on this occasion that the fateful cropping of the picture must have taken place. Three figures were cut away on the left, together with a major section of the extreme foreground and a smaller strip on the right. This mutilation severely impaired the composition's expressive power. Seventy years later the painter and restorer Jan van Dijk still flew into a rage whenever he thought of this outrage and of the "boiled oil and varnish" with which the picture was mistreated time and again. Yet the power of the admirable brushwork survived.

Strong sunlight prevails in the picture. Rembrandt applied his pigments with a vigorous brush, and one can only marvel that such roughness blends into such painstaking care. The trimming of the lieutenant's doublet is dabbed on so thickly that one could almost grate a nutmeg on it.

Note that through all the mayhem this painter and professional restorer was still able to appreciate the work's surpassing virtues. Note also that he speaks of sunlight rather than of a "night" watch.[12]

Bartholomeus van der Helst THE COMPANY OF CAPTAIN ROELOF BICKER. 1639
Amsterdam, Rijksmuseum

Other artists were disappointed, especially Sir Joshua Reynolds: "It was with difficulty I could persuade myself that it was painted by Rembrandt; it seemed to me to have more of the yellow manner of Bol." A visit to the Amsterdam Town Hall was a must in any 18th-century Dutch itinerary—but Rembrandt had a hard time standing up to the facing group picture by van der Helst, a bright, colorful, brilliant production painted to a mirror-smooth finish (see Illustration). The French painter Nicolas Cochin relates that van der Helst's work put all else in the shade, Rembrandt's above all. He is the embodiment of nature, exclaimed a woman painter, his people are alive, one is truly in their presence. It would almost seem that the playing card simile

fitted Rembrandt in the early 19th century, as his painting languished beside van der Helst's *tour de force*.[13]

Whether or not we view THE NIGHT WATCH as the greatest monument of Rembrandt's art, it remains an extraordinary venture. A work of true grandeur, it continues to work so powerful a spell that its history has become almost the epitome of Rembrandt's art. Awe and cavil, neglect and care, emerge from contemporary sources as for scarcely another of his works. Indeed, the story of THE NIGHT WATCH may fittingly exemplify the story of other paintings whose fate, owing to our lack of documentary evidence, is hidden in obscurity.

THE RECONCILIATION OF DAVID AND ABSALOM [207]
NICOLAAS VAN BAMBEECK [232] and AGATHA BAS [233]

The 1640's

The dramatic idiom of THE NIGHT WATCH with its urgent sense of movement thrusting from the picture, its willful lights and shadows, is actually an anachronism within the context of Rembrandt's art in the 1640's. By the time the great painting was finished, in 1642, Rembrandt had outgrown this showy Baroque style. His intimate Bible stories of about 1640, together with his self-portraits from this period are more on the reserved and harmonious side. THE NIGHT WATCH is the last and almost laggard utterance of a time of boundless energy and creative vigor, a happy phase in which Rembrandt enjoyed good fortune and renown. Although it was not completed until 1642, the great group portrait was probably planned and laid out in the late thirties.

On May 1, 1639 Rembrandt had moved into a large house in the St. Anthonisbreestraat. It had cost him 13,000 guilders, a considerable sum even for a successful painter. No wonder his letters kept pressing Constantijn Huygens for payment of the Passion pictures. Rembrandt continued to live in this house until the late fifties. Here he kept his art collection, which included casts of ancient sculptures and volumes of drawings and engravings. Two of Saskia's children had already died—a third was born in the new house, only to die within a matter of weeks. Titus alone, born in September 1640, lived. Saskia herself died in the year THE NIGHT WATCH was finished, 1642. Her fortune went in equal parts to Titus and Rembrandt, who was also for the time being to enjoy the usufruct of Titus' share. Saskia's will provided that in the event of Rembrandt's remarriage half of the estate should revert to one of her sisters, a clause that was to be the source of a great deal of trouble for Rembrandt.

To look after his child, Rembrandt took in Geertje Dircx, the widow of a trumpet player. She must have grown very fond of Titus, for in her own will, dated 1648, she bequeathed him her small possessions, including some of Saskia's jewelry that Rembrandt had given her. A portrait Rembrandt had painted of her, on the other hand, was left to a legatee in Hoorn. Soon after Geertje drew up her will a quarrel broke out between the two. Geertje left Rembrandt's home, charging him with breach of promise. The courts did not adjudicate this particular issue, but Rembrandt was ordered to pay a yearly alimony in excess of what he had offered Geertje who, on her part, was enjoined from revoking her bequest to Titus.

This settlement would have worked quite well had not Rembrandt learned that Geertje had incurred debts and pawned Saskia's jewels. He now moved heaven and earth—using some rather doubtful methods—to have the woman prosecuted on account of her dissolute way of life; and she was committed for twelve years to the bridewell at Gouda, whence friends were able to effect her release after five years. The litigants were unevenly matched. In a settlement draft a notary describes Geertje simply as the widow of Abraham Claesz. while he speaks of "the far-famed painter Rembrandt van Rijn."[1]

A woman named Hendrickje Stoffels, a member of Rembrandt's household, gave evidence on his behalf. She made an affidavit confirming that Rembrandt had offered to pay the widow a lump sum and an annual allowance for life, on the understanding that she would keep in force her will in Titus' favor. This was on October 1, 1649. Hendrickje Stoffels had plainly supplanted Geertje. She too was a simple woman and she too cared devotedly for the growing boy Titus. Rembrandt never married her. It has been pointed out that the widower of Saskia van Uylenburgh, a painter of wide renown and the owner of a large house, could scarcely have remarried so far beneath his station. But even had he been willing to sacrifice his social position, it is unlikely that Rembrandt could have raised the sum of money he would have been required to pay his in-laws in the event of his remarriage, according to the terms of Saskia's will.

The consequences of his living with Hendrickje were not all pleasant. When she became pregnant, she was summoned before the church council, where she "confessed to the sin of fornication with the painter Rembrandt, was severely punished, admonished to repentance, and excluded from the Lord's supper." But Hendrickje stayed with Rembrandt, and bore him a daughter, Cornelia, who was baptized in the Old Church in Amsterdam on October 30, 1654.

When we compare the few surviving documents from the thirties with those after 1640, we find that the latter reflect Rembrandt's growing troubles. Saskia died a bare three years after they moved into the fine house; children were born and died; payments on the property faltered; the records show that debts were contracted; there was the unpleasantness with Geertje Dircx—until at last the warmhearted Hendrickje came to share

Rembrandt, after Leonardo da Vinci THE LAST SUPPER. Drawing
New York, The Lehman Collection

the painter's misfortunes. Is this loss of everyday security reflected in Rembrandt's art?

It was once the custom to contrast the extrovert Rembrandt of the thirties with the "inward" painter of the later years, whose art, ripened in adversity, gathered weight, gravity, and maturity, who turned his back on the Flemish Baroque and became truly himself. It is true that the impact of life is reflected in the growth and the output of every artist. Yet what really governs such careers is the experience not so much of life as of art. Artistic experience entails in the main the encounter with the work of other artists, sharing the creative ferment of time and place. We have seen how young Rembrandt, in league with Jan Lievens, broke with the pretty pathos of the Lastman school and swept aside the Caravaggesque vogue. Plausibly, young painters who begin so rebelliously could be expected to remain at odds with the artistic traditions of their time; yet somehow both Rembrandt and Lievens managed to earn full recognition and enjoy rich careers.

In fact, the changes that took place in Rembrandt's style around 1640 were anything but a personal, self-willed development. The momentum of the Baroque, with the emphasis on concentrated movement, had pervaded all Dutch art in the thirties, while in the ensuing decade the stylistic approach was dominated by classicism with its sense of harmony. We must leave unresolved here the question of what forces are responsible for this constant ebb and flow in history—the great personalities of the time or the intangible *Zeitgeist*.

Rembrandt's own development as an artist was entirely in accord with the stylistic impulses of his time, both in the thirties and, as we shall see, the forties. His turn toward classical repose, about 1640, was in no way associated with his troubled domestic circumstances. These new paintings are serene and harmonious, radiant with joyous colors that melt into the delicate background chiaroscuro. As for THE NIGHT WATCH with its riot of color and movement, though it was completed in the year of Saskia's death, it certainly cannot be called either gloomy or tranquil, nor does it bespeak the artist's vicissitudes. Life and art are much more tenuously linked than is often thought.

Rembrandt's borrowings from Italian models are illuminating. In his copies after Leonardo's LAST SUPPER, done in the early thirties, the sense of movement and expression in that masterpiece is deepened (see Illustration). The focal point is emphasized by the addition of a canopy, while the interior with the painstakingly constructed linear perspective of which the Renaissance was so fond has been suppressed. It simply did not fit in with Rembrandt's dramatic Baroque treatment of the composition.[2]

On April 9, 1639 a shipload of Italian paintings brought together by the art dealer Lucas van Uffelen was auctioned in Amsterdam. Rembrandt attended the event. He had often made purchases at auctions in the preceding years, but on this occasion he was unable to acquire anything. He did, however, make a swift sketch of Raphael's famous portrait of BALDASSARE CASTIGLIONE (Illustration a, p. 88), which sold, he noted, for 3,500 guilders; and he added the date, 1639. Rembrandt knew the buyer, the art dealer Alphonso Lopez, a Spanish Jew who lived in Amsterdam, where he was engaged in business on a large scale, not limiting himself to the art market. It was Lopez who had sold one of Rembrandt's earliest paintings, THE ASS OF BALAAM BALKING BEFORE THE ANGEL [6], to a purchaser in Paris. Rembrandt must also have seen Titian's so-called portrait of ARIOSTO in Lopez's possession. Both the Raphael and the Titian left their traces in Rembrandt's own work of these years, though with an accent rather different from Leonardo's LAST SUPPER. They appealed to his new-found sense of quiet dignity and sublimity.[3]

An etched SELF-PORTRAIT from this same year of 1639 (Illustration b, p. 88) follows the example of Raphael quite closely. The cocked beret not only underlines a certain elegance and self-possession but echoes the diagonals that are part and parcel of Rembrandt's powerful virtuosity during the thirties. But the Italian influence emerges fully only in a SELF-PORTRAIT [238; Colorplate, p. 89] of the following year. Here, Rembrandt's arm rests on a stone ledge that no longer serves as the jumping-off point for a forward thrust, but simply as a steadying support for the whole structure of the picture. All sharpness has fled from the contours of body and beret, creating an impression of easy repose. Originally the artist's left hand was also shown, the fingers resting on the balustrade, but Rembrandt himself overpainted it, presumably to avoid breaking the compact composition by still another bright patch.

THE RISEN CHRIST AT EMMAUS [218]

a Rembrandt, after Raphael BALDASSARE CASTIGLIONE
Drawing. 1639. Vienna, Albertina

b Rembrandt SELF-PORTRAIT. Etching. 1639
Amsterdam, Rijksmuseum

One might think that SASKIA WITH A FLOWER [226], dating
from the following year, 1641, was meant as a pendant to this
SELF-PORTRAIT. But although the dimensions almost correspond,
this is probably not the case, at least not in the ordinary sense.
Rembrandt seems to have painted himself with Saskia in a double
portrait or in pendant portraits only on rare occasions. The exceptions are noteworthy: one is a "disguised" biblical picture,
THE PRODIGAL SON IN THE TAVERN [79]; another a pair of
portraits in fancy dress, of which only the SASKIA [184] survives.
It was these glamorous portraits that inspired Govaert Flinck's
gentle gibe at Rembrandt—his portraits of his master and Saskia
as shepherd and shepherdess (Illustrations a, b, p. 134), in the
same poses as the romantic portraits by Rembrandt of the year
before.

An artist is always at a certain disadvantage when he paints his
own portrait. He must resort to the mirror, which inevitably introduces an element of unreality, a kind of distortion that is bound
to affect the finished picture's emotional tone, and particularly its
relation to a pendant painted directly from life. The last of the
rare cases in which Rembrandt painted himself with Saskia is the
portrait pair of 1643 [240, 241]. This pair is doubly exceptional,
for Saskia was by then dead, and Rembrandt had to paint her
from memory, introducing a distinct dimension of unreality.
Both of these portraits are therefore in a special sense introspec-
tive. Both are renderings of an inner vision.

There are fewer portraits of couples from the forties, and they
are more reserved in gesture than the earlier ones, from which the
sitters seem to be regarding us attentively. THE FRAMEMAKER
HERMAN DOOMER [230] and his wife BAARTJEN MARTENS
[231] are joined by neither glance nor gesture—their union is
more subtly implied by turn of body, equal filling of the picture
area, and correspondence of lighting. The bodies are still seen in
full depth, standing out clearly but not obtrusively against a
gently lit back wall. These two portraits, alas, are no longer in
the same hands and the total effect is thus lost. Separation has
worked even greater mischief in the case of a pair of portraits done
the following year, NICOLAES VAN BAMBEECK [232] and his
wife AGATHA BAS [233; Colorplates, pp. 82, 83]. The total
effect suffers even when these two paintings are temporarily re-
united, at special exhibitions; for a coat of yellow varnish veils the

husband in Brussels, while the wife, in the Royal Collection in
England, has enjoyed painstaking care, and still shines forth in
her original beauty. It is not a flashy picture, however; the brushwork is delicate and the lighting subdued. The total effect of the
pair gains from the different postures of the spouses. Both in dress
and pose the husband seems to display greater animation. Yet,
compared with the HERMAN DOOMER of the preceding year, let
alone the SELF-PORTRAITS from the same years [229, 236], he
seems almost to float in space. Both figures are bathed in gentle
light. But for Rembrandt's painted frame and the familiar balustrade, the figures would be adrift in a space with no fixed points.
These painted frames, unlike the illusionistic painted frames so
common in Dutch painting, are not meant to deceive the eye.
That effect is intended when a painted frame passes itself off as a
window and seeks to present its occupant not as a painted image
but a glimpse of a real person. Rembrandt's painted frames are
never intended to deceive; they serve rather as a subtle means of
support, bracing the figure within the picture, so to speak. Nor is
Agatha Bas' fan, held outside the painted frame, intended to
create a false sense of depth. On the contrary, this wedge of color
glittering in the light serves a frankly decorative function. It is
only Rembrandt's students and imitators who misused the frame
motif for illusionist purposes.

The use of architectural elements for framing purposes begins
somewhat earlier in Rembrandt's work, occurring for the first
time in the portrait of MARIA TRIP [194], done in 1639. In this
painting and its preparatory drawing (Illustration a, p. 304),
however, Rembrandt had not yet learned to use the device to full
purpose. The archway and what looks like the tail end of a stair
rail give no more than a hint of movement. This can be said also
of the oil sketch of EPHRAIM BUENO [263], which served as a
study for the 1647 etching (Illustration a, p. 349). But in the etching the architectural elements seem to be more purposefully
worked out and give the portrait fiber. The problem seems to be
not so much one of providing a frame but rather of investing the
figure with a certain monumental character and an air of movement, a problem that preoccupied Rembrandt only after 1645.

Some caution is indicated when considering the chronological
development of the frame motif. The 1646 etching of JAN COR-
NELISZ SYLVIUS (Illustration b, p. 349) is presented in straight-

a Rembrandt JAN SIX. Etching. 1647
Amsterdam, Rijksmuseum

b Rembrandt JAN SIX. Drawing
Amsterdam, Six Foundation

forward terms of *trompe l'œil*; and its rather crude effects do not fit in well with our overall impression of the forties as a decade during which Rembrandt was given to harmony and delicacy. These etched portraits of preachers do have a tradition of their own, however, involving captions that deplore the artist's inability to depict the act of speaking; and rhetorical gestures like that of Sylvius in the etching of 1646 are thus entirely appropriate. Jan Emmens has recently examined this whole subject in great depth—the long controversy over the respective roles of eye and ear, with the implied competition between words and visual images.[4] Rembrandt's first essay in this special genre was his 1641 etched portrait of the Mennonite minister CORNELIS CLAESZ. ANSLO (Illustration b, p. 335), which carries a rhymed legend by Vondel challenging the artist to "paint the voice of Cornelis." That Rembrandt regarded this as more than a mere phrase is demonstrated by his painting of the same year [234] showing Anslo earnestly lecturing an enraptured woman, probably a maid servant. The bond of the word between the preacher's exhortation and the woman's absorption is rendered explicit by the speaker's hand, and this gesture—virtually a "painted word"—strikes us, like the gesture of Sylvius, as being at odds with Rembrandt's quiet, even inexpressive portrait style of the forties, as first exemplified in the 1641 pendants [230, 231]. But it is nothing unusual, after all, for an artist to progress unevenly, to produce advanced works, then to backtrack in the face of the problem presented by his latest challenge.

If we were asked to name a painting thoroughly representative of Rembrandt's art of the forties, it would probably be the YOUNG GIRL LEANING IN A WINDOWSILL [228], done in 1645. Its upper termination was originally a semicircle with a diameter somewhat smaller than the width of the painting as a whole. This shape, originally a Flemish invention, can still be made out in our illustration of the SELF-PORTRAIT in the Wallace Collection [237], though the shape of this panel has been changed. In the Dulwich picture there is no longer any proper "framing" on any side, yet a clear-cut architectural structure is retained. It is not the oblique lines that create the feeling of space but rather the full modeling of the face turning toward us. The sense of line is much firmer and surer than in the 1641 portrait pair. Added to this, the firm masonry structure securely encloses the space, while the

unambiguous architecture is matched by equally clear-cut brush-work. There is no fussy hatching to the yellow-white tints of the girl's shift, which are applied in broad impasto. This increasingly monumental brushwork constitutes a new element in Rembrandt's art that was to come to full maturity in the ensuing years.

What unfolds before our eyes when we regard Rembrandt's portraiture of the forties—the likenesses officially commissioned as well as the studies of friends and children—is a picture of joyous and radiant harmony, of serene contemplation and inner peace. All pomp has dropped away; Rembrandt gives up painting the fierce, fancifully dressed Levantines. Let the etched portrait of JAN SIX (Illustration b), done in 1647, serve as the final example of this bright, warm portrait art. Six was a poet as well as a merchant. He published a play, *Medea*, for which Rembrandt designed a title page (Illustration a, p. 318), and it is the poet who is depicted in Rembrandt's fine sheet. The interior, hinted at rather than explicit, enhances the sense of intimacy and harmony surrounding Six and his world. A preliminary drawing for the etching is still preserved in the Six Collection (Illustration a). A first swift sketch, it is coarser and more excited than the etching. Rembrandt is seen to have made many changes in Six's stance and expression when he moved on to the etching; and the playful dog was eliminated. Yet the draftsmanship is not as different as it seems at first glance. But for Rembrandt's sure sense of line the etching would lack inner structure. The firmness of design is laid bare in the drawing, as in an X-ray picture of a painting that penetrates beneath the smooth surface layers.

An account book of the House of Orange carries an authorization, dated November 29, 1646, for payment to "N. Rembrandt, painter at Amsterdam" of 2,400 guilders for two paintings —"a NATIVITY and CIRCUMCISION OF CHRIST"—the artist made for Prince Frederick Henry. The honorific description "far-famed" is lacking in this official document, as it is in the summons by the church council a few years later, to which only Hendrickje responded. The two paintings for Frederick Henry "accorded"—to use Rembrandt's own term—in size with the Passion pictures he had delivered earlier [64, 65, 80, 87, 88]. The "NATIVITY" is THE ADORATION OF THE SHEPHERDS [215] in Munich; the "CIRCUMCISION" is lost, though it is known from a

a Copy after Rembrandt THE CIRCUMCISION OF CHRIST Brunswick, Herzog Anton Ulrich Museum

b X-ray photograph of THE ADORATION OF THE SHEPHERDS [216]. Detail. London, National Gallery

copy (Illustration a). In the 17th century, however, the whole series of "seven pictures by Rembrandt, each in a black frame rounded at the top, the whole enclosed in a frame decorated with gilt foliage," was assembled in the Stadholder's palace at The Hague.[5]

Actually, the two later paintings "accorded" only outwardly with the Passion series. In spirit and pictorial form they are very different. In THE ADORATION OF THE SHEPHERDS the faces of the Virgin, Joseph, and two shepherds, ringing the child in a circle of loving devotion, shine by reflected candlelight. Other shepherds approach from the depth of the stable, while still another busies himself in the hayloft. The gentle radiance of candle and stable lanterns suffuses all the faces, lighting the interior just enough for the solid verticals and horizontals to emerge. Once again the soft brushwork nestles within a firm structure. A sense of inner grandeur marks the intimate scene.

The similar painting in London [216; Colorplate, p. 93] may be regarded as a first version of this same commission. It has a rather more sketchy and direct character with greater contrast in movement and lighting. The two shepherd groups—gathered about the child and approaching this time from the right—display their awe and humility with greater eloquence. The painting in Munich is marked by greater unity of line, composition, and lighting, but the London canvas is livelier in conception, and this vitality was present from the very outset, as shown in the X-ray photograph of this work, which has a beauty all its own (Illustration b). Like the portraits done during these years, these paintings are rounded at the top. In the Munich ADORATION this was done to keep the whole series uniform in format, while in other paintings with this shape (many of which have since been altered), the rounding was used deliberately, for expressive purposes. A gentle arc does admirably "round out" the story of the Nativity.

The finest example of a composition with a frame painted into the picture is THE HOLY FAMILY [212] in Cassel, which even carries a second framing element, a painted curtain. Both frame and curtain take on special meaning in this painting, for the modest-sized representation of THE HOLY FAMILY is conceived as an everyday Dutch domestic scene, utterly unpretentious in composition and palette. Homely details are lovingly dwelt on—

the child nestling against the mother, the cat purring by the blazing logs that warm the Virgin's bare feet, and the feeding dish. By contrast, the rather ornate framing elements fulfill a dual function. They not only lend strength and support to the loose, dabbing brushwork but elevate the whole scene to the level of a solemn occasion. The composition itself, moreover, contains elements—like the barred window, the ceiling beams, and the flooring—that make up a delicate gridwork to enhance the outspoken horizontal and vertical lines of the framing elements enclosing this genrelike scene.

It was not uncommon in Holland to hang a real curtain in front of a picture; and the addition of a painted drape was a popular device intended to enhance the realistic effect and, especially, the illusion of depth. Actually, this illusion can scarcely be said to be present in Rembrandt's picture, where the curtain, whatever its value in adding realism, serves chiefly to invest the everyday scene with an air of solemnity. Drapes as a rule are meant to protect from everyday use what is reserved for Sundays—for special occasions. Here the devout beholder is vouchsafed a glimpse of the Holy Family itself. What lends frame and curtain such felicity is that these elements underline both the dignity and the intimacy of the scene, bringing out its essence in the most appropriate fashion. The drape, moreover, serves as a screen for echoing in abstract form all the warm tints in the main group.

Rembrandt's sensitive works of the forties were sometimes based on earlier compositions. An example is CHRIST AND THE WOMAN TAKEN IN ADULTERY [208; Colorplate, p. 63] of 1644; in lighting and interior construction it harks back to the 1631 PRESENTATION [17; Colorplate, p. 17], though dramatic concentration on a narrowly circumscribed zone has now given way to a more detailed narrative that occupies most of the picture's middleground. ANNA ACCUSED BY TOBIT OF STEALING THE KID [209] of 1645, on the other hand, tells the story of the aged couple in an altogether new fashion, though the incident depicted is precisely the same as in the 1626 version [4]. The two small figures are caught in the half-light of their cottage, scarcely touched by the radiance streaming in through the window, which illuminates the back wall much more strongly. Half hidden in the gloom, they are further hemmed in by the ceiling beams, their lively

Pieter Lastman SUSANNA SURPRISED BY THE ELDERS. 1614
Berlin-Dahlem, Gemaeldegalerie

quarrel dwarfed by the picturesque interior. Unless one knows the story one can scarcely discern the old man's horror and his wife's protestations.

Many pictures of this period are small and precious works, radiating peace and intimacy by the very modesty of their format and mood. On occasion Rembrandt's terseness actually gives rise to misinterpretations. The true meaning of the picture in London, called "THE CASTING OUT OF HAGAR" was recognized only a few years ago by C. Tümpel—it actually represents THE DEPARTURE OF THE SHUNAMITE WIFE [202; Colorplate, p. 85], though in conception the composition is, of course, related to traditional renderings of the Hagar incident as well as the Flight into Egypt, and even the Triumph of Mordecai (Illustration a, p. 312).[6] It is noteworthy that here once again a group—this time emerging from a warm brown glow—is held together by an arch, though here the arch is painted on a rectangular field—one of the earliest examples of this device.

The creative background of SUSANNA SURPRISED BY THE ELDERS [221], done in 1647, also reaches back to the thirties. It actually utilizes a prior work by Rembrandt's teacher, Lastman (see Illustration), a fact of considerable significance in Rembrandt's development. In the late thirties, at a time when Rembrandt's approach to pictorial organization was growing more austere, he resumed his habit of making drawings of Lastman's compositions (Illustration a, p. 327). Lastman's skill in achieving an impression of dynamic balance was bound to be an element of renewed interest to Rembrandt, who nevertheless suppressed Lastman's dramatic gesticulations as out of character in his own works of the forties.

THE HOLY FAMILY WITH ANGELS [211; Colorplate, p. 65] may serve as an example of a Bible picture in large format from these years. Once again we catch an intimate glimpse of the carpenter's family, and once again the interior is enriched with picturesque narrative detail. The intimation of divinity is here inherent in the very structure of the painting—the Virgin and the descending angels are linked by a diagonal flow of light, echoed in the opposing diagonals of the Virgin's movements, as she glances up from her book and reaches out toward the child. All the suspended, hovering elements come to rest in the focus on the sleeping child, and the scene of peaceful solemnity in the foreground

contrasts with Joseph's busy wood-chopping in the background. The warm red of the child's coverlet forms the dominant color accent.

In the late forties the architectonic assembly of Rembrandt's paintings becomes more and more emphatic. Grace and intimacy yield to the monumental, firmly joined structure supplants the former feeling of unresolved suspense in space. In THE RISEN CHRIST AT EMMAUS [218; Colorplate, p. 87] of 1648 a huge masonry niche forms a kind of protective mantle about the figure of Christ, a use of background new to Rembrandt. Christ's unexpected and baffling appearance thus gains inward and outward plausibility—it is as if the niche were prepared beforehand to enclose Christ in majesty at the moment that he reveals himself. The consternation of the disciples, the dramatic climax in the earlier EMMAUS [14; Colorplate, p. 15], is now suggested only in the figure with his back toward the beholder. More central to the mood of the picture is the quiet horizontal expanse of the white tablecloth which contrasts with the many verticals. The two figures at the right fit effortlessly into this scheme. Doubtless Rembrandt's new feeling for the monumental drew strength from paintings of the High Renaissance in Venice.

The assumption that artistic growth proceeds in a straight line would lead us to conclude that the somewhat simpler RISEN CHRIST IN EMMAUS [219] in Copenhagen preceded the version in the Louvre we have just discussed. The curtain motif is still used here, though with considerable reserve, while the disciples, united in the act of recognition, form a quiet group with the two approaching servants, a group not nearly so well integrated with the architectural elements. Indeed, the composition itself is no longer as closely tied to the construction of the interior as in the earlier large HOLY FAMILY WITH ANGELS. It now rests rather on the figures themselves, which strikes us at once as a sign of even deeper mastery. This raises the alternative possibility of regarding the Copenhagen picture as the extraction of the figure group from the Paris picture, with the abandonment of the dramatic architecture. Fortunately, our speculations are not likely to lead us into gross factual error in this case: both paintings are, in fact, dated 1648.

THE HUNDRED-GUILDER PRINT (Illustration a, p. 358) represents a turning-point in Rembrandt's religious imagery. The

Rembrandt THE BRIDGE. Etching. 1645
Amsterdam, Rijksmuseum

biblical subjects of the thirties were violent; those of the forties tender. All of them were dramatic. A new, more detached approach to the Bible makes itself felt in THE HUNDRED-GUILDER PRINT, an etching of the late forties that illustrates several scenes from the 19th chapter of *The Gospel According to Saint Matthew*: the sick are healed, the Pharisees challenge Christ, the children come to him, and in the background a real camel appears, image of the camel that shall go through the eye of a needle more easily than a rich man shall enter the kingdom of heaven. From now on Rembrandt was to illustrate the Bible with this kind of directness and lack of affectation, abstracting the essence of a story rather than seeking to dramatize it.

Considering Rembrandt's career by decades and dividing his works into portraits, history paintings, and the like could easily mislead one into thinking of these periods and categories as separate entities when in fact the complex cross-currents between these arbitrarily distinguished phases are essential to an understanding of Rembrandt's art. "Landscape," for example, was a sphere closely allied to other themes in his work. His first great landscape was, as we have already seen, the large river valley that is the scene of the Baptism of the Eunuch [195]. There followed a small series of fanciful landscapes which, in their wild forms and swirling lights and shadows, correspond to the stormy Bible pictures of the thirties. In the forties Rembrandt begins to organize and strengthen his landscapes with romantic buildings that rise from the rough soil. Perhaps the finest example from this period is the LANDSCAPE WITH A CASTLE [268; Colorplate, p. 97]. The landscape paintings do not stem from immediate outdoors experience, nor do they have any direct connection with the landscape sketches and drawings of the period in point. They do, on the other hand, have close links with the history paintings. One might even go so far as to suggest that Rembrandt painted these landscapes with an eye to his Bible pictures—so close, for example, is the correspondence between the landscape just mentioned and the background in THE RECONCILIATION OF DAVID AND ABSALOM [207; Colorplate, p. 81], a resemblance that extends even to the general structure of the two panels. The rich landscape detail in the RECONCILIATION—the swiftly and freely

sketched trees and shrubs in the right foreground—recur in the nocturnal REST ON THE FLIGHT INTO EGYPT [220], done in 1647. There is a sense of enchantment to this interweaving of light and dark, these tiny dots of pigment against the dark wood, these reflections dying away over the water and into the foliage. At the same time, the basic structure is firm and clear enough to keep rocks and woods from drifting away into uncertainty, even though they are pulling the darkness about themselves. The shepherd with the broad-brimmed hat is the very same who, lantern in his left hand, is approaching the kneeling circle in the London ADORATION [216] of the year before. In the Dublin painting the figures move with even greater delicacy, blending completely into the countryside.

It is an odd fact that Rembrandt was 30 before he felt the impact of nature as a creative visual experience to be transmuted through the medium of drawing. Domestic life, children and old people in the street, actors and mendicants—all these had long since drawn his attentive gaze by the time he came to sketch the environs of Amsterdam, with their rivers and mills and villages and fortifications. Rembrandt's home was not far from St. Anthonispoort, from which it was easy to reach nearby villages such as Diemen or the hamlets along the Amstel River. Why it was only during these years that he discovered the beauty of the countryside and captured it in his drawings is hard to say. Possibly he sought sustenance in nature at a time when his domestic life had grown oppressive because of Saskia's illnesses—and even more difficult after her death. Again, the very fact that he had moved to a new home may have been the occasion for looking at the environment with new eyes. However that may have been, a new world of visual experience did open up for Rembrandt. With a few lines he would capture a village on the horizon or a group of buildings in the foreground. The white areas of the paper are allowed to retain their brightness, helping the impression of distance (Illustrations a, b, p. 353). Let us consider the degree to which his draftsmanship may have affected his overall style in the forties.

As we have already established, it had no effect on his landscape paintings. These are essentially imaginary rather than realistic. Yet, recalling Rembrandt's general progression from a dra-

LANDSCAPE WITH A CASTLE [268]
JACOB BLESSING THE SONS OF JOSEPH [277] Two details

a Rembrandt VIEW OF DIEMEN. Etching
   Amsterdam, Rijksmuseum

b Rembrandt VIEW OF DIEMEN. Drawing
   Rotterdam, Museum Boymans-van Beuningen

matic approach to one of quiet poetic transparency, we can see how the experience of the light-drenched countryside could add radiant, glowing warmth to the new pictorial forms that came with the forties. Conversely, it may be even more appropriate to say that only the new and quieter classicist vision opened the way for Rembrandt to capture the countryside in loose and airy drawings.

But if Rembrandt's drawings and paintings of landscapes each have their own function—their special sphere in shaping his creative style—his landscape etchings blend direct visual experience with imaginative projection, sometimes on the very same sheet. The medium of etching served Rembrandt for many different purposes. Study heads that are little more than sketches stand alongside commissioned portraits, large Bible compositions mingle with small title-page designs for books by his friends, and plates etched after paintings (in the manner of Rubens' studio) are found next to original compositions intended exclusively for this medium.

Some of Rembrandt's etchings do indeed have the fleeting and spontaneous character of sketches, and he even etched landscape sketches in this manner. The author of the first catalogue of Rembrandt's etchings (1751), Gersaint, tells of an incident which, like so many apocryphal anecdotes, may hold a kernel of truth—or at least significance: While visiting his friend Six in the country, Rembrandt sketched his etching THE BRIDGE (Illustration, p. 96) directly on the copper plate, during a brief interval between dinner courses, while a servant was dispatched to a neighboring village to fetch mustard.

Rembrandt's landscape etchings showing scenes in the vicinity of Amsterdam also have this sketchy character (Illustration b). There is really no essential difference between drawings and

etchings in this style. In a similar vein and possessing the same eloquence as his drawings are Rembrandt's many etched self-portrait studies, his scenes of everyday life, and his many study heads. A curious gap obtrudes, however—there are no etchings depicting his own household: Saskia, Titus, Hendrickje, all of whom figure so eloquently in his drawings.

Of great power and splendor is a landscape etching of 1643, built around three trees (Illustration a, p. 355). In expression and feeling for the monumental it is the equal of a painting. Its swirling vapors bear comparison with the cloud structures above the Virgin's deathbed (Illustration b, p. 359), except that in the landscape the trails are frothier and of even greater delicacy. The upper left corner is vigorously and obliquely hatched, lending an element of firm support and serving as a counterpoise to the tree group on the right. The countryside stretches far and wide beneath lowering skies, its breadth proclaiming peace and calm.

In sheer sense of drama the LANDSCAPE WITH THREE TREES is almost without parallel among etchings, even while it preserves its character of a direct visual record fleshed out into a work of art with independent form. In the drawing VIEW OF DIEMEN (Illustration b) the village emerges from the background of itself, drawn out by the act of viewing, while in the etched view of the same village (Illustration a) we find a clear and carefully calculated contrast between the emphatic motif of the tree in the right foreground and, on the other side, the delicate outlines of the village seen, beyond an intervening canal, on the horizon. The differences between the two works, however, go only so far. Essential to both is an approach based on visual clarity and harmony, on a gentle ordering of the visible world into a delicate texture of forms in repose.

The Later Works

The 1650's mark the heroic era of Dutch painting. Works from this period include Jacob Ruisdael's VIEW OF THE CASTLE OF BENTHEIM (1653), Frans Hals' PORTRAIT OF A MAN in the Metropolitan Museum, Philips Koninck's RIVER VALLEY newly acquired by the Rijksmuseum, and THE WATCH (1654) by Carel Fabritius (Illustrations a, b, p. 102; a, p. 104). Other landmarks are the early works of Jan Vermeer and the last works of Jan van Goyen. This is the exclusive group that defines our notion of the classic decade. We may add some works of the forties that seem to belong here: the small painting by Terborch, THE SIGNING OF THE TREATY OF MUENSTER (1648), and van der Helst's brilliant BANQUET OF THE CIVIL GUARD, done in the same year and on the same occasion. To link the names of van der Helst and Terborch with those of Ruisdael, Hals, and Koninck may seem to betray a lack of sophistication. But, though the works of the latter three may appeal to us more strongly today, van der Helst and Terborch too were brilliant artists who made vital contributions to the art of the fifties. We can go even further and honor two more names, lately out of fashion, as eminent exponents of their country's art: Caesar van Everdingen and Paulus Potter. Van Everdingen was given an important slice of the great commission of the late forties—the mural decoration of the Huis ten Bosch, the modish little palace of Amalia van Solms, widow of Frederick Henry; and Potter's BULL (1647) was long honored as the great masterpiece of its time. These works have today come to elicit a condescending smile that is quite undeserved. They are just as successful, in their own genres, as the landscapes and portraits of the great masters; at least, if we judge them through the eyes of their own age, as products of a popular culture.

The great commission of the late fifties was the decoration of Jacob van Campen's new Town Hall of Amsterdam, especially the great hall, one of the finest of Baroque interiors. The classic architecture of van Campen seems not to have interested Rembrandt; he drew the ruins of the old Town Hall after it was destroyed by fire in 1652 (Illustration, p. 106), but he made no drawing of the new one. On the other hand, the prospect of painting the great hall was an exciting one, and Rembrandt looked forward to participating, but that story is better saved for our next chapter.

Whereas no place could be found in the Huis ten Bosch for the "romantic" landscapes of Ruisdael and Koninck, Rembrandt was still regarded, in the fifties, in Amsterdam, as a leading spirit of the popular and highly esteemed classic-heroic style, despite his "romantic" side and his apparent distaste for classic-heroic architecture.

Much of what was done after 1659 still breathes the spirit of the fifties—in the work of Rembrandt himself as in that of his contemporaries Jan Steen, Aelbert Cuyp, Jan van de Cappelle, Emanuel de Witte, and Willem Kalf; but bit by bit a more niggling style, suspicious of heroics, supplanted the proud sublimity that was the great achievement of an older generation. There is no doubt that this late phase was still able to produce enchanting pictures of considerable artistic value, as we see in the polished and poetic works of Jan van der Heyden, Adriaen van de Velde, and Philips Wouwerman.

The heroic period in the art of Rembrandt was anything but a heroic period in his life. Many factors combined to aggravate his economic straits. Rembrandt had never paid off the full purchase price of the great house on St. Anthonisbreestraat. By 1653 he still owed more than half of the 13,000 guilders to Christopher Thijs, the seller. At the time he acquired the house in 1639, the transaction was certainly not above his means. There were the various sources of income mentioned by Sandrart—tuition, the sale of his students' work; and then, much more important, there was his direct income from painting commissions, which is bound to have brought in substantial sums. True, Saskia's family was irritated by Rembrandt's "profligacy" in buying works of art, but Rembrandt was able to prove that he earned plenty of money for such luxuries. At Saskia's death he estimated his fortune at close to 41,000 guilders. In 1640, by the way, he had inherited a by no means inconsiderable share of his mother's estate.[1]

Christopher Thijs had the greatest confidence in Rembrandt. Under the terms of the arrangement Rembrandt was to pay three-quarters of the purchase price within five or six years, at his pleasure and in any installments he chose. There was no provision for what should be done in the event of default. But almost 15 years had now elapsed, and Thijs pressed for the balance, with interest due. Rembrandt must have visited him some time before this, at his country estate of Saxenburg near Haarlem; and it was on that occasion that he did the etching known by the misleading title THE GOLDWEIGHER'S FIELD (Illustration b, p. 409).[2]

Rembrandt now borrowed money from several leading citizens of Amsterdam—Cornelis Witsen, who had just become burgo-

a Philips Koninck RIVER VALLEY. 1655
Amsterdam, Rijksmuseum

b Carel Fabritius THE WATCH. 1654
Schwerin, Gemaeldegalerie

master, a certain Isaac van Hertsbeeck, and Jan Six. Except for a residue of about 1,000 guilders he was able to settle with Christopher Thijs; but in the meantime his debts had grown to the point where he was compelled to file a petition for a *cessio bonorum* with the high court at The Hague, to appease his creditors. As reasons he gave "losses in trade, including overseas trade." Unless this was merely customary legal verbiage, we are tempted to conclude that Rembrandt, like so many other artists, had dabbled in the art market and engaged in other speculative deals. It is a fact that there was an economic recession in Holland during the first Anglo-Dutch war (1652–4). Commerce was badly hit and shipping was paralyzed for months on end.[3]

To this unfortunate development we owe a document of great importance to us—an inventory of Rembrandt's possessions in the house on St. Anthonisbreestraat. They added up to an impressive art collection, including ancient relics and art objects from Asia, works of fine craftsmanship, weapons, musical instruments—and, of course, paintings. There were Italian pictures bearing the names of the greatest artists, as well as works by Dutchmen whom Rembrandt held in particularly high esteem. Of special value to us are the themes and titles of Rembrandt's own works that remained unsold—and may not even have been for sale. The collection of etchings and drawings by other artists was particularly large—they were not enumerated individually, only as portfolios. The first auction, at which Rembrandt was present, lasted for three weeks. Next came the house itself and lastly the priceless collection of drawings and etchings, which fetched far too little, whether because times were bad or there had been too little publicity.[4]

Distribution of the yield brought on many legal complications. The fascination these documents have for us lies in the names of Rembrandt's friends and patrons, the insight they afford us into the works of art he owned and what value was put on them. In the settlement of creditors' claims it was important to show that Rembrandt's income before his financial collapse had been high, since this would raise Titus' share in the proceeds. Thus, friends testified as to Rembrandt's ability to acquire valuable jewelry for Saskia and works of art for his collection. It was on this occasion, by the way, that the cloth merchants Jan Pietersz. and Nicolaes van Cruysbergen appeared to testify in their different

ways that "the painting in the great hall of the Civic Guard" (i.e. THE NIGHT WATCH) had cost 1,600 guilders. The "rarities," engravings, drawings, and paintings Rembrandt owned about 1650 were estimated by two experts to be worth more than 17,000 guilders. The actual auction did not realize even one-third of this sum.[5]

During these years Rembrandt etched portraits of several of the friends who stood by him. He even did a likeness of the man whose job it was to serve as auctioneer of his art treasures, Thomas Jacobsz. Haringh. Of other helpful friends, such as Lodewijk van Ludick, we have, unfortunately, no portraits.

The house in St. Anthonisbreestraat was signed over to the new owners on December 18, 1660, and at that time Rembrandt moved to another home in another part of town. Three days earlier he, Titus, and Hendrickje (who signed herself with a small cross) confirmed an earlier agreement under which they were to continue together trading in Rembrandt's paintings, drawings, and etchings "so long as the abovementioned Rembrandt van Rijn shall be alive, and for six years after his death." This clause was followed by special arrangements among the three parties, a complicated device rendered necessary in order to protect Rembrandt from other creditors and to enable him to continue to work. For it so happened that the Guild of St. Luke (the painter's guild) had pushed through a municipal ordinance under which a painter who had gone bankrupt in Amsterdam was enjoined from practicing his profession. In the eyes of many people, however, Rembrandt remained Amsterdam's premier painter even after his financial ruin. Indeed, a poem by Jan Vos written in 1662, celebrating the reestablishment of the Guild of St. Luke, has Rembrandt marching in the front rank of Amsterdam artists.[6]

But let us turn back to the heroic period in Dutch art and more specifically to Rembrandt's contribution during the fifties. There is no better example than the YOUNG GIRL AT A WINDOW [285; Colorplate, p. 105], previously mistaken for "LA SERVANTE," a painting acquired by Roger de Piles and described by him.[7] What really is the new element in this painting, compared with the similar YOUNG GIRL LEANING IN A WINDOWSILL [228] of 1645? A single term will serve to describe the difference—a tendency toward the monumental. The picture's strength and structure are based upon the powerful brushwork that heaps up

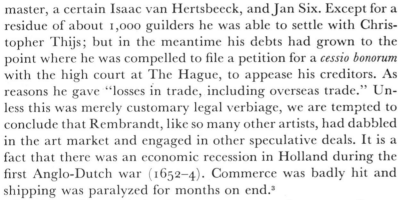

a Frans Hals PORTRAIT OF A MAN
New York, Metropolitan Museum of Art

b Rembrandt GIRL AT A WINDOW. Drawing
Stockholm, Nationalmuseum

block upon block of pigment. In the 1645 painting, the lines of ledge and wall still receded evasively into depth; but in the Stockholm painting of 1651 they are presented as directly as the girl's frank stare. The window motif is stated here in its ultimate form, reached after many years of preparation and a series of intermediate solutions in some splendid drawings (Illustration b) and paintings [228, 301].

In Rembrandt's male portraits the frame motif does not recur after the portrait pair of 1641—unless one were to count the delicate TITUS AT HIS DESK [325; Colorplate, p. 117]. Perhaps it would be more appropriate to suggest that frames and related motifs—balustrade, side wall—are added only to those pictures most likely to need such support because of a certain inner delicacy—portraits of women and children, for example.

Not that all male portraits are strongly expressive or depict large and well-poised figures facing us openly head-on, as the OLD MAN IN A FUR-LINED COAT [254]. Indeed, Rembrandt shows a marked fondness for portraits in which the subject seems barely able to sit still, veering toward us from profile [246], halting on a stairway [263], or regarding us from beneath lowered eyelids (Illustration a, p. 381). All these examples were done around 1650. They are soft and delicate in feeling. Even casual sketches are utterly lacking in pomp and circumstance—indeed in anything reminiscent of the earlier Baroque period. Slowly these pictures ripen into portraits of distinctly monumental character. Stages along this road are the portraits of NICOLAES BRUYNINGH [307], of 1652, and JAN SIX [309], done two years later. Light strikes the surfaces so glancingly that it seems at first to be dissolving the originally firm structure. Nicolaes Bruyningh is shown in an almost lighthearted mood, leaning confidentially toward us, an informal posture that serves only to underline the verisimilitude of the likeness. Yet it is by no means this spontaneity of observation alone that determines the overall impression. Of equal importance is the firm structure hinted at in the background (the chair) and more clearly expressed by the carefully placed vertical at the painting's left. Even more essential to the effect of radiant serenity is the firm brushwork, particularly manifest in the face and hair, the very elements that primarily convey the inner mood of a portrait to the viewer. One might describe Bruyningh's expression as one of untroubled thoughtfulness.

In the portrait of JAN SIX the fleeting moment is captured and enhanced to monumental dimension, though with a rather different set of vectors. The slight inclination of the head, the gloves being drawn on, the leftward bias (counter to the direction we habitually take in reading a painting), the coat drooping over the sitter's left shoulder—all these elements seem to effect a sense of movement toward the left and out of the picture, a trend momentarily halted as we are permitted to survey the scene. Six's features, framed by his hair, are modeled with great care and delicacy, in keeping with his thoughtful gaze that slides past us into the vague distance. Even more than in the NICOLAES BRUYNINGH, the monumental power of Rembrandt's brush here serves as the fitting vehicle for delicacy of expression. Wide brushstrokes struggle up the hem of Six's cloak, almost like abstract color patches. Gloves and hands have merged into almost cubical form, and the collar of the cloak arches up toward the face, a splash of red resplendent in the light.

Yet it is unwise to overemphasize abstract form elements in the interpretation of a 17th-century portrait. There was then no motivation—nor, for that matter, even the possibility—for breaking up pictorial structure into geometrical forms, as Cézanne did some 200 years later. The mere craft of painting was rich enough to absorb all striving for creative form; and perhaps it is this that gives so much realism and humanity to Dutch art, elements that seem to have become less accessible in later times. Even in Holland this optimistic period of heroic portraiture lasted only a short time. Frans Hals and Rembrandt—artistically these two came closer to each other during this decade than ever before—are among the very few to have created sublime portraits then.

The heroic touch emerges even more compellingly in pictures that do not bear so unequivocal a portrait character. A major example is the so-called POLISH RIDER [287; Colorplate, p. 109] which must have been done in the mid-fifties. Lately, careful study has been devoted to the meaning of this picture, and its title has been shown to be well-founded in that all its elements—dress, weapons, breed of horse, even the rider's seat in the saddle—accord with Polish tradition. On the other hand, the picture seems so clearly out of character with a commissioned portrait that one would expect it to yield some deeper meaning. Many of its aspects point beyond the canvas—the horseman is simply passing by and

YOUNG GIRL AT A WINDOW [285]

Rembrandt THE RUINS OF THE OLD TOWN HALL, AMSTERDAM. Drawing. 1652
Amsterdam, Rembrandt-Huis

even looks past us. There is no relation between background and figure, unless the massive and large-dimensioned color strata are taken to enhance the whole composition with their abstract quality.

By comparison, the commissioned portrait of FREDERICK RI-HEL ON HORSEBACK [410; Colorplate, p. 157] features a well-bred party in a coach looming from the dark and a hint of a city gate. "THE POLISH RIDER" lacks even the slightest reference to the world of the 17th century. Does it represent a historical personage, or is it perchance intended to personify an idea, a virtue become a legend, as in Duerer's KNIGHT, DEATH, AND DEVIL? Julius Held looks for a solution along the latter lines. He sees the horseman simply as a *miles christianus*, a Christian soldier, the matter of the Polish character being quite irrelevant. Białostocki, on the other hand, has been able to make out a case that the painting idealizes a certain group of martyrs of the faith with Polish associations, the so-called Socinians. This Dutch-Polish congregation was persecuted for its anti-trinitarian views both in Holland and Poland. Recent research has shown that Rembrandt seems to have been in touch with this sect as well as with the more moderate wing of the Mennonites.

As it happened, an edict directed against the Socinians was issued in 1653, at the instigation of the Calvinist church, only to be bitterly attacked the following year in a pamphlet published in Amsterdam by the Pole Jonasz Szlichtyng, who decried coercion and favored tolerance. The controversy dragged on, but it does not seem likely that Rembrandt ever intervened in these polemics. That his creative imagination should have been fired by such a controversy, however, is by no means implausible. Earlier studies of Polish dress and of an equine skeleton (Illustration a, p. 371) may well have laid the groundwork for an equestrian picture symbolizing the valiant struggle for freedom of conscience.

A self-portrait shows not only how the painter sees himself but how he wishes to be seen. At this stage Rembrandt's self-portraits grew firmer, their expression graver [308]—which need not necessarily be taken to reflect the vicissitudes of his life. Rembrandt's vision of himself in this portrait and its preliminary drawing, showing him dressed in painter's smock, is marked by largeness of perspective. The figure, seen almost head-on, is again built up

along monumental lines, and again the brushwork gives the painted image its air of assurance. Broad streaks of deep hue are laid over the figure, enclose the head, fill the background.

In the seated SELF-PORTRAIT [343; Colorplate, p. 121] dated 1658, the heroic aspect is even further deepened. The painter's maulstick becomes his scepter, the broad-brimmed beret his crown. The clear emphasis on the horizontals in this painting shows that the aim is to achieve a sense of breadth. The figure completely fills the lower part of the picture, lending the composition all the immobile assurance of a pyramid.

The SELF-PORTRAIT [376] of the following year, in Washington, is less lordly in feeling, for the viewer's eyes are drawn to the face as the only part that emerges into light. The painter is looking at us (or at himself, in the mirror?) with a piercing gaze. Hands and body play only a minor part. The head, almost caught in the act of turning, puts this self-portrait in the category of Rembrandt's "stop-motion" pictures, of which the portrait of JAN SIX is a fine example. In the Washington SELF-PORTRAIT, the sensitive skin with its dimples, furrows, and scars, and the thinning hair on either side are dabbed on thickly in large blobs, to capture the sense of solid structure under the fragile surface.

The inventory of Rembrandt's art collection, already mentioned, affords us particular insight into his store of his own paintings and those by his students. The latter, by the way, are never listed as copies by particular students, although the various copies after Rembrandt—and even after Rembrandt drawings—may well represent the work of his apprentices. It is, of course, disconcerting that we have been unable to identify such works among our present-day corpus of paintings attributed to Rembrandt. Among pictures by the older generation of contemporaries, the names of Hercules Seghers, Jan Lievens, Adriaen Brouwer, and Pieter Lastman are prominent. We must assume that any pictures by Lievens in Rembrandt's possession dated back to the Leyden period, as was probably the case with those by his teacher Lastman as well. Conspicuous among the Italians are works ascribed to Giorgione, Palma, Lelio Orsi, Raphael, and Carracci. Ancient sculptures, Roman portrait busts, Oriental weapons, and the like—these were probably among the objects of which Rembrandt, with his taste for the extraordinary, grew so inordinately fond.

BATHSHEBA WITH KING DAVID'S LETTER [271]

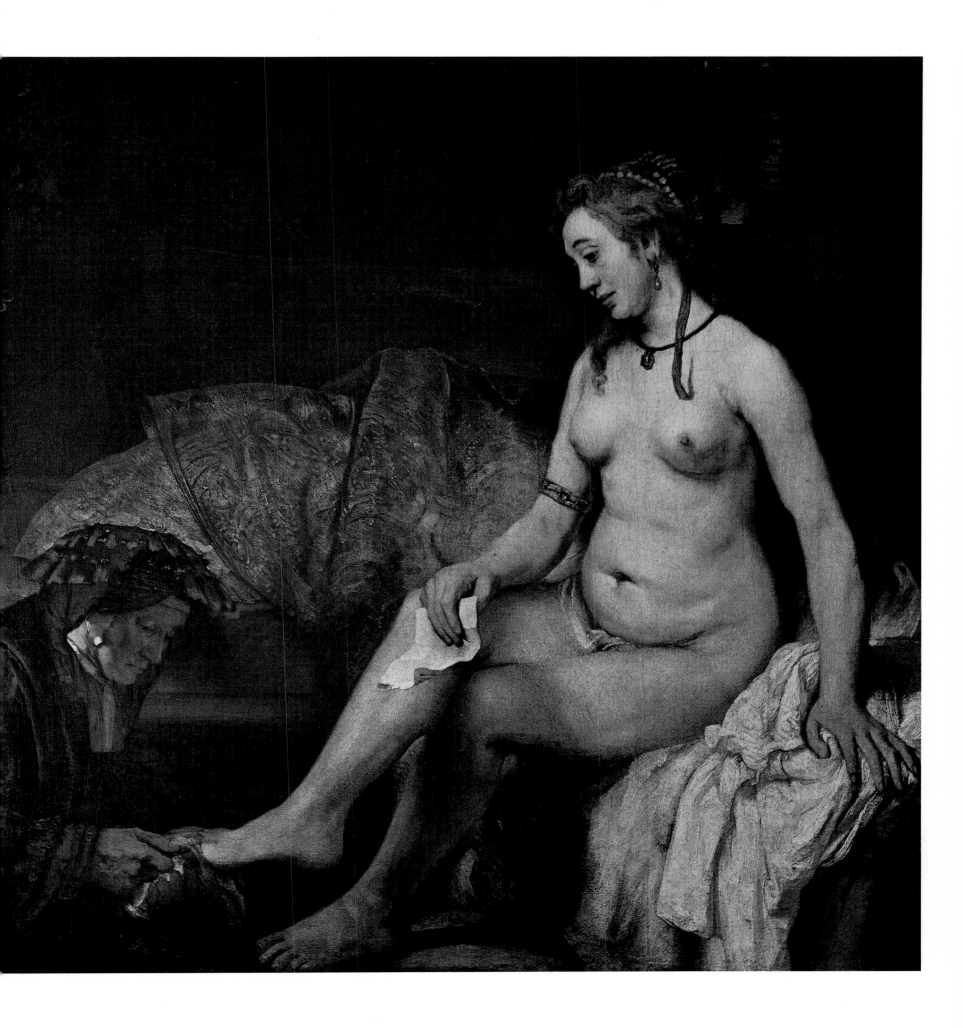

Hercules Seghers and Rembrandt, after Elsheimer THE FLIGHT OF THE HOLY FAMILY INTO EGYPT. Etching
Amsterdam, Rijksmuseum

Much more important as study materials were the portfolios with drawings and engravings after Dutch and foreign masters. Certain portfolios and works by major masters are enumerated separately. One is described as being "full of curious miniatures" —could these have been the Indian miniatures of the Mogul school which Rembrandt copied (Illustrations b, p. 365; b, p. 371)?[8]

The artists and schools mentioned in Rembrandt's inventory are the very ones we were called on to invoke when we discussed his own art. Hercules Seghers and the Venetians, Roman portrait busts, Raphael, engravings after ancient sculptures—all these were elements of Rembrandt's visual world during these years; but the fact that he owned the works of others and was influenced by them does not necessarily mean to say that he actually copied them first. The treatment of the "Persian" miniatures constitutes an exception. About 1655, perhaps anticipating their early sale, Rembrandt copied his favorites among them, at a single effort. To him they represented the world of the Orient, the world in which dwelt the prophets of the Old Testament and the apostles of the New. ABRAHAM SERVING THE THREE ANGELS, an etching of 1656, is plainly derived from the copy after the four "Persians" (Illustrations a, b, p. 365).

Yet it was not merely the novelty of this alien world that fascinated Rembrandt, but the elegance and delicacy in even these mediocre specimens. The sketch of Homer Rembrandt drew in Six's album in 1652 is another token of his shrewd appropriation of various cultural traditions.[9] The sketch has long been thought to echo a composition by Raphael; but an equally important inspiration—evidenced in the delicate draftsmanship with its large light areas—must derive from the East. This new drawing style also began to invade Rembrandt's paintings, softening and transfiguring the vigorous brushwork of his heroic period. A moving example is JUPITER AND MERCURY VISITING PHILEMON AND BAUCIS [278; Colorplate, p. 103], dating from 1658, directly linked, even in the group arrangement, with the etching, ABRAHAM SERVING THE THREE ANGELS, and, of course, the model from India. So carefully integrated are the ceiling beams, the profiles obscuring the light or lighted by it, so subtle is the whole alternation of light and dark that the picture seems almost to be woven of gossamer.

Kenneth Clark has pointed to the "magical remoteness of the profile" that invests the works of this period with a timeless quality beyond the "flux of action" of everyday life. Rembrandt found this cool approach to the representation of the human form not only in his miniatures from India but also in his Italian medallions and other Renaissance works.[10]

PHILEMON AND BAUCIS also bespeaks a new understanding of the art of Adam Elsheimer, who did many such cabinet paintings: quiet mythological scenes taking place in hushed evening landscapes and intimate candle-lit interiors. Comparing this revived interest in Elsheimer with Rembrandt's earlier interpretations of his art [7, 8, 14, 24] one gains the conviction that only now could Rembrandt draw from Elsheimer's art its deepest values. Elsheimer actually enters into Rembrandt's work in many guises. Rembrandt worked over the copperplate of Hercules Seghers' etching, THE FLIGHT INTO EGYPT (see Illustration), a composition that was in turn a free copy after a small painting by Elsheimer (Illustration a, p. 58). Seghers and Elsheimer both create landscapes gently bewitched onto the sheet, so to speak, with trees, shrubs, and bright waters interwoven. Light sky and dark countryside are carefully balanced within the picture area, giving rise to a firm and vigorous texture. The urge toward abstraction is felt in the treetops outlined against the bright background. Dignity and intimacy are blended in equal parts.

There is, lastly, the Venetian component. Whether or not the attributions in Rembrandt's inventory to such as Palma Vecchio, the Bassanos, and Giorgione ("a large painting of the Samaritan Woman") command credence is of small importance. They do in any event testify to Rembrandt's admiration of Venetian painting, which was manifest long before 1650. The Palma and the Giorgione, by the way, belonged to Rembrandt and Pieter de la Tombe jointly; and the small sum realized when they were sold suggests they may not have been genuine. For that matter, they may have been, like so many others, simply trade stock—we have spoken of Rembrandt's activities on the Amsterdam art market before.[11]

Curiously, the Rembrandt painting that most clearly embodies the Venetian spirit is also a CHRIST AND THE WOMAN OF SAMARIA [273]. The landscape with its palm trees, the foreground display before this backdrop, the architecture with its

a Rembrandt SAINT JEROME. Etching
Amsterdam, Rijksmuseum

b Rembrandt LANDSCAPE WITH A TOWER. 1650. Etching
Amsterdam, Rijksmuseum

niches, the parallel arrangement of the figures, the interrupted gestures—all these are elements of the Venetian pictorial idiom, with the figures embedded in the gentle countryside and the monumental architecture. In places Rembrandt allowed his brush free rein and it tended toward ornamental abstraction—the masonry of the well, the woman's skirt, indeed larger areas of stone and fabric are the loci of such unrealistic "abstract" painting. There are similar picturesque doodles in the landscape as well, somewhat subduing the sense of realism in the picture, but also softening its heroic character and making the Bible story more accessible. Many of Rembrandt's works done during the fifties owe their new harmony of contained power and peaceful narrative to this Venetian influence.

Rembrandt's landscape etchings from these years are likewise often Venetian in mood. The etched SAINT JEROME (Illustration a) is distinctly reminiscent of an engraving by Campagnola. The buildings in it are clearly in the Italian manner and the hill formations are anything but Dutch. But even more than these topographic details, the whole structure of the sheet with its surfaces and masses blocking off the distances is an Italian invention, here enhanced to heroic proportions.[12] Yet these landscapes do not at all represent a foreign body in Rembrandt's art of this period. There is a clear-cut Venetian feeling even to purely Dutch motifs like the LANDSCAPE WITH A TOWER (Illustration b) or the small landscape with a boat in the foreground, a feeling that extends both to the composition as such and to the firm painterly mode of execution.[13]

Actually Venetian art as exemplified by Titian and his circle—whose works provided the models in point for Rembrandt's pictures during the fifties—does not by any means embody the strongest expression of the heroic mood to be found in Italian art. It so happens, however, that Rembrandt—and with him many other northerners—felt particularly close to Venetian art because it seemed so much in accord with the Dutch feeling of how painters should interpret the world. In BATHSHEBA WITH KING DAVID'S LETTER [271; Colorplate, p. 107], dated 1654, the warm Venetian palette and surface sumptuousness have always excited admiration, as has the way in which the figures are isolated from the background, underlining their monumentality. All anecdotal frills have been dispensed with—not even the figure of King

David, so essential to the Bible story, appears in the background. One important influence in the emphasis on the two women is an ancient relief with which Rembrandt may have been acquainted through an engraving by François Perrier and which probably would have impressed him with its purity of form. Oddly enough, the curtain motif is also reasserted in the painting, this time not to frame or terminate it in an effort to create a sense of intimacy, but as a focus of the color range within the painting itself.

As so often in his later works, Rembrandt, in finishing the painting, interrelated the figures more strictly than in the first design. Bathsheba's head was originally erect. As it turns out, however, the picture derives its ultimate sense of solemnity from the fact that her gaze remains within its confines. It is possible, of course, that the lines, and indeed the whole draftsmanship of the painting, have sharpened with age, for physical damage has made inroads on the surface, impairing the balance of hues.

Dated in the same year, HENDRICKJE BATHING IN A STREAM [289; Colorplate, p. 113] is an unpretentious painting that is little more than a sketch in oils. The cleaning of this picture has been unfairly condemned. Actually, it enables us to appreciate the sense of unity, color harmony, and fine firm brushwork of the painting in almost pristine form. Once again the background is warmed and enriched by a length of Oriental fabric in red and gold. Firm modeling and bold pigment application raise even this sketch to the level of monumentality. Hendrickje's cautious groping becomes transfigured into a self-sufficient act. A casual moment is here given the same kind of heroic truth that puts the portrait of JAN SIX head and shoulders above ordinary Dutch portraits. By the same token, HENDRICKJE BATHING IN A STREAM certainly cannot be described as a typical Dutch genre picture.

In these years, which saw a new monumentality of form in Rembrandt's female nudes, the artist revised an older composition of his, the DANAE [270; Colorplate, p. 95]. The grace of the beautiful nude body and the state of mind of a woman expecting her lover preoccupied Rembrandt to the point where other details of the story are left vague. The unusual spirituality of the scene made scholars reluctant to accept the obvious identification of the subject and led them to propose various biblical heroines. But Panofsky has shown that Danae need not be an

a Rembrandt THE ARTIST DRAWING A NUDE. Drawing
Oxford, Ashmolean Museum

b Rembrandt BUST OF A ROMAN EMPEROR. Drawing
Vienna, Albertina

emblem of carnal corruptness; she can also be a figuration of the Virgin, and her lover—Jupiter in a shower of gold lucre—an image of God himself in a heavenly blaze of light.

The painting is dated 1636, the year in which it was originally painted. The showy drapes of the bedstead, the Baroque carvings, and the oblique lighting accord in structure with THE BLINDING OF SAMSON [76] done at about the same time—though even in its original condition the DANAE could hardly have matched the expressive power of the SAMSON. The message to be conveyed by the two paintings was too different for that. But in the fifties Rembrandt repainted the figure of Danae completely, changing the position of the hand and lending the picture a more mature sense of beauty, a warmth and fullness in keeping with the great nudes of the fifties (such as BATHSHEBA) rather than the bland sheen of ABRAHAM'S SACRIFICE of 1635.

It is taken for granted, probably rightly, that Hendrickje served as a model for these history paintings. Rembrandt did many life studies, often after Hendrickje, in these years. Until the last he was fascinated by the nude human body with its large bright areas, its soft flow of lines, the gentle roundings of its flesh. These light-drenched drawings now became works of art in their own right. Once they had merely been a by-product of Rembrandt's art school. On one occasion Rembrandt showed himself in the act of drawing; and even this sheet is primarily a study in light filling the room and enveloping the model (Illustration a). On another occasion he showed his seated model wearing the same exotic headdress that adorns the old crone in his BATHSHEBA (Illustration a, p. 361).[14]

Rembrandt's retreat from narrative detail, combined with his increasing emphasis on the individual figure, often makes it hard for us to identify the proper themes of his late history paintings. In time, as his expressive power steadily grew, the narrative element came to be limited to the barest minimum. Side by side, another process took place whose beginnings we have already observed—the marvelous, the inner vision was to be combined with the contemporary world. Vision and everyday experience moved closer and closer together. Rembrandt's first encounter with a model—and for that matter with any aspect of the world—was capable of translating him to the higher reaches of awareness, something by no means typical of the Dutch character.

Dutch artists ordinarily used their art to record visual experience, which they liked to present with every refinement of technical skill. Rembrandt, on the other hand, elevated the most casual sketch to the level of pure expression, by his skill with lighting, his brushwork, his flair for monumental composition. In the course of the years, Rembrandt seemed to grow more and more selective in his models, whether they were people around him, works of art from the past, or simply topics that interested him. Sketch and painting, portrait and history—they all tended to merge, imperceptibly, one into the other.

An instructive example is provided by Rembrandt's many studies we call CHRIST [255, 256, 257, 258, 321, 322, 323, 378]. Are they really evocations of Rembrandt's own image of Christ, or simply portrait heads of a young Jew? This sequence of idealized heads has been thought to be preliminary to the Emmaus pictures of the late forties [218, 219], yet a few of them were almost certainly done later, without any direct connection at all with Bible paintings. The only reason the bust-length PORTRAIT OF A YOUNG JEW [392], dated 1661, is not considered a Christ figure is because the model wears a skull-cap—otherwise, in frontal aspect and lowered gaze, it is entirely in the manner we know Rembrandt reserved for Christ. THE RISEN CHRIST [360] and CHRIST [369] are no more than enlarged adaptations of that searching and spiritualized portrait study. In keeping with tradition, Rembrandt always showed Christ at a youthful age, and the preliminary studies leading to his Christ type are probably all portraits of young Jews.[15]

It is no accident that Rembrandt had so close an affinity for Jewish models, for the house he had bought in St. Anthonisbreestraat lay near the Jewish quarter. To Rembrandt the Jews were part of the Old Testament world that—however humanistically inclined Rembrandt's faith may have been—still occupied a firm place in the Christian universe to which his art was devoted. And at the same time it was precisely the Jewish types who satisfied Rembrandt's taste for the exotic. For it remains true that all his life Rembrandt was in search of the exotic, of what lay beyond the pale of Amsterdam bourgeois society with its bland and cheerful concept of art. To Rembrandt the Jews were the embodiment of another culture, and he availed himself of their features almost as a matter of course when it came to conjuring up images of the

HENDRICKJE BATHING IN A STREAM [289]

Barent Fabritius THE PRODIGAL SON. 1663
Amsterdam, Rijksmuseum

past, whether of biblical or classical antiquity. The ideals of the wise man, the prophet, the apostle all stem from this same visual environment, and in Rembrandt's late works they coalesce more and more into a single type of human dignity and loving-kindness.

In the course of the year 1652 Rembrandt was commissioned by Antonio Ruffo, a nobleman from Sicily, to paint a picture of Aristotle. The correspondence concerning this commission has been preserved—though, of course, it does not include any letters by Rembrandt himself, only by Ruffo's agent in Amsterdam and the nobleman himself. Rembrandt was no polyglot Rubens who could converse with Italian patrons in their own tongue. But these letters reflect Rembrandt's views and offer an interesting commentary on them. ARISTOTLE CONTEMPLATING A BUST OF HOMER [286; Colorplate, p. 111] met with approval—Ruffo was to order two other pictures from Rembrandt. Much in the first pictures must have appeared strange and old-fashioned to Italian eyes; indeed, even the half-length format as such. On the other hand, Ruffo may have had fewer prejudices than other collectors who lived in the centers of Baroque classicism, and he may have heard of Rembrandt's reputation in Rome as "spectacularly skillful in painting" (*stravagantissimo nel modo del dipingere*). He certainly looked forward to receiving Rembrandt's paintings as an extraordinary event.[16]

Linking Aristotle with Homer, the philosopher's wisdom with the poet's illumination, was not a new idea. The philosopher, the expositor, the theorist of traditional thought—he was a figure familiar to Dutch intellectual life in the second half of the 17th century; for one of the triumphant trends of the time was the systematization of all phenomena, their reduction to mathematical measure. Rembrandt's world view—or perhaps we had better say his mode of seeing and painting—did not fit into this framework. If we do wish to look for an appropriate reflection in Dutch art of the kind of thinking that was then current, we are more likely to find it in the works of Jan Vermeer. Rembrandt's Aristotle steps forth in the garb of a priest, with faint echoes of fanciful 16th-century styles. Rembrandt's light never attains the daytime clarity of Vermeer.[17] Faces and fabrics shine in a glancing light that symbolizes illumination and enlightenment. The room is shut off by a drape, keeping our gaze and our thoughts from wandering off into the shadowy interior. A few tomes in the left

background bespeak knowledge—or is this the base of a pillar? Either way the culture of antiquity is hinted at.

Rembrandt himself owned ancient portrait busts, or copies of them (Illustration b, p. 112). A bust of Homer and a bust of Aristotle are enumerated one after the other in his inventory, together with still others.[18] He drew some of these busts. The one of Homer, being pondered by Aristotle in Rembrandt's painting, is of a well-known antique type. The features of Aristotle, on the other hand, are certainly not in the image of an ancient sculpture. No, the philosopher stems from quite another culture. His antecedents are those self-same portrait studies of bearded Jews [283] who came to symbolize prophetic wisdom to Rembrandt. The slight bow of the head not only suggests thoughtful contemplation but perplexity at the blindness of Homer, whose bust looms erect, as though the bard's veiled gaze probed the mysteries of the world.

The mood of the painting is heavy, as is the brushwork, which has a touch of unreality. For the first time we encounter here large white areas shot through with gold, while the expanse of black robe is cut through by a glittering gold chain. Green and blue-green shadows blend in the white cassock. There is little emphasis on the hands as the indicators of action. Even the almost square format of the painting may not be fortuitous. Its balanced dimensions seem to resist all centrifugal force.

One might imagine that themes of outward tranquillity would have accorded particularly well with Rembrandt's stylistic tendencies of these years—themes like the Holy Family, Bathsheba, Homer. Yet he also managed to render more dramatic Bible stories in the heroic style of the fifties—a style in which Rembrandt, as we have seen, also found a place for the warm color magic of Venetian art. The major example is JOSEPH ACCUSED BY POTIPHAR'S WIFE [274, 275], which has come down to us in two versions. What seems to have chiefly preoccupied Rembrandt was the posture and gestures of Joseph. In the Washington version [275] he stands humble and despairing, one hand placed atop the other. In the Berlin version [274] his hand is raised imploringly. Originally, Joseph covered his face in the Berlin painting, still a third expressive possibility; but Rembrandt himself painted this out. In terms of color and expression, the Berlin painting is the richer and more carefully considered version. Figures and

a Samuel van Hoogstraten VANITAS. 1644
Rotterdam, Museum Boymans-van Beuningen

b Barent Fabritius REMBRANDT
Leipzig, Museum der bildenden Kuenste

action are shown against the background of what seems to be a state chamber in the royal palace. The Washington painting, on the other hand, might very well have been a workshop product which Rembrandt worked over. It has less detail, without thereby gaining in monumentality. In it, for example, so significant a detail as Joseph's red cloak, held down under the foot of his accuser, is omitted. Among the unique elements in the Berlin picture are the magnificent cubic color masses that lend it such radiance and inner assurance. The X-ray photograph that reveals the original position of Joseph's hands also allows the firm sketching of the whole underdrawing to emerge.

The anecdotal accents in these Joseph pictures, we note, are only hinted at lest they detract from the compact composition of the three figures. In JACOB BLESSING THE CHILDREN OF JOSEPH [277; Colorplates, pp. 98, 99], the iconographic motif of the crossed arms which played so important a part in previous representations of this theme is all but suppressed. Of course, even Rembrandt cannot completely ignore the crux of the story, Joseph's intervention in order to secure the grandfather's blessing for his first-born; but despite Joseph's guidance, Jacob places his right hand in blessing on the younger child, who looms larger in the picture. This is Ephraim whom the Gentiles invoke—the elder boy, Manasseh, small and dark, is blessed with the left hand.

Rembrandt's audience, thoroughly familiar with the Bible story, will have appreciated these subtleties. The dominant elements in the picture are the act of the old man's blessing and the inner strength and gravity that shine forth from the proud patriarch. Joseph, his children, and his father form a compact group, with Joseph's wife Asenath (whose presence is quite unusual) merely serving to strengthen the elongated composition. As in other later works, the sense of depth (accentuated by the lines of the bed) is counteracted, in this case by the broad expanse of the red coverlet. The coverlet contrasts—even competes—in tone with the lighter figures, but its contours bring our attention back to the picture surface, for they follow the outline of the group of figures at a lower level; the drapes perform the same function at the left margin. Just as movement is arrested in portraits done at this time, so a dramatic story is here raised to the level of quiet contemplation, given body by the firm brushwork and inner stress by the glowing palette.

We can readily understand why Rembrandt's students of those years were unable to fathom, let alone develop further, this stylistic phase, which marks the work of the fully mature Rembrandt. Samuel van Hoogstraten, who must have been Rembrandt's student about 1641, discussed the basic questions of artistic training and the correct manner of depicting the world in paint with his fellow students Carel Fabritius and Abraham Furnerius. How does one get to be a good painter? When is a story well told in paint? and other questions of the kind. On one occasion, when he besieged his master with these problems, Rembrandt is said to have told van Hoogstraten: "Learn to put to the right use what you already know; what is now hidden from you will soon enough become clear." [19]

Jan Emmens, who has delved particularly deeply into problems of 17th-century art theory, believes this Rembrandt dictum to be a recommendation of Practice, *exercitatio*, one of the three basic principles on which a good education in art was thought to rest— the other two being Inspiration, *ingenium*, and the Science of Art, *ars*. This it certainly is. But does this mean that Rembrandt consciously balanced Practice against Theory and decided against the latter? Probably not. If he shrank from making theoretical utterances, it is more likely for the reasons stated by van de Waal: Dutch artists and critics of the 17th century, including Rembrandt, had simply not yet developed concepts and terms to describe what they were doing. The "problems" Rembrandt refused to discuss with the young van Hoogstraten were indeed intangible to the art terminology of the day. How could we expect Rembrandt, whose work encompassed worlds never dreamed of by the critics of his time, and who was not very articulate, to have discussed them? [20]

However that may have been, there were no Rembrandt students after Carel Fabritius who might have used Rembrandt's art as their own point of departure. Like so many other contemporaries, Carel's brother Barent continued to be diverted by the warm interplay of Rembrandt's colors. They are echoed even in Barent's late pictures, in which the figures dance through the compositions in Mannerist curlicues (Illustration, p. 114). Barent's most impressive works are his self-portraits done in the early 1650's. Among study heads wrongly ascribed to Rembrandt are a few that may very well have been painted by Barent in Rem-

a Nicolaes Maes A STUDENT
Panshanger, Collection of Lady Desborough

b Nicolaes Maes A FAMILY GROUP
Toledo, Ohio, Museum of Art

brandt's studio—e.g. the portrait of Rembrandt in Leipzig (Illustration b, p. 116) and the two replicas after a lost Rembrandt original, now in Glasgow and Groningen.[21] Lighting effects associated with Carel Fabritius—dark head against a light wall, for example—coupled with a certain loose brushwork, support such an attribution.

Samuel van Hoogstraten's portrait art likewise rests on his study of Rembrandt, though it is not easy to point to the particular Rembrandt portrait type that served as his model. In the early fifties van Hoogstraten was still blending the gentle Rembrandt style of the forties with a vigorous and colorful manner that belongs only to a much later Rembrandt phase (Illustration a, p. 116). But neither Barent Fabritius nor Samuel van Hoogstraten was gifted with a feeling for monumental composition. Neither wielded a sweeping and self-assured brush.

Nicolaes Maes (1634–93) is perhaps the figure whose development becomes most tangible to us, both as a painter and a draftsman. Maes reveled in a soft painterly style he must have borrowed from Rembrandt's Bible pictures done during the forties. He was particularly skillful in rendering soft white skin and the nuances of warmth and brightness. Maes always tells his stories well, though without his master's depth of expressiveness, gravity, and austerity, and never going out of his way to avoid anecdotal ornament. In Maes' hands, in other words, Rembrandt's style was tailored to suit the taste of contemporary collectors (Illustration b). He, too, lent his own interpretation to the portrait with a painted frame, more oratorical in spirit than Rembrandt's original creation (Illustration a).[22] It is scarcely necessary to add that in his later years, when he became almost exclusively a portrait painter, Maes also developed a fashionable portrait style of his own. A noteworthy feature of that style is its cultivated and extremely subtle palette, which must be considered an outgrowth of the Rembrandt tradition.

Maes' interpretation of Rembrandt's art made an extraordinary appeal to the generation born around 1625–30, as a style that preserved all of Rembrandt's sensitivity and picturesqueness, including his gentle lighting—all qualities belonging to Rembrandt's art of the forties. What it did not adopt, of course, was Rembrandt's sense of grandeur in composition, his sweeping, heroic brushwork. Jan Victors, Willem Drost, Karel van der

Pluym, and Abraham van Dijck are painters that belong to this group. Some of them were Maes' seniors, suggesting that their interpretation of Rembrandt was not coined by Maes and handed over to them. Yet Maes did tower above all of them, by virtue of his extraordinary productivity and the enhanced sensibility of his style. Now and then a work of extraordinary charm would come from this group, such as Drost's BATHSHEBA in the Louvre (Illustration a, p. 120)—at least this is true in terms of finish and technique. The element of internal power is another matter.

Abraham van Dijck was a specialist in the rendering of old people; and at first glance his oldsters closely resemble Rembrandt's—a resemblance that has occasionally led to wrong attributions.[23] Jan Victors (1620–76) had the odd ambition to paint Bible pictures of huge format, pictures that irritate by their dryness and vacuousness. Yet here, too, a question of correct attribution sometimes arises, particularly in the case of paintings done in Rembrandt's studio that have come down to us with Rembrandt's own revisions—his drawings indeed often providing the starting-point for the whole composition. The large ANGEL ASCENDING IN THE FLAMES OF MANOAH'S SACRIFICE [204], quite beautiful in parts, may well be such a school work by Jan Victors, though designed and retouched by Rembrandt.

By the 1650's Rembrandt's fame had spread to the far ends of Europe. It was primarily his etchings, sold in the large centers of the art trade, that served as ambassadors of his style—though, as we have seen, some of his paintings had already gone to France, among other places. We note further that a number of painters from abroad, especially from Germany, received training in his Amsterdam studio, only to purvey a watered-down Rembrandt style of chiaroscuro and warm coloration once they had returned home. The charm that even such pictures can exert is shown in the sensitive still lifes and palish hermits and old men done by Christoph Paudiss (Illustration b, p. 120). Bernard Keil, a Dane, moved on from Holland to Italy. As a painter in the Rembrandt tradition he is of small importance, but we are eternally indebted to him for having described Rembrandt's life and art to Filippo Baldinucci, a story which Baldinucci included in his *Cominciamento e Progresso dell'Arte dell'intagliare in Rame* (1686). Baldinucci, as a matter of fact, was familiar with paintings in Italian collections which were either by Rembrandt or from his school.

a Willem Drost BATHSHEBA. 1654
Paris, Louvre

b Christoph Paudiss STILL LIFE. 1660
Rotterdam, Museum Boymans-van Beuningen

Let us return to the observation made at the outset of this chapter: the 1650's are indeed a period of greatness in the history of Dutch art. Paintings of this time have a certain grandeur and heroic expressiveness, a firmness of structure emerging in the emphasis on vertical and horizontal elements, in keeping with the ideals of Baroque classicism. Rembrandt possessed this sense of inward power and noble construction in high measure. His students, by contrast, seem to have been receptive largely to the sheer abundance of his creative invention. In their hands Rembrandt's sublime vision turns into the same old familiar view; even the picturesque themes are cliché-ridden. The students missed Rembrandt's muscle and sinew, capturing only the surface beauty of his work.

The Final Years

The late works of great artists weave a strange magic for the sensitive beholder. One regards them with a certain awe, as though the imminence of death might have brought intimations of visions beyond the frontiers of life. One looks for a last message that would embody in a single work everything the artist's eyes had seen, all he had striven for. It is hard to accept the possibility that his life's work might remain unfinished, that his creative powers might have waned.

Rembrandt died in his 63rd year. He had greatly aged in body—his self-portraits document that beyond doubt. Yet his late works reach such a pinnacle of perfection, such a true consummation that it is hard to envisage how his creative work might have been sustained or prolonged. In any case, we are not used to thinking of Rembrandt's death as an interruption of his career.

The sturdy and heroic character to which we have become accustomed drops away from the style of Rembrandt's old age. His paintings open up and gain in transparence. Large, thick clots of pigment, imperfectly integrated into the whole picture, occasionally glisten from his canvases. Yet we do not sense any slackening of creative power in this greater structural looseness.

Rembrandt's growing loneliness is a disturbing thought. Saskia was followed into death by Hendrickje in 1667 and by Titus the following year—the year of his marriage. For the last year of his life, Rembrandt dwelt alone in the house on the Rozengracht that had served him as a dwelling and workshop combined, and also as an office for the art gallery Hendrickje and Titus had been running to protect and support Rembrandt. Partly responsible for his growing isolation must have been the decline in his social position. We think of the last days of Rubens, whom Rembrandt had emulated as a collector in better days—his dignified retirement to his country home, the solicitous enquiries of his royal patrons after his health. But when it comes to that, Rembrandt never had the same need nor the capacity for mingling with the great as that prince among painters. Baldinucci's report, based on the evidence of Bernard Keil, who was with Rembrandt in the 1640's, says that when Rembrandt was working he would not admit even the greatest monarch in the world into his presence, let alone interrupt his work on account of such a visit.[1] In contrast to Rembrandt, who worked in a plain smock that he would use as a brushrag when absorbed in his work, Rubens, in his spacious

home and large studio, is described to us in rather different terms. While working "he listened to someone reading aloud from Tacitus and also dictated a letter. He would greet a visitor and converse with him, while continuing to paint and dictate and listen to Tacitus."[2]

Intellectual acrobatics of this sort were a Rubens specialty; but the anecdotes tell us more than the idiosyncrasies of Rembrandt and Rubens: they highlight the basic difference in cultural level between Holland and Flanders. In many respects, painting as practiced in the northern Netherlands was still very much a craft like any other. Despite his rise in social position during the thirties, Rembrandt never assimilated the "princely" manner of Rubens, and he did not consider it beneath his dignity to seek diversion and inspiration among the common people. This greatly irked such sophisticated artist-critics as Joachim von Sandrart and Arnold Houbraken, who were very concerned to raise painting from a "craft" to an "art."[3]

J. G. van Gelder has repeatedly emphasized that Rembrandt's work as a teacher must have been an important creative stimulus to him, no matter how untalented his students may have been.[4] If this is so, Rembrandt must have preferred delivering his artistic message to a group of students to mingling with his patrons. At the same time, Rembrandt surely realized that the deeper values of his art could only be compromised by students who did not understand him or grasped only the surface elements of his art. Typical examples are the variable interpretations they gave to his window and curtain motifs, which we have analyzed in some detail.

We do not know much about Rembrandt's relations with the people who gave him commissions, and what little we do know hints of a certain awkward unworldliness. The commission for the Stadholder, for example, dragged on for years. When a certain Diego Andrada complained that a portrait did not sufficiently resemble the sitter, Rembrandt gave a peppery reply.[5] Yet there are plenty of works from every period of Rembrandt's career that were done on commission.

Are we really justified in speaking of Rembrandt's growing artistic isolation? How extensive were the changes in his approach and vision during the last decade of his life? It is true that he failed in certain commissions, like that for the new Town Hall. It

a Jan Lievens FIVE MUSES. 1650
The Hague, Huis ten Bosch

b Caesar van Everdingen FOUR MUSES
The Hague, Huis ten Bosch

is also true that his concepts often violated the tenets of decorum accepted by the classicistic criticism of the sixties, and that he failed to provide the blandly decorative canvases bought so eagerly in those days. Ten years earlier, when it came to decorating the Huis ten Bosch, no use had been found for Rembrandt either, though he was well known to the Stadholder's circles. The new style Jan Lievens had acquired in Antwerp (Illustration a) and the art of Caesar van Everdingen (Illustration b) fitted the decorative scheme better.

One fact that militates against the theory of Rembrandt's isolation is that a whole series of handsome commissions continued to come his way during the last years of his life, from civic groups as well as individuals. As we shall see, Antonio Ruffo placed additional orders for paintings and for a whole series of etchings. When the Grand Duke of Tuscany visited Amsterdam he tried to buy a Rembrandt self-portrait.[6] And, of course, many citizens of Amsterdam still liked to have their portraits painted by Rembrandt. Even if he was not a central figure in the city's art life, then, Rembrandt was by no means altogether isolated. Indeed, he may well have taken a certain satisfaction in his established position as an artist of European rank. Rembrandt is far less likely to have been profoundly affected by the loss of his social position, by having to move out of his fine house, than would have been the case with many other Dutch painters—the kind who were rooted in society body and soul.

And what about the question of students? There were indeed fewer than before, but Rembrandt could take that blow, too, with better grace than many another artist. All aging artists learn by painful experience that the growing generation prefers to study with the fathers rather than the grandfathers—rebelling against both, by the way! That was as true in Rembrandt's day as it is today—the phenomenon hardly requires explanation.

The fact is, Rembrandt did have disciples, even in his old age—men like Aert de Gelder, who joined his workshop about 1660. He also had friends who had once been his students—men like Gerbrandt van den Eeckhout (1621–74) who, in a highly personal way, carefully cultivated Rembrandt's late style. Further, Houbraken tells us that the landscape painter Roelant Roghman was a great friend of both Rembrandt and Gerbrandt van den Eeck-

hout. Out of friendship for Roghman, we are told, Rembrandt on one occasion declined to accept a student who had run away from Roghman to study with Rembrandt.[7]

Still another landscape painter, Philips Koninck, must have kept up his personal friendship with Rembrandt for many years after his apprenticeship in Rembrandt's studio. On the back of a Rembrandt drawing he owned, Koninck wrote: "This drawing represents the Buitenamstelkant, well drawn by Mijnheer Rembrandt's own hand."[8] The painter Jan van de Cappelle (1623/5–79) also knew Rembrandt well, probably down to the last year of Rembrandt's life. Not only were both he and his father portrayed by Rembrandt, he even owned four portfolios with about 500 Rembrandt drawings![9]

Such considerations persuade us to revise the picture of Rembrandt as an aged and lonely artist, forgotten and misunderstood. In certain respects, his situation was quite typical of that of the aging artist whose personal style reaches its climax only after the period style has moved away from him. But if the distance that separates Rembrandt from his younger contemporaries seems inordinate we should also seek reasons in his own character, and the character of his art. In any case we can scarcely put the responsibility on any lack of understanding on the part of his fellow citizens. The sentimental notions once prevalent about Rembrandt were no doubt inspired in part by the romantic stereotype of the misunderstood genius, further dramatized in his case by the decline in his fortunes. The great esteem in which the art of his declining years was held is reflected in the biographies that began to appear soon after his death. They had a good deal of fault to find with him, but though the classicist ideal was then dominant they praised him as "a most eminent artist" with great powers of imagination, whose art was "d'une force, d'une suavité et d'une vérité surprenante."[10] The most eloquent testimony to his standing, however, is provided by the many portrait commissions to which we shall now devote our attention.

Three group portraits of very different character form important landmarks in Rembrandt's late style. The first, THE ANATOMY LESSON OF DOCTOR JOAN DEYMAN [326], was done as early as 1656. Stylistically, it still belongs to the heroic manner of the

MOSES WITH THE TABLES OF THE LAW [347]
THE CONSPIRACY OF JULIUS CIVILIS [354] Two details

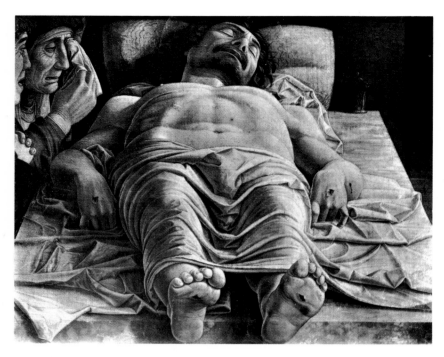

a Andrea Mantegna THE DEAD CHRIST
Milan, Brera

fifties, yet comparison with the late works is illuminating. We must take into account that this painting suffered serious damage by fire, about half of it being destroyed outright. A drawing Rembrandt made of the whole painting and its frame (Illustration a, p. 398) will help us in our judgment.

The cadaver under dissection thrusts out powerfully toward the viewer, the soles of its feet prominent. Rembrandt may have taken over the idea of this sharply foreshortened figure from Mantegna, Borgianni, or Goltzius (see Illustration). The outward resemblance to Mantegna's nobly proportioned body of Christ adds a ghoulish effect to this dreadfully mutilated cadaver. In compositional terms, this sprawling corpse probably formed the major—one is almost tempted to say the living—accent in the picture. It is supported on the broad plate of a dissecting table which emphasizes the main horizontal dimension. The assistant and other doctors are grouped on either side in careful symmetry. The torchbearer of science, the anatomist himself, stands four-square behind the cadaver, like a lord over life and death. His hands are at their cautious work. The drawing, which fills us in on the mere shell of the painting, is no preliminary sketch. As J. Q. van Regteren Altena has shown, it was meant to record how the picture hung in the hall of the Amsterdam medical guild. Here the character of the picture clearly emerges—a group portrait that is more static than the earlier DOCTOR NICOLAAS TULP DEMONSTRATING THE ANATOMY OF THE ARM [100] and without the eloquent rhetorical gesture of that work. Despite the exaggerated foreshortening of the dead man, the portrait group in the DEYMAN is rhythmically organized in surface terms of horizontals and verticals rather than in depth.

Our interpretation of this Amsterdam fragment must also take into account the later portrait group THE SAMPLING OFFICIALS OF THE DRAPERS' GUILD [404; Colorplate, p. 131] of 1662. A somewhat similar compositional principle is used in this painting, a group of five persons (not counting the attendant), arranged about a forward-thrusting element that again works its effect by harmoniously organizing the picture surface rather than its depth. To van de Waal must go the credit for having properly read the ordinance of this painting. The main character is seated at the short posterior end of a table, flanked on each side by two other members of the woolen manufacturers' control commission. The foremost gentleman at the left (from the viewer's point of view) has pushed his chair back from the table, while his neigh-

bor has risen. Perspective in depth is thus transformed into juxtaposition in almost the same plane. The two figures at the extreme ends, by their inward-facing posture, serve to bracket the picture, so to speak. The paneling, like the forward edge of the table, contributes further to the dominance of the horizontal, so that the foreshortened elements and the rise and fall of the black hats are projected against a pattern of inert parallels.

Here too Rembrandt took into account the way the picture was to be hung. It was to be high, good reason for the foreshortened perspective from below. The viewer raises his eyes and grows aware that from behind a glowing red table-rug five formidable gentlemen are regarding him intently, barely able to restrain themselves from bursting into speech. The impression is so vivid that Schmidt-Degener was led to interpret this group portrait as a "snapshot" taken at a public session. Someone in the audience (which is seated at a lower level in the hall) has just charged the board with some failing, and they are on the point of replying to the accusation. Undeniably this interpretation comes closer to the group's compelling animation than our analysis by pictorial structure alone. Yet Schmidt-Degener's theory must be rejected on historical grounds: the "staalmeesters," as the sampling officials are called in Dutch, were not accountable to the public. Their eloquent gestures—like that of the man "ostentatiously grasping the money-bag"—have nothing to do with speech or inward agitation. They are designed as easily readable indications of the sitter's rank and office.

In visual terms, nevertheless, these eloquent hands serve a function that transcends individual or official characterization. This becomes plain from a comparison with the older ANATOMY LESSON OF DOCTOR JOAN DEYMAN. There the hands of the doctor do their work on the cadaver, followed with more or less attention by the other figures (the drawing does not tell us enough on this point). In THE SAMPLING OFFICIALS the book on the table joins the main figure and his neighbor into a single compositional unit; but it is the hand of the leading official, visible only in part, that ties the group together, as becomes clear when it is covered up. Its gesture permits the man on his right to rise, and conducts all attention to a common focus. X-ray studies have shown that Rembrandt made a number of important changes in the process of painting the picture. Only after several endeavors, for example, was the attendant assigned to his definitive place, strengthening the central group as against the framing figures.

Rembrandt experimented with this composition in preliminary studies, both of groups of figures and of individual sitters. This is unusual in respect of his group portraits. We know of no single compositional or portrait study for THE NIGHT WATCH. The fragmentary study for THE SAMPLING OFFICIALS in Berlin (Illustration a, p. 445) shows the left-hand group in more vigorously contrasted postures than in the quieter final version. Surviving pen-and-ink figure studies (Illustration a, p. 445) open our eyes to the soft delicacy of Rembrandt's touch and the gentle light in which the figures are bathed. Such is the grandeur of the painting that we incline to overlook the sensitive brushwork on the faces, the silky hair in all its perfection, the black cloth with its color reflections.

In THE SAMPLING OFFICIALS we find familiar elements of Rembrandt's art as well as innovations. Rembrandt had used the gesture of the leading figure as a keynote in his very first group portrait, the TULP of 1632. A main accent shifted toward the left, against the grain of our habitual "reading bias," is something we already saw in THE NIGHT WATCH. Just such a foundation of radiant red fabric as appears in THE SAMPLING OFFICIALS shines forth in JACOB BLESSING THE SONS OF JOSEPH. Harmonious organization of the picture area in defiance of its forward thrust we know from THE ANATOMY LESSON OF DOCTOR JOAN DEYMAN. But the grandeur and unity of THE SAMPLING OFFICIALS are not founded on a rigid adherence to principle but on the interplay of many forces, controlled with sovereign mastery, investing the work with a human warmth transcending the perpetuation of one moment in time.

The Brunswick FAMILY GROUP [416; Colorplate, p. 165] is a work from the last years of Rembrandt's life. It lacks even the slightest hint of an interior that would help to fix the domestic circumstances of the sitters. This temporal and spatial disengagement is sharply at odds with the physical obtrusiveness of the pigments. The paint is piled on in thick dabs, often with the palette knife rather than the brush. One can sense the creative excitement imparted directly to the medium.

Rembrandt's contemporaries often chided him for leaving his paintings "unfinished," a reproach to which he is said to have replied: "A picture is done when the master has expressed his intent in it." [11] It would be hard to imagine that he could have given this one greater perfection by abiding by conventional techniques. Nor is it any easier to decide whether it is a commission or a purely personal creation. Rembrandt trespasses many of the limits he once imposed on his portraits, in a last ardent flowering of imagination and freedom, a triumphant rise above the limitations of pictorial genres, above the confines of the medium.

Scanning the series of Rembrandt's late portraits—excluding the self-portraits and family portraits—we find them falling into two groups: polished society portraits; and those that are fancifully elaborated, leading in turn to idealized figures from the Bible and antiquity. His likenesses of leading citizens are in no way more superficial or less expressive than the creations of his imagination. The commissioned portraits of the sixties retain the lofty spiritual tone of THE SAMPLING OFFICIALS. The PORTRAIT OF A YOUNG MAN [405; Colorplate, p. 153] of 1663 is marked by the same nobility and delicacy that distinguishes the officials. The husband and wife in Washington [411, 412; Colorplates, pp. 158, 159], probably done somewhat later, are even more spiritual in approach. In outward appearance they are related to the works of such Amsterdam and Haarlem portraitists as Ferdinand Bol and Jan de Bray, to which, however, they are vastly superior in profundity of expression and in the suppression of anecdote and embroidery. The warm humanity of the sitters is not in the least impugned by their formal and stylized poses.

It is unfortunate that we are so poorly informed about the identity of these sitters. Who is the elegant horseman in the London portrait [410]? We suspect he must have been Frederick Rihel, an Amsterdam patrician who took part in the state reception given young Prince William III. Oddly enough, the Baroque stage setting of this cavalier portrait is dominated by the elegiac style of Rembrandt's late pictures other than portraits. No display of ostentatious splendor is made. Instead, by the magic of its deep color glow, the picture breathes a spirit of thoughtful gravity. The horseman seems to appear from nowhere, like a specter —though it must be admitted that this effect of unreality is deepened by the damage the picture has suffered, and especially the darkening of the background directly about the rider.

The portraits of JEREMIAS DE DEKKER [413] and GERARD DE LAIRESSE [407] are rescued from anonymity only by chance. In the case of the poet de Dekker an epigram written upon the painting plays artfully on the sitter's image and his words, and weighs their relative importance in assuring him immortality— as in the ANSLO etching (Illustration b, p. 335). De Dekker's fame rests on his writings rather than on his portrait painted by the

a Adriaen van der Werff SELF-PORTRAIT. 1699
Amsterdam, Rijksmuseum

b Michiel van Musscher THOMAS HEES AND HIS STAFF. 1687
Amsterdam, Rijksmuseum

great painter-phoenix Rembrandt, says the epigram. De Lairesse, subject of the other portrait, laid down in the *Groot Schilderboeck* (1707) a theory of art rooted entirely in French-Italian soil. In this work, Rembrandt, Lievens, and even Rubens are reproached on account of their deep shadows, and Rembrandt's impasto technique is ridiculed, though his palette is called the equal of Titian's. But when Rembrandt painted his portrait of de Lairesse in 1665, there were surely no hard feelings between the two men, who already stood as far apart as possible in the spectrum of Dutch painting in the late 17th century. On the contrary, the ugly features, disfigured by disease, are softened rather than emphasized by the appealingly delicate brushwork.

Besides these formal portraits of persons of substance at their best, Rembrandt also felt the need to capture the transitory essence of sitters in far more casual poses, indeed, almost at a slouch. Earlier, from the YOUNG MAN AT A DESK [54] to the portrait of JAN SIX [309], Rembrandt sought to catch an evanescent state, to make the viewer aware that the sitter was on the point of moving. Through the years these portraits gain the spontaneity of casual sketches successfully carried into finished and polished portrait paintings. The PORTRAIT OF AN OLD MAN [409] and PORTRAIT OF A FAIR-HAIRED MAN [414; Colorplate, p. 163], both dated 1667, are among the very last portraits. The firm formulation of earlier portrait compositions—even the "casual" ones—is gone and the figures seem to be placed within the picture area almost at random; yet the impetuous brushwork achieves astonishing expressiveness, especially in the faces and hands. The features are painted with the utmost intensity, the hands seem almost to clutch the forward picture plane. Surely one cannot speak of any weakness in creative grasp here, as some writers have done, intent on demonstrating Rembrandt's senility in his later years. At worst what has happened is that the mood of comfort and social assuredness so often serving to conceal the inner personality has been neglected.

These are by no means the only commissioned portraits during the sixties. In wills and art sales in the years from 1660 to 1680 there is mention of portraits by Rembrandt of Adriaen Bank, Jan van de Cappelle (father and son), Salomon Walens, Jan de Caullery Jr., Koert Kooper, and Anna Huybrechts (mother-in-law to Titus), pictures either lost or unidentified among the number

that survives. It is true, of course, that paintings figuring in legacies and sales during the 1660's may well have been done in earlier years. This must certainly be the case with the portrait pair of Abraham van Wilmerdonx "and his housewife." At the behest of Titus' guardian, van Wilmerdonx declared at the time of the *cessio bonorum* that Rembrandt had painted the couple about 1642, prior to Saskia's death. These pictures too are unknown or unidentified.[12]

On the other hand, Hofstede de Groot succeeded 40 years ago in running down the portraits of JACOB TRIP [383] and his wife, MARGARETHA DE GEER [384]. Jacob Trip was a merchant of Dordrecht. He and his wife were kin to one of the largest arms dealers and ore magnates, and Jacob Trip had had a share in the business ever since 1626. In 1660/1 his sons had the huge Trip House built for them in Amsterdam. Rembrandt's portrait of JACOB TRIP, done just before the sitter's death in 1661, looks like an Old Testament prophet rather than a leading merchant of Holland. Business and shipping magnates were quite likely to have themselves painted in elegant morning robes of Japanese silk (Illustration b); but Trip's fur-trimmed robe and white scarf are more likely to have come from Rembrandt's studio prop chest. The whole get-up fits in better with the apostle pictures that were painted in these very years. The dignity and wisdom of age speak eloquently from this portrait, assimilated to a biblical personage. The sitter's erect posture is underlined by the verticals of chair and walking-stick.

Much less enchantment attaches to the portrait of MARGARETHA DE GEER. Her old-fashioned dress expresses her allegiance to the established social values of an older generation. Rembrandt seated her in severely frontal aspect before us, omitting any reference to the male pendant, in keeping with Flemish portrait convention (Illustration a, p. 132). The half-length portrait of the same lady [385] and its preparatory drawing (Illustration b, p. 132) exert an extraordinary fascination by virtue of the portraitist's concentration on capturing every line and blemish in her face. The painting, moreover, is in an impeccable state of preservation, making it a feast to the eyes.

Looking at these late works has shown us that Rembrandt's magic touch extended even to portraits of wealthy merchants, ennobling them to the level of creatures from another world—a

THE SAMPLING OFFICIALS OF THE DRAPERS' GUILD [404] Detail

a Jacob Jordaens PORTRAIT OF A WOMAN. 1641
Brussels, Musée Royal des Beaux-Arts

b Rembrandt MARGARETHA DE GEER. Drawing
Rotterdam, Museum Boymans-van Beuningen

transmogrification that must surely have met with the approval of his patrons. The most appealing instance in which portrait and biblical motif are blended, lifting the sitters beyond the mundane world, is ISAAC AND REBECCA [356], where the Bible theme becomes the haunting picture of a betrothed couple (the painting has long been known as "THE JEWISH BRIDE"). Now portraits in which the sitters are shown in the guise of shepherds, or as mythological or biblical figures, are by no means uncommon in Dutch painting. Usually such works carry a playful touch, however—a *bergerie*, a toying with learned allegory, joy in dressing up in Oriental finery. Openhanded patrons were at times even willing to have themselves portrayed among the flock of children being blessed by Christ. Rembrandt himself, in earlier years, painted Saskia decked out as the goddess Flora [92, 96], while Flinck showed his master and Saskia in shepherd's garb (Illustrations a, b, p. 134). In THE PRODIGAL SON IN THE TAVERN [79] it is a moot point which has precedence, the Bible story or the portrait in fancy dress.

The grave spirit of the painting, the ambiguity of time and place seem to me to suggest that a Bible story formed the basis for Rembrandt's ISAAC AND REBECCA. Further evidence is found in a related drawing, plainly representing Abimelech eavesdropping on Isaac and Rebecca (Illustration a, p. 421). In the painting too the figures were originally shown seated, as proved by X-ray studies; but the anecdotal element of the eavesdropping king is missing, allowing the couple's fond affection to emerge undiluted, in posture, hand, and expression.

Once again, in this late painting, the *matière* of the dress colors takes on a life of its own, enhancing the sense of the precious and marvelous, far above any facile conformity with the everyday world. Nothing is smoothed out to please. Faces and hands are sensitively depicted, with a feeling for the gentle stirrings of affection. If the couple can rise, for us, above their identity as particular biblical personages to become symbols of the very essence of love, it is because of the immediacy of the portraits. These characters are no phantoms, no nondescript models. Rembrandt saw them in the flesh as man and wife and he painted them as such. Perhaps they were friends from his own circle, or perhaps he came upon them by chance and they inspired him to lend new life and humanity to the old Bible story. Yet despite its unusual

creative freedom, despite the liberties taken with tradition, the painting may well have been commissioned or sold to a collector.

Even though so many of Rembrandt's late paintings seem to transcend their time and place, they must have been valued by a circle of Dutch collectors; to have occupied a distinct place in the framework of Dutch painting. It may very well have been that some shrewd art dealers and *marchands d'amateurs* sensed the extraordinary quality of Rembrandt's art. This seems to be hinted at in financial transactions with Lodewijk van Ludick and Harmen Becker, where various pictures are mentioned.[13] Becker, for example, had commissioned Rembrandt to do a JUNO, which had not been finished by 1664. The JUNO has come down to us [374; Colorplate, p. 133]. It belongs among Rembrandt's late large-format figure-pieces, like the two versions of THE SUICIDE OF LUCRETIA [372, 373]. None of these pictures breathes the spirit of nobility and antiquity of traditional iconography. Yet the women depicted are enormously appealing, and again the brush-work with its massive and luminous color patches is marked by a powerful sense of expressive immediacy. In all three paintings the colors seem to swell up from the lower edge to the retreating countenances. Not the slightest hint is given of space or domestic background, enhancing the power of these superhuman heroines.

Our discussion of the late commissioned portraits and their heroic biblical and mythological counterparts has cut across Rembrandt's final decade both chronologically and thematically, giving us a framework for discussing his other works of the sixties. While the large-scale history paintings are the most important part of Rembrandt's work during this period, the small histories should not be overlooked. The last of these intimate paintings we encountered, from the late fifties, was JUPITER AND MERCURY VISITING PHILEMON AND BAUCIS [278], done in 1658. This mood is continued in THE CIRCUMCISION OF CHRIST [350], of 1661; by good fortune, both paintings are to be admired in the National Gallery of Art in Washington. The feature that identifies Rembrandt's late style in THE CIRCUMCISION is the prominence given the figures within the picture area. The subsidiary figures seem to ebb away into the background and the only hint of the locale—the stable—is a piece of tenting that shelters the Virgin and the kneeling priest. Light no longer illumines the in-

JUNO [374]

a Govaert Flinck REMBRANDT AS A SHEPHERD. 1636
Amsterdam, Rijksmuseum

b Govaert Flinck SASKIA AS A SHEPHERDESS. 1636
Brunswick, Herzog Anton Ulrich Museum

terior and the supporting beams that structure the space. It clings instead to the bright dabs of paint of which the images now consist.

Rembrandt's final version of CHRIST AND THE WOMAN OF SAMARIA [349] was done a bit earlier, his last RISEN CHRIST AT EMMAUS [352] a little later than THE CIRCUMCISION. Particularly appealing is the EMMAUS with its triad of luminous figures and its interior organized solely by shadows and lines of light. Somehow we have the feeling of being able to see through the paint to the preliminary drawing. Just how such a drawing might have looked we may infer from a small page in Jacobus Heyblock's friendship album (Illustration a, p. 423), showing Simeon with the Christ child. Its special importance lies in the fact that the final painted version of this theme [358] was unfinished at the time of Rembrandt's death and has come down to us in a wretched state of preservation. Both the drawing and the painting show the main figures in half-length, isolated from the temple interior, conveying by their bearing alone the full burden of the story. Even the small drawing breathes a spirit of solemnity. Once again Rembrandt's delicacy of line brings to mind the sophisticated art of the Far East. It is a sensitive, almost disembodied style that Rembrandt seems to find waiting for him in the moments of his last years when he turned away from material things. Yet during this same period Rembrandt could also make sweeping drawings with a broad nib, such as ACTAEON TURNED INTO A STAG BY DIANA (Illustration, p. 136). This altogether different draftsmanship may have been motivated by the nature of the challenge, the recording of an Italian model; but then too, we may see these extravagant lines as the equivalent, in terms of draftsmanship, to the "rough" brushwork in certain details of Rembrandt's late paintings.[14]

Rembrandt also went back once more to the story of Esther, to produce a small work [351] filled, like THE RISEN CHRIST AT EMMAUS, with a sense of dramatic tension, even in the absence of overt action. The figures are grouped about a table, as in an Indian miniature, two profiles face to face. Ahasuerus points his scepter to the accusing hand of Esther whose delicate figure in its wide brocade mantle comes so close to his that their silhouettes blend menacingly into a single mass of glowing color.

The human condition is depicted with even greater intensity in the major biblical paintings. The same powerful construction that underlies JACOB BLESSING THE SONS OF JOSEPH [277] of 1656 forms the foundation of THE APOSTLE PETER DENYING CHRIST [353], which rises to even greater heights. The figures loom larger, the frame constrains the auxiliary details more severely. The apostle, as vast and as white as a monument, is replying to the maid whose questioning gaze is echoed by the two soldiers. From the background Christ glances over his shoulder at the scene, as though from another world. The covered candle no longer silhouettes the figures like puppets in a shadow play—the light catches the surfaces of the pale fabrics. Even the reflections on the metal are applied with a wide brush; color fills the picture area continuously as a living unit. In a sense this DENIAL is not presented as a biblical narrative at all—as was, for example, Rembrandt's youthful version of the same theme from the Leyden period [7]. It depicts instead the weakness of this huge man exposed to inquisitive looks. Pictorial abstraction and concentration serve to intensify and humanize a moral dilemma.

In a number of paintings of the late fifties and early sixties—images of apostles, evangelists, and Christ himself [295–298, 359–366, 368, 369]—Rembrandt probes the human character for the qualities that would make a man a bearer of divine tidings. This is no rounded sequence of the kind Rubens painted in Antwerp 50 years earlier. There are two subgroups, one of paintings from 1657 and another from 1661; and one apostle, Bartholomew, as well as Christ, is represented more than once. One would like to think that they all hung in Rembrandt's studio together for some time, including perhaps the SELF-PORTRAIT AS THE APOSTLE PAUL [403] and THE VIRGIN MARY [367]. These paintings vary widely in mood and expressiveness. THE EVANGELIST MATTHEW INSPIRED BY THE ANGEL [359] (with Titus serving as the model for the angel) is a composition of great solemnity with rich pictorial nuances. THE APOSTLE BARTHOLOMEW [366], on the other hand, is so rough and rude a study that the question has been raised whether it belongs with this group. But all these paintings break away from the traditional—Flemish—scheme for the depiction of single biblical figures. They are not simply "apostles with attributes," as is often the case in Rubens and van Dyck. They are men lost in thought, praying or writing, listening raptly. Some draw erect before us, others remain shut off in contemplation. Their attire is subdued in tone; only Jesus shines in

ISAAC AND REBECCA [356] Detail

Rembrandt, after Antonio Tempesta DIANA AND ACTAEON. Drawing
Dresden, Kupferstichkabinett

red-and-white splendor. Here Rembrandt's sheer mastery in laying on the colors produces pictorial unity and painterly charm. There is no further need now for that basic structure of verticals and horizontals he deemed so important in the 1650's.[15]

One of Rembrandt's projects of these years failed completely—his share in the adornment of the new Amsterdam Town Hall. Modern art historians have reacted badly to the refusal of the city fathers to accept Rembrandt's representation of THE CONSPIRACY OF JULIUS CIVILIS [354; Colorplates, pp. 126, 127]. Yet van de Waal, in a comprehensive study, has shown that this rejection was all but inevitable. Rembrandt and the magistrates simply did not see eye to eye on matters of historical fact and artistic principle. Rembrandt seems to have been altogether indifferent to the new Amsterdam that was rising all about him. He drew the ruins of the old Town Hall after it had been consumed by fire (Illustration, p. 106), but never depicted the new building that replaced it, a creation the proud Amsterdamers considered the eighth wonder of the world (Illustration, p. 138). Rembrandt preferred the old city gates to the new Westerkerk, and when he drew the gates he even ignored the additions and refinements added in the 17th century.[16]

We have already mentioned the circumstances surrounding this great municipal commission of the late fifties. It is not clear whether the city fathers solicited Rembrandt's participation in the decoration of the new Town Hall or whether Rembrandt tried on his own to secure a share in this great undertaking. Originally Govaert Flinck had been given a commission to execute provisional decoration, for a visit to Amsterdam by the Prince of Anhalt was expected and the work of interior decoration had not even begun. Within a matter of days Flinck painted huge lengths of linen in water color and these were fitted into the arches of the galleries. Flinck might well have got the final contract, but he died unexpectedly on February 2, 1660.

Other painters must have been employed subsequently, but Rembrandt's name does not appear in the city accounts. Yet Melchior Fokkens' *Beschrijvinge der Wijdtvermaerde Koop-Stadt Amstelredam* (1662) describes a painting of THE OATH OF THE BATAVIANS as one of the four vast canvases then installed in the north and south lunettes of the great hall. This could only be

Rembrandt's painting, soon to be removed from its place of honor. The theme of the cycle was the early national aspirations of the Netherlanders, in their attempted revolt against their Roman conquerors, under Julius Civilis (wrongly called Claudius Civilis in the 17th century). Rembrandt's episode was the banquet of Julius Civilis, the high point of the abortive revolt. The one-eyed leader challenges the Batavian nobles to swear on the sword to fight the Romans.

For more than 200 years Fokkens' important testimony was completely forgotten. Not until 1891 did the eminent archivist N. de Roever rediscover and publish it; and the following year eager investigators rigged ladders to inspect—to no result—the place Fokkens had designated, now occupied by a painting by Jurriaen Ovens first described in later city guides.[17] We can reconstruct what must have happened. Rembrandt had been under the necessity of taking back his painting, in order to make changes and improvements. This must have happened in that same year of 1662, for as early as August 28, in an elaborate contract, Rembrandt undertook to remit to Lodewijk van Ludick a quarter of all income he might receive for the Town Hall painting, whether from further monies for the work if it were finally accepted or from any other disposition after overpainting.[18] The picture never returned to its place. Rembrandt may have grown discouraged and lost interest in the whole project. Ultimately the giant canvas was cut down and the central area sold.

The painting was originally 16 feet square, the largest work Rembrandt ever did, larger than THE NIGHT WATCH. Even in its present fragmentary form, preserved in Stockholm, it remains among Rembrandt's largest. From a sketch in Munich, made on the back of a death notice dated October 25, 1661, we can envisage the grand design (Illustration a, p. 419)—the conspirators are grouped about a long table, their hands and swords raised as they swear their oath. The table stands on a rostrum to which steps lead up across the full breadth of the picture, and on either side are stone balustrades, shown only indistinctly in the sketch. The rear wall is crowned by an immense vault. The wash shading indicates that the assembled company is meant to emerge into the full light from a dark or shadowy background, and this is confirmed in the surviving fragment. Rembrandt evidently took into account that the viewer would look up at the painting from a dis-

Gerrit Berckheyde THE NEW TOWN HALL OF AMSTERDAM. 1673
Amsterdam, Museum de Waag

tance. It is on such an expansive and grandiose scale that it engages and commands the eye even from a distance.

Rembrandt must have based his version of the story on a fresh reading of the passage in Tacitus that describes the one-eyed Julius Civilis and the oath sworn on their swords by the chieftains, inflamed by wine. In earlier cycles, this scene was only an episode in a quarrel that ended in an alliance with the Romans. True, the revolt had historic importance as a parallel to the revolt of the Netherlands against Spain in the 16th century; but the subsequent bond with Rome was also a matter of national pride as showing the Dutch to be worthy of Roman civilization.

Right here, most likely, lay the dividing line between Rembrandt and the city fathers of Amsterdam. No doubt they had looked for a dignified historical pageant, decorous and orderly and in keeping with the classic proportions of the new Town Hall. Rembrandt on his part immersed himself in the realities of history as he saw them, and as he did when he dealt with stories from the Bible, awakening the past to new life.

The surviving fragment, worked over by Rembrandt, represents approximately the central portion of the original canvas. To make it salable, large sections were trimmed away, especially at the top. The particular enchantment to our eyes lies in the color broadly applied with a loose brush, a technique usually seen only in Rembrandt's studies. The lighting is treated in much the same way as in THE APOSTLE PETER DENYING CHRIST. Obscured by the figures in front, the light source casts its bright glow on the white and yellow and gold of the fabrics. The swords gleam as though they came fresh from the forge. Not only in concept but also in its freedom of execution, this work forms a complete antithesis to the decorative style of Amsterdam classicism, exemplified in the history paintings of Ferdinand Bol or Gerard de Lairesse (Illustration, p. 142).

A happier outcome awaited another commission, though here too the patron found fault with its unfinished state and negligent execution. We have seen that in 1652 Antonio Ruffo commissioned Rembrandt to do a picture of Aristotle. By 1661 he wanted a companion piece, a picture of Alexander the Great. Since Aristotle was Alexander's tutor, this supplement to Rembrandt's ARISTOTLE CONTEMPLATING A BUST OF HOMER made good sense. Still later there was to be a third commission, a picture of Homer himself. Rembrandt delivered an ALEXANDER THE GREAT to Ruffo in 1661, but on its arrival Ruffo found fault with

the picture. Originally only a head, the canvas had been pieced out to make a half-length figure. Rembrandt at once agreed to paint a second version; and indeed two pictures with the appropriate perquisites of antiquity have come down to us and may very well have formed part of this commission. The version in Glasgow [294], called MARS or more discreetly MAN IN ARMOR, is actually pieced out on all sides, though this is believed to have been done only in the 18th century. The very similar second version [293] in the Gulbenkian Foundation is in a single piece. There has been much dispute over the relation of these two pictures to each other and to the Ruffo commission. Some have insisted that the model is male, others female. The date of 1655, appearing on the Glasgow version, seemed definitely to rule out its identity with the original Ruffo commission. Two observations have lately contributed to solving the problem. The irksome date of 1655 cannot (or can no longer) be made out on the Glasgow picture. An archaeologist, moreover, has pointed out that there was traditional confusion between Alexander and Athena, derived from a misreading of ancient coins. Likenesses of Alexander were commonly based on an Athena type. Both the Rembrandt pictures, in fact, represent men. Neither the long hair, the pearl earring, the owl, nor the shield of Medusa are exclusively feminine in character or exclusive attributes of Athena. The jousting spear, on the other hand, never occurs in images of Athena.

Apparently, what Rembrandt did, upon receiving the Ruffo commission, was to rework a 1655 portrait of Titus into an ALEXANDER THE GREAT. When Ruffo balked at this, objecting to the piecing out of the canvas, Rembrandt did the second version with its magnificent helmet, "a marvelous child of Rembrandt's imagination, completely recreated in paint," in the words of Kenneth Clark.[19] A close stylistic comparison of the two works supports this hypothesis: we discover that the Gulbenkian version is clearly the later one. The soft brushwork in the first, stiffened by an architectural framework, has been supplanted by thickly dabbed-on colors over the whole surface, superseding the need for any spatial organization and emphasizing the figure on its own, without any regard to how it fitted into the environment.

The last of the Ruffo commissions, HOMER DICTATING TO A SCRIBE [371; Colorplate, p. 141], is dated 1663. This picture too was returned to the artist with the request that it be finished, and the date probably marks the time of Rembrandt's reworking. Here the uncompromisingly tough brushwork is even more absolute—freer and at the same time less flexible than in the other two pictures. The golden yellow of the figure draws it forth from the indeterminate background. The present fragmentary state of the painting may be thought to enhance the image of the solitary blind poet. But before it suffered damage by fire, the picture showed a scribe or two on the right—one may be seen in a drawing in Stockholm, perhaps a preliminary sketch (Illustration a, p. 430); and two disciples appear in a painting by Aert de Gelder, probably based in essence on Rembrandt's rendering (Illustration, p. 140).

Unlike the gentlemen of Amsterdam, Ruffo did not pretend to discover inadequacies in Rembrandt's art. His criticisms dealt with faults in the canvas, incorrect dimensions, the unfinished character of the execution. On one occasion Rembrandt wrote rather rudely that there must be few art connoisseurs in Sicily, if such flaws were picked. But he did heed Ruffo's criticism, perhaps because he did not wish to give his client cause for reducing the price to be paid. Compared with what Ruffo paid the painters of Naples and Bologna, Rembrandt's pictures did not come cheap. Yet the year before Rembrandt's death, Ruffo placed a final order for a complete set of the artist's etchings. Rembrandt assembled the series himself, dispatching 189 sheets.

To accuse Ruffo of artistic Philistinism was scarcely fair. The Sicilian collector left Rembrandt entirely free to compose the themes as he pleased. He merely asked for a picture of a philosopher, and Rembrandt sent him ARISTOTLE CONTEMPLATING A BUST OF HOMER. Ruffo may have envisaged something like a gallery of scholars, to which poets and other wise men might later be added—the kind of gallery that was very much in the Italian tradition. Commissions along these lines went to Guercino, Preti, Giacinto Brandi, and Salvator Rosa.

When Guercino saw a sketch after Rembrandt's ARISTOTLE, he took it for a member of such a series of representatives of the various sciences. He thought it was a "physiognomist"—a student of facial features as the marks of character—and offered to execute a "cosmographer in my early expansive style that will fit in well with Rembrandt's picture" in order to satisfy Ruffo's desire for a continuation of his series. The painting was actually delivered, but meanwhile Ruffo had commissioned Rembrandt himself to do counterparts to the ARISTOTLE, leaving the choice of subject to the judgment of the artist. However that may have been, Guercino, himself an artist in his sixties, felt honored to be commissioned to do a pendant to Rembrandt's picture. He admired the perfection, artistic sense, and excellent technique of Rembrandt's etchings, never doubting that his paintings must therefore also be of great perfection. "In short," he said, "I admire him in all sincerity as a great artist." [20]

On the other hand, the painter and art dealer Abraham Brueghel, who filled many orders for Ruffo from Rome, had no high opinion of Rembrandt's art, "which is not held in high esteem here in Rome." He complained of

the draped figure in half-length, with a tiny light falling solely on the tip of the nose, nor does one know whence comes the light, since all else is shrouded in darkness. Now when it comes to great painters, they let you see a beautiful nude. [21]

Brueghel made no bones about his contempt for Rembrandt's ignorance, the dark and lumpy costumes in his paintings, his poor draftsmanship. Brueghel was not merely protecting his interest as an art dealer, he was applying to Rembrandt the esthetic tenets of Roman classicism, with its admiration for even light and clarity of outline. But Ruffo himself was more interested in contemporary painting in Naples, a school based—like the art of Rembrandt and the young Guercino—on non-classicistic Caravaggesque principles. Thus, Brueghel's criticism could not have mattered very much to Ruffo, who admired Rembrandt for the very reasons for which Brueghel despised him.

The late works of Rembrandt show less and less of what we may call iconographic fidelity—presenting biblical and mythological themes in such a way that contemporaries could readily identify them. Of course Rembrandt did not completely recast all the traditional themes, nor was he forever searching for new themes. Quite the contrary, a methodical study of his Bible pictures has shown that he keeps reverting to the same themes. What did change, particularly as Rembrandt grew older, was the precision of narrative detail, which now grew too vague to pinpoint the subject beyond doubt. Athena, Mars, or Alexander?—it is no accident that we can identify the youthful figure from antiquity only from the context of the Ruffo commission. The true meaning of another such picture—the so-called COUNT FLORIS OF HOLLAND [370]—still remains obscure, in the absence of any helpful documentation like the Ruffo papers. The paintings embodying the wisdom of Rembrandt's old age—the evangelists, Homer, Aristotle—all resemble portrait studies of aged Jews or Orien-

Aert de Gelder HOMER DICTATING TO SCRIBES
Boston, Museum of Fine Arts

tals. Isaac and Rebecca become the epitome of a Jewish bridal couple. Titus brings Alexander back to life, and Rembrandt's own features underlie his rendering of THE APOSTLE PAUL [403; Colorplate, p. 149].[22]

Of course Rembrandt had always been in the habit of dressing up his models; and even in Leyden he sought to translate them from their everyday environment to the boundless realm of his imagination; but in his old age this urge to encompass the world in visionary terms deepened. It is quite true, as we have seen in the case of the JULIUS CIVILIS, that Rembrandt immersed himself in history and sought to present its essential truth; but at the same time he tended more and more to place the burden of expressing that historical truth on individual figures in his paintings, at the expense of documentary detail. Who is the condemned man in the Leningrad picture [357]? Interpretation has varied widely. The fact is that all of Rembrandt's characters have a great deal in common, whether they belong to the world of the Bible or to the world of mythology. The way in which Rembrandt's images of men gain allegorical value marks even his commissioned portraits, as we have seen in the case of his JACOB TRIP.

One of Rembrandt's last Bible pictures, THE RETURN OF THE PRODIGAL SON [355; Colorplate, p. 143], is an exercise in pure compassion. In spare concentration it goes beyond the biblical parable itself. Tümpel has discovered that the silent witnesses to the father's loving forgiveness are borrowed from a woodcut by Maerten van Heemskerck; but their stature is enlarged here—their devout participation in the scene has become symbolic. Like ourselves, they are deeply moved at the sight of the ragged figure, aching for the love bestowed. The impression of union and reunion emanates not merely from the looming group of father and son, blending into one. Rembrandt's dabbing brushwork juxtaposes—and dissolves into one another—rich clothes and ragged; old skin and young. In isolating this occurrence so totally, Rembrandt succeeds in setting its meaning against the meaning of all the rest of the world. Pictorially, this is achieved by the most conscientious respect for the individuality of each figure and its position in the space of the painting. No artificial diagonals imply false relationships between the figures, nor are they bound to their environment, which is barely suggested.

How did Rembrandt see himself in the last decade of his life? The SELF-PORTRAIT of 1660 [389], showing Rembrandt at work, still displays the self-possession of the preceding years, though the artist has plainly aged and become frailer. The firm foundation at the picture's lower border has gone by the board. The bodily contours are but cautiously revealed toward the head. For the first time the brow is covered by a light-colored cap, its pure white emitting an unreal radiance. White pigment as such generally introduces a mood of the abstract. Here, too, it refuses to work with the warm color harmony and thus counteracts the portrait's pictorial unity and realism. In Rembrandt's late Bible pictures too a whitish tinge points to another level of reality. In the Paris SELF-PORTRAIT the palette in the painter's left hand and the maulstick in his right are directive elements in structuring the picture as a whole. They perform this function with even greater clarity in the SELF-PORTRAIT at Kenwood House [380; Colorplate, p. 145], where an even stronger abstract element is brought in as a contrast to the living figure— two great arcs mark off the background wall. This picture is particularly firm in structure, but unlike the SELF-PORTRAIT of 1658 [343], the firmness does not lend a heroic air to Rembrandt himself, who is rather withdrawn, no longer projecting himself into our presence. The delicately dabbed brushwork lies like a cloud of skin, hair, and clothing over the hard skeleton that forms the painting's real structure.

The unreal element of the circles in the background has given rise to many interpretations. Have these "signs" allegorical or symbolic meaning, or are they, as we incline to believe, no more than compositional elements? We should, of course, beware of lapsing into a kind of constructivist interpretation more appropriate to the Cubist strain in the art of Cézanne and Picasso than to the 17th century. It has indeed been said of this picture that "Cézanne springs to the mind," and quite understandably too. Emmens, on the other hand, reads this self-portrait as representing the artist in the role of mediator between the world of theory, symbolized by the circle at the left, and the world of practice, symbolized by the circle and ruler at the right.

Such explanations cannot be dismissed as mere sophistry, for emblems and symbols, complex or naïve, had a very definite place in 17th-century Dutch culture and art. The claims of any

Ferdinand Bol REST ON THE FLIGHT INTO EGYPT. 1644
Dresden, Gemaeldegalerie

interpretation, however, must be measured against the visual evidence provided by the work of art itself. In the present case, the circles simply seem to be too barren of symbolism to support the interpretation. The lines drawn with a ruler in the right circle, moreover—if that is indeed what they are—are far too indistinct to serve as an effective contrast to the other, pure circle.

The explanation offered by van de Waal and Bauch seems to fit the circumstances no better. The two circles, they say, are all that is left of a map of the world. Such double-circular maps were indeed popular wall decorations in Holland and they appear not infrequently in pictures of Dutch interiors. Rembrandt himself showed one, on an oblong sheet, in one of his early paintings [130]. But in the Kenwood SELF-PORTRAIT, the circles are void of all informational or decorative content, presenting themselves as pure geometric forms. This kind of abstractionism is also expressed in the palette, brushes, and maulstick, though these remain legible as objects. Thus, there remains little visual corroboration for the map theory.

Rembrandt has left us two self-portraits from the year of his death, one in London [415; Colorplate, p. 167] and the other in The Hague [420]. It has been said that poets and painters always present themselves as they wish to be seen by others. The last informal SELF-PORTRAIT, in The Hague, is probably an exception in this respect. More than any other, it is a mirror image, the artist groping for his own features in the looking-glass. It is more delicate in pictorial values, more tentative, richer in nuances, more carefully worked than the Brunswick FAMILY GROUP [416] with its opulent colors. The thinly painted receptacle of hair and skin is barely able to contain a fragile life at the brink of dissolution. The London picture, by contrast, might well take its place in a gallery of representative self-portraits. It originally included the attributes of the painter's trade, brush and maulstick, but Rembrandt painted these out in the final state. The posture with the folded hands is reminiscent of the fine SELF-PORTRAIT done ten years earlier [376]. In both pictures the sitter is proudly erect, and if in the later work the expression seems wearier, the brushwork more reticent, X-ray analysis nevertheless confirms that the underpainting displays the same power and assurance that marked the heroic years of the fifties.

The last portrait of Hendrickje [382] was done in 1660. Titus

was probably painted for the last time a few years later [406; Colorplate, p. 155]. This rendering shows little change from the childhood portraits in painterly aspect and delicacy of hair and features, but the joyful reveling in color is gone. The figure emerges from the dark foreground, without the crutch of a balustrade or desk. The face looms larger in the picture than ever before, and it is paler too, less linked to the ambience. To the viewer it thus seems more remote from life, despite its nearness.

Alienation in the sense of dematerialization is surely a mark of Rembrandt's late style. More and more the tangible and the anecdotal are repressed. This process is less conspicuous in portraiture than in the history paintings, where the main figures are often given such prominence that the story itself is not easy to grasp. While in formal portraits and self-portraits there are natural limits to the process of alienation, it marks nearly all of Rembrandt's works: during the earlier periods, through disguise and fancy dress, in the later through austerity of structure, symbolism, and autonomy of palette.

It has long been thought that a "mask" of this kind is superimposed on the laughing SELF-PORTRAIT in Cologne [419]. Stechow has presented a closely argued iconographic and historical thesis to the effect that Rembrandt is here meant to represent Democritus, the philosopher who laughs at the world, while the shadowy and indistinct bust represents Heraclitus, moved to tears by the same spectacle. This would accord perfectly with our picture of Rembrandt in those years. X-ray study has shown, however, that the painter's hand originally rested on the breast of the blurred sculpture, which destroys the impression of opposition we expect in any image of the two philosophers.

There must therefore be another relation between the living Rembrandt and the mysterious figure, which, by the way, was also simplified (and thus rendered more obscure) in the final state—a relation perhaps not unlike that between Aristotle and the bust of Homer in the great painting of 1653 [286]. To Białostocki must go the credit for having identified the shadowy sculpture as the god Terminus. Terminus represents the ultimate end of all. Terminus gives way to none. To him Rembrandt opposes

his ripe painterly perfection of color and light; to the death symbolism of Terminus [he opposes] his brushwork scintillating with life and his

serene philosophical smile. Rembrandt's late self-portrait with its masterly form proclaims—in the artist's own field—the old impresa *of Terminus:* Concedo nulli.

As Bialostocki has shown, what Rembrandt did here was to revert to a pictorial tradition of the Renaissance, applying it for the first time to a self-portrait. This immersion into the ideas of antiquity and of the Renaissance becomes comprehensible when we bear in mind the Ruffo commissions and Rembrandt's familiarity with works of art from those periods. Yet here as before,

Rembrandt's painterly expression remains untouched by the formal idioms and ideologies of the past. The last message we hoped to find is the fateful motto discovered by Bialostocki in the Cologne SELF-PORTRAIT: I yield to none. Rembrandt's smile speaks of steadfastness in the face of inexorable destiny—an attitude that underlines his whole approach toward the image of his fellow man, and himself, in art. As his life ebbed, he sought once for all to supplant its cheap, transitory forms with personal artistic ideas of enduring value.

Rembrandt and his Century

Rembrandt died on October 4, 1669. For some ten years, ever since the big house on St. Anthonisbreestraat had passed into the hands of its new owner, he had lived in the western part of town, on the Rozengracht. Here in this small home the "firm" of Rembrandt, Hendrickje, and Titus had its seat; its object was to sell Rembrandt's output, its true purpose to protect Rembrandt from importunate creditors. It is from the circumstantial description of a notary who drew up Hendrickje's will on August 7, 1661, that we know Rembrandt lived in this street, opposite the new Doolhof, a small park.

Another legal document tells us that Hendrickje's neighbors looked on her as the "housewife of Mijnheer Rembrandt van Rijn, art painter." She left her small property to her daughter Cornelia; in the event Cornelia died without issue, everything was to go to Titus, Rembrandt's son by his first wife, Saskia. Titus had already made a similar will—if he were to have no heirs, his half sister was to inherit his property. Destiny was to leave these familial dispositions unfulfilled. Hendrickje died the following year—she was buried on July 24, 1662—Titus, the year of his marriage, in September, 1668.

The girl Titus married was Magdalena, daughter of his father's friend Jan van Loo. A posthumous child sprang from this union, Rembrandt's granddaughter Titia, born half a year before the painter's own death. The guardians of the two girls, both still under age, fought over Rembrandt's estate for some time. Unfortunately, the surviving inventory lists only the furnishings and not the art works and antiques owned by Rembrandt or, in the legal sense, by the "firm" of Rembrandt-Hendrickje-Titus. Yet there is reason to believe that Rembrandt did not die penniless. His funeral was a respectable affair, nor had Titus' share of his father's property been altogether trivial at the time of his marriage. The funeral register of the Westerkerk carries a straightforward entry under the date of October 8, 1669: "Rembrandt van Rijn, of Rozengracht, opposite the Doolhof, 16 pallbearers. Two surviving children. Costs 20 guilders." Titus had been buried almost exactly a year before, at half the cost.[1]

Neither in Amsterdam nor elsewhere at home or abroad was Rembrandt's death particularly noted—but that was probably true of all Dutch painters, even those who enjoyed the greatest vogue. In the cultural life of the time they occupied a position far below city officials, for example. Having lost the patronage of both the church and the nobility, Dutch artists no longer shared the glamour that issued from such dignitaries. Nor did they think of each other in the flattering terms the sophisticated Rubens could bestow on his colleagues, as when he wrote this eloquent obituary for Adam Elsheimer: "Surely, after such a loss, our entire profession ought to clothe itself in mourning. It will not easily succeed in replacing him."[2] Words at this articulate level of praise are found only in contemporary correspondence among the small elite of cultural leaders, to which Rubens belonged.

One might have expected a word of condolence on Rembrandt's death from Constantijn Huygens, or some form of eulogy— he had been in Amsterdam as recently as August 1669; but Huygens had lost touch with Rembrandt. In his diary for 1669 he noted the death of his friend Pieter Post, an architect at The Hague, where both Post and Huygens lived, and also of many other people at home and abroad; but the aged diplomat no longer knew his way about in the world of Rembrandt, the lone wolf of Amsterdam.[3]

Six years after Rembrandt's death, Joachim von Sandrart's *Teutsche Academie* appeared (1675), and three years thereafter Samuel van Hoogstraten's *Inleyding tot de Hooge Schoole der Schilderkonst* (1678). Both works make it plain that despite occasional criticism Rembrandt was accounted *the* great Dutch painter. Sandrart calls him the "excellent Rembrandt van Rijn"; van Hoogstraten for some incomprehensible reason, the *verzierlijke* Rembrandt. Filippo Baldinucci, also already known to us, included a comprehensive biography in his history of the graphic arts (1686), pronouncing judgment on Rembrandt's technique and chiaroscuro. Particular praise is lavished on the etchings, which had spread Rembrandt's fame at an early stage. The two foreigners dwell in the main on Rembrandt's art of the 1630's and 1640's. Those were the years when Sandrart was in Amsterdam; while Baldinucci's knowledge rested in part on the reports of Bernard Keil, who had been Rembrandt's pupil before he came to Rome in the 1650's. Their image of Rembrandt is the popular one, plainly based on the socially successful and flamboyant Rembrandt of the thirties.[4]

In 1718 appeared Arnold van Houbraken's *Groote Schouburgh* with its discursive Rembrandt biography, including many anec-

Aert de Gelder THE BOERHAVE FAMILY
Amsterdam, Rijksmuseum

dotes and some of the author's own observations and theories on art, served up in story form. J. A. Emmens and other critics have examined the picture of Rembrandt projected by Houbraken and his contemporaries, finding it rather one-sided and marked by classicist bias; I must agree that Houbraken's oppressive influence on all the Rembrandt literature of the 18th and 19th centuries is deplorable. But at the moment we need cite only one aspect of his account—one that was surely based on fact: the large number of students from Holland and abroad Houbraken tells us flocked to the studio of the "far-famed" painter.[5]

In old Amsterdam guides Rembrandt's two anatomy pictures— TULP [100] and DEYMAN [326]—are singled out as "surpassing all others, being by the famous Rembrandt."[6] In 1711 the German antiquary Zacharias Uffenbach inspected the Amsterdam *Schneykamer oder Theatro Anatomico*, preferring the TULP to the other "where the dead man lies in foreshortening so that one sees the undersides of his soles." Uffenbach, by the way, neglected to note Rembrandt's name—or was he perchance not even told it? A few days later he visited the collection of Sibert van der Schelling in The Hague and there saw "an incomparable likeness of Rembrandt, very large and painted by himself, which surely is worthy of admiration and cannot be regarded enough."[7]

Uffenbach was assuredly no connoisseur with a personal viewpoint. He did little more than reflect current opinion among the collectors, bibliophiles, and antiquarians whom he visited. Within these circles the art of Rembrandt continued to command awe and admiration, and this most likely extended to works of his late period. Rembrandts fetched respectable prices at the good auctions. We even find art inventories in which only works by Rembrandt rate the distinction of being mentioned by title.[8]

But perhaps the most tangible sign of veneration for Rembrandt's art is found in the paintings of Aert de Gelder. Not that this disciple ever equaled the full grandeur and significance that inheres in the pictures of his master—compared directly with Rembrandt, he seems superficial. Yet his intoxication with color, the unorthodox structure of his pictures, his utter contempt for smoothing out his provocative brushwork give his paintings a deserved place beside those of Rembrandt as works beyond the pale of late 17th-century Dutch art with its bright, noble, and ingratiating classicism.

Whether de Gelder was painting the renowned BOERHAVE FAMILY (see Illustration) or the PASSION OF CHRIST (Illustrations a, b, p. 150), the spontaneity of his visual approach sweeps the viewer off his feet. His Passion series is not only romantic in aspect but deeply moving in the rough, indeed almost savage way the story is told. The painterly play of torches in the background, winding paths, and fanciful processions is effectively integrated with the narrative itself, whose message is thus brought closer to us. And the family portrait, despite its informality, carries a sense of enchantment in no way detracting from the famous physician's dignity. But for Rembrandt's example of independence from the fixed tenets of "decent" art, Aert de Gelder would never have achieved so dynamic a brush. It is to the credit of both painter and patrons that this nonconformist Baroque style practiced by Rembrandt and de Gelder could flourish in an Amsterdam in which an altogether different main trend dominated.

It was about 1660/1 that Aert de Gelder worked in Rembrandt's studio. Against the background of the meticulous style of Leyden and the cultivated classicism of Amsterdam, he was the only one in the 1660's—and indeed into the next century—who let his colors run riot and his imagination explode in this fashion. By good fortune, society in his home town of Dordrecht must have been receptive to his art, and he probably found purchasers there even for his most unorthodox works—the large Old Testament pictures.

Dordrecht, as a matter of fact, knew other eccentric painters. It was there that Aelbert Cuyp worked until 1691. His huge and expansively painted pictures with their warm and bright luminosity also were, in a sense, anachronisms, compared with the rarified cabinet works of Adriaen van de Velde and Jan van der Heyden. Nicolaes Maes (1634–93) also came from Dordrecht before settling in Amsterdam as Rembrandt's pupil. The urbanity of his late portraits is often overstressed, while it is overlooked that the broad painterly style of these late pictures always retains the profound grasp of character Maes had acquired under Rembrandt's tutelage (Illustration, p. 152).[9]

Then there was Gerbrandt van den Eeckhout (1621–74), whose distinctly Rembrandtesque style confirms a friendship with the master which is also attested by the documents.[10] Remarkably enough, van den Eeckhout's art retained its warmth and sim-

SELF-PORTRAIT AS THE APOSTLE PAUL [403] Detail

a Aert de Gelder THE CARRYING OF THE CROSS
Aschaffenburg, Gemaeldegalerie

b Aert de Gelder CALVARY
Aschaffenburg, Gemaeldegalerie

plicity into the painter's late maturity (Illustration, p. 154). Beyond these direct pupils, moreover, Rembrandt seems to have inspired the relaxed approach of a number of major Dutch painters of the latter half of the 17th century. Not only Aelbert Cuyp, but Philips Koninck and Jacob Ruisdael as well reveled in color at a time when the official Amsterdam style clung to a neat classicist idiom.

Rembrandt exerted an influence on the art of his time, near and far, during every phase of his career. As we have seen, he was never completely isolated, either in an artistic or a social sense. On the other hand, his painting was at all times in a special sense "different" from anything that was done around him. THE STONING OF SAINT STEPHEN [2], THE PRESENTATION IN THE TEMPLE [17], the two anatomy pictures [100, 326], THE BLINDING OF SAMSON [76], THE NIGHT WATCH [239], THE HOLY FAMILY WITH ANGELS [211], "THE POLISH RIDER" [287], THE RETURN OF THE PRODIGAL SON [355], the SELF-PORTRAITS, THE SAMPLING OFFICIALS [404]—all these and many more are in high degree incommensurable with what was done in Holland in the 17th century. We keep coming back to Rembrandt's complete autonomy as the essential element in our picture of him, the core around which all the positive features of his art are grouped.[11]

What we have done so far is to report in the main on Rembrandt's growth, to follow his path to maturity, to trace the changes in his style, coordinating them with the development of Dutch art itself. Now the time has come to consider the elements in his art that remained constant, a relative term, as the historian has reason to know. It might be objected, for example, that the notion of autonomy belongs to our mental image of all great artists, applying with equal force to any judgment of Frans Hals, Vermeer, or Ruisdael, to name only Dutch artists. Yet we are constrained to admit that Vermeer had much more intimate ties with the Delft school and Ruisdael with that of Haarlem, than Rembrandt did with Amsterdam. Admirers of Vermeer may reject any comparison of Vermeer's art with Pieter de Hooch who also came from Delft, but the stylistic approach of these two masters shows greater kinship than can be found between Rembrandt and any other painter.

Our awareness of the singular grandeur of Rembrandt's art often tempts us to exalt his personality beyond the meager evidence that documents his life. We like to read into his religious paintings the profession of the creed of Rembrandt the man, to identify in the esthetic approach of his art an ethical approach in his life.[12] This mixing of esthetic and ethical considerations, of art and life, carries the reciprocal dangers of turning purely visual interpretations into personal insights and of projecting into Rembrandt's art large elements of his personality which to tell the truth, remains a closed book to us. This does violence not only to our art historical conclusions but to the mere historical facts of Rembrandt's career.

The notion that a great artist should have an impeccable moral character often flies in the face of the facts. The rude, not to say illegal tactics Rembrandt used against Geertje Dircx—who had to make way for Hendrickje—do not gibe with the kind of upright character we feel should grace a great artist. The early investigators of documents relating to Rembrandt's life simply blinked these facts. Shortly before he went into bankruptcy, for example, Rembrandt tried to evade his long-suffering creditors by signing over his house to his son Titus. And can Houbraken's malicious anecdote about Rembrandt's avarice be a complete invention?—how his students painted realistic coins on the floor of his studio and the master tried to rake them in. We must, of course, make allowances for the folklore of art, which has always been fond of dwelling on its *trompe l'œil* possibilities. Yet Rembrandt's money-mindedness can scarcely be pure fiction. In the eyes of the Amsterdam city fathers and the stilted Joachim von Sandrart, he was a parvenu, an upstart who shoveled in money by the labor of his own hands and that of his students, who spent an inordinate amount on jewels for his wife and art works for himself. There were other incidents that can be interpreted to the detriment of Rembrandt's character. It is scarcely necessary to say that Rembrandt's artistry was in no way affected by any of this. The question of whether he was thrifty or profligate, respectable or bohemian, may be of interest in connection with contemporary mores; but it has little to do with 17th-century art. Nor can we be any more certain that Rembrandt's attitude toward religion was more closely related to his art.

We actually have no statement by Rembrandt on how he felt about God and Christianity. His numerous paintings, etchings, and drawings of biblical themes are widely taken as conclusive

Nicolaes Maes A FAMILY GROUP
The Hague, Art dealer G. Cramer

evidence of his devoutness, but it is not clear whether he adhered to the dominant Calvinistic creed or to some other doctrine. This question has lately drawn particular attention, and some searching studies have rather upset traditional views. In purely numerical terms, of course, biblical themes bulk very prominently in Rembrandt's *œuvre*, but this does not mean very much in a painter who felt his vocation to be that of history painter. The work of Rembrandt's teacher, Lastman, contains an even larger proportion of subjects from the Bible. It is possible to compile a connected picture story of the Bible from Rembrandt's works—indeed, it has been said that no other artist has left us such complete illustrative material. Theologians, however, have pointed out that there are significant gaps—the miracle of Pentecost is missing, and so are the *Revelation of St. John* and any confrontation between New Testament and Old. Perhaps the most noteworthy omission is the Last Supper. Bruyn and Tümpel have shown that in iconographic terms Rembrandt's Bible themes are rooted entirely in 16th-century tradition—he never chose a theme that was really out of the way. Theologians may dispute the issue of whether he was a Calvinist or a Baptist, but to art historians the details of Rembrandt's Bible themes provide little immediate evidence of his personal faith. They make up a pictorial world rooted primarily in traditional religious representation.[13]

All inquiry into Rembrandt's faith must go back to the only contemporary statement on the matter, a remark made by Filippo Baldinucci (1686):

Rembrandt professed for some time the religion of the Mennonites which, false as it is, is none the less opposed to Calvinism, in that the Mennonites are baptized only after the age of thirty.

There is a kernel of truth to this report. Rembrandt came from a Reformed family and like Saskia van Uylenburgh belonged to the Reformed Church (which later on punished Hendrickje); but from an early stage onward both Rembrandt and Saskia moved in Mennonite and Remonstrant circles. The art dealer Hendrick van Uylenburgh, in whose house Rembrandt had his studio during his first years in Amsterdam, was a member of the Waterlandish congregation of the Mennonites. Rembrandt's pupils Govaert Flinck and Jacob Backer came from the same background, and it is scarcely surprising that at a distance Rembrandt should have been reckoned to belong to the same sect.

Actually, church discipline was much stricter among the Mennonites than in the Reformed Church, virtually precluding Rembrandt's membership.[14]

If Rembrandt's Bible pictures fail to testify to his denominational allegiance, what do they exemplify in his work? It is noteworthy that his representations from the Old Testament seem to carry the same authority as those from the New; and Greek and Roman mythology take their place beside the Bible themes, without sharp distinction. Rembrandt, in a word, painted biblical subjects because he practiced history painting—a perfectly honorable, though distinctly old-fashioned genre. That meant, in the terms of the fashionable contemporary school of painting, that Rembrandt was anything but "modern." Not even as a landscape painter did he belong among the pioneers of the new realism, like Esaias van de Velde and Jan van Goyen. "Creative vision"—to use the term van Hoogstraten applied to THE NIGHT WATCH—was more important to Rembrandt than the increasingly official vision of the new Holland and the new Amsterdam. He simply turned his back on the bourgeois world, creating another world of fanciful dress and unreal architecture—above all, with a lighting entirely its own. Jakob Burckhardt, for one, condemned this world of gloom, and even Jan Huizinga was not persuaded that it represented reality.[15]

Where else could a bent toward dramatic narrative have found wider scope than in the traditions of the Bible and mythology, worlds long gone? Rembrandt immersed himself in these stories, sought out the 16th-century illustrations of them. In his early works and those from the 1630's he was intent on stirring the viewer by dramatic action; in the 1640's quiet devotion was the dominant effect.

With advancing age, Rembrandt's representations from the Christian sphere and those from pagan mythology tend to grow towards each other in visual and narrative terms. At the outset such pictures as THE ABDUCTION OF PROSERPINA [57] and THE RAISING OF THE CROSS [64] shared only a certain Baroque approach, a gloomy romantic background from which light erupted dazzlingly. DANAE [270] and BATHSHEBA [271] have more in common—they share the same ponderous gravity and expressiveness. But when it comes to works from the last years, it is hard to decide whether the Christian theme of THE CIRCUM-

Gerbrandt van den Eeckhout THE APOSTLE PETER HEALING THE LAME. 1667
San Francisco, M. H. de Young Memorial Museum

CISION OF CHRIST [350] carries the greater sense of solemnity, or the mythological PHILEMON AND BAUCIS [278]. Rembrandt's Christian faith has been rightly called humanistic, for his essential humanity is always evident, whether he is depicting pagan or Christian faith—or Jewish.[16]

Rembrandt's interest in the Jews of Amsterdam sprang from his ingrained longing to depict a world different from that of the merchants and dignitaries of the city. The Jews lived by traditions that were essentially alien. Rembrandt saw in them models not only for his Bible stories, but also for his ancient philosophers dressed in precious robes. He can scarcely be expected to have immersed himself in the learned sophistries of Jewish theology, any more than he is likely to have sided with one or another of the opposing Protestant interpretations of the Bible.[17]

In short, traces of adherence to a particular religious sect are to be found neither in Rembrandt's own scanty words, nor in his approach to Bible themes, nor in what we know of his relations with clients and pupils. Dutchmen were quick to embitter each other with polemic pamphlets in the religious controversies of the 17th century; looking at Rembrandt's portrait gallery of prominent clerics, we can only conclude that he was not himself a partisan: we find the Calvinists Swalmius and Sylvius side by side with the Remonstrant Uytenbogaert, the dogmatic Mennonite Anslo, and suspect sympathizers of the Socinians.

Rembrandt portrayed the worldly CATRINA HOOGHSAET [336], who blithely ignored church discipline, and the pious Portuguese Jews EPHRAIM BUENO [263] and MANASSEH BEN ISRAEL (Illustration b, p. 156). Differences in creed, by the way, did not keep Amsterdamers from joining in order to serve their city. Seated fraternally around the same table in Rembrandt's SAMPLING OFFICIALS are "five gentlemen of very different religious persuasion, a telling symbol of Amsterdam's tolerance and commercial power in the heyday of the republic." There were two Catholics, a Remonstrant, a Mennonite and, as chairman, a strict member of the Reformed Church.[18]

Rembrandt seems to have had a thorough knowledge of the Bible; and his curriculum in Latin School and at the university was the same many humanists of his day enjoyed. His culture and learning, nevertheless, did not compare with the antiquarians, writers, and philologians of the time. His house was full of art works, but inscriptions, medallions, and books were lacking. If Rembrandt declined to visit Italy, the decision embodied a sure instinct that he stood to gain little from contact with the remnants of ancient culture. His repudiation of literary culture also weighed upon Rembrandt's relations with poets and scholars. Huygens, as we have seen, lost touch with him after the 1630's. Vondel took no notice of Rembrandt, a failure for which later generations of historians have taken him severely to task, wrongly constructing a split down the middle of Dutch cultural life.[19] When Rembrandt read the Bible, Tacitus, Livy, or the *Jewish Histories* of Flavius Josephus, he did so with the sensibility of the artist, letting them inspire his visual imagination. He did not study them with the scholarly insight of the educated Baroque historian or the feeling of pathos a contemporary poet might have brought to the task.

It is a curious fact that in the 17th century creative artists were seldom considered—even by themselves—as members of the cultured class. Poussin, Rubens, and the great architects were exceptional in attaining high social position. In Holland it was the architects who had the best chance of improving their status because of their direct contact with clients. Jacob van Campen, gentleman architect of the Amsterdam Town Hall, collaborated with the humanist Huygens to design the decorative program of the princely Huis ten Bosch. Van Campen, who had visited Italy, was the recognized leader of Dutch classicism. He ended his days not in an Amsterdam studio, but on his country estate, Randenbroek.

Even for architects a career on the grand scale was more difficult in Holland than it was in Catholic countries, for the municipalities were seldom in a position to place commissions that could compare in scope and splendor with the possibilities offered farther south—grandiose palaces of princes and ecclesiastical buildings intended to represent the full might of the church. Even wealthy Amsterdam never rivaled impoverished Antwerp in staging such a welcoming procession as that given for the Cardinal Infante Ferdinand. In Flanders, moreover, the corporations and wealthy burghers competed with the princely patrons in decorations for their chapels and town halls. In Amsterdam's one great project, the building and adornment of its new Town Hall, Flemish artists were employed. The Calvinist republic was

PORTRAIT OF A YOUNG MAN (TITUS?) [406]

a Govaert Flinck MANASSEH BEN ISRAEL. 1637
The Hague, Mauritshuis

b Rembrandt MANASSEH BEN ISRAEL. Etching. 1636
Amsterdam, Rijksmuseum

a rather half-hearted patron of arts no longer considered appropriate to religious edification nor even simple festive pleasure. What did flourish were the new specialized branches of painting, intended to adorn the homes of even plain citizens—allegories, still lifes, landscapes, genre scenes. Themes from the Old and New Testament were also popular. Rembrandt painted such scenes for the bourgeois world, as he did his portraits—though he held more and more aloof from it.

Originally, his hold on the public was based on the Baroque sweep of his works, their dazzling glamour, their *naetureelste beweechgelijkheijt*. But despite its romantic character, his art was not in the proper sense Dutch. He was seeking to rival Rubens; he fell in love with imaginary dream landscapes—which looked back on a Flemish rather than a Dutch tradition. Even in his portraits of solid citizens, his vision added the exotic glow of fancy dress, or at least of extraordinary bold lighting effects that invested the sitters with an air of grandeur amid their domestic background. His patrons must have surely seen the difference between his work and the sober, admittedly descriptive productions of run-of-the-mill painters, and they probably appreciated the sense of enchantment only Rembrandt seemed able to convey. His style met a secret need for creative exaltation and proud magnificence, for which the young Dutch school of painting had not yet found appropriate forms.

In a certain sense it might be said that Rembrandt lost his direct grip on the current trend within that school in direct measure to its own growing autonomy, its success in becoming a truly national art. What he did was to create his own world, rooted in the biblical and mythological past, a world that was on occasion quite able to accommodate the likenesses of his contemporaries. ISAAC AND REBECCA [356] is an appealing example of that dual

character. If, despite its contrast with Amsterdam's new classicist style, Rembrandt's art did not pass unassimilated through the busy art mill, this was perhaps for two reasons. Rather than his learning, it was Rembrandt's rich store of European and Oriental art objects, from which his vision could always take fire anew, that made him aware of a broader world of art than his provincial Dutch colleagues could perceive. And Rembrandt had one quality the Dutch understood and admired: international status. Alone among Dutch artists, he spanned in his work the whole visual range of European art. Before his death, his works were already collected in all of Europe, from Stockholm to Sicily. The breadth of his vision accounts for this universal dissemination of his influence; it also kept impelling him to deepen and fathom his own creative experience.

On the other hand, the "Dutch commonwealth of merchants" deserves credit for allowing scope—within the limits of what was possible in the 17th century—to dissidents from orthodox art, to those who stood outside the church, to strangers. Such men did, of course, encounter hostility in Holland, but small groups of people of like mind could always find a home there nonetheless. Rembrandt himself can scarcely be counted among those who suffered persecution; yet it is hard to see where else his supremely independent late style could have enjoyed such freedom and exerted such influence. He always found company, moreover, at whatever level of Dutch society he sought it. As an ambitious young man, his friends were men of note: rich merchants, ministers, scholars, and poets. In his final years, he preferred to mingle with plain people who, while they might not have understood much about his art, could share with him the human values of a Christian way of life.

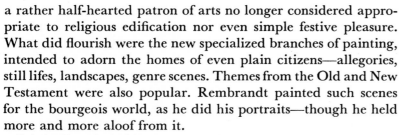

FREDERICK RIHEL ON HORSEBACK [410]
A MAN HOLDING GLOVES [411] and A WOMAN HOLDING AN OSTRICH-FEATHER FAN [412]

Rembrandt and Posterity: The Broken Tradition

History is a dialogue that never ends. New insights come to us as we study the past, and new perspectives. One thing that never comes is certainty.[1] Is this true of the history of art as well? Do art historians too merely lend their own shape to what is of itself shapeless (G. Ritter) or give meaning to the meaningless (T. Lessing)?[2] At first blush we art historians seem to be in a more favorable situation. The objects with which we deal really exist—or at least many of them do. They are not mere memories enshrined in books, documents, and oral tradition. They are tangible things rather than myths. Yet their material existence does not guarantee objective knowledge. Even the history of scholarly description of the objects, whether in chronological, esthetic, or functional terms, has the character of an unending dialogue that keeps adding insight but offers no promise of certainty. No one can jump over his own shadow.

We drew attention at the very outset of our study to the tenacity with which modern art criticism has fastened on its own history. In part this single-mindedness springs from a hope that analysis of the subjective methods by which art historians have proceeded may give birth to a working theory that promises objective results. In part this preoccupation with the history of history is no more than a flight from the direct impact of art. For the truth that resides in works of art is often so hard to decipher that even the connoisseur is driven to distraction. Even so, our critique of recent work in the history of art has surely driven home the lesson that our own knowledge and insight are in large measure dependent on the historical situation in which we live. We have repeatedly cited the study by J. A. Emmens of the changes our image of Rembrandt has undergone, of the limitations from which successive generations have suffered in trying to bring him into focus. This approach has only recently been echoed by Kenneth Clark in his brilliant essay on Rembrandt's relation to the Italian Renaissance, though Clark's art historical analysis reflects some aspects of slightly older but still contemporary trends in art.[3]

Every historian must eventually decide what value his conclusions may have as positive statements of fact. To speak of my own, I recognize distinctly their relativistic—even tentative—claim to truth. It would surely be naïve to place any deeper faith in the authority of present-day statements on art. True, the painstaking work of connoisseurs, added to tradition, has spread out before us a Rembrandt *œuvre* of great abundance—paintings, drawings, etchings; faced with this wealth we are prone to forget how flimsily the individual works are documented, how thin are the arguments by which stylistic criticism has ascribed many of them to Rembrandt. The "truth quotient" varies among the several categories of Rembrandt's work. When it comes to the etchings we are usually on sound ground, but with the drawings we are always keenly aware of the question of authenticity, for serious research in this area is of comparatively recent date. As for the paintings, the rather overoptimistic criteria of the older stylistic criticism, superimposed on the uncertainties of tradition, have created a precarious situation.

Oddly enough, we are more secure in our knowledge of the great 16th-century painters than those of the 17th century, even though the documentary evidence is slenderer and the losses have been greater, from the assaults of the iconoclasts and other destructive forces. The reason is that the surviving store was lovingly attended to by real connoisseurs, before dealers, speculators, and collectors had a chance to build their edifice of dubious tradition. Yet even with respect to the earlier century there has been increasing reticence in making final attributions to certain masters.[4] Our own predilection is for insights of smaller scope but greater certainty, rather than for broad generalizations. It should perhaps be mentioned in passing that art historians have not been able to rely very heavily on signed works from the 16th century, for the custom of an artist signing his work came in but slowly. This has actually turned out to be a boon for scientific inquiry, since it was less likely to be led down the garden path by spurious signatures.

British art collectors have a peculiar talent for self-mockery and understatement, and what they are prone to say about the 17th century remains largely true: "Nearly half the old masters are wrongly attributed and the others are not old at all." In retrospect, we can sympathize with the American J. C. van Dyke, who in 1923 published a book under the title of *Rembrandt and his School*, in which he blissfully ignored the weight of tradition in Europe and radically cut back Rembrandt's authentic *œuvre* to a small group of pictures. Connoisseurs have condescendingly belittled this bold foray, but despite van Dyke's less than adequate research and his arbitrary attributions and de-attributions, his work has not been without value as a warning and protest.

But let us return to our problem. Is the documentation of 17th-century Dutch painting really less extensive, less reliable, harder to tie in with the surviving works than is true in other branches of art? I think the answer must be an unequivocal yes. The reasons lie in the artist's social status then—indeed in the whole Dutch social order itself, rather in contrast to neighboring Flanders, as has already been pointed out. Is it a mere accident that we have no more than seven letters from Rembrandt's hand, whereas so very much larger a number have survived from Rubens'? It has been said, of course, that Rembrandt was simply not the kind of man to engage in theoretical discussions on art.[5] But was this really a matter of personal choice, or did the deeper causes reside in his social situation?

Rubens was a court painter, with the church as one of his major patrons. He had friends abroad who acted as his agents. He was a wealthy collector himself, as well as a knowledgeable antiquarian and a state official. The traces of his work—commissions, contracts, correspondence, state papers—were bound to be preserved in far greater abundance in the archives and in the files of his contemporaries than those of Rembrandt in his bourgeois milieu. The Stadholder was niggardly with commissions to Rembrandt, preferring to buy Flemish pictures.[6] The church in Holland was opposed to religious images and even music. In Holland art collecting and patronage remained the province of the middle class for the first half of the 17th century; that may be the reason why art was misprized by the more class-conscious society of the later 17th and the 18th century.

Rembrandt's career is typical in this respect. The number of public commissions received by the greatest painter of his time can be counted almost on the fingers of one hand—commissions for which documents have survived, works accessible to the broad public that might have proclaimed his glory for all time. That the Stadholder Frederick Henry in the course of time commissioned Rembrandt to do a whole Passion series we learn only from the seven Rembrandt letters—preserved in Huygens' files—and from a few payment orders in the account books of the House of Orange. There never seems to have been a full-fledged contract in which the details were laid down. Nor do we know how these pictures passed into the possession of the Electors at Duesseldorf. Even for these conspicuous works it has proved impossible to reconstruct an unbroken provenance.

From the moment they were delivered until the early 19th century the two anatomy paintings remained continuously in the anatomy theater at Amsterdam and there is thus no shadow on their past. Yet we have not a single document that would tell us how these commissions came about. Even the origins of THE NIGHT WATCH, Rembrandt's most famous work today, are shrouded in darkness. The theory that ascribes its genesis to the state visit of Maria de Medici in 1638 is now shown to be false. Its original title, THE MILITIA COMPANY OF CAPTAIN FRANS BANNING COCQ, was lost somewhere en route. Sir Joshua Reynolds could actually doubt that Rembrandt had painted it! But for Melchior Fokkens, the only one to mention Rembrandt's name in connection with the commission for the Amsterdam Town Hall, we should have not the least proof that the fragment now in Stockholm once served to adorn that eighth wonder of the world.[7] No official document tells us anything of the circumstances. Was it indeed an official commission or did Rembrandt do it on speculation? Was the work flatly rejected, or did Rembrandt take it back himself, refusing to concede to demands to alter it? We do not know.

Rembrandt, to be sure, was a famous man from 1632 on. "Artful and far-famed" are the words proudly applied by Orlers (1641), Burgomaster and historian of Leyden, to that town's eminent native son. By the time Orlers wrote, Rembrandt's pictures had hit the Paris market and Charles I of England had acquired some for his collection (as later on did Archduke Leopold William for his large, choice collection at Brussels). Poets composed verses on works by Rembrandt, but while these inform us about the sitters and what their portraits meant to them and their friends, they tell us nothing about the authenticity of the surviving paintings. Our difficulties are compounded by the vagueness of 17th-century inventories and by our knowledge that even then many copies of Rembrandts were in circulation.[8]

On the other hand, some portraits survive for which we have a complete history above all suspicion. We know, for example, that Jan Elison commissioned Rembrandt in 1634 to paint his clergyman father, John, and his mother, Maria Bockenolle [162, 163]. The elder Elisons later returned to Norwich in England, where John Elison was a vicar. After the son's death the portraits passed into the hands of his brother-in-law in Norwich and remained in the possession of the family until the middle of the 19th century. They are signed so boldly and unmistakably, moreover, that we really need no other authentication (Illustration a, p. 162).

Thus it is possible to identify an indubitable core of genuine Rembrandts, as against all the others that are ascribed to him

a Rembrandt, signature on portrait of JOHANNES ELISON [162]

b Rembrandt, signature on YOUNG MAN WITH A POINTED BEARD [119]

with lesser degrees of certainty, solely by comparison. In this process we must, of course, take into account a not inconsiderable group of documented works, sometimes hard to recognize, actually painted by Rembrandt's pupils but worked over by the master, sold under his name, and sometimes even signed by him.

Ah, that signature! By present-day standards nothing should testify so eloquently to a painting's genuineness as the painter's own mark. He signs his name to it, so we feel, in unmistakable token of the fact that it is the creation of his brush and his imagination. What we have to bear in mind is that in 17th-century practice a master might sign any painting issuing from his studio that was deemed to be worthy of going out into the world under his name. Rembrandt may have followed this custom during the early period, but by and large determining the distinction between "autograph" and "studio" works is not the kind of problem that dogs the Rembrandt scholar. On the other hand Rubens—who seldom signed his pictures—maintained not only students but assistants, some of them for the specific purpose of executing paintings after his sketches and designs. In the case of Rembrandt and his school, the major difficulty is that signatures not only have a tendency to fade with time, but are all too easy to imitate. A genuine though (to the dealer) irksome signature—say, that of a student—is readily scraped away or trimmed off during "relining." The loss is readily repaired with the brand-new signature of the master himself. Close inspection and even laboratory tests are seldom able to authenticate a signature beyond all doubt. Neither paleography nor modern handwriting analysis can do very much with a single word, and there is the additional problem that writing with a brush is something quite different from ordinary writing with a pen. Still, the signature carries such authority in the mind of most people that even genuine paintings often display signatures that have been tampered with or are spurious. During cleaning, the retouched portions of the signature *Rembrant f. 1632* on the TULP was carefully removed, only to reveal the master's genuine (?) signature. When the portrait of MANASSEH BEN ISRAEL (Illustration a, p. 156) was cleaned, traces were found of a signature of Govaert Flinck, previously scraped away and covered with a *Rembrandt*. To this day, on the male portrait in Brunswick [119], one can make out, under the spurious *Rembrandt*, an original *RHL van Rijn* (Illustration b).[9]

But the little deceits practiced on signatures are the least of the traumas Rembrandt's paintings have suffered. The history of THE NIGHT WATCH has shown what damage repeated cleaning and restoring can do. When we look at old illustrations of picture galleries, moreover, we cannot help being dismayed at the way the panels and canvases are crowded together.[10] Often they could be accommodated only after they had been cropped and trimmed —the cavalier way in which THE NIGHT WATCH was treated is proof, if any were needed. All too often the art works we gaze at today are no more than the butchered remains of the past. Overpainting and thick coats of varnish may in some measure hide the scars and improve appearances; but yellowing varnish can also obscure masterpieces that have otherwise remained intact, and when the grime is removed, the pristine effect can be overwhelming. Whether the effect is pleasing or disappointing, works of the past should stand revealed in all their frailty, like beautiful ruins and ancient torsos.

In the view of the classicistic criticism dominant throughout the 18th century, the art of Rembrandt was regarded as almost the prototype of "bad taste," which did not help assure his works the fastidious care they deserve. Of course, the criticism was intermingled with admiration for the bizarre and picturesque elements; yet even Arnold Houbraken who, early in the 18th century, included the up-to-then most comprehensive biography of Rembrandt in his book on painting, gives an account of only a few works in the hands of Dutch collectors. It was rather the etchings on which Rembrandt's fame rested in the 18th and 19th centuries. None of his paintings ever caused the kind of stir that attended Rubens' Medici cycle in Paris. The animated arguments between the *Poussinistes* and *Rubénistes* kept Rubens' prestige alive in the art world, whichever artist one sided with. By comparison, THE NIGHT WATCH was but one of many civic guard pieces in Amsterdam, and in the eyes of the 18th-century travelers it was by no means the best.[11] The anatomy pictures were curiosities, and the remnant of the Town Hall painting had gone to Sweden.

In the course of the 18th century, nevertheless, Netherlandish art became the vogue in Paris collector circles, though official art doctrine accorded ultimate respect to nobility of theme and thus looked down on the "vulgar" scenes from everyday life that dominated Dutch painting. In the marketplace, however, among col-

Salomon Koninck INTERIOR WITH A SCHOLAR
Paris, Louvre

lectors big and small, the "picturesque" Dutchmen Berchem, Wouwermans, and Ostade stood in high esteem. Fabulous prices were paid for their pictures. Nor was Rembrandt left out—his bizarre chiaroscuro works in particular were to the taste of these collectors. We can scarcely be surprised that apprentice works and imitations intruded among the genuine paintings at a time when there was as yet no traditional *œuvre* firmly attached to the name of Rembrandt. It was the fashion to copy Rembrandt, to paint pendants for his portraits or provide them with mates from the works of other Dutch masters. I am afraid the aftermath of these doctored groups is still with us today. It was not so very long ago, after all, that a portrait of an aged scholar in the Louvre (see Illustration), which had been thought to be a pendant to a Rembrandt [91], was unmasked as a student work of Salomon Koninck. We know, for example, that Hyacinthe Rigaud painted two copies of Rembrandts, a *portrait de Rimbran et de sa fille en ovalle*, and *une teste de paisanne*—but where are they now? Lost or unrecognized among genuine Rembrandts, or vanished among the nameless mass of nondescript Rembrandt copies?

It was in this age, too, that the German princes in Duesseldorf (whose collections are now in Munich), Cassel, Brunswick, and Dresden started their collections of Dutch paintings. Catherine the Great made her purchases principally in France, while the English collectors bought both in Holland and in Paris. The pictures passed from hand to hand through auctions and dealers, with all the attendant hazards of mistakes, inadvertent or intentional. All the same, a Rembrandt painting coming from a famous 18th-century collection has a respectable pedigree. The collectors and dealers of that period were highly knowledgeable, able to tell good works from bad, and this justifies our giving weight to their choices. Yet we must not overlook that even then the authentic word-of-mouth traditions on which these admirers of Rembrandt and of Dutch art based themselves had begun to dry up. Nor must we forget what events of recent years should have impressed upon us: a vogue for a certain school or style, past or present, serves as a stimulus not only for connoisseurs and serious critics, but also for forgers and imitators. This perennial annoyance seems to be the ineradicable heritage of art collecting in Europe.

In the 19th and 20th centuries two new elements affected the development of Rembrandt research. Wealthy capitalist collectors, especially from America, began to get into the art market; and scholarly art criticism with its *œuvre* catalogues began to take over the guidance of collectors and museums from the art dealer-connoisseurs. Especially on the Continent, the newer scientific approach contrasted with the amateurism that still prevailed in England, yet it is not necessarily true that the approach of the professional scholars was always superior. For many years the *Catalogue Raisonné* (1836) of John Smith, a knowledgeable art dealer, formed a more reliable guide to Rembrandt than the learned treatises of the new generation.

Hofstede de Groot paid tribute to this predecessor. In his lists of the works of Dutch painters, which began to appear in 1906, he openly stated that he had proceeded "on the model of John Smith's *Catalogue Raisonné*." Beyond doubt the documentary researches of A. Bredius and the profound scholarship of Wilhelm von Bode, W. R. Valentiner, and many others stimulated the growth of scholarly art criticism. It was owing to their knowledge and zeal that many of the previously unrecognized works unearthed by alert art dealers were authenticated. Of course these scholars too knew of imitators and forgeries, some of whom they exposed; but by and large they tended to err on the generous side, and we can no longer today share their optimism, which was indeed deprecated by less sanguine critics even at the time.[12]

More in keeping with our present moderate attitude are the cautious and balanced judgments voiced by Neil MacLaren in his 1960 catalogue of the Dutch paintings in the National Gallery, London. But it must be said, to the credit of English collectors and art lovers, that the quality of this Rembrandt collection is of such stature that there is seldom any need in this exemplary catalogue to pose the question of attribution. The disturbing divergences of opinion among Rembrandt scholars simply do not come into play here.

The Rembrandt corpus reached its all-time peak in the various catalogues of Valentiner. Bredius' *Rembrandt Paintings* of 1936–37 considerably reduced the *œuvre* amassed by Valentiner. It added only a few attributions, and of the nine pictures added in a second English edition (which has remained virtually unknown) only a few have stood up to more recent criticism. In his *Rembrandt Gemaelde* (1966), Kurt Bauch condemned outright some 70 of about

A FAMILY GROUP [416] Detail

Copy after Rembrandt, JUDAS RETURNING THE THIRTY PIECES OF SILVER [12]
Whereabouts unknown

620 paintings reproduced by Bredius, and cast doubt on many more. By and large, this purge of the Rembrandt corpus accords with the present state of our knowledge, and it seems to have met with greater approval than some of Bauch's new attributions. Perhaps the situation can best be summed up in the statement that nowadays more Rembrandts are being disqualified than discovered. An exception to this trend is found in the works of Jakob Rosenberg who, in the second edition of his Rembrandt monograph (1964), rejected only half as many paintings as Bauch, while he reincorporated 30 older works that Bredius had previously eliminated. Among living Rembrandt scholars Rosenberg is perhaps the most conservative; he eliminates paintings from the traditional corpus only after careful deliberation, and with the greatest restraint.

The conventions of art research and the social (and economic) structure of collecting hinder any radical regrouping of the works that are traditionally ascribed to Rembrandt; no serious experiment of this sort has yet been published. It should not be too difficult, however, to single out the paintings that bear genuine signatures and those that are convincingly documented; that effort has been made in the CATALOGUE. Yet it does not seem right to give these pictures pride of place over "attributed" pieces (especially since the reader is conditioned by a sad twist of usage to assume that "attributed" paintings are not quite genuine) that are often works of surpassing creative power whose sole flaw is that they lack proper credentials. Of course, there are those who believe that only stylistic analysis can yield a conclusive attribution; they disregard the distinction between "documented" and "attributed" works.

Possibly the standards of scientific connoisseurship will be more universally applied once the migrations of old masters have come to a halt, so that the question of prejudicing the current owner's interests will no longer arise. In such a utopian art world of tomorrow, we should look at paintings as we now do at ancient buildings—solely for the sake of their innate beauty. A change in attribution would have no greater economic consequences than a change in the identity of the architect of an old church.

The CATALOGUE that follows cannot but reflect the many questions that still remain unanswered. With their numbered lists and air of systematic assurance, catalogues tend to take on an impersonal, authoritative look, stripped of all sentiment and subjectivity. This may be true, but let the reader—and the Rembrandt owner—take warning: the CATALOGUE is not intended as a definitive list of "All the Paintings of Rembrandt." In many cases my resolute convictions on questions of authenticity are at odds with current opinion. In many more cases, I have weighed my own hesitation against the firmly held opinions of colleagues, and struck a compromise. But I have taken special care to mention all recently published opinions on authenticity, especially those that disagree with my own judgments. There are paintings in the CATALOGUE of whose authenticity I am not certain: paintings deemed (mainly by others) to be documents essential to our understanding of the whole corpus of Rembrandt and his followers; others that I have seen—and discredited—since the CATALOGUE ILLUSTRATIONS were printed; and finally, questionable paintings to which I give the benefit of the doubt if only because I have not seen them myself in the original.

Are all the traditional Rembrandt attributions not included in the CATALOGUE false? I believe that most of them are falsely attributed, whatever considerable merits they may possess; some of those I have discussed elsewhere.[13] Other paintings that might have found a place in the CATALOGUE are provisionally omitted —in the final weighing of the pros and cons they simply did not look good enough. These borderline cases, in and out of the CATALOGUE, disturb me deeply.

Those who have pondered the documentary evidence will know that the portraits and studies are more heavily represented in the borderline group than the history paintings or landscapes. Stylistic analysis does not help us very much—in the case of the portraits, especially those of the early Amsterdam period, style criticism has failed to pinpoint the dividing line between the early works of students and those of the young Rembrandt himself.

In the CATALOGUE doubt is cast on many of the signatures. Repeated comparisons of Rembrandt signatures with the few perfectly convincing specimens has taught me that the authenticity of a painting does not guarantee that its signature is genuine. Many of the signatures found today on perfectly good Rembrandts are false or touched up. Progress here is slow: no systematic work on signatures has been attempted, and no one scholar has yet seen all the Rembrandt paintings and their signatures.

I have also made use whenever possible of X-ray photographs. When these are held up alongside the original, one is often able to make out underlying layers of paint that can provide important evidence in judging a painting—and may even lead to its immediate condemnation.

Soon enough, we shall no longer have cause to complain about the yellowed varnish on old paintings. Techniques of restoration will no doubt be further perfected before long. While I myself stand behind the museums that are committed even now to the cleaning of pictures—even when this reveals a damaged surface—I also understand the feelings of those who refrain from cleaning. But I feel correspondingly compelled to refrain from offering a definitive opinion on a picture whose beauties or weaknesses go unseen behind a yellow mask.

Many colleagues and museum officials have allowed me access to their papers. It is an agreeable duty to express to these friends and fellow students my heartfelt thanks for entrusting to me treasures in their safekeeping, for such crucial favors as finding ladders and lights and removing protective glass panes—and not least for sparing me time for instructive and illuminating talk. It is to their help that I owe many insights contributing to the image of Rembrandt I have tried to project in these pages. I hope the image is an up-to-date one. My wish implies, of course, that the future—Rembrandt years to come—will bring new images of Rembrandt each "up to its own date." In this reflection I find the single reassuring certitude of history: the books of the past are never closed.

Catalogue Illustrations

Rembrandt's paintings have been reproduced before in the valuable reference works of Bode, A. Rosenberg, Valentiner, Bredius, and Bauch. In their various books the paintings are filed, usually one to a page, either in "pure" chronological order or—again chronologically—under more or less arbitrary classifications designed to help the reader locate quickly any given painting. The first system gives the false impression that the works were painted by Rembrandt one after the other, in the order given. The second system blunts this impression somewhat, but it introduces other distractions: by separating "Portraits of Men" from "Portraits of Women" from self-portraits, companion pictures of couples are divorced from one another; by segregating Old Testament from New Testament from mythological and historical subjects, the history paintings take on an unfortunately parochial character.

The present CATALOGUE is designed in another spirit than a file of reproductions: it is intended as a visual commentary on the paintings, a presentation of some of the formal and iconographic themes of Rembrandt's work in their general chronological progression. Within five periods, the paintings are grouped roughly by their 17th-century genres:

HISTORY PAINTINGS. 17th-century art theory treated all narrative and allegorical compositions, regardless of their subject, under the heading "history." Breaking Rembrandt's history paintings down further, as has always been done before, into Old Testament, New Testament, and mythological and historical subjects, only introduces artificial distinctions into an organic body of work. The reader searching for a particular painting will find an iconographical breakdown in the INDEX OF REMBRANDT PAINTINGS.

THE LIFE OF MEN AND SAINTS. Rembrandt's friend, the painter Jan van de Cappelle, had a large collection of Rembrandt drawings which he kept in portfolios labeled: HISTORIES, LANDSCAPES, SKETCHES (probably including figure and face studies), and THE LIFE OF WOMEN AND CHILDREN. We paraphrase his last title for a section of the CATALOGUE with depictions of a rich group of characters—based on life, mythology, history, the Bible, the painter's own imagination—which are not quite history paintings, but more than portraits or studies. The 17th-century Dutch art theorist, Gerard de Lairesse, in explaining that the creative painter need not feel constricted by his field of specialization, lists the variety of types that could provide a *Beeldschilder*, a face and figure painter, with subject matter for a rich career:

Not only are there male and female saints, but philosophers, prophets, and prophetesses or sybils, illustrious men and women in civilian as well as military dress, worldly rulers, jurors of the civil and sacred law, the four continents of the earth, the five senses, and more noteworthy personages and subjects.

Many of these characters—and other, more humble ones—were painted by Rembrandt. They remain to be identified among the *Beelden* of this section of the CATALOGUE and the next.

PORTRAITS AND STUDIES. All the self-portraits, commissioned portraits, "face paintings" (*tronie* in Dutch; we include the heads of Christ, one of which was described in a catalogue of the time as "Head of Christ, painted from life"), and studies. Companion pieces are always reproduced opposite each other.

LANDSCAPES. Including those with historical subjects.

The dimensions of paintings have been controlled scrupulously against the most reliable sources available and have been proofread with special care. The reader may assume that the dimensions of paintings in public collections are taken from the most recent catalogue of the collection concerned. As for paintings in private collections, the dimensions have been controlled whenever possible against recent published information or the advice of the owner. Dimensions of etchings and drawings are taken from the catalogues of Münz and Benesch (see Bibliography). Dimensions are given in the unit of the source. When this is in centimeters, the measurement is converted into inches, in brackets, to the nearest quarter-inch. The paintings are reproduced as they are seen in their frames. In the rare cases where photographs of paintings removed from the frame were used, the marginal damage exposed was cropped off in the reproduction.

CATALOGUE ILLUSTRATIONS composed by GARY SCHWARTZ.

1625–1631

THE PAINTINGS LISTED IN THE CHRONOLOGY ARE FIRMLY DATED BY DOCUMENT OR INSCRIPTION.

1606. July 15: Rembrandt is born in Leyden.

1620. May 20: Matriculated in Leyden University, after completing a 7-year course at the Latin School preparing him for classical studies. Later in the year he apparently left the University to study painting with Jacob van Swanenburgh, a Leyden painter of hell scenes.

1624. Completed his formal training as a painter with the Amsterdam history painter Pieter Lastman. Returned to Leyden.

1625. THE STONING OF SAINT STEPHEN [2], the first dated painting. The presumed date of 1626 on CONSUL CERIALIS [1] is not clearly legible, and in fact the picture seems earlier than THE STONING OF SAINT STEPHEN, a more accomplished work. The inscribed date 1625 on DAVID PRESENTING THE HEAD OF GOLIATH TO SAUL [3] is not clearly legible, though the painting may well have been executed in that year.

1626
  4 ANNA ACCUSED BY TOBIT OF STEALING THE KID
  5 CHRIST DRIVING THE MONEY-CHANGERS FROM THE
    TEMPLE
  6 THE ASS OF BALAAM BALKING BEFORE THE ANGEL
  18 THE MUSIC-MAKERS

1627
  8 THE FLIGHT OF THE HOLY FAMILY INTO EGYPT
  19 THE MONEY-CHANGER
  22 THE APOSTLE PETER IN PRISON

1628. Around 1628, the Utrecht humanist Arnout van Buchell inscribed this line in his notebook on art:
Molitoris etiam Leidensis filius magni fit, sed ante tempus. (The Leyden miller's son is much praised, but before his time). This is the first recorded comment on Rembrandt's art. It tells us that Rembrandt had a reputation as an *enfant terrible* at the age of 18. Van Buchell apparently felt that such early success could do a young painter no good.

  7 THE APOSTLE PETER DENYING CHRIST (?)
  9 SAMSON BETRAYED BY DELILAH
  11 TWO SCHOLARS DISPUTING

1629. Probably in 1629, Constantijn Huygens wrote his enthusiastic report on Rembrandt in his autobiographical sketch. By this time, Rembrandt's name was made in the circles of the wealthy Dutch collectors and connoisseurs. There was a lag of about two years, however, before he began to receive vast numbers of commissions.
  12 JUDAS RETURNING THE THIRTY PIECES OF SILVER
  15 THE TRIBUTE MONEY
  32 SELF-PORTRAIT

1630. April 27: Harmen Gerritsz. van Rijn is buried in the Pieterskerk, Leyden.
  24 THE PROPHET JEREMIAH LAMENTING THE DESTRUCTION OF JERUSALEM (REMBRANDT'S FATHER)
  42 AN OLD MAN IN A FUR HAT
  45 SELF-PORTRAIT
  50 OLD MAN WITH A JEWELED CROSS

1631. June 20: Hendrick van Uylenburgh, Amsterdam art dealer, acknowledges receipt of a 1,000-guilder loan from Rembrandt in Leyden (surely an investment disguised as a loan—Uylenburgh was a wealthy man). Toward the end of the year, in all likelihood, Rembrandt moved to Amsterdam, where he lived with van Uylenburgh and had a studio in his home.
  17 THE PRESENTATION OF CHRIST IN THE TEMPLE
  25 THE APOSTLE PETER IN PRISON
  26 A SCHOLAR IN A LOFTY ROOM ("SAINT ANASTASIUS")
  27 THE PROPHETESS HANNAH (REMBRANDT'S MOTHER)
  48 OLD MAN WITH A GOLD CHAIN
  51 YOUNG OFFICER
  52 YOUNG MAN IN A PLUMED HAT
  53 THE AMSTERDAM MERCHANT NICOLAES RUTS
  54 YOUNG MAN AT A DESK
  56 CHRIST ON THE CROSS
  106 YOUNG MAN IN A TURBAN

I CONSUL CERIALIS AND THE GERMAN LEGIONS (?) 1626 (?)
Panel. 89.8 x 121 cm. (35¼ x 47½ in.)
Leyden, Stedelijk Museum "De Lakenhal"

2 THE STONING OF SAINT STEPHEN. 1625
Colorplate, page 9
Panel. 89.5 x 123.6 cm. (35¼ x 48½ in.)
Lyons, Musée des Beaux-Arts

a THE REST ON THE FLIGHT INTO EGYPT
Etching. 21.7 x 16.5 cm. (8½ x 6½ in.)
Amsterdam, Rijksprentenkabinet

The earliest paintings we know to be the work of Rembrandt are not timid trial pieces but self-assured and ambitious history paintings with many figures. The similarity of scale and structure of both paintings suggest that they were part of a rather grand series. Rembrandt's style may be awkward, and his goals too high, but even in these confusing compositions we recognize his eagerness to give history painting emotional force and free it from conventionality.

2

a

3

4

5

3 DAVID PRESENTING THE HEAD OF GOLIATH TO SAUL.
   162(5)
   Panel. 27.5 x 39.5 cm. (10¾ x 15½ in.)
   Basel, Oeffentliche Kunstsammlung

4 ANNA ACCUSED BY TOBIT OF STEALING THE KID. 1626
   Colorplate, page 11
   Panel. 39.5 x 30 cm. (15½ x 11¾ in.)
   Amsterdam, Rijksmuseum (on loan from Baroness Bentinck-
   Thyssen)

5 CHRIST DRIVING THE MONEY-CHANGERS FROM THE
   TEMPLE. 1626
   Colorplate, page 13
   Panel. 43 x 33 cm. (17 x 13 in.)
   Moscow, Pushkin Museum

6 THE ASS OF BALAAM BALKING BEFORE THE ANGEL. 1626
   Panel. 65 x 47 cm. (25½ x 18½ in.)
   Paris, Musée Cognacq-Jay

6

7

8

a

7 THE APOSTLE PETER DENYING CHRIST (?) 1628
   Copper. 21.5 x 16.5 cm. (8½ x 6½ in.)
   Tokyo, Bridgestone Gallery
8 THE FLIGHT OF THE HOLY FAMILY INTO EGYPT. 1627
   Panel. 26.4 x 24.2 cm. (10½ x 9½ in.)
   Tours, Musée des Beaux-Arts
9 SAMSON BETRAYED BY DELILAH. 1628
   Panel. 59.5 x 49.5 cm. (23½ x 19½ in.)
   Berlin-Dahlem, Gemaeldegalerie
a THE FLIGHT OF THE HOLY FAMILY INTO EGYPT
   Etching (I). 14.6 x 12.2 cm. (5¾ x 4¾ in.)
   Amsterdam, Rijksprentenkabinet

After his first vast and violent history paintings [1, 2], Rembrandt
took another tack in his depiction of dramatic narrative. His history paintings of 1626–8 no longer make the unpleasant impression of *tableaux-vivants*—they bring the action to us in the
more evocative terms of direct personal experience. The small
night scenes [7, 8] and the studies in dramatic action [5, 6] and
interior space [4] are crowned by the mysterious SAMSON BE-
TRAYED BY DELILAH, a masterpiece of terror and suspense.

9

10

a

b

10 THE PRESENTATION OF CHRIST IN THE TEMPLE
Panel. 55.5 x 44 cm. (21¾ x 17¼ in.)
Hamburg, Kunsthalle

11 TWO SCHOLARS DISPUTING. 1628
Panel. 28⅞ x 23½ in.
Melbourne, National Gallery of Victoria

a THE APOSTLES PETER AND JOHN AT THE GATE OF THE
TEMPLE
Etching. 22.1 x 17 cm. (8¾ x 6¾ in.)
Amsterdam, Rijksmuseum

b OLD MAN WITH A BOOK
Red and black chalk drawing. 29.5 x 21 cm. (11½ x 8¼ in.)
Berlin-Dahlem, Kupferstichkabinett

The open arms of the apostle Peter in the etching foreshadow the
paternal embraces of KING DAVID [207] and the father of THE
PRODIGAL SON [355], while the more impersonal gesture of the
prophetess Hannah (probably Rembrandt's mother), expressing
wonder in the face of a mystery, reminds us of the praying figures
in the Early Christian catacombs, which Rembrandt can scarcely
have known.

11

12

12 JUDAS RETURNING THE THIRTY PIECES OF SILVER. 1629
   Panel. 31½ x 40¼ in.
   Mulgrave Castle, Yorkshire, Normanby Collection
13 DAVID PLAYING THE HARP BEFORE SAUL
   Panel. 62 x 50 cm. (24½ x 19¾ in.)
   Frankfurt, Städelsches Kunstinstitut

JUDAS RETURNING THE THIRTY PIECES OF SILVER was praised
by Rembrandt's first important patron for the powerful visual
impact of Judas' sheer misery. No less impressive are the hyster-
ically rejecting gestures of the priests and the placing of the figures
in the composition—the repulsive mound of senile hunchbacks
retreating fearfully into the shelter of the temple, leaving Judas
isolated in his despair. At the very moment Rembrandt found his
way to this gripping style of history painting, which he had sought
for years, Huygens and other connoisseurs were beginning to
crave more stark drama in painting, of the sort they found in the
modern Flemish and Italian schools. As the only Dutchman who
breathed the spirit of Rubens and Caravaggio, in the history
paintings of the later Leyden period, Rembrandt was acclaimed
as the wonder of the age.

14

15

a

14 THE RISEN CHRIST AT EMMAUS
   Colorplate, page 15
   Paper stuck on panel. 39 x 42 cm. ($15\frac{1}{4}$ x $16\frac{1}{2}$ in.)
   Paris, Musée Jacquemart-André

15 THE TRIBUTE MONEY. 1629
   Panel. 41 x 33 cm. ($16\frac{1}{4}$ x 13 in.)
   Ottawa, National Gallery of Canada

16 THE RAISING OF LAZARUS
   Panel. 93.7 x 81.1 cm. (37 x 32 in.)
   California, Private Collection

a THE ENTOMBMENT OF CHRIST. 1630
   Red chalk drawing. 28 x 20.3 cm. (11 x 8 in.)
   London, British Museum

In these remarkable scenes from the life of Christ Rembrandt brings together in an integrated style the most striking features of his earlier history paintings: powerfully dramatic lighting; brilliantly lit figures contrasted with figures in shadow or in silhouette; expressive realism of gesture; plunges from the foreground to the background; islands of impasto that break surface into our world, setting off the flat expanse of the picture plane and the depths of the space behind it.

16

a

17 THE PRESENTATION OF CHRIST IN THE TEMPLE. 1631
  Colorplate, page 17
  Panel. 61 x 48 cm. (24 x 19 in.)
  The Hague, Mauritshuis
 a THE RAISING OF LAZARUS
  Etching (II). 36.7 x 25.7 cm. ($14\frac{1}{2}$ x 10 in.)
  Amsterdam, Rijksprentenkabinet

Rembrandt made his first reputation as a "naturalist." Paradoxically enough, naturalism in art tends to go hand in hand with downright romanticism. Rembrandt observes physical and emotional reality closely in these years, but he does it in a rapturous mood. The results are uncanny, like photographs of a vision.

17

18

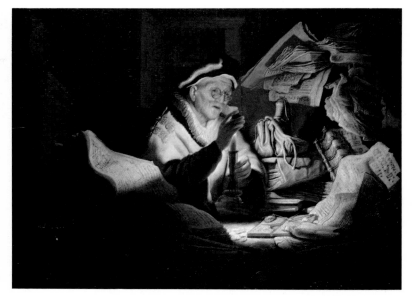

19

20

1625–1631: THE LIFE OF MEN AND SAINTS

18 THE MUSIC-MAKERS. 1626
   Panel. 63 x 48 cm. (24¾ x 19 in.)
   Sold at N. Katz auction: Paris, April 25, 1951
19 THE MONEY-CHANGER. 1627
   Panel. 32 x 42 cm. (12½ x 16½ in.)
   Berlin-Dahlem, Gemaeldegalerie
20 AN ARTIST IN THE STUDIO ("THE EASEL")
   Panel. 10 x 12½ in.
   Boston, Museum of Fine Arts
21 A SCHOLAR IN A LOFTY ROOM
   Panel. 21 11⁄16 x 18 5⁄16 in.
   London, National Gallery

These early scenes from daily life betray Rembrandt's unusual approach to genre painting. His figures are filled with the same dramatic concentration that marks the personages of his history paintings—their involvement with daily life is no less intense than the struggles of the historical characters in their more charged situations. With few exceptions, the other Dutch painters treated subjects from daily life either with a patronizing smile or with journalistic descriptiveness. Rembrandt never applied a double standard to "history" and "life." To him, history had all the immediacy of life, and life all the dignity of history.

21

22

a

c

b

22 THE APOSTLE PAUL IN PRISON. 1627
   Panel. 72.8 x 60.3 cm. (28¾ x 23¾ in.)
   Stuttgart, Staatsgalerie
23 THE APOSTLE PAUL AT HIS DESK (REMBRANDT'S
   FATHER)
   Panel. 47 x 39 cm. (18½ x 15¼ in.)
   Nuremberg, Germanisches Nationalmuseum
 a THE APOSTLE PAUL AT HIS DESK
   Red chalk and wash drawing. 23.6 x 20.1 cm. (9¼ x 8 in.)
   Paris, Louvre

b THE DRUNKEN LOT. 1633
  Black chalk drawing. 25.1 x 18.9 cm. (10 x 7½ in.)
  Frankfurt, Städelsches Kunstinstitut
c REMBRANDT'S FATHER
  Red and black chalk and wash drawing. 18.9 x 24 cm.
  (7½ x 9½ in.)
  Oxford, Ashmolean Museum

The Oxford drawing (Illustration c) offers a tentative guide for
the identification of Rembrandt's father among the old men who
served as models in the Leyden years. To the study head in Wassenaar [29] we would add two biblical figures [23, 24].

23

24

24 THE PROPHET JEREMIAH LAMENTING THE
DESTRUCTION OF JERUSALEM (REMBRANDT'S FATHER).
1630
Colorplate, page 19
Panel. 58 x 46 cm. (22¾ x 18 in.)
Amsterdam, Rijksmuseum

25 THE APOSTLE PETER IN PRISON. 1631
Panel. 58 x 48 cm. (22¾ x 19 in.)
Brussels, Collection of the Prince of Mérode-Westerloo

a A BEGGAR ASKING FOR AN ALMS. 1630
Etching. 11.6 x 6.9 cm. (4½ x 2¾ in.)
Amsterdam, Rijksprentenkabinet

b OLD MAN WITH CLASPED HANDS
Red and black chalk drawing. 22.6 x 15.7 cm. (9 x 6¼ in.)
Berlin-Dahlem, Kupferstichkabinett

JEREMIAH [24], PETER [25], "ANASTASIUS" [26], and HAN-
NAH [27]—which are all nearly the same size—may have belonged to a still larger series of religious personages. "Sets" of the
twelve apostles, the four evangelists, the first twelve Roman em-
perors, and other groups were popular collectors' items in the
17th century. We cannot identify the binding principle of this
group, since the titles of three of the four surviving members [24,
26, 27] are uncertain.

25

a

b

26

26 A SCHOLAR IN A LOFTY ROOM ("SAINT ANASTASIUS").
    1631
    Colorplate, page 21
    Panel. 60 x 48 cm. (23½ x 19 in.)
    Stockholm, Nationalmuseum
27 THE PROPHETESS HANNAH (REMBRANDT'S MOTHER).
    1631
    Panel. 60 x 48 cm. (23½ x 19 in.)
    Amsterdam, Rijksmuseum
 a REMBRANDT'S MOTHER IN FANCIFUL DRESS. 1631
    Etching (I). 14.5 x 12.9 cm. (5¾ x 5 in.)
    London, British Museum

27

a

28

1625–1631: PORTRAITS AND STUDIES

28 SOLDIER IN A PLUMED CAP
   Panel. 39.6 x 29.3 cm. (15½ x 11½ in.)
   Lugano-Castagnola, Switzerland,
   Collection of Countess Batthyany

29 REMBRANDT'S FATHER
   Colorplate, page 23
   Panel. 24.1 x 20.5 cm. (9½ x 8 in.)
   Wassenaar, Holland, Collection of Mr. S. J. van den Bergh

30 SELF-PORTRAIT
   Panel. 23.4 x 17.2 cm. (9¼ x 6¾ in.)
   Cassel, Gemaeldegalerie

31 HEAD OF A MAN
   Panel. 48 x 37 cm. (19 x 14½ in.)
   Cassel, Gemaeldegalerie

a SELF-PORTRAIT
   Brush and pen drawing. 12.7 x 9.5 cm. (5 x 3¾ in.)
   London, British Museum

b SELF-PORTRAIT. 1629
   Etching. 17.8 x 15.4 cm. (7 x 6 in.)
   Amsterdam, Rijksprentenkabinet

29

31

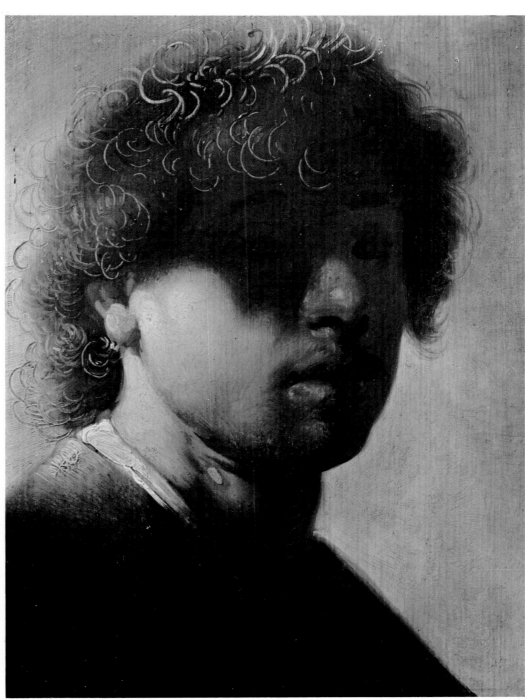

30

a

b

32

a

33

32 SELF-PORTRAIT. 1629
   Panel. 15.5 x 12.7 cm. (6 x 5 in.)
   Munich, Alte Pinakothek
33 SELF-PORTRAIT
   Colorplate, page 25
   Panel. 41.2 x 33.8 cm. (16¼ x 13¼ in.)
   Amsterdam, Rijksmuseum
34 REMBRANDT'S MOTHER READING
   Canvas. 74 x 62 cm. (29 x 24½ in.)
   Wilton House, Salisbury, Collection of the Earl of Pembroke
   and Montgomery

35 REMBRANDT'S MOTHER
   Colorplate, page 27
   Panel. 35 x 29 cm. (13¾ x 11½ in.)
   Essen, Collection of Mr. H. von Bohlen und Halbach
a SELF-PORTRAIT. 1630
   Etching. 9 x 7.2 cm. (3½ x 2¾ in.)
   London, British Museum
b REMBRANDT'S MOTHER. 1628
   Etching (I), corrected by Rembrandt in chalk. 8.5 x 7.2 cm.
   (3¼ x 2¾ in.)
   Amsterdam, Rijksprentenkabinet

b

34

35

36

37

36 AN OLD MAN IN A CAP
    Colorplate, page 29
    Panel. 47 x 39 cm. (18½ x 15¼ in.)
    The Hague, Mauritshuis
37 REMBRANDT'S MOTHER
    Panel. 23½ x 18 in.
    Windsor Castle, Royal Collection
38 SELF-PORTRAIT
    Panel. 35 x 29 in.
    Boston, Isabella Stewart Gardner Museum

Rembrandt's early portrait style, like his style of history painting, first crystallized around 1629. These three portraits—none of them commissioned pieces—show many of the same features as the scenes from the life of Christ from that and the following year [14, 15, 16], such as the exaggerated chiaroscuro and bold thrusts into depth. These works all show a variably finished surface—selected details are brought to jewel-sharp focus, while others are merely suggested. This juxtaposition of clear and obscure in the drawing corresponds to the chiaroscuro of the lighting. Such overstated contrasts were soon to disappear from Rembrandt's work.

38

39

39 SELF-PORTRAIT
   Panel. 37.5 x 29 cm. (14¾ x 11½ in.)
   The Hague, Mauritshuis
40 SELF-PORTRAIT
   Panel. 61 x 47 cm. (24 x 18½ in.)
   Sold at N. Katz auction: Paris, December 12, 1950
41 SELF-PORTRAIT
   Panel. 28½ x 22¾ in.
   Liverpool, Walker Art Gallery
42 AN OLD MAN IN A FUR HAT. 1630
   Panel. 22 x 17 cm. (8½ x 6¾ in.)
   Innsbruck, Museum Ferdinandeum

43 "THE REPENTANT SAINT PETER"
   Panel. 29½ x 23½ in.
   Boston, Museum of Fine Arts

A more mellow chiaroscuro, which no longer cuts heedlessly
across faces and forms, marks the portraits and studies of 1630-1.
The SELF-PORTRAITS [39, 40, 41, 44, 45] show Rembrandt in a
range of moods, but in presentation they are all more modest
than the rather pompous SELF-PORTRAIT of 1629 [38].

40

41

42

43

44

45

44 SELF-PORTRAIT. 1630 (?)
   Copper. 15 x 12 cm. (6 x 4¾ in.)
   Stockholm, Nationalmuseum
45 SELF-PORTRAIT. 1630
   Colorplate, page 31
   Panel. 49 x 39 cm. (19¼ x 15¼ in.)
   Aerdenhout, Holland, Collection of Jhr. J. H. Loudon
46 OFFICER WITH A GOLD CHAIN
   Canvas. 32⅞ x 29¾ in.
   Chicago, Art Institute

47 AN OFFICER
   Panel. 25½ x 20 in.
   London, Collection of Sir Brian Mountain
48 OLD MAN WITH A GOLD CHAIN. 1631
   Panel. 23¾ x 20¼ in.
   Birmingham, England, City Museum and Art Gallery (on
   loan from Mrs. Oscar Ashcroft)

46

47

48

49

The ambiguous OLD MEN and OFFICERS are joined in 1631 by equally evasive YOUNG MEN and YOUNG OFFICERS. These unpretentious pictures are the only prelude we know to Rembrandt's full-scale commissioned portraits, aside from the "practice portraits" [36, 37, 38]. Strangely enough, they are starker and more withdrawn than the rather flamboyant portraits of the same year [53, 54].

50

51

52

53

53 THE AMSTERDAM MERCHANT NICOLAES RUTS. 1631
Panel. 46 x 34⅜ in.
New York, The Frick Collection

54 YOUNG MAN AT A DESK. 1631
Canvas. 113 x 92 cm. (44½ x 36¼ in.)
Leningrad, Hermitage

In his first commissioned portraits, Rembrandt demonstrates an instinctive feeling for portraying likenesses. Although his only previous essays in formal portraiture were the rather stiff and mannered family portraits of 1629, he somehow succeeds in coining a spontaneous and engaging portrait style in his very first commissions. He may very well have turned to Jan Lievens for help in working out the problems of the portrait, a field in which Lievens was expert. But in these two dynamic likenesses, Rembrandt surpasses Lievens in flash and liveliness.

54

1632-1639

1632. Fifty paintings are dated 1632 and 1633—more than in any other two years in Rembrandt's career. All but four are portraits or studies. In the deluge of portrait commissions, Rembrandt simply had no time for history paintings, which were generally painted on speculation, for the market. He surely earned a small fortune in these years.

62 THE ABDUCTION OF EUROPA
99 SELF-PORTRAIT
100 DOCTOR NICOLAAS TULP DEMONSTRATING THE ANATOMY OF THE ARM
101 YOUNG MAN WITH A GOLD CHAIN
102 SAINT JOHN THE BAPTIST
103 MAN IN FANCIFUL DRESS ("THE NOBLE SLAV")
104 MAURITS HUYGENS, SECRETARY OF THE STATE COUNCIL OF HOLLAND
105 THE PAINTER JACOB DE GHEYN III
107 BALD-HEADED OLD MAN
108 YOUNG MAN WITH A WIDE COLLAR
109 BEARDED OLD MAN WITH A GOLD CHAIN
110 THE AMSTERDAM MERCHANT MARTEN LOOTEN
112 AMALIA VAN SOLMS
114 YOUNG WOMAN IN A PEARL-TRIMMED BERET
115 YOUNG WOMAN WITH AN EMBROIDERED ROBE
116 YOUNG WOMAN WITH A GOLDEN NECKLACE
117 YOUNG WOMAN WITH AN EMBROIDERED ROBE
118 YOUNG WOMAN WITH A FAN
119 YOUNG MAN WITH A POINTED BEARD
120 PORTRAIT OF A MAN
121 PORTRAIT OF A WOMAN
122 A FORTY-YEAR-OLD MAN
124 JORIS DE CAULLERY
125 AELBERT CUYPER
127 OLD WOMAN IN A WHITE CAP
128 PORTRAIT OF A YOUNG WOMAN

1633
59 DANIEL AND CYRUS BEFORE THE IDOL OF BEL
60 CHRIST IN THE STORM ON THE SEA OF GALILEE
123 PORTRAIT OF A WOMAN
126 CORNELIA PRONCK, WIFE OF AELBERT CUYPER
129 SELF-PORTRAIT
130 PORTRAIT OF A FASHIONABLE COUPLE

132 SASKIA WITH A VEIL
134 SASKIA
135 BEARDED OLD MAN WITH A CAP
136 OLD MAN
137 THE PREACHER JOHANNES UYTTENBOGAERT
138 THE POET JAN HERMANSZ. KRUL
139 "THE SHIPBUILDER AND HIS WIFE"
140 MAN RISING FROM A CHAIR
141 YOUNG WOMAN WITH A FAN
143 YOUNG WOMAN WITH A GOLD CHAIN
145 RICHLY DRESSED CHILD
146 WOMAN WITH A LACE COLLAR
147 THE ROTTERDAM MERCHANT WILLEM BURCHGRAEFF
148 MARGARETHA VAN BILDERBEECQ, WIFE OF WILLEM BURCHGRAEFF
149 BEARDED MAN IN A WIDE-BRIMMED HAT
151 BEARDED MAN WITH A FLAT BROAD COLLAR
152 MAN IN ORIENTAL COSTUME
155 PORTRAIT OF A YOUNG WOMAN

1634. June 22: Rembrandt marries Saskia van Uylenburgh, the niece of Hendrick van Uylenburgh, in the Reformed Church at St. Anna Parochie, Frisia, where Saskia's sister lived.

66 THE DESCENT FROM THE CROSS
67 THE RISEN CHRIST SHOWING HIS WOUND TO THE APOSTLE THOMAS
69 SOPHONISBA RECEIVING THE POISONED CUP (?)
72 CHRIST BEFORE PILATE AND THE PEOPLE
92 SASKIA AS FLORA
93 A SCHOLAR IN HIS STUDY
150 PORTRAIT OF A YOUNG WOMAN
156 PORTRAIT OF AN 83-YEAR-OLD WOMAN
157 SELF-PORTRAIT
158 SELF-PORTRAIT
159 BEARDED MAN IN A WIDE-BRIMMED HAT
161 BOY WITH LONG HAIR
162 THE PREACHER JOHANNES ELISON
163 MARIA BOCKENOLLE, WIFE OF JOHANNES ELISON
164 MAERTEN SOOLMANS
166 YOUNG MAN WITH A MOUSTACHE
167 YOUNG WOMAN WITH FLOWERS IN HER HAIR
168 MAN OF THE RAMAN FAMILY

1635. December 15: Rembrandt's first child is born, a boy he named Rumbartus after Saskia's father, Rombertus van Uylenburgh. The baby died after two months.

70 KING UZZIAH STRICKEN WITH LEPROSY
73 THE ABDUCTION OF GANYMEDE
74 THE ANGEL STOPPING ABRAHAM FROM SACRIFICING ISAAC TO GOD
94 MINERVA
96 SASKIA AS FLORA
170 MAN IN ORIENTAL COSTUME
171 SELF-PORTRAIT
172 MAN IN FANCIFUL COSTUME
173 MAN WITH DISHEVELED HAIR
178 PHILIPS LUCASZ., COUNCILLOR OF THE DUTCH EAST INDIA COMPANY
179 PETRONELLA BUYS, WIFE OF PHILIPS LUCASZ.
180 MAN IN A WIDE-BRIMMED HAT
181 PORTRAIT OF A YOUNG WOMAN
183 THE DIPLOMAT ANTHONIS COOPAL
185 A 70-YEAR-OLD WOMAN SEATED IN AN ARMCHAIR

1636. The first two of Rembrandt's seven letters to Constantijn Huygens were written in 1636. The first informs Huygens that of the three Passion scenes yet to be delivered to Frederick Henry, THE ASCENSION OF CHRIST [80] was finished and the other two "half done." The second letter, following on the delivery of THE ASCENSION, is a request for payment.

1636–8 mark the low tide in Rembrandt's activity as a portraitist and his debut as a landscape painter.

75 TOBIAS HEALING HIS FATHER'S BLINDNESS
76 THE BLINDING OF SAMSON BY THE PHILISTINES
80 THE ASCENSION OF CHRIST
95 THE STANDARD BEARER
169 WOMAN OF THE RAMAN FAMILY
195 LANDSCAPE WITH THE BAPTISM OF THE EUNUCH
270 DANAE

1637
81 THE ANGEL LEAVING TOBIAS AND HIS FAMILY
83 THE PARABLE OF THE WORKERS IN THE VINEYARD
97 SAINT FRANCIS AT PRAYER
186 MAN IN POLISH COSTUME

187 A MAN SEATED IN AN ARMCHAIR

1638. July 16: Rembrandt's lawyer—his brother-in-law Ulricus Uylenburgh—appears at the courthouse in Leeuwarden to lodge a charge of libel against a relative of Saskia's who had accused the young couple of squandering Saskia's inheritance from her parents (which, under certain circumstances, was to pass to other members of the family). Rembrandt was outraged. He himself, claimed his lawyer, earned "richly and *ex superabundanti* (for which he can never thank the Almighty sufficiently)" and had no need of his wife's money. This was true at the time. No document tells us how the case was settled.

82 THE RISEN CHRIST APPEARING TO MARY MAGDALENE
85 SAMSON POSING THE RIDDLE TO THE WEDDING GUESTS
199 LANDSCAPE WITH THE GOOD SAMARITAN

1639. January 5: Rembrandt buys a house in the Breestraat, two doors from that of Hendrick van Uylenburgh. The house was a rather grand affair. The purchase price was 13,000 guilders, of which one fourth was to be paid within a year of taking possession and the rest "within five or six years." Rembrandt never managed to shake off the debt he now incurred.

The last five letters to Huygens were written in January and February 1639. They deal with delivery of THE ENTOMBMENT [87] and THE RESURRECTION [88]; payment therefore; and the bestowal of a gift on Huygens for his help with the commission.

190 REMBRANDT'S MOTHER
191 SELF-PORTRAIT WITH A DEAD BITTERN
192 MAN STANDING IN FRONT OF A DOORWAY
193 ALOTTE ADRIAENSDR.
194 MARIA TRIP, DAUGHTER OF ALOTTE ADRIAENSDR.

55

55 ANDROMEDA CHAINED TO THE ROCK
   Colorplate, page 33
   Panel. 34.5 x 25 cm. (13½ x 9¾ in.)
   The Hague, Mauritshuis
56 CHRIST ON THE CROSS. 1631
   Canvas. 100 x 73 cm. (39½ x 28¾ in.)
   Le Mas d'Agenais, France, Parish Church

Although CHRIST ON THE CROSS is dated 1631, it should not be separated from the paintings of the Passion series [64, 65, 80, 87, 88], for which it may be a trial piece or an experimental beginning.

ANDROMEDA CHAINED TO THE ROCK is a much smaller painting than CHRIST ON THE CROSS, but it is very similar in structure and technique. Both paintings strike a new note of lyric grandeur. Rembrandt suppresses the sensuality of the nude bodies. The nakedness of these fragile victims proclaims physical helplessness—an aspect of nudity conventionally ignored in art. In fact, Rembrandt never painted a figure without covering unless the narrative demanded it, even in mythological subjects.

56

57

57 THE ABDUCTION OF PROSERPINA
Panel. 83 x 78 cm. (32¾ x 30¾ in.)
Berlin-Dahlem, Gemaeldegalerie

58 ESTHER PREPARING TO INTERCEDE WITH AHASUERUS.
163(3)
Panel. 43 x 37 in.
Ottawa, National Gallery of Canada

59 DANIEL AND CYRUS BEFORE THE IDOL OF BEL. 1633
Panel. 22.5 x 28.7 cm. (8¾ x 11¼ in.)
Great Britain, Private Collection

The new brilliance that comes into Rembrandt's biblical and
mythological scenes after his move to Amsterdam may be due in
part to the richer costumes and more resplendent decors that
became available to him in the studio of Hendrick van Uylenburgh.

The violent lighting effects of the history paintings of 1629 [14–
16] are now a thing of the past, but the tendency toward decorative splendor of those panels is developed much further.

61

62

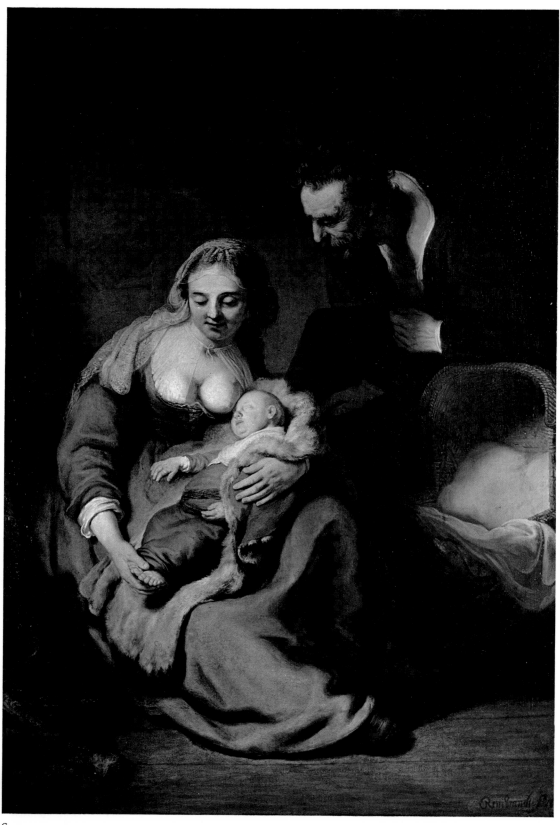

63

63 THE HOLY FAMILY
   Canvas. 183.5 x 123 cm. (72¼ x 48½ in.)
   Munich, Alte Pinakothek
64 THE RAISING OF THE CROSS
   Canvas. 96.2 x 72.2 cm. (38 x 28½ in.)
   Munich, Alte Pinakothek

The Passion series for the Stadholder begins on a more robust note than its rather poetic prelude, CHRIST ON THE CROSS [56]. As was often the case with the House of Orange, the taste and feelings of the court were out of tune with the bourgeois culture of the land as a whole. Even in the years that saw the birth of a great national style in Holland, Frederick Henry's artistic interests lay elsewhere—in the aristocratic art of Rubens and van Dyck. Rembrandt knew this very well, and accommodated his style, in the first two paintings of the Passion series [64, 65], to the taste of his important patron. But there were lesser men—especially Honthorst—who could do this much better, and Rembrandt never became a favored painter at court.

64

65

65 THE DESCENT FROM THE CROSS
   Colorplate, page 47
   Panel. 89.4 x 65.2 cm. (35¼ x 25¾ in.)
   Munich, Alte Pinakothek

66 THE DESCENT FROM THE CROSS. 1634
   Canvas. 158 x 117 cm. (62¼ x 46 in.)
   Leningrad, Hermitage

THE DESCENT FROM THE CROSS [65] is the companion to THE RAISING OF THE CROSS [64] in the Passion series. The subject seems to have inspired ideas Rembrandt could not work into the commissioned piece, so that he painted, in the same year, a larger and more tragic DESCENT [66]. The sheer weight of Christ's body—attested by the struggles of the men lowering him to the ground—sets the depressing emotional tone in this version. The cross is moved to the center of the stage, and turned parallel to the picture plane. In this respect, and in its more forthright emotionality, THE DESCENT FROM THE CROSS [66] is very close to CHRIST ON THE CROSS [56]. These two pieces show us Rembrandt's personal vision of the Passion in these years. Comparing them with the commissioned pictures [64, 65], we can gauge just how much Rembrandt compromised this vision to please his patron.

66

67

67 THE RISEN CHRIST SHOWING HIS WOUND TO THE
APOSTLE THOMAS. 1634
Colorplate, page 37
Panel. 53 x 51 cm. (20¾ x 20 in.)
Moscow, Pushkin Museum
68 THE FLIGHT OF THE HOLY FAMILY INTO EGYPT. 1634 (?)
Panel. 20½ x 16¼ in.
London, Collection of Lord Wharton
a THE RISEN CHRIST AT EMMAUS. 1634
Etching. 10.2 x 7.2 cm. (4 x 2¾ in.)
London, British Museum

b CHRIST AND THE WOMAN OF SAMARIA. 1634
Etching (I). 12.1 x 10.6 cm. (4¾ x 4¼ in.)
Amsterdam, Rijksprentenkabinet
c THREE STUDIES FOR A DISCIPLE AT EMMAUS
Pen drawing. 17.4 x 16 cm. (6¾ x 6¼ in.)
Paris, Institut Néerlandais, F. Lugt Collection

68

a

b

c

69

69 SOPHONISBA RECEIVING THE POISONED CUP (?) 1634
Canvas. 142 x 153 cm. (56 x 60¼ in.)
Madrid, Prado

70 KING UZZIAH STRICKEN WITH LEPROSY. 1635
Colorplate, page 45
Panel. 40 x 30½ in.
Chatsworth, Derbyshire, Devonshire Collection

The subject of the secular scene—which we call secular only by elimination of the known biblical themes—has not been identified convincingly. The same was true of the biblical subject [70] until Dr. Robert Eisler (see the CATALOGUE) came up with a solution. The anguished figure is KING UZZIAH who, filled with vanity at his great successes, entered the temple on a festival day in the garb of a priest and tried to offer a sacrifice to God on the high altar, a function reserved for the priests. They tried to stop him, but Uzziah threatened them with death.

But, while he spoke, Flavius Josephus describes the scene, *a great tremor shook the earth, and, as the temple was riven, a brilliant shaft of sunlight gleamed through it and fell upon the king's face so that leprosy at once smote him.*

The flecks of white on Uzziah's face can be seen on the painting, though they are not easy to make out in reproductions.

70

71

71 SAINT JOHN THE BAPTIST PREACHING
Canvas laid down on panel. 62 x 80 cm. (24½ x 31½ in.)
Berlin-Dahlem, Gemaeldegalerie

72 CHRIST BEFORE PILATE AND THE PEOPLE. 1634
Paper stuck on canvas. 21 7/16 x 17½ in.
London, National Gallery

a CHRIST AND HIS DISCIPLES. 1634
Black and red chalk, pen, and wash drawing. 35.5 x 47.6 cm.
(14 x 18¾ in.)
Haarlem, Teyler Museum

b CHRIST BEFORE PILATE AND THE PEOPLE. 1635/6
Etching (III). 55 x 44.6 cm. (21¾ x 17½ in.)
Amsterdam, Rijksprentenkabinet

Painted in gray and brown, these exciting biblical scenes [71, 72] are preparatory sketches for etchings, of which only one was executed (Illustration b). The etchings may have been intended as companion pieces, to judge by the similar size and setting of the sketches in oil, and the scale of the figures. When Rembrandt decided not to etch JOHN THE BAPTIST, he pieced out the canvas on all sides, touched it up, and mounted it on panel to be sold as a finished painting.

a

72

b

a

73

b

73 THE ABDUCTION OF GANYMEDE. 1635
  Canvas. 171 x 130 cm. (67¼ x 51¼ in.)
  Dresden, Gemaeldegalerie

74 THE ANGEL STOPPING ABRAHAM FROM SACRIFICING
  ISAAC TO GOD. 1635
  Canvas. 193 x 133 cm. (76 x 52½ in.)
  Leningrad, Hermitage

a THE ANGEL STOPPING ABRAHAM FROM SACRIFICING
  ISAAC TO GOD
  Red and black chalk and wash drawing. 19.4 x 14.6 cm.
  (7¾ x 5¾ in.)
  London, British Museum

b THE ABDUCTION OF GANYMEDE
  Pen and wash drawing. 18.3 x 16 cm. (7¼ x 6¼ in.)
  Dresden, Kupferstichkabinett

The ABRAHAM is just as full of Baroque pathos, as boldly direct
in its depiction of physical detail, as THE ABDUCTION OF GANY-
MEDE of the same year. In none of Rembrandt's 16th-century
models for the ABRAHAM do the grasping hands of the angel and
the patriarch play so great a role. It would seem that Rembrandt
sought to convey the disruptive effect of divine interference—in
both stories—in terms of physical violence and fear.

74

75

a

A story from *The Book of Tobit* that Rembrandt painted once and drew a number of times is TOBIAS HEALING HIS FATHER'S BLINDNESS. Rembrandt dwells tenderly on the special intimacy between the men at the moment Tobias touches his father's eye. The motif seems to have fascinated Rembrandt—not surprising in a man to whom the sense of sight meant so much more than it does to ordinary people—for in the same year he gave expression to its dark side, in THE BLINDING OF SAMSON. Both paintings are intensely graphic—a Stuttgart physician even claims that Tobias is performing a creditable cataract removal—lending the one the gentleness of a carefully controlled daydream, the other the involuntary self-torture of a nightmare.

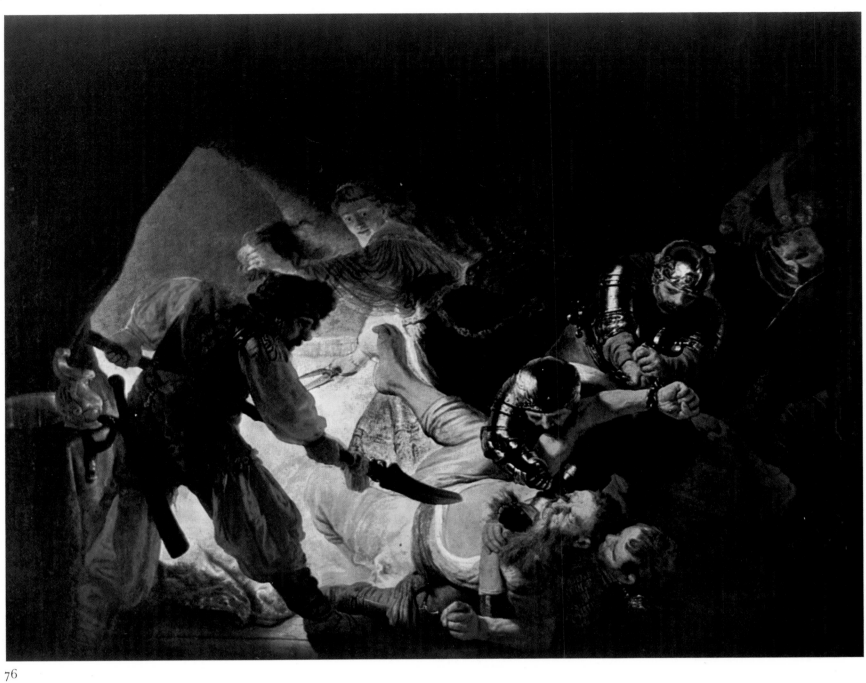

76

77

77 BELSHAZZAR SEES THE WRITING ON THE WALL
   Colorplate, page 41
   Canvas. 66 x 82⅜ in.
   London, National Gallery
78 SAMSON THREATENING HIS FATHER-IN-LAW. 163(5)
   Canvas. 156 x 129 cm. (61½ x 50¾ in.) Cut down
   Berlin-Dahlem, Gemaeldegalerie

Rembrandt's acquaintance with the great Jewish scholar Manas-seh ben Israel, whose portrait he etched in 1636, had conse-quences for his work. When Rembrandt painted BELSHAZZAR, Manasseh ben Israel was preparing a treatise on the subject, which was published in 1639. In it he suggests that Belshazzar's wise men were unable to read the writing on the wall because the words—cryptic even when read properly—were written from above to below rather than from right to left. Rembrandt adopted this theory in his BELSHAZZAR, which was painted, in all proba-bility, two or three years before the book was published.

78

a

b

79 THE PRODIGAL SON IN THE TAVERN
Canvas. 161 x 131 cm. (63¼ x 51½ in.)
Dresden, Gemaeldegalerie

a REMBRANDT AND SASKIA. 1636
Etching (I). 10.4 x 9.6 cm. (4 x 3¾ in.)
London, British Museum

b THE RETURN OF THE PRODIGAL SON. 1636
Etching. 15.6 x 13.6 cm. (6¼ x 5¼ in.)
Amsterdam, Rijksprentenkabinet

The portrait character of THE PRODIGAL SON still puzzles scholars. Emmens claims that it is irrelevant to the painting's message, but in doing so he ignores an important piece of evidence—
the etching (an undoubted double portrait) where Rembrandt
and Saskia face us in much the same manner as in the painting.
The contrast between the sober expressions of the couple in the
etching, where Rembrandt is shown busy at work, and the painting, with its many tokens of profligacy and extravagance, gives
us pause for thought: is the "old-fashioned" reading of the painting as Rembrandt's confession of the worldly side of his own nature so easy to dismiss? Bergström's interpretation of the picture
as THE PRODIGAL SON—a theme Rembrandt was thinking
about in 1636 (Illustration b)—underlines this reading.

79

a

80 THE ASCENSION OF CHRIST. 1636
   Canvas. 92.7 x 68.3 cm. (36½ x 27 in.)
   Munich, Alte Pinakothek
 a THE ANGEL APPEARING TO THE SHEPHERDS. 1634
   Etching (11). 26.2 x 21.9 cm. (10¼ x 8½ in.)
   Amsterdam, Rijksprentenkabinet

THE ASCENSION is the third scene of the Passion series for the Stadholder. It was probably begun immediately after the first two scenes [64, 65] were completed, in 1634, which would account for its close ties in conception and in many details to the etching of 1634 THE ANGEL APPEARING TO THE SHEPHERDS. Rembrandt seems to have experienced difficulties in finishing off the canvases for Frederick Henry. His two letters to Huygens must have been responses to tactful inquiries as to when the remaining pieces were to be delivered. Huygens shook Rembrandt into sending one piece along, but he was not to receive the last two for another three years.

81

81 THE ANGEL LEAVING TOBIAS AND HIS FAMILY. 1637
Panel. 68 x 52 cm. (26¾ x 20½ in.)
Paris, Louvre

82 THE RISEN CHRIST APPEARING TO MARY MAGDALENE.
1638
Panel. 24 x 19½ in.
London, Buckingham Palace, Royal Collection

83 THE PARABLE OF THE WORKERS IN THE VINEYARD.
1637
Panel. 31 x 42 cm. (12¼ x 16½ in.)
Leningrad, Hermitage

a THE ANGEL ASCENDING IN THE FLAMES OF MANOAH'S
SACRIFICE
Pen drawing. 17.5 x 19 cm. (7 x 7½ in.)
Berlin, Kupferstichkabinett

b THE ANGEL ASCENDING IN THE FLAMES OF MANOAH'S
SACRIFICE
Pen and wash drawing. 23.3 x 20.3 cm. (9¼ x 8 in.)
Stockholm, Nationalmuseum

a

b

82

83

84

84 SUSANNA SURPRISED BY THE ELDERS. 1637 (?)
   Panel. 47.5 x 39 cm. (18¾ x 15¼ in.)
   The Hague, Mauritshuis
85 SAMSON POSING THE RIDDLE TO THE WEDDING GUESTS.
   1638
   Canvas. 126 x 175 cm. (49½ x 69 in.)
   Dresden, Gemaeldegalerie

SAMSON POSING THE RIDDLE TO THE WEDDING GUESTS was
described admiringly by the Leyden painter Philips Angel in
1641:

In Rembrandt's WEDDING FEAST OF SAMSON *(Judges 10:14)
you can see how that keen mind observed, with deep thoughtfulness, the way
the guests would really have sat (rather—lay) at the table. The ancients,
you see, lay on little beds, rather than sitting at the table the way we do;
they reclined on their elbows, as is still the custom in the countries under the
Turks, and Rembrandt showed this very nicely.*

Angel's assumption that things in the 17th-century East were
not much changed from biblical times was probably shared by
Rembrandt—and his Orientals of the thirties are profitably compared with the auxiliary figures in such "archaeologically accurate" works as this.

85

b

a

86 JOSEPH RELATING HIS DREAMS
   Paper. 51 x 39 cm. (20 x 15¼ in.)
   Amsterdam, Rijksmuseum

a OLD MAN SEATED IN AN ARM-CHAIR. 1631
   Red and black chalk drawing. 22.5 x 14.5 cm. (8¾ x 5¾ in.)
   Haarlem, Teyler Museum

b JOSEPH RELATING HIS DREAMS. 1638
   Etching (11). 10.8 x 8.1 cm. (4¼ x 3¼ in.)
   Amsterdam, Rijksprentenkabinet

The grisaille oil sketch of JOSEPH RELATING HIS DREAMS is probably a preparatory study for the etching (Illustration b). Jacob is based on a drawing dated as long before as 1631.

86

87

87 THE ENTOMBMENT OF CHRIST
Canvas. 92.5 x 68.9 cm. (36½ x 27¼ in.)
Munich, Alte Pinakothek

88 THE RESURRECTION OF CHRIST. 163(9)
Canvas transferred to panel. 91.9 x 67 cm. (36¼ x 26½ in.)
Munich, Alte Pinakothek

After years of delay, Rembrandt delivered the last of the Passion series. Rembrandt and Frederick Henry may have momentarily seen eye to eye about the Rubensian Baroque in 1632, but in the seven years that had elapsed the painter's style and the prince's taste had grown away from each other. The official painting style had found its distinctive tone by 1639: a cooler classicism than that of Rubens, its stylistic and iconographic specifications prescribed by the courtly committee of experts, Huygens, Jacob van Campen, Pieter Post, Honthorst, and the Prince himself. The Passion series, on the other hand, had grown ever more "passionate." Rembrandt even excused himself for the delay by pointing out to Huygens that the extra time went into filling the figures with "the greatest and most natural *beweechgelickheijt*." Whether the last word means motion or emotion, the explanation must have seemed terribly out of date to Huygens. All the same, the courtiers knew a good painting when they saw one, and two more pieces were eventually ordered from Rembrandt.

88

a

b

89 THE LAMENTATION OVER THE DEAD CHRIST
   Paper and canvas stuck on panel. 12 9/16 x 10½ in.
   London, National Gallery
 a CALVARY
   Pen and wash drawing. 21.8 x 17.9 cm. (8½ x 7 in.)
   Berlin, Kupferstichkabinett
 b CALVARY
   Etching. 9.5 x 6.7 cm. (3¾ x 2¾ in.)
   Amsterdam, Rijksprentenkabinet

This grisaille version of THE LAMENTATION (the thieves and the rest of Calvary seem to have been added by Rembrandt later) bears much the same relation to THE ENTOMBMENT [87] as the Leningrand DESCENT FROM THE CROSS [66] to that in Munich [65]—both are by-products of the Passion series. Like the Leningrad DESCENT, THE LAMENTATION is more personal and less theatrical than its commissioned counterpart.

89

90

91

90 MINERVA
   Panel. 59 x 48 cm. (23¼ x 19 in.)
   Berlin-Dahlem, Gemaeldegalerie
91 SCHOLAR IN A ROOM WITH A WINDING STAIR.
   Panel. 29 x 33 cm. (11½ x 13 in.)
   Paris, Louvre
92 SASKIA AS FLORA. 1634
   Colorplate, page 43
   Canvas. 125 x 101 cm. (49¼ x 39¾ in.)
   Leningrad, Hermitage

Splendid figures like MINERVA, with her self-conscious brilliance, lead to the more mature FLORAS [92, 96] and the MINERVA of 1635 [94]. These three-quarter-length females of the mid-thirties (SOPHONISBA [69] may be included here) are grander in scale and less brash than the sharp young women, in full length, of 1632–3 [58, 90].

93

93 A SCHOLAR IN HIS STUDY. 1634
    Canvas. 141 x 135 cm. (55½ x 53¼ in.)
    Prague, Národní Gallery
94 MINERVA. 1635
    Canvas. 137 x 116 cm. (54 x 45¾ in.)
    London, Julius Weitzner
a   ESTHER PREPARING TO INTERCEDE WITH KING
    AHASUERUS
    Pen and wash drawing. 23.2 x 18.2 cm. (9 x 7¼ in.)
    Stockholm, Nationalmuseum

b   ESTHER PREPARING TO INTERCEDE WITH KING
    AHASUERUS ("THE GREAT JEWISH BRIDE"). 1635
    Etching (11). 22 x 16.8 cm. (8¾ x 6½ in.)
    Amsterdam, Rijksprentenkabinet

THE GREAT JEWISH BRIDE has been identified recently as Queen
Esther; but she is more closely related to this MINERVA than to
the ESTHER of 1633 [58]. Perhaps both women seemed alike to
Rembrandt in that they exemplify the virtues of wisdom and
courage. The similarities between A SCHOLAR IN HIS STUDY and
MINERVA are suggestive, but it would probably be going too far
to propose that they are companion pieces.

94

a

b

95

95 THE STANDARD BEARER. 1636
    Canvas. 125 x 105 cm. (49¼ x 41½ in.)
    Paris, Collection of Baron Elie de Rothschild
96 SASKIA AS FLORA. 1635
    Canvas. 48⅝ x 38¾ in.
    London, National Gallery

The paintings of SASKIA AS FLORA [92, 96] have more than the usual degree of ambiguity. Without diminishing the portrait character of the works at all, Rembrandt presents a complete image of the Roman goddess in her 17th-century guise. And Flora herself is an ambiguous creature—a goddess of flowers who is the patroness of prostitutes. Rembrandt posed Saskia as a prostitute in another painting of this period, THE PRODIGAL SON IN THE TAVERN [79]. Scholars have pointed out resemblances between Saskia and Samson's faithless wives: the bride from Timnath [85] and Delilah [76]. The stalwart STANDARD BEARER, on the other hand, bears a suspicious resemblance to Rembrandt himself. The personal meanings Rembrandt may have attached to these images of himself and Saskia remain a closed book to us.

96

97

a

b

97 SAINT FRANCIS AT PRAYER. 1637
   Panel. 23¼ x 18¾ in.
   Columbus, Ohio, Gallery of Fine Arts
98 CHILD WITH DEAD PEACOCKS
   Canvas. 145 x 135.5 cm. (57 x 53½ in.)
   Amsterdam, Rijksmuseum
a TWO STUDIES OF A BIRD OF PARADISE
   Pen and wash drawing. 18.1 x 15.4 cm. (7 x 6 in.)
   Paris, Louvre
b AN ELEPHANT. 1637
   Black chalk drawing. 23 x 34 cm. (9 x 13½ in.)
   Vienna, Albertina

Rembrandt never painted a straight still life, that we know of.
CHILD WITH DEAD PEACOCKS is sometimes called that, but
here the child pre-empts our interest. The "still life" changes its
meaning under her fascinated gaze. Once we have seen her, how
can we, any more than she, consider the dead birds as mere visual
display? We are bound to see them with her eyes, as extrava-
gantly beautiful creatures killed for some reason of which we are
ignorant. A feeling of tenderness for nature is also implied by the
choice of SAINT FRANCIS as a subject, and Rembrandt's debut as
a landscape painter in these years.

98

99

99 SELF-PORTRAIT. 1632
   Colorplate, page 35
   Panel. 25 x 18½ in.
   Glasgow, Art Gallery and Museum (on loan from the
   Burrell Collection)

100 DOCTOR NICOLAAS TULP DEMONSTRATING THE
   ANATOMY OF THE ARM. 1632
   Colorplate, page 51
   Canvas. 169.5 x 216.5 cm. (66¾ x 85¼ in.)
   The Hague, Mauritshuis

a SELF-PORTRAIT. 1631
   Etching (VII). 14.6 x 13 cm. (5¾ x 5 in.)
   Amsterdam, Rijksprentenkabinet

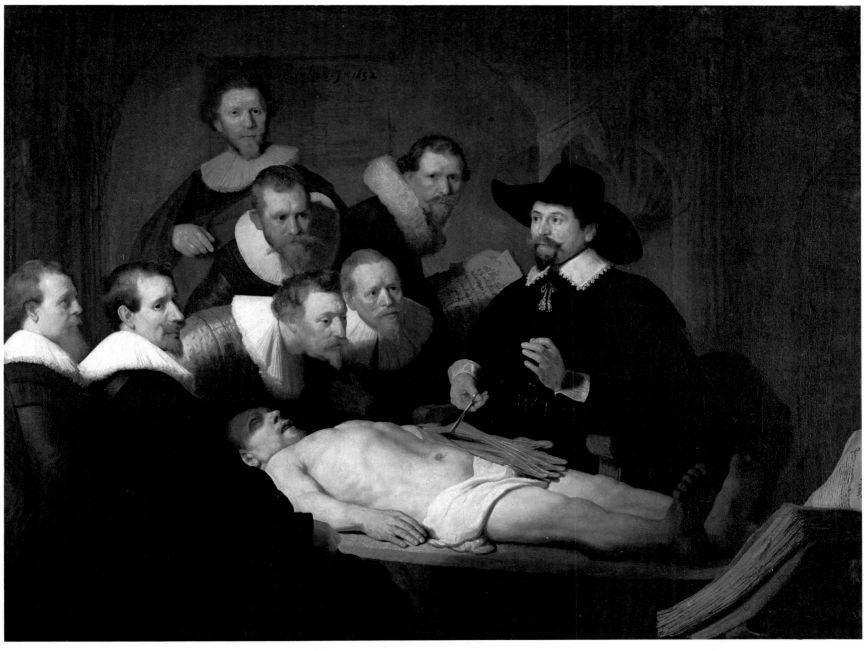

100

a

101

102

101 YOUNG MAN WITH A GOLD CHAIN. 1632
     Panel. $22\frac{3}{4}$ x $17\frac{1}{4}$ in.
     Cleveland, Ohio, Museum of Art
102 SAINT JOHN THE BAPTIST. 1632
     Panel. $25\frac{1}{2}$ x 19 in.
     Los Angeles, County Museum of Art
103 MAN IN FANCIFUL COSTUME ("THE NOBLE SLAV"). 1632
     Canvas. $60\frac{1}{8}$ x $43\frac{3}{4}$ in.
     New York, Metropolitan Museum of Art

Rembrandt's brilliant new portrait techniques now were at the service of his character studies as well. The old man last seen in Leyden as a humble OFFICER [49] is now decked out in Oriental splendor and posed with the bearing of an aristocrat to become "THE NOBLE SLAV." The smaller oval studies also gain new depth, emotional enrichment, and painterly refinement.

103

104

105

104 MAURITS HUYGENS, SECRETARY OF THE STATE
COUNCIL OF HOLLAND. 1632
Panel. 31.2 x 24.6 cm. (12¼ x 9¾ in.)
Hamburg, Kunsthalle

105 THE PAINTER JACOB DE GHEYN III. 1632
Panel. 11⅞ x 9⅞ in.
London, Dulwich College Gallery

106 YOUNG MAN IN A TURBAN. 1631
Panel. 25½ x 20 in.
Windsor Castle, Royal Collection

107 BALD-HEADED OLD MAN. 1632
Panel. 50 x 40.5 cm. (19¾ x 16 in.)
Cassel, Gemaeldegalerie

108 YOUNG MAN WITH A WIDE COLLAR. 1632
Panel. 63 x 46 cm. (24¾ x 18 in.)
Wanås, Sweden, Collection of Count Wachtmeister

109 BEARDED OLD MAN WITH A GOLD CHAIN. 1632
Panel. 59.3 x 49.3 cm. (23¼ x 19½ in.)
Cassel, Gemaeldegalerie

106

107

108

109

110

110 THE AMSTERDAM MERCHANT MARTEN LOOTEN. 1632
   Colorplate, page 53
   Panel. 36 x 29½ in.
   Los Angeles, County Museum of Art
111 YOUNG MAN SHARPENING A QUILL
   Canvas. 101.5 x 81.5 cm. (40 x 32 in.)
   Cassel, Gemaeldegalerie
112 AMALIA VAN SOLMS. 1632
   Canvas. 68.5 x 55.5 cm. (27 x 21¾ in.)
   Paris, Musée Jacquemart-André

113 YOUNG MAN WITH A BROAD COLLAR
   Canvas. 63.5 x 49.5 cm. (25 x 19½ in.)
   New York, Collection of Mr. T. Fleitman
114 YOUNG WOMAN IN A PEARL-TRIMMED BERET. 1632
   Canvas. 27 x 21 in.
   Zurich, Collection of Dr. A. Wiederkehr
115 YOUNG WOMAN WITH AN EMBROIDERED ROBE. 1632
   Panel. 22¾ x 16⅞ in.
   Boston, Museum of Fine Arts (on loan from Mrs. Richard
   C. Paine)

111

112

113

114

115

116

117

116 YOUNG WOMAN WITH A GOLDEN NECKLACE. 1632
    Panel. $25\frac{1}{8}$ x $19\frac{3}{8}$ in.
    Allentown, Pennsylvania, Art Museum
117 YOUNG WOMAN WITH AN EMBROIDERED ROBE. 1632
    Panel. 55 x 48 cm. ($21\frac{3}{4}$ x 19 in.)
    Milan, Brera
118 YOUNG WOMAN WITH A FAN. 1632
    Canvas. 72 x 54 cm. ($28\frac{1}{4}$ x $21\frac{1}{4}$ in.)
    Stockholm, Nationalmuseum

In Leyden Rembrandt had never painted the portrait of any woman but his mother. Now that he had become a fashionable portrait painter overnight (he was to paint the princess, AMALIA VAN SOLMS [112], before his first full year in Amsterdam was out), Rembrandt practiced painting the likenesses of a number of chic young women of his acquaintance [114–8]. The results are charming indeed, but from the first Rembrandt's portraits of women lack the animation and spontaneity of his men.

118

119

119 YOUNG MAN WITH A POINTED BEARD. 1632
    Colorplate, page 39
    Panel. 63.5 x 48 cm. (25 x 19 in.)
    Brunswick, Herzog Anton Ulrich Museum
120 PORTRAIT OF A MAN. 1632
    Canvas. 44 x 35 in.
    New York, Metropolitan Museum of Art
121 PORTRAIT OF A WOMAN. 1632
    Canvas. 44 x 35 in.
    New York, Metropolitan Museum of Art

122 A FORTY-YEAR-OLD MAN. 1632
    Panel. 29¾ x 20½ in.
    New York, Metropolitan Museum of Art
123 PORTRAIT OF A WOMAN. 1633
    Panel. 26¾ x 19¾ in.
    New York, Metropolitan Museum of Art

120

121

122

123

124

124 JORIS DE CAULLERY. 1632
   Canvas. $40\frac{1}{4}$ x 33 in.
   San Francisco, M. H. de Young Memorial Museum
125 AELBERT CUYPER. 1632
   Panel. 60 x 47 cm. ($23\frac{1}{2}$ x $18\frac{1}{2}$ in.)
   Paris, Louvre
126 CORNELIA PRONCK, WIFE OF AELBERT CUYPER. 1633
   Panel. 60 x 47 cm. ($23\frac{1}{2}$ x $18\frac{1}{2}$ in.)
   Paris, Louvre
127 OLD WOMAN IN A WHITE CAP. 1632
   Panel. 75 x 55.5 cm. ($29\frac{1}{2}$ x $21\frac{3}{4}$ in.)
   Paris, Private Collection

128 PORTRAIT OF A YOUNG WOMAN. 1632
   Canvas. 92 x 71 cm. ($36\frac{1}{4}$ x 28 in.)
   Vienna, Akademie der bildenden Kuenste

125

126

127

128

129

129 SELF-PORTRAIT. 1633
    Panel. 58 x 45 cm. (22¾ x 17¾ in.)
    Paris, Louvre
130 PORTRAIT OF A FASHIONABLE COUPLE. 1633
    Canvas. 51¾ x 42 in.
    Boston, Isabella Stewart Gardner Museum

Wall maps often serve an expressive function in Dutch interior paintings and portraits. In Vermeer's interiors with letter-reading women, the map hints at husbands voyaging far from home, but it also implies a contrast between the cozy enclosed interior and the endless space outside it. Rembrandt's interior is strangely uncozy. It does not evoke the sense of comfortable at-homeness that is the ideal of the Dutch household. In its bareness, and in the tense poses of its inhabitants, it seems like a corridor or waiting-room. The rich costumes and fascinating faces of the people contrast with the emptiness of their environment—including the not very decorative map, which suggests continuity, not contrast, between the indoors and out. Holding their capes and gloves, the couple too form a link between the outer world and the inner.

130

131

a

131 RICHLY DRESSED YOUNG BOY
 Panel. 67 x 47.5 cm. (26½ x 18¾ in.)
 Leningrad, Hermitage
132 SASKIA WITH A VEIL. 1633
 Colorplate, page 55
 Panel. 66.5 x 49.7 cm. (26¼ x 19½ in.)
 Amsterdam, Rijksmuseum
 a SASKIA. 1633
 Silverpoint drawing on vellum. 18.5 x 10.7 cm. (7¼ x 4¼ in.)
 Berlin-Dahlem, Kupferstichkabinett

The technique of Rembrandt's delicate drawing of Saskia enhances its preciousness and sense of intimacy. Drawing with a silver needle (and chalk) on prepared vellum was anything but a casual procedure. But even this drawing has a freer touch than the portraits of young women of 1632 [116–8]. The painted portrait is all the more direct. The fussy details of embroidery and jewelry in the earlier paintings were static, competing with the shy faces behind them for attention. The corresponding details in SASKIA WITH A VEIL only add brilliance to Saskia's bold gaze.

133

133 SELF-PORTRAIT
   Panel. 55 x 46 cm. (21¾ x 18 in.)
   Berlin-Dahlem, Gemaeldegalerie
134 SASKIA. 1633
   Panel. 52.5 x 44.5 cm. (20¾ x 17½ in.)
   Dresden, Gemaeldegalerie

These charming paintings are here reproduced as companion pieces for the first time. Their many similarities—in pose, dress (Rembrandt and Saskia wear the same hat), mood and, not least, size—make it at least possible that they were intended as pendants, perhaps as engagement portraits. The vigorous tech-nique of the SELF-PORTRAIT harks back to the rough examples of 1629 [30, 32], while the SASKIA is thin and gingerly.

Rembrandt's patrons were merchants, theologians, doctors, poets—everyone but soldiers, who preferred to have their portraits painted by masters with a more sensitive eye for such details as decorations and the sheen of polished gold. Yet Rembrandt delighted in painting himself in armor, at least in the thirties. Sometimes this adds dash to his appearance, and other times it has quite the opposite effect [157].

134

135

136

135 BEARDED OLD MAN WITH A CAP. 1633
   Panel. 65 x 42 cm. (25½ x 16½ in.)
   Metz, Musée
136 OLD MAN. 1633
   Panel. 9.5 x 6.5 cm. (3¾ x 2½ in.)
   New York, Collection of Mr. Arthur A. Houghton, Jr.
137 THE PREACHER JOHANNES UYTTENBOGAERT. 1633
   Canvas. 52 x 40¼ in.
   Mentmore, Buckinghamshire, Collection of the Earl of
   Rosebery

Johannes Uyttenbogaert was the leader of one of Holland's em-
battled religious minorities, the Remonstrants. He played a
central role in the great struggles of the 1610's, which led to the
condemnation of his party at the Synod of Dort in 1618. At the
age of 76, he was the great pleader for religious tolerance in
Holland. Constantijn Huygens, who knew both men, said that
the greatest preachers of his day were Uyttenbogaert and John
Donne.

Uyttenbogaert recorded in his diary on April 13, 1633: "Painted by Rembrandt for Abraham Anthonisz." Apparently Uyttenbogaert sat for Rembrandt as a favor to this friend, who
wanted to own a portrait of him.

137

138

138 THE POET JAN HERMANSZ. KRUL. 1633
       Colorplate, page 57
       Canvas. 128.5 x 100.5 cm. (50½ x 39½ in.)
       Cassel, Gemaeldegalerie
139 "THE SHIPBUILDER AND HIS WIFE." 1633
       Canvas. 45 x 66½ in.
       London, Buckingham Palace, Royal Collection
140 MAN RISING FROM A CHAIR. 1633
       Canvas. 49 x 39½ in.
       Cincinnati, Taft Museum

141 YOUNG WOMAN WITH A FAN. 1633
       Canvas. 49½ x 39¾ in.
       New York, Metropolitan Museum of Art

The portraits of the 1630's often seem to have programs. Why does Jan Krul have himself painted in an archway? Why is the young man rising from his chair and gesturing toward his spouse? What is the message being handed to the busy shipwright? More work will have to be done on the iconography of 17th-century portraits before we can answer these questions.

139

140

141

142

142 SELF-PORTRAIT. 163(4)
Panel. 68 x 53 cm. (26¾ x 21 in.)
Paris, Louvre

143 YOUNG WOMAN WITH A GOLD CHAIN. 1633
Canvas. 62 x 55.5 cm. (24½ x 21¾ in.)
South America, Private Collection

144 SELF-PORTRAIT
Panel. 67 x 54 cm. (26½ x 21¼ in.)
Florence, Uffizi

145 RICHLY DRESSED CHILD. 1633
Panel. 44 x 33 cm. (17¼ x 13 in.)
France, Private Collection

146 WOMAN WITH A LACE COLLAR. 1633
Panel. 25 x 19 in.
Santa Barbara, California, Collection of Mr. C. M. Converse

143

144

145

146

147   148

149

150

151

152

153

Vinken and de Jongh rightly object to the sort of criticism that reads the character of sitters out of their portraits, on the basis of personal reaction. Communication by facial expression is not so much a language as an infinite number of related dialects, one for each person. But art cannot deal with the human face in all its complexity; there arose rules, in the Renaissance, for showing emotions and personal characteristics through physiognomy—and these systems have to be taken into account in the study of 16th- and 17th-century portraits. Until we understand the meaning of conventional gestures and poses, clothing and accessories, as well as facial expressions, we cannot know whether 17th-century portraits, including those of Rembrandt, were intended as descriptions of character or not.

154

155   156

157

158

159

160

161

162

162 THE PREACHER JOHANNES ELISON. 1634
  Canvas. 68¼ x 48⅞ in.
  Boston, Museum of Fine Arts
163 MARIA BOCKENOLLE, WIFE OF JOHANNES ELISON. 1634
  Canvas. 68¾ x 48⅞ in.
  Boston, Museum of Fine Arts

Two pairs of life-size portraits of a husband and wife [162–3, 164–5] illustrate two of the possibilities for grand full-length portraits in 1634. JOHANNES ELISON, a minister in the Church of England, is shown with his wife, seated, soberly dressed, gesturing with restraint and earnestness. Like JOHANNES UYT-

TENBOGAERT [137] in the portrait of the year before, the preacher holds his hand over his heart (in token of his faith?). The 21-year-old MAERTEN SOOLMANS and his bride make quite another impression. He was surely the most foppish of Rembrandt's sitters. Rembrandt did not grudge Soolmans a worthy display of his extravagant wardrobe: the result is a portrait where the remarkable lace ruffles at the young man's knees and on his shoes compete successfully for our attention with his bland face. Even with the perspective effect of the tiled floor (with a separate vanishing point for each spouse), MAERTEN SOOLMANS and OOPJEN COPPIT are placed in their surroundings less convincingly than the Elisons, with their neutral backdrop.

163

164

165

164 MAERTEN SOOLMANS. 1634
   Canvas. 209.8 x 134.8 cm. (82½ x 53 in.)
   Paris, Private Collection
165 OOPJEN COPPIT, WIFE OF MAERTEN SOOLMANS
   Canvas. 209.4 x 134.3 cm. (82¼ x 52¾ in.)
   Paris, Private Collection
166 YOUNG MAN WITH MOUSTACHE. 1634
   Panel. 70 x 52 cm. (27½ x 20½ in.)
   Leningrad, Hermitage

167 YOUNG WOMAN WITH FLOWERS IN HER HAIR. 1634
   Panel. 28 x 21 in.
   Edinburgh, National Gallery of Scotland (on loan from
   the Duke of Sutherland)
168 MAN OF THE RAMAN FAMILY. 1634
   Panel. 67 x 52 cm. (26¼ x 20½ in.)
   Wassenaar, Holland, Collection of Mr. H. Kohn
169 WOMAN OF THE RAMAN FAMILY. 1636
   Panel. 27 x 21 in.
   Rossie Priory, Perthshire, Collection of Lord Kinnaird

166

167

168

169

170

170 MAN IN ORIENTAL COSTUME. 1635
Panel. 72 x 54.5 cm. (28¼ x 21½ in.)
Amsterdam, Rijksmuseum
171 SELF-PORTRAIT. 1635
Panel. 92 x 72 cm. (36¼ x 28¼ in.)
Formerly Vaduz, Collection of the Prince of Liechtenstein
172 MAN IN FANCIFUL COSTUME. 1635
Panel. 70 x 61 cm. (27½ x 24 in.)
Hampton Court Palace, Royal Collection
173 MAN WITH DISHEVELED HAIR. 1635
Panel. 26¼ x 20¾ in.
New York, Acquavella Galleries

a SELF-PORTRAIT. 1634
Etching (II). 12.4 x 10.2 cm. (5 x 4 in.)
Amsterdam, Rijksprentenkabinet

The mass of commissioned portraits accounts for nearly all the portraits and studies of the first Amsterdam years. Not until 1634–5 did Rembrandt again begin to paint studio models in costume. At the same time his self-portraits regain their exotic flavor. In 1632–3 Rembrandt compared himself with his fashionable patrons; in 1634–5 with the characters created by his imagination.

171

a

172

173

174

a

174 SASKIA
Panel. 23¾ x 19¼ in.
Washington, D.C., National Gallery of Art
175 SASKIA
Colorplate, page 61
Panel. 99.5 x 78.8 cm. (39¼ x 31 in.)
Cassel, Gemaeldegalerie
a SASKIA. 1634
Etching. 8.6 x 6.6 cm. (3¾ x 2½ in.)
Amsterdam, Rijksprentenkabinet

In Saskia's ambivalent pose [175], her body is turned toward us, but her face is flattened against the background into an ideal profile. The remoteness of her profile and the decorative richness of her garment contrast with the sensuous colors of her dress and the suppressed liveliness of her expression.

Like the self-portraits, Rembrandt's portraits of Saskia are experimental applications of his changing ideas of portraiture rather than records of physical appearance. The belle dame sans merci of the portraits of 1635 [175, 184] is more like an impersonal image of femininity than the woman who confronts us so candidly in the other portraits—not nearly so devastating, and likewise not so forbidding.

175

176

177

176 JAN PELLICORNE AND HIS SON, CASPAR
   Canvas. 61 x 48¼ in.
   London, Wallace Collection

177 SUSANNA VAN COLLEN, WIFE OF JAN PELLICORNE, AND
   HER DAUGHTER, EVA SUSANNA
   Canvas. 61 x 48¼ in.
   London, Wallace Collection

178 PHILIPS LUCASZ., COUNCILLOR OF THE DUTCH EAST
   INDIA COMPANY. 1635
   Colorplate, page 67
   Panel. 31 5/16 x 23 3/16 in.
   London, National Gallery

179 PETRONELLA BUYS, WIFE OF PHILIPS LUCASZ. 1635
   Panel. 29⅞ x 22⅞ in.
   New York, Collection of Mr. André Meyer

180 MAN IN A WIDE-BRIMMED HAT. 1635
   Canvas transferred to panel. 30½ x 25½ in.
   Indianapolis, Collection of Mr. Earl C. Townsend, Jr.

181 PORTRAIT OF A YOUNG WOMAN. 1635
   Panel. 30½ x 25½ in.
   Cleveland, Museum of Art

178

179

180

181

182

182 MAN IN ORIENTAL COSTUME
   Canvas. $38\frac{3}{4}$ x $29\frac{1}{8}$ in.
   Washington, D.C., National Gallery of Art

183 THE DIPLOMAT ANTHONIS COOPAL. 1635
   Panel. 83 x 67 cm. ($32\frac{3}{4}$ x $26\frac{1}{2}$ in.)
   Greenwich, Connecticut, Neumann de Vegvar Collection

184 SASKIA IN FANCY COSTUME. 163(5)
   Panel. 98 x 70 cm. ($38\frac{1}{2}$ x $27\frac{1}{2}$ in.)
   Switzerland, Private Collection

185 A 70-YEAR-OLD WOMAN SEATED IN AN ARMCHAIR.
   1635 (?)
   Canvas. $50\frac{3}{8}$ x $39\frac{1}{8}$ in.
   New York, Metropolitan Museum of Art

a SELF-PORTRAIT (?) 1634
   Etching (I). 19.7 x 16.2 cm. ($7\frac{3}{4}$ x $6\frac{1}{4}$ in.)
   Amsterdam, Rijksprentenkabinet

183

184

a

185

186

We sometimes suspect that Rembrandt's portraits—even his most stately commissioned works—are filled with unexpressed feelings. Noting the resemblance of the old preacher [187] to the ABRAHAM of the etching (Illustration a), we sense a patriarchal love and anxiety for his descendants in the grave look of the minister. But when we take the etching away, we are left with the portrait of a quiet and reserved old man who does not invite us to share his thoughts.

a

b

189

189 SELF-PORTRAIT (?)
Panel. 62.5 x 47 cm. (24½ x 18½ in.)
The Hague, Mauritshuis
190 REMBRANDT'S MOTHER. 1639
Panel. 79.5 x 61.7 cm. (31¼ x 24¼ in.)
Vienna, Kunsthistorisches Museum

191

191 SELF-PORTRAIT WITH A DEAD BITTERN. 1639
    Panel. 121 x 89 cm. (47½ x 35 in.)
    Dresden, Gemaeldegalerie
192 MAN STANDING IN FRONT OF A DOORWAY. 1639
    Canvas. 200 x 124.2 cm. (78¾ x 49 in.)
    Cassel, Gemaeldegalerie

The SELF-PORTRAIT WITH A DEAD BITTERN was done in the same years as CHILD WITH DEAD PEACOCKS [98]. Rembrandt does not decline to demonstrate his virtuosity in reproducing the various colors and textures of avian plumage, but the birds serve a larger function than mere visual display: they are related to a figure, in this case to Rembrandt himself. He raises the bird to hang it on the hook of a gallowslike post bearing his signature. An approach to the interpretation of the painting might begin with the speculation that it reflects the relation between art and nature: the artist captures animate beauty and decorates the shingle of his fame with its remains.

MAN STANDING IN FRONT OF A DOORWAY is a life-size full-length portrait. We do not know who the man is who has thrown down his gauntlet, nor to whom his challenging gesture and gaze are addressed.

192

193

a

193 ALOTTE ADRIAENSDR. 1639
Panel. 64.7 x 55.3 cm. (25½ x 21¾ in.)
Rotterdam, Willem van der Vorm Foundation

194 MARIA TRIP, DAUGHTER OF ALOTTE ADRIAENSDR. 1639
Panel. 107 x 82 cm. (42 x 32¼ in.)
Amsterdam, Rijksmuseum (on loan from the van Weede Family Foundation)

 a MARIA TRIP
Pen, wash, and red chalk drawing. 16 x 12.9 cm. (6¼ x 5 in.)
London, British Museum

Portrait commissions by a family could lead to unrelated individual portraits such as those of ALOTTE ADRIAENSDR. and MARIA TRIP or to closely integrated pictures of families such as the pendants JAN PELLICORNE AND HIS SON, CASPAR and SUSANNA VAN COLLEN AND HER DAUGHTER, EVA SUSANNA [176–7]. The money changing hands probably refers to the gifts the parents hope to bestow on their children: the boy receives a full money-bag, the fortune of his father, and the girl a single coin, no doubt a "trouwpenningh" (marriage coin), standing for the dowry that will bring her a good husband.

304

194

195

195 LANDSCAPE WITH THE BAPTISM OF THE EUNUCH. 1636
Canvas. 85.5 x 108 cm. (33¾ x 42½ in.)
Hanover, Niedersaechsisches Landesmuseum (on loan)

196 LANDSCAPE WITH A STONE BRIDGE
Panel. 29.5 x 42.5 cm. (11½ x 16¾ in.)
Amsterdam, Rijksmuseum

197 STORMY LANDSCAPE WITH AN ARCHED BRIDGE
Panel. 28 x 40 cm. (11 x 15¾ in.)
Berlin-Dahlem, Gemaeldegalerie

Rembrandt's contribution to Dutch landscape painting is small
but superb. He never dabbled in branches of painting that he
could not practice with total mastery: architectural painting and
still life he left to the specialists. In fact, no non-specialist seemed
equal to producing good paintings in these genres, while Rembrandt's early landscapes can only be compared to the most advanced works of Salomon van Ruisdael and Jan van Goyen.
Still, Rembrandt's starting point was different from that of these
specialists. They were committed to modern Dutch naturalism,
however rich in feeling their work may be, while to Rembrandt,
the history painter and student of the 16th century, problems of
expression always precede the motif.

196

197

198

199

200

201

1640-1649

1648. January 24: Geertje Dircx makes her testament, leaving all her property but 100 guilders and her portrait to Titus. Geertje apparently joined Rembrandt's household some years before this date as Titus' nurse, soon to become Rembrandt's mistress as well. Her testament speaks eloquently of her affection for them both.

1649. Hendrickje Stoffels seems to have replaced Geertje Dircx in Rembrandt's affections early in this year, while Geertje was still living in the house on St. Anthonisbreestraat. The ensuing difficulties made life painful for all concerned for a period of years. Geertje was not one to surrender her prerogatives easily, and she sued Rembrandt for breach of promise. The court was not sympathetic: Rembrandt was not required to marry her, while Geertje was enjoined from changing her will in favor of Titus. (Rembrandt was worried that Saskia's jewels, which he had given to Geertje, would be lost to him forever.) She was awarded an annual alimony of 200 guilders, an amount Rembrandt would earn from two portrait commissions. There are, however, no portraits—or any paintings at all, for that matter—dated in 1649.

202

a

1640–1649: HISTORY PAINTINGS

202 THE DEPARTURE OF THE SHUNAMITE WIFE. 1640
Colorplate, page 85
Panel. 39 x 53 cm. (15¼ x 21 in.)
London, Victoria and Albert Museum

203 THE MEETING OF MARY AND ELIZABETH (THE
VISITATION). 1640
Panel. 22¼ x 18⅞ in.
Detroit, Institute of Arts

a THE TRIUMPH OF MORDECAI
Etching. 17.4 x 21.5 cm. (6¾ x 8½ in.)
London, British Museum

203

204

204 THE ANGEL ASCENDING IN THE FLAMES OF MANOAH'S
    SACRIFICE. 1641
    Canvas. 242 x 283 cm. (95¼ x 111¼ in.)
    Dresden, Gemaeldegalerie
205 THE HOLY FAMILY. 1640
    Panel. 41 x 34 cm. (16 x 13½ in.)
    Paris, Louvre

205

206

206 "DE EENDRAGT VAN 'T LANT" (THE CONCORD OF THE
STATE). 1641
Colorplate, page 75
Panel. 74.6 x 101 cm. (29½ x 39¾ in.)
Rotterdam, Museum Boymans-van Beuningen
207 THE RECONCILIATION OF DAVID AND ABSALOM. 1642
Colorplate, page 81
Panel. 73 x 61.5 cm. (28¾ x 24¼ in.)
Leningrad, Hermitage

Though "concord" is intended, the general impression of the
action in THE CONCORD OF THE STATE is anything but unified.
In fact, while one procession is already marching off toward the
left, the group in the right foreground, though mounting up,
seems undecided: the captain and the colors both face right. This
is very different from THE NIGHT WATCH [239], which has a
distinct forward accent (much stronger before the painting was
cut down). There are other ambiguities in the details of THE
CONCORD OF THE STATE for which no suitable explanation is
known. Fortunately, knowing the title Rembrandt gave to the
painting keeps speculation as to its meaning within bounds: all
interpretations must take it into account.

207

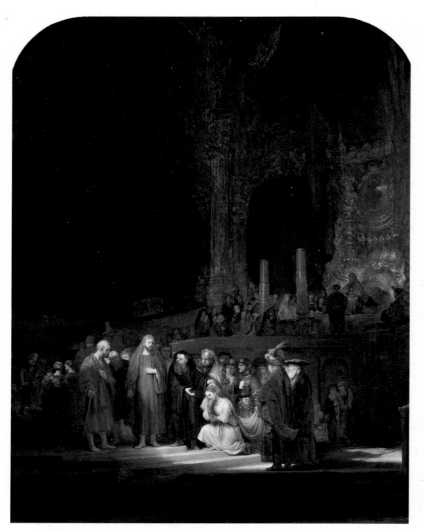

208

a

The light in the two small biblical pictures of 1645 has a more complicated relation to space and figures than formerly, following laws of its own, touching everywhere, dissolving surfaces here, resolving lines of construction there. As a result, the interior space has a new warmth, the figures a new gentleness, and the whole picture a satisfying wholeness. CHRIST AND THE WOMAN TAKEN IN ADULTERY shows many of the same features when compared to THE PRESENTATION [17] of 1631.

209

210

211

212

a

213

214

215

The tenderly illuminated interior space first encountered in the small paintings of 1645 [209, 210] becomes the scene of monumental compositions in these pictures of the following year. Light itself forms the structural and thematic framework of the paintings: space becomes dense and measurable only in the bright areas, losing its very ability to receive forms in the shadows. The action is defined in terms not of figures but of areas of light that bind together fragments of figures into whole images, leaving the individual actors further undefined. Comparison with THE ENTOMBMENT [217] of the previous decade underlines these qualities, which were seldom again applied so consistently as in these experimental examples.

216

217

218

218 THE RISEN CHRIST AT EMMAUS. 1648
Colorplate, page 87
Panel. 68 x 65 cm. (26¾ x 25½ in.)
Paris, Louvre

219 THE RISEN CHRIST AT EMMAUS. 1648
Canvas. 89.5 x 111.5 cm. (35¼ x 44 in.)
Copenhagen, The Royal Museum of Fine Arts

220 THE REST ON THE FLIGHT INTO EGYPT. 1647
Panel. 34 x 48 cm. (13½ x 19 in.)
Dublin, National Gallery of Ireland

219

220

221

221 SUSANNA SURPRISED BY THE ELDERS. 1647
Panel. 76 x 91 cm. (30 x 35¾ in.)
Berlin-Dahlem, Gemaeldegalerie
222 BIBLICAL FIGURE. 1643
Panel. 70.5 x 53.5 cm. (27¾ x 21 in.)
Budapest, Museum of Fine Arts
223 HANNAH IN THE TEMPLE AT JERUSALEM. 16(50)
Panel. 16 x 12½ in.
Edinburgh, National Gallery of Scotland (on loan from
the Duke of Sutherland)

a SUSANNA SURPRISED BY THE ELDERS
Red chalk drawing. 23.5 x 36.4 cm. (9¼ x 14¼ in.)
Berlin-Dahlem, Kupferstichkabinett

The drawing, after Lastman's SUSANNA (Illustration, page 94),
was the starting point for Rembrandt's SUSANNA of 1647.

a

222

223

224

225

224 YOUNG GIRL. 1641
    Panel. 104 x 76 cm. (41 x 30 in.)
    Formerly Vienna, Collection of Count Lanckoronski
225 A SCHOLAR AT HIS DESK. 1641
    Panel. 104 x 76 cm. (41 x 30 in.)
    Formerly Vienna, Collection of Count Lanckoronski
226 SASKIA WITH A FLOWER. 1641
    Panel. 98.5 x 82.5 cm. (38¾ x 32½ in.)
    Dresden, Gemaeldegalerie

The combination of old men and young girls has a long history in northern art. The couple is usually related in the obvious way: she is making a fool of him. This does not seem to be the case with Rembrandt's pendants. The old man is not aflame with desire, nor the girl with cupidity. Judging from the writer's reflective gaze, we might guess that she is his muse, the genius of his inspiration.

The last portrait of Saskia before her death has a straightforward warmth that reminds us more of the engagement drawing (Illustration a, p. 270) than of any of the intervening portraits.

226

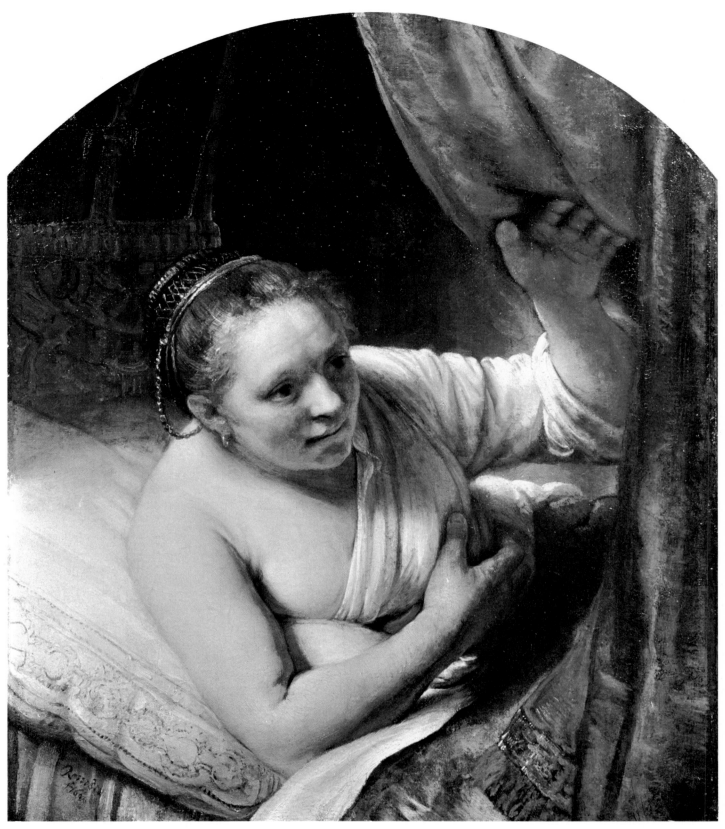

227

227 HENDRICKJE IN BED
   Canvas. 32 x 26½ in.
   Edinburgh, National Gallery of Scotland
228 YOUNG GIRL LEANING IN A WINDOWSILL. 1645
   Canvas. 32⅛ x 26 in.
   London, Dulwich College Gallery

HENDRICKJE IN BED goes back to a figure by Pieter Lastman of
SARAH AWAITING TOBIAS ON THEIR WEDDING NIGHT (Boston, Museum of Fine Arts). Sarah had been married seven times
before, but each time her husband had been destroyed by the
devil Asmodeus on the wedding night before the marriage could

be consummated. Sarah watches in wonder and increasing joy
as Tobias burns ash of perfume and the innards of a fish, and the
angel Raphael appears to despatch Asmodeus. Tobias and Sarah
spend the rest of the night in prayer, and she is finally freed from
her curse.

Ferdinand Bol illustrated this story (Brunswick, Herzog Anton
Ulrich Museum), using Rembrandt's figure of DANAE [270] for
Sarah. Rembrandt's HENDRICKJE IN BED and DANAE are both
closely related in mood and expression as well as pose to the
representations of Sarah by Lastman and Bol and may well be
Sarahs themselves.

228

229

229 SELF-PORTRAIT
Panel. 62.5 x 50 cm. (24½ x 19¾ in.)
Liverpool, Walker Art Gallery (on loan from Lieut.-Col.
A. Heywood-Lonsdale)

230 THE FRAMEMAKER HERMAN DOOMER. 1640
Panel. 29⅝ x 21¾ in.
New York, Metropolitan Museum of Art

231 BAARTJEN MARTENS, WIFE OF HERMAN DOOMER
Panel. 76 x 56 cm. (30 x 22 in.)
Leningrad, Hermitage

232 NICOLAAS VAN BAMBEECK. 1641
Colorplate, page 82
Canvas. 105.5 x 84 cm. (41½ x 33 in.)
Brussels, Musée Royal des Beaux-Arts

233 AGATHA BAS, WIFE OF NICOLAAS VAN BAMBEECK. 1641
Colorplate, page 83
Canvas. 41½ x 33 in.
London, Buckingham Palace, Royal Collection

230

231

232

233

a

234 THE MENNONITE MINISTER CORNELIS CLAESZ. ANSLO
   IN CONVERSATION WITH A WOMAN. 1641
   Canvas. 176 x 210 cm. (69¼ x 82¾ in.)
   Berlin-Dahlem, Gemaeldegalerie

235 ANNA WIJMER (?) 1641
   Panel. 96 x 80 cm. (37¾ x 31½ in.)
   Amsterdam, Six Foundation

 a CORNELIS CLAESZ. ANSLO. 1640
   Red chalk, pen, and wash drawing. 24.6 x 20.1 cm.
   (9¾ x 8 in.)
   Paris, Louvre

 b CORNELIS CLAESZ. ANSLO. 1641
   Etching (11). 18.6 x 15.7 cm. (7¼ x 6¼ in.)
   Amsterdam, Rijksprentenkabinet

THE MENNONITE MINISTER CORNELIS CLAESZ. ANSLO IN
CONVERSATION WITH A WOMAN is Rembrandt's reply to the
challenge of Vondel to "paint Cornelis' voice," in a rhyme on the
somewhat earlier etching (Illustration b). Given the context, we
perceive an attempt in the painting to render a man engaged in
persuasive speech. But Anslo's gesture is no more rhetorical than
that of the SEATED MAN [153] in Vienna. Is he, too, speaking, to
his attentive wife [154]?

234

235

b

335

237

236

236 SELF-PORTRAIT
   Canvas. 37 x 29¼ in.
   Ottawa, National Gallery of Canada
237 SELF-PORTRAIT
   Panel. 25 x 19⅜ in.
   London, Wallace Collection
238 SELF-PORTRAIT. 1640
   Colorplate, page 89
   Canvas. 40⅛ x 31½ in.
   London, National Gallery

In the SELF-PORTRAITS of around 1640 [229, 236–8] Rembrandt regains a certain aloof dignity. He preens his self-image to an even greater extent than any of his paying patrons dared to request in those days. In his search for an appropriate mode of self-portraiture—a problem he alone in Holland considered vital—Rembrandt turns to 16th-century Italian models, notably Titian's "ARIOSTO," possibly considered by Rembrandt a self-portrait. Rembrandt cannot match Titian in unembarrassed self-glorification. A sense of personal reserve tempers the candor of physical observation and the freedom of fantasy.

238

239

239 THE MILITIA COMPANY OF CAPTAIN FRANS BANNING
COCQ ("THE NIGHT WATCH"). 1642. Cut down
Colorplate, page 73
Canvas. 363 x 437 cm. (143 x 172 in.)
Amsterdam, Rijksmuseum
a Detail of 239

a

240

241

240 SELF-PORTRAIT
   Panel. 28½ x 23 in.
   Boston, Museum of Fine Arts (on loan)

241 SASKIA (POSTHUMOUS PORTRAIT). 1643
   Panel. 72 x 59 cm. (28¼ x 23¼ in.)
   Berlin-Dahlem, Gemaeldegalerie

242 OLD MAN WITH A BERET
   Panel. 51 x 42 cm. (20 x 16½ in.) Originally 18½ x 14½ in.
   Leningrad, Hermitage

243 AN OLD MAN IN RICH COSTUME. 1643
   Panel. 29 x 23½ in.
   Woburn Abbey, Collection of the Duke of Bedford

244 YOUNG MAN HOLDING A SWORD. 1644
   Canvas. 40½ x 34 in.
   Brunswick, Maine, Bowdoin College Museum of Art (on
   loan from Eunice, Lady Oakes)

245 MAN HOLDING A GLOVE
   Panel. 31¾ x 26½ in.
   New York, Metropolitan Museum of Art

242

243

244

245

246

246 MAN STANDING IN A DOORWAY
    Canvas. 41 x 30 in.
    Tisbury, Wiltshire, Collection of Lord Margadale
247 OLD MAN WITH A STICK. 1645
    Canvas. 128.2 x 112.1 cm. (50½ x 43¾ in.)
    Oeiras, Portugal, Calouste Gulbenkian Foundation
248 YOUNG WOMAN AT A DOOR. 1645
    Canvas. 40⅛ x 33⅛ in.
    Chicago, Art Institute
249 WOMAN SEATED IN AN ARMCHAIR. 1644
    Canvas. 49 x 39½ in.
    Toronto, Art Gallery of Ontario

The portraits and studies of the mid-forties are less forceful and expressive than those of the late thirties (compare MAN STANDING IN FRONT OF A DOORWAY [192] with the present man's portrait), but more mellow in lighting and warmer in their approach to the sitter.

247

248

249

250

250 THE ART DEALER CLEMENT DE JONGHE (?)
   Canvas. 37 x 29 in.
   Buscot Park, Berkshire, Faringdon Collection
251 THE PAINTER HENDRICK MARTENSZ. SORGH. 164(7)
   Colorplate, page 79
   Panel. 74 x 67 cm. (29¼ x 26½ in.)
   London, Westminster Collection
252 ARIAENTJE HOLLAER, WIFE OF HENDRICK MARTENSZ.
   SORGH. 1647 (?)
   Panel. 74 x 67 cm. (29¼ x 26½ in.)
   London, Westminster Collection

253 SELF-PORTRAIT
   Panel. 67.5 x 57.5 cm. (26½ x 22½ in.)
   Windsor Castle, Royal Collection
254 OLD MAN IN A FUR-LINED COAT. 1645
   Canvas. 110 x 82 cm. (43¼ x 32¼ in.)
   Berlin-Dahlem, Gemaeldegalerie

251

252

253

254

255

256

346

257

258

259

260

261

262

a

b

263

264

a

b

1640–1649: LANDSCAPES

265 LANDSCAPE WITH A CHURCH
   Panel. 42 x 60 cm. (16½ x 23½ in.)
   Madrid, Collection of the Duke of Berwick and Alba
266 LANDSCAPE WITH A COACH
   Panel. 18 x 25⅛ in.
   London, Wallace Collection
 a LANDSCAPE WITH A COTTAGE. 1641
   Etching. 12.5 x 32 cm. (5 x 12½ in.)
   Amsterdam, Rijksprentenkabinet
 b THE OMVAL. 1645
   Etching (11). 18.5 x 22.5 cm. (7¼ x 8¾ in.)
   Berlin-Dahlem, Kupferstichkabinett

265

266

267

267 WINTER LANDSCAPE. 1646
Panel. 17 x 23 cm. (6¾ x 9 in.)
Cassel, Gemaeldegalerie
a COTTAGE NEAR A WOOD. 1644
Pen, wash, and red and black chalk drawing. 29.8 x 45.2
cm. (11¾ x 17¾ in.)
New York, The Lehman Collection
b VIEW OVER THE NIEUWE MEER (?)
Pen and wash drawing. 8.8 x 18.1 cm. (3½ x 7 in.)
Chatsworth, Derbyshire, Devonshire Collection

a

b

353

268

268 LANDSCAPE WITH A CASTLE
Colorplate, page 97
Panel. 44.5 x 70 cm. ($17\frac{1}{2}$ x $27\frac{1}{2}$ in.)
Paris, Louvre
a THE THREE TREES. 1643
Etching. 21.1 x 28 cm. ($8\frac{1}{4}$ x 11 in.)
Amsterdam, Rijksprentenkabinet

a

1650-1658

1650. Rembrandt takes revenge on Geertje Dircx. On July 4 he had a notary draw up a collection of nasty stories about Geertje gathered by the painter himself among her new neighbors. With the help of these notarized rumors, Rembrandt sought and obtained the connivance of Geertje's brother, a ship's carpenter, in having Geertje put away for moral delinquency. The law lent its authority to the cruel plan, and Geertje was sentenced to twelve years in the bridewell at Gouda, a reform house for anti-social elements. Rembrandt put up 140 guilders in order to have her transported to and installed in her new home, though the brother was the one legally required to provide the cash to implement the court order. Some alert friends of Geertje from Edam got wind of her predicament the following year, and began trying to get her released. They succeeded only after five years, and then on account of Geertje's having fallen ill. Rembrandt reacted to these attempts to free Geertje with violent threats. When Geertje died, within a year and a half of her release, Rembrandt owed her at least one year's alimony. Naturally, his further indebtedness ceased with her death.

280 A MAN IN FANCIFUL COSTUME
301 MAN LEANING IN A WINDOWSILL
304 PORTRAIT OF A MAN

1651
282 KING DAVID
285 YOUNG GIRL AT A WINDOW
299 AN OLD MAN IN FANCIFUL COSTUME
306 AN OLD MAN IN A LINEN HEADBAND

1652
305 AN OLD MAN IN AN ARMCHAIR
307 NICOLAES BRUYNINGH
308 SELF-PORTRAIT

1653. Rembrandt's financial debacle begins. After 14 years, he still owed his creditors 7,000 guilders on the purchase price of his house in addition to interest on the loan. They now began pressing for payment. Rembrandt tried to escape them with various manoeuvres, but it was too late; his income was no longer sufficient to allow him to raise the necessary funds.

286 ARISTOTLE CONTEMPLATING A BUST OF HOMER

1654. February 23: The Portuguese merchant Diego Andrada complained that a girl's portrait he commissioned from Rembrandt bore insufficient likeness to the sitter and refused to pay for it. Rembrandt offered to retouch it if and when the painters' guild concurred in Andrada's judgment and then only when full payment had been made. We don't know how the affair ended, nor can we identify the painting.

July 23: Hendrickje appears before the Reformed church council after ignoring two previous summonses. She "confesses to fornication with Rembrandt the painter, is gravely punished for it, admonished to penitence, and excluded from the Lord's Supper."

October 30: Baptism of Cornelia, Hendrickje's and Rembrandt's daughter.

302 AN OLD MAN WITH A BERET
303 AN OLD WOMAN WITH A HOOD
309 JAN SIX
312 AN OLD WOMAN IN AN ARMCHAIR
313 AN OLD MAN IN AN ARMCHAIR
317 THE STANDARD BEARER
345 EVENING LANDSCAPE WITH COTTAGES

1655
272 CHRIST AND THE WOMAN OF SAMARIA
273 CHRIST AND THE WOMAN OF SAMARIA
274 JOSEPH ACCUSED BY POTIPHAR'S WIFE
276 THE TRIBUTE MONEY
291 THE SLAUGHTERED OX
292 AN OLD WOMAN READING
320 SELF-PORTRAIT
325 TITUS AT HIS DESK

1656. Rembrandt is granted a *cessio bonorum*, a disposal of his goods by the court for the benefit of his creditors, on a voluntary basis. The action was not considered in the same category as outright bankruptcy.

July 25-6: Inventory is taken of Rembrandt's house and its contents, for the municipal auctioneer. The inventory is the most valuable of all the Rembrandt documents.

277 JACOB BLESSING THE SONS OF JOSEPH
326 THE ANATOMY LESSON OF DOCTOR JOAN DEYMAN

1657. December 4: The contents of Rembrandt's house sold at auction. The sale lasted three weeks.
296 THE APOSTLE BARTHOLOMEW
329 SELF-PORTRAIT
332 AN OLD MAN WITH A GOLD CHAIN
336 CATRINA HOOGHSAET

1658. February: Rembrandt's house sold at auction. He was not required to move out, however, until almost two years later.
278 PHILEMON AND BAUCIS
340 A MAN HOLDING A MANUSCRIPT
341 A MAN HOLDING A LETTER
342 A MAN WITH ARMS AKIMBO
343 SELF-PORTRAIT

269

1650–1658: HISTORY PAINTINGS

269 THE RISEN CHRIST APPEARING TO MARY MAGDALENE.
  165(1)
    Canvas. 65 x 79 cm. (25½ x 31 in.)
    Brunswick, Herzog Anton Ulrich Museum
  a CHRIST RECEIVING THE LITTLE CHILDREN ("THE
    HUNDRED-GUILDER PRINT")
    Etching (1). 27.8 x 39.6 cm. (11 x 15½ in.)
    Amsterdam, Rijksprentenkabinet
  b THE DEATH OF THE VIRGIN. 1639
    Etching (1). 40.9 x 31.5 cm. (16 x 12½ in.)
    Amsterdam, Rijksprentenkabinet

The Dutch poet H. F. Waterloos wrote four epigrams on the back
of his copy of THE HUNDRED-GUILDER PRINT (now in Paris,
Bibliothèque Nationale). The first and last ones read:
This is how Rembrandt etches a living image of God's son
And places him among a crowd of the sick:
To let the world see, after 16 centuries,
What miracles he performed for one and all.

He who seemed so gentle to Israel, clothed in our flesh,
Now shines above the clouds in all his majesty,
To be adored by the angels in his triune self
Until he comes again, to judge all the nations.

a

b

270

270 DANAE. 1636
   Colorplate, page 95
   Canvas. 185 x 203 cm. (72¾ x 80 in.)
   Leningrad, Hermitage
271 BATHSHEBA WITH KING DAVID'S LETTER. 1654 (?)
   Colorplate, page 107
   Canvas. 142 x 142 cm. (56 x 56 in.)
   Paris, Louvre
 a SEATED FEMALE NUDE
   Pen and wash drawing. 26.3 x 20 cm. (10¼ x 8 in.)
   London, Victoria and Albert Museum

The drawing in London (Illustration a) is a study containing elements both of Bathsheba and her woman servant: her pose and weightly physical presence are like Bathsheba, her head and hat like the servant's. But despite its derivation from a life study, BATHSHEBA WITH KING DAVID'S LETTER is directly inspired by a French engraving after an ancient relief. The painting is more ideal than the drawing, more human than the engraving, and towers above them both in dignity and monumentality.

The nudes of the fifties have infinitely greater sensual richness— DANAE is the most erotic of Rembrandt's paintings—than the harshly observed bodies of ANDROMEDA [55] and CHRIST ON THE CROSS [56].

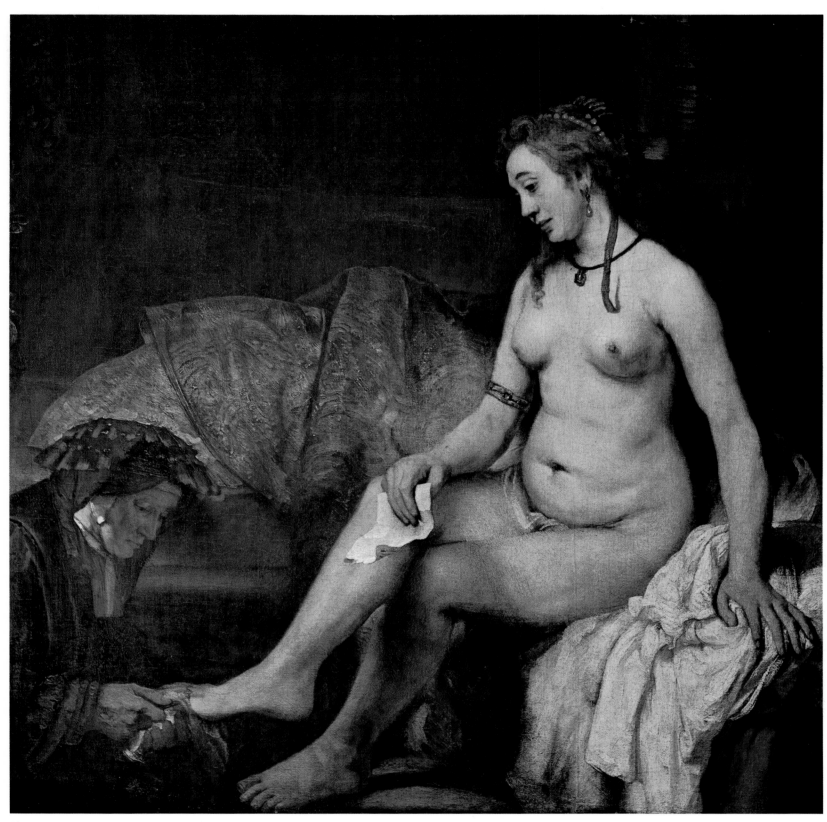

271

a

272

273

272 CHRIST AND THE WOMAN OF SAMARIA. 1655
Panel. 46.5 x 39 cm. (18¼ x 15¼ in.)
Berlin-Dahlem, Gemaeldegalerie

273 CHRIST AND THE WOMAN OF SAMARIA. 1655
Panel. 25 x 19¼ in.
New York, Metropolitan Museum of Art

274 JOSEPH ACCUSED BY POTIPHAR'S WIFE. 1655
Canvas. 110 x 87 cm. (43¼ x 34¼ in.)
Berlin-Dahlem, Gemaeldegalerie

275 JOSEPH ACCUSED BY POTIPHAR'S WIFE. 165(5)
Canvas. 41⅝ x 38½ in.
Washington, D.C., National Gallery of Art

276 THE TRIBUTE MONEY. 1655
Canvas. 63 x 84 cm. (24¾ x 33 in.)
Bywell, Northumberland, Collection of Viscount Allendale

Art historians often revert to the axiom that Rembrandt was in-
capable of repeating himself. On this basis the "best of the surviving versions" of compositions known in more than one replica
is given admittance to the Rembrandt corpus, while the rest are
relegated to the most convenient student. Only one pair of nearly
identical twin compositions has survived this process: the Washington and Berlin JOSEPHS, both of too high quality to be
sacrificed to a rule of thumb.

274

275

276

277

The groups of figures in these four great works share a single superpersonal existence that does not, however, completely submerge the personality of each figure. In the concentration of the individuals on the common action, a perfect dramatic unity results that puts to shame the outlandish behavior of many of the characters in earlier history paintings.

278

a

b

279

280

281

1650–1658: THE LIFE OF MEN AND SAINTS

279 A YOUNG WOMAN AT HER MIRROR. 165(4)
     Panel. 39.5 x 32.5 cm. (15½ x 12¾ in.)
     Leningrad, Hermitage
280 A MAN IN FANCIFUL COSTUME. 1650
     Panel. 50⅜ x 40⅞ in.
     Cambridge, England, Fitzwilliam Museum
281 A WOMAN IN FANCIFUL COSTUME
     Panel. 54 x 40 in.
     Sarasota, Florida, John and Mable Ringling Museum of Art
282 KING DAVID. 1651
     Panel. 30.2 x 26 cm. (12 x 10¼ in.)
     New York, Collection of Mr. Louis Kaplan

283 OLD MAN IN AN ARMCHAIR (THE PATRIARCH JACOB?)
     Canvas. 51 x 37 cm. (20 x 14½ in.)
     Berlin-Dahlem, Gemaeldegalerie

In the forties there were not very many paintings of models in costume. With the century's halfway mark, Rembrandt again sought the freedom of fancy this genre offered, in contrast to portraiture. His paintings of THE LIFE OF MEN AND SAINTS in the fifties form one of the richest groups of paintings in his entire œuvre.

282

283

284

284 YOUNG GIRL HOLDING A BROOM. 1651 (?)
Canvas. 42¼ x 36 in.
Washington, D.C., National Gallery of Art
285 YOUNG GIRL AT A WINDOW. 1651
Colorplate, page 105
Canvas. 78 x 63 cm. (30¾ x 24¾ in.)
Stockholm, Nationalmuseum

285

286

286 ARISTOTLE CONTEMPLATING A BUST OF HOMER. 1653
    Colorplate, page 111
    Canvas. 56½ x 53¾ in.
    New York, Metropolitan Museum of Art
287 "THE POLISH RIDER"
    Colorplate, page 109
    Canvas. 46 x 53⅛ in.
    New York, The Frick Collection
  a A HUMAN SKELETON MOUNTED ON THE SKELETON OF
    A HORSE
    Pen drawing. 15.3 x 14.8 cm. (6 x 5¾ in.)
    Darmstadt, Hessisches Landesmuseum

b AN ORIENTAL CAVALIER
    Pen, wash, red chalk, and water-color drawing. 20.6 x 17.7
    cm. (8 x 7 in.)
    London, British Museum

Before documents were published establishing the romantic title
ARISTOTLE CONTEMPLATING A BUST OF HOMER, art historians
called this painting a portrait of the poet P. C. Hooft. We are not
so fortunate as to have documents concerning "THE POLISH
RIDER," but exotic interpretations are not to be rejected out of
hand. Rembrandt's sources of inspiration are exotic enough (Illustrations a, b).

287

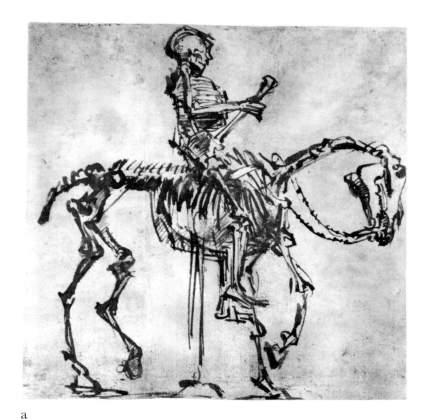

a

b

288

288 HENDRICKJE AS FLORA
   Canvas. 39⅜ x 36⅛ in.
   New York, Metropolitan Museum of Art
289 HENDRICKJE BATHING IN A STREAM. 1654 (1655?)
   Colorplate, page 113
   Panel. 24 5/16 x 18½ in.
   London, National Gallery

The nearly identical poses of HENDRICKJE AS FLORA and
SASKIA [175] invite a comparison that leads to the discovery of
the vast difference between the two works. All the outward signs
that can affect the emotional tone of an idealized portrait are
antithetical: the closed outline of SASKIA is set against a dark
void, bedecked as richly as a cult object; HENDRICKJE's shadow
falls on the backdrop of her shallow stage. She holds a handful of
flowers taken from her skirt in a gesture of giving. Her dress and
jewelry are simple. If these outward signs refer to inner meaning,
we are justified in calling Rembrandt's HENDRICKJE a vision of
woman more directly human, less colored by romantic infat-
uation and the mystique of feminine beauty than SASKIA. This
may or may not reflect the various dispositions of the two women,
but it surely reflects a change in Rembrandt, who was 26 years
old when he met Saskia, and 43 when he met Hendrickje.

289

290

290 THE SLAUGHTERED OX
Panel. 28⅞ x 20⅜ in.
Glasgow, Art Gallery and Museum
291 THE SLAUGHTERED OX. 1655
Colorplate, page 119
Panel. 94 x 67 cm. (37 x 26½ in.)
Paris, Louvre

Emmens has studied "The Slaughtered Ox in Art" as a means of controlling the relevance of our emotional reactions to 17th-century paintings. He found not a trace of the revulsion we are apt to experience in looking at these paintings before the 18th century, nor the least hint that they were considered "ugly." The motifs that *were* called ugly by later 17th-century critics were dilapidated houses, unreconstructed ruins, shabby clothing, mis-formed bodies, etc.—subjects later admitted to the esthetically positive realm of the picturesque. A cautionary lesson is to be drawn from this: we must beware of giving too much heed, in interpreting the emotional content of old art, to the "universal" esthetic, emotional, or moral criteria we take so much for granted. Rembrandt's universe had laws of its own still hazy to us. We do not know, for example, what his slaughtered oxen might betoken.

292

292 AN OLD WOMAN READING. 1655
    Canvas. 31½ x 26 in.
    Drumlanrig Castle, Scotland, Collection of the Duke of
    Buccleuch
293 ALEXANDER THE GREAT
    Canvas. 118 x 91.1 cm. (46½ x 35¾ in.)
    Oeiras, Portugal, Calouste Gulbenkian Foundation
294 ALEXANDER THE GREAT
    Canvas. 54⅛ x 41⅛ in. Enlarged from approx. 45½ x 34½ in.
    Glasgow, Art Gallery and Museum

One of the two versions of ALEXANDER THE GREAT was painted
in 1661, but the other one is an elaboration of an earlier painting,
possibly a portrait of Titus. The contrast between the military
getup of the figure and its soft, womanish expression has always
puzzled scholars. The most likely explanation is that the figures
indeed represent Alexander, whose iconography in the Renaissance was based upon antique coins of Athena.

293

294

295

295 THE APOSTLE PAUL AT HIS DESK
   Canvas. 50¾ x 40⅛ in.
   Washington, D.C., National Gallery of Art
296 THE APOSTLE BARTHOLOMEW. 1657
   Canvas. 64¾ x 55¾ in.
   San Diego, California, Timken Art Gallery
297 A BEARDED MAN
   Canvas. 70.5 x 58 cm. (27¾ x 23 in.)
   Berlin-Dahlem, Gemaeldegalerie
298 THE APOSTLE PAUL
   Canvas. 40⅛ x 33⅝ in.
   London, National Gallery

The late series of apostles has an altogether different character than that of the Leyden period [24–7]. The figures are brought closer to us, and background and picturesque detail are left aside. What remains the same is the grim intensity of these men, cursed in their inability to forget for even a moment the plight of man on earth.

296

297

298

299

1650–1658: PORTRAITS AND STUDIES

299 AN OLD MAN IN FANCIFUL COSTUME. 1651
Canvas. 43¾ x 34¾ in.
Chatsworth, Derbyshire, Devonshire Collection

300 A FRANCISCAN MONK
Canvas. 35 1/16 x 26 3/16 in.
London, National Gallery

301 MAN LEANING IN A WINDOWSILL. 1650
Canvas. 82 x 68.5 cm. (32¼ x 27 in.)
Cincinnati, Taft Museum

a THE ART DEALER CLEMENT DE JONGHE. 1651
Etching (II). 20.6 x 16.1 cm. (8 x 6¼ in.)
Amsterdam, Rijksprentenkabinet

a

300

301

302

303

302 AN OLD MAN WITH A BERET. 1654
     Canvas. 74 x 65 cm. (29 x 25½ in.)
     Moscow, Pushkin Museum

303 AN OLD WOMAN WITH A HOOD. 1654
     Canvas. 74 x 63 cm. (29 x 24¾ in.)
     Moscow, Pushkin Museum

304 PORTRAIT OF A MAN. 1650
     Canvas. 80 x 67.1 cm. (31½ x 26½ in.)
     The Hague, Mauritshuis

304

305

306

305 AN OLD MAN IN AN ARMCHAIR. 1652
Canvas. 43⅝ x 34⅝ in.
London, National Gallery

306 AN OLD MAN IN A LINEN HEADBAND. 1651
Canvas. 77 x 66 cm. (30¼ x 26 in.)
Wanås, Sweden, Collection of Count Wachtmeister

307 NICOLAES BRUYNINGH. 1652
Canvas. 107.5 x 91.5 cm. (42¼ x 36 in.)
Cassel, Gemaeldegalerie

Most portraits and studies of the fifties show unsmiling, uncommunicative old men and women—and young ones [328, 331]. The forward liveliness of NICOLAES BRUYNINGH, we feel, must stem from the ebullience of the sitter himself. Rembrandt's own mood was quite different.

307

308

308 SELF-PORTRAIT. 1652
    Canvas. 112 x 81.5 cm. (44 x 32 in.)
    Vienna, Kunsthistorisches Museum
309 JAN SIX. (1654)
    Canvas. 112 x 102 cm. (44 x 40¼ in.)
    Amsterdam, Six Foundation

A good many of the commissioned works of the fifties—paintings
and etchings alike—are portraits of Rembrandt's creditors. This
is no accident: Rembrandt traded on his art, and used portrait
commissions as capital. In 1655, for example, he bought a house
from Dirk van Kattenburgh. The purchase price of 4,000 guilders

was to be made up of works of art by Rembrandt and others. One
item was "a portrait of Otto van Kattenburgh [Dirk's brother],
to be etched from life by the aforementioned van Rijn, of the
same quality as the portrait of Mr. Jan Six, in the amount of 400
guilders." The portrait of Jan Six intended is the etching of 1647
(Illustration a, p. 90), not the present painting. But if the etching
depicts Six the poet, as a contemporary epigram has it, the
painting shows us the businessman—the creditor who no doubt
accepted this supreme work in partial settlement of Rembrandt's
financial debt to him.

309

310

311

310 SELF-PORTRAIT. 165(4)
Canvas. 73 x 60 cm. (28¾ x 23½ in.)
Cassel, Gemaeldegalerie

311 HENDRICKJE
Canvas. 72 x 60 cm. (28¼ x 23½ in.)
Paris, Louvre

312 AN OLD WOMAN IN AN ARMCHAIR. 1654
Canvas. 109 x 84 cm. (43 x 33 in.) Enlarged from 35 x 30 in.
Leningrad, Hermitage

313 AN OLD MAN IN AN ARMCHAIR. 1654
Canvas. 109 x 84.8 cm. (43 x 33½ in.) Enlarged from
35 x 30 in.
Leningrad, Hermitage

314 AN OLD MAN IN AN ARMCHAIR
Canvas. 108 x 86 cm. (42½ x 33¾ in.)
Leningrad, Hermitage

315 AN OLD WOMAN SEATED
Canvas. 82 x 72 cm. (32½ x 28¼ in.)
Moscow, Pushkin Museum

312

313

314

315

316

316 A MAN IN A FUR-LINED COAT
    Canvas. 45 x 34¼ in.
    Boston, Museum of Fine Arts (on loan from the Fuller
    Foundation)
317 THE STANDARD BEARER. 1654
    Canvas. 55¼ x 45¼ in.
    New York, Metropolitan Museum of Art

THE STANDARD BEARER was likely the ensign in one of Amsterdam's militia companies. The portraits of Jan Six seem to have set the style for Rembrandt commissions of the fifties (see p. 386 for the etched portrait). We can easily imagine that this commission too read: "a portrait of the same quality as that of Mr. Jan Six," in reference to the painting of the same year [309].

317

318

318 HENDRICKJE
   Canvas. 65.5 x 54 cm. (25¾ x 21¼ in.)
   Los Angeles, Collection of Mr. and Mrs. Norton Simon
319 BOY IN FANCIFUL DRESS
   Canvas. 65 x 56 cm. (25½ x 22 in.)
   Fullerton, California, Norton Simon Foundation

319

320

320 SELF-PORTRAIT. 1655
    Panel. 66 x 53 cm. (26 x 21 in.)
    Vienna, Kunsthistorisches Museum
321 CHRIST
    Panel. $9\frac{3}{4}$ x $7\frac{7}{8}$ in.
    Philadelphia, John G. Johnson Collection
322 CHRIST
    Panel. 25.2 x 19.9 cm. (10 x $7\frac{3}{4}$ in.)
    Cambridge, Massachusetts, Fogg Art Museum

323 CHRIST
    Colorplate, page 115
    Panel. 25 x 20 cm. ($9\frac{3}{4}$ x 8 in.)
    Berlin-Dahlem, Gemaeldegalerie
a CHRIST PREACHING ("LA PETITE TOMBE")
    Etching. 15.5 x 20.7 cm. (6 x $8\frac{1}{4}$ in.)
    Amsterdam, Rijksprentenkabinet

321

322

323

a

324

324 SELF-PORTRAIT
Colorplate, page 91
Panel. 49.2 x 41 cm. (19½ x 16¼ in.)
Vienna, Kunsthistorisches Museum

325 TITUS AT HIS DESK. 1655
Colorplate, page 117
Canvas. 77 x 63 cm. (30¼ x 24¾ in.)
Rotterdam, Museum Boymans-van Beuningen

In the fifties Rembrandt stopped affecting the costume of his models [262] and the airs of his patrons [99] to paint self-portraits in his proper social and personal guise. Only at this point do the self-portraits become different in sort from the other portraits and studies. Except for the grandiose SELF-PORTRAIT AS THE APOSTLE PAUL [403], the works from 1652 on show us Rembrandt as the man himself or as the artist.

Titus must have become Rembrandt's pupil around the time of this, first portrait of him at the age of 14. He became increasingly important to Rembrandt in the years of adversity, and never left his father until his marriage at the age of 27.

325

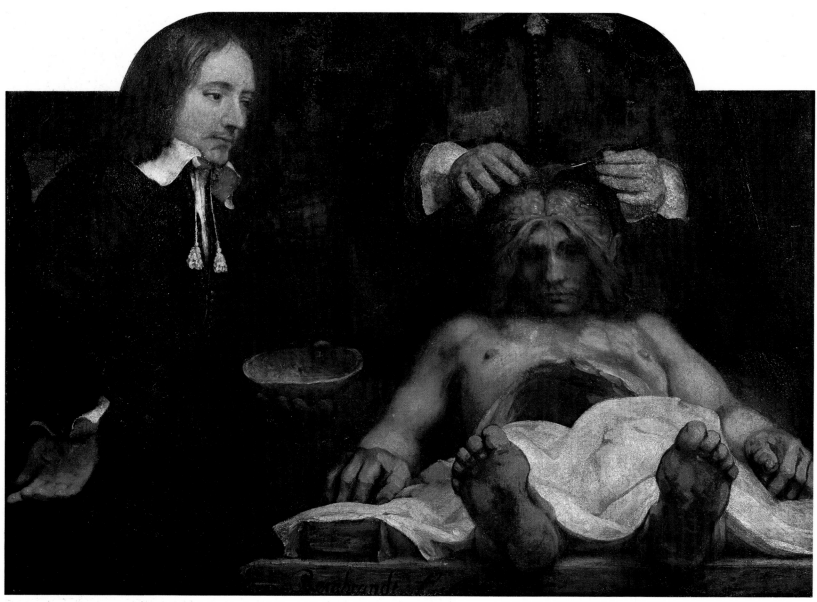

326

326 THE ANATOMY LESSON OF DOCTOR JOAN DEYMAN. 1656
Canvas. 100 x 134 cm. (39½ x 52¾ in.) Fragment
Amsterdam, Rijksmuseum

327 THE AMSTERDAM PHYSICIAN ARNOUT THOLINX. 1656
Canvas. 76 x 63 cm. (30 x 24¾ in.)
Paris, Musée Jacquemart-André

328 A YOUNG MAN WITH A BERET
Canvas. 76 x 61 cm. (30 x 24 in.)
New York, Collection of Mr. and Mrs. Charles S. Payson

a THE ANATOMY LESSON OF DOCTOR JOAN DEYMAN
Pen drawing. 11 x 13.3 cm. (4¼ x 5¼ in.)
Amsterdam, Rijksprentenkabinet

The symmetrical setting of THE ANATOMY LESSON OF DOCTOR
JOAN DEYMAN as well as the distinctive placing of the cadaver
conform to the model of the first modern ANATOMY: the frontis-
piece to Andreas Vesalius' *De Humani Corporis Fabrica* (1543) by
J. J. van Calcar. But Vesalius is shown probing the female uterus,
"the seat of corruption," while Doctor Deyman has moved from
the ventral cavity of his male cadaver to its brain, the seat of the
soul.

a

327

328

329

330

329 SELF-PORTRAIT. 1657
Canvas. 20 x 17 in.
Edinburgh, National Gallery of Scotland (on loan from the
Duke of Sutherland)

330 TITUS
Canvas. 26½ x 21¾ in.
London, Wallace Collection

331 A YOUNG WOMAN WITH A CARNATION
Canvas. 78 x 68.5 cm. (30¾ x 27 in.)
Copenhagen, The Royal Museum of Fine Arts

332 AN OLD MAN WITH A GOLD CHAIN. 1657
Canvas. 31 x 25½ in.
San Francisco, California Palace of the Legion of Honor

333 AN OLD MAN IN A CAPE
Canvas. 32½ x 26 in.
Kenosha, Wisconsin, Collection of Mr. R. Whitacker

334 A BEARDED MAN IN A CAP
Canvas. 30¾ x 26¼ in.
London, National Gallery

331

334

335

335 TITUS READING
    Canvas. 70.5 x 64 cm. (27¾ x 25¼ in.)
    Vienna, Kunsthistorisches Museum
336 CATRINA HOOGHSAET. 1657
    Canvas. 49½ x 38 in.
    Penrhyn Castle, Wales, Collection of Lady Janet Douglas-
    Pennant

336

337

337 A YOUNG WOMAN
Canvas. 22$\frac{3}{16}$ x 18$\frac{11}{16}$ in.
Montreal, Museum of Fine Arts
338 PORTRAIT OF A MAN
Canvas. 32$\frac{7}{8}$ x 25$\frac{3}{8}$ in.
New York, Metropolitan Museum of Art
339 HENDRICKJE AT AN OPEN DOOR
Canvas. 86 x 65 cm. (34 x 25$\frac{1}{2}$ in.)
Berlin-Dahlem, Gemaeldegalerie

340 A MAN HOLDING A MANUSCRIPT. 1658
Canvas. 42$\frac{3}{4}$ x 34 in.
New York, Metropolitan Museum of Art
341 A MAN HOLDING A LETTER. 1658
Canvas. 113 x 95.5 cm. (44$\frac{1}{2}$ x 37$\frac{1}{2}$ in.)
Switzerland, Private Collection

338

339

340

341

342

342 A MAN WITH ARMS AKIMBO. 1658
Canvas. 42 x 34½ in.
New York, Columbia University

343 SELF-PORTRAIT. 1658
Colorplate, page 121
Canvas. 52⅝ x 40⅞ in.
New York, The Frick Collection

Creighton Gilbert has shown that in the 16th century (and this is probably true of the 17th century as well), men resignedly began calling themselves old at a much earlier age than we do. Rembrandt seems to have done the same in paint. The vigor he still possessed in the painting of 1652 [308], when he was 46, has diminished sharply by 1655 [320]. In 1658 (age 52), he no longer considers vigor appropriate. He sits, presenting himself for the first time in an altogether new image: the old master painter.

343

344

344 RIVER LANDSCAPE WITH RUINS
   Colorplate, page 123
   Panel. 67 x 87.5 cm. ($26\frac{1}{2}$ x $34\frac{1}{2}$ in.)
   Cassel, Gemaeldegalerie

345 EVENING LANDSCAPE WITH COTTAGES. 1654
   Panel. 10 x $15\frac{1}{2}$ in.
   Montreal, Museum of Fine Arts

 a "THE GOLDWEIGHER'S FIELD." 1651
   Etching. 12 x 31.9 cm. ($4\frac{3}{4}$ x $12\frac{1}{2}$ in.)
   Chicago, Art Institute

b LANDSCAPE WITH A COTTAGE
   Pen and wash drawing. 11.8 x 17.9 cm. ($4\frac{3}{4}$ x 7 in.)
   Groningen, Museum

Rembrandt practiced two alternate modes of landscape painting in the fifties. RIVER LANDSCAPE WITH RUINS is a romantic landscape of the italianate sort; EVENING LANDSCAPE WITH COTTAGES almost a plein-air painting, a drawing in oils. In THE GOLD-WEIGHER'S FIELD we sense the common ground, in Rembrandt's creative imagination, shared by these two modes.

345

a

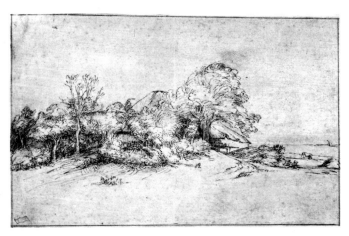

b

1659-1669

1660. December 15: Titus and Hendrickje form a company to trade in art. Since Rembrandt was no longer allowed to sell his own works, after the painters' guild had passed a ruling—apparently aimed at Rembrandt—prohibiting any painter who had held a general sale of his works from operating independently in the art market, Rembrandt had to become the employee of his mistress and his son, turning over all his works to them in exchange for support. This demeaning arrangement lasted until the death of the partners, and the company itself even survived Rembrandt by six years.

1661. August 7: Hendrickje makes her testament. She gives her address as Rozengracht, indicating that she, Rembrandt, Titus, and Cornelia had moved to the Rozengracht sometime before this date.

1662. July 24: Hendrickje is buried in the Westerkerk.

THE CONSPIRACY OF JULIUS CIVILIS: THE OATH was reported by Fokkens to be hanging in the Town Hall of Amsterdam in 1662. Rembrandt took part, then, in the great artistic project of the day, though his canvas did not remain in its place. Rembrandt's last important portrait commission [404] is dated 1662.

1665. November 5: Titus, having applied for and been granted *veniam aetatis* (official recognition of his majority of years), is paid out the 6,952 guilders and five stuivers that were his share of the sale of Rembrandt's goods in 1657–8.

1668. February 10: Titus marries Magdalena van Loo, the daughter of old family friends, the goldsmith Jan van Loo and his wife Anna Huybrechts.

September 7: Titus is buried in the Westerkerk.

1669. March 22: Baptism of Titia van Rijn, Titus' posthumous daughter.

October 4: Rembrandt dies. He was buried in the Westerkerk on October 8.

346

1659–1669: HISTORY PAINTINGS

346 JACOB WRESTLING WITH THE ANGEL
Canvas. 137 x 116 cm. (54 x 45¾ in.)
Berlin-Dahlem, Gemaeldegalerie

347 MOSES WITH THE TABLES OF THE LAW. 1659
Colorplate, page 125
Canvas. 167 x 135 cm. (65¾ x 53 in.)
Berlin-Dahlem, Gemaeldegalerie

347

348

348 OLD TOBIT AND ANNA WAITING FOR THEIR SON. 1659
Panel. 40.3 x 54 cm. ($15\frac{3}{4}$ x $21\frac{1}{4}$ in.)
Rotterdam, Willem van der Vorm Foundation

349 CHRIST AND THE WOMAN OF SAMARIA. 1659
Canvas. 60 x 75 cm. ($23\frac{1}{2}$ x $29\frac{1}{2}$ in.)
Leningrad, Hermitage

a THE APOSTLES PETER AND JOHN AT THE GATE OF THE
TEMPLE. 1659
Etching (II). 17.9 x 21.6 cm. (7 x $8\frac{1}{2}$ in.)
Amsterdam, Rijksprentenkabinet

The distinctive difference between indoor and outdoor lighting
falls away in the later paintings. Illumination becomes a property
of individual details and figures, not of the space as a whole. In
unilluminated details the texture of the painted surface is heavy
and intractable; in lighted details the *matière* is lively, contributing to the literal meaning of the painted image instead of
resisting it.

349

a

350

350 THE CIRCUMCISION OF CHRIST. 1661
  Canvas. 22¼ x 29½ in.
  Washington, D.C., National Gallery of Art

351 HAMAN AND AHASUERUS AT THE FEAST OF ESTHER.
  1660
  Canvas. 73 x 94 cm. (28¾ x 37 in.)
  Moscow, Pushkin Museum

352 THE RISEN CHRIST AT EMMAUS
  Canvas. 48 x 64 cm. (19 x 25¼ in.)
  Paris, Louvre

Here one sees Haman eating with Ahasuerus and Esther
But in vain—his breast is full of regret and pain.
He bites into Esther's dishes, but deeper into her heart.
The king is obsessed by wrath and revenge;
A ruler's ire is terrible in full rage.
The terror of all men, shocked by one woman.
So one falls from the heights to the depths of adversity.
The wrath that grows slowly works the cruelest punishment.

This poem by Jan Vos, published in 1662, shows that Rembrandt's contemporaries were much more sensitive than we are to the suppressed emotions of characters in history paintings.

351

352

353

353 THE APOSTLE PETER DENYING CHRIST. 1660
Canvas. 154 x 169 cm. (60½ x 66½ in.)
Amsterdam, Rijksmuseum
354 THE CONSPIRACY OF JULIUS CIVILIS: THE OATH (1661)
Colorplates, pages 126, 127
Canvas. 196 x 309 cm. (77¼ x 121¾ in.) Cut down
Stockholm, Nationalmuseum
a THE CONSPIRACY OF JULIUS CIVILIS: THE OATH
Pen and wash drawing. 19.6 x 18 cm. (7¾ x 7 in.)
Munich, Graphische Sammlung

Interplay between the main action in the foreground and a subsidiary background scene was characteristic of the religious
pictures of the Leyden years [esp. 14, 24]. Rembrandt's use of the
device in THE APOSTLE PETER DENYING CHRIST is unique for
his later period, when he favored inexpressive backgrounds,
whose staffage function only as observers. Our recognition of the
dimly lit figure behind the apostle as the betrayed Christ en-
genders a dramatic tension absent from other paintings with
similar figures [350, 355].

354

a

355

355 THE RETURN OF THE PRODIGAL SON
Colorplate, page 143
Canvas. 262 x 206 cm. (103 x 81 in.)
Leningrad, Hermitage

356 ISAAC AND REBECCA ("THE JEWISH BRIDE")
Colorplate, page 135
Canvas. 121.5 x 166.5 cm. (48 x 65½ in.)
Amsterdam, Rijksmuseum

a ISAAC AND REBECCA SPIED UPON BY ABIMELECH
Pen drawing. 14.5 x 18.5 cm. (5¾ x 7¼ in.)
New York, Private Collection

The gesture of embracing begun by the apostle Peter in the early etching (Illustration a, p. 178) is completed 40 years later by the father of the Prodigal Son. Kenneth Clark has spoken movingly of the embrace as a "motive" that western artists seize upon—and their audiences perceive—at a nearly intuitive level. In the earlier history of art, however, this degree of physical expressiveness was attainable only to sculptors. Rembrandt was the first painter to evoke, in both these masterpieces, the full emotional release of the embrace on the flat surface of a picture.

356

a

357

357 THE DISGRACE OF HAMAN
    Canvas. 127 x 117 cm. (50 x 46 in.)
    Leningrad, Hermitage
358 SIMEON WITH THE CHRIST CHILD IN THE TEMPLE.
    (1669)
    Canvas. 98 x 79 cm. (38½ x 31 in.)
    Stockholm, Nationalmuseum
  a SIMEON WITH THE CHRIST CHILD IN THE TEMPLE. 1661
    Pen and brush drawing. 12 x 8.9 cm. (4¾ x 3½ in.)
    The Hague, Royal Library

The retreat of each of the figures in THE DISGRACE OF HAMAN
into isolated reflection raises problems regarding the actual
subject of the picture. However, the identity of the two main
figures with the Ahasuerus and Haman in THE FEAST OF
ESTHER of 1660 [351]—a likeness that even extends to the unexpectedly subdued gestures and facial expressions (though see
Jan Vos' poem)—has to be fully accounted for before any alternate explanation, such as DAVID AND URIAH, can be considered.

358

a

359

359 THE EVANGELIST MATTHEW INSPIRED BY THE ANGEL.
1661
Colorplate, page 137
Canvas. 96 x 81 cm. (37¾ x 32 in.)
Paris, Louvre

360 THE RISEN CHRIST. 1661
Canvas. 78.5 x 63 cm. (31 x 24¾ in.)
Munich, Alte Pinakothek

361 THE APOSTLE JAMES. 1661
Canvas. 90 x 78 cm. (35½ x 30¾ in.)
New York, Metropolitan Museum of Art (on loan)

THE EVANGELIST MATTHEW INSPIRED BY THE ANGEL has a certain obvious formal similarity to TWO NEGROES [390] of the same year: in both we see one figure looking over the shoulder of another. Moreover, the main figure in both paintings seems to ignore the secondary one. In the case of the MATTHEW this one-sidedness is rooted in the pictorial tradition for the treatment of attributes, which are always taken for granted by those who bear them. But in TWO NEGROES we have no clue to the relationship between the figures. Bauch and others think the painting shows two studies of one and the same man—but this does not clear up the problem.

360

361

352

362 THE APOSTLE SIMON. 1661
Canvas. 98.3 x 79 cm. (38¾ x 31 in.)
Zurich, Kunsthaus (Ruzicka Foundation)

363 AN EVANGELIST WRITING
Canvas. 102 x 80 cm. (40¼ x 31½ in.)
Rotterdam, Museum Boymans-van Beuningen

364 AN EVANGELIST WRITING
Canvas. 40¼ x 33 in.
Boston, Museum of Fine Arts

365 AN APOSTLE PRAYING
Canvas. 32¾ x 26½ in.
Cleveland, Ohio, Museum of Art

366 THE APOSTLE BARTHOLOMEW. 1661
Canvas. 87.5 x 75 cm. (34½ x 29½ in.)
Sutton Place, Surrey, Getty Collection

The individuality of each of the various evangelists and apostles
of 1661 is so strongly expressed that it is hard to see how the
paintings could ever have functioned as a group. The recognition
that such a series exists helped to establish the correct identity of
these subjects, previously interpreted as "THE AUCTIONEER"
[363] and "REMBRANDT'S BUTCHER" [366].

363

364

365

366

367

368

367 THE VIRGIN MARY ("PORTRAIT OF A NUN"). 1661
Canvas. 107 x 81 cm. (42 x 32 in.)
Epinal, France, Musée des Vosges
368 CHRIST
Canvas. 108 x 89 cm. (42½ x 35 in.)
Glens Falls, New York, The Hyde Collection
369 CHRIST. 1661
Canvas. 37½ x 32½ in.
New York, Metropolitan Museum of Art
370 MAN WITH A FALCON (COUNT FLORIS OF HOLLAND?)
Canvas. 98 x 79 cm. (38½ x 31 in.)
Gothenburg, Sweden, Konstmuseum

1661 was the year of the heroic half-figure for Rembrandt. Who knows if some of these works were not aimed at a particular patron—Rembrandt's best of those years, Don Antonio Ruffo, who had bought the ARISTOTLE [286] in 1654 and ALEXANDER THE GREAT [293?] in 1661. The Sicilian nobleman must have seemed to Rembrandt to have an unlimited appetite for series of half-figures. If this is so, could the MAN WITH A FALCON not be the Holy Roman Emperor Frederick II—the "Sicilian Alexander the Great"—who was well known in the 17th century as the author of a manual on hunting with the falcon? There is no evidence, however, that the painting was ever offered to Ruffo for sale.

369

370

371

371 HOMER DICTATING TO A SCRIBE. 1663
    Colorplate, page 141
    Canvas. 108 x 82.4 cm. (42½ x 32½ in.) Fragment
    The Hague, Mauritshuis
372 THE SUICIDE OF LUCRETIA. 1666
    Canvas. 43 x 36½ in.
    Minneapolis, Institute of Arts
373 THE SUICIDE OF LUCRETIA. 1664
    Canvas. 47¼ x 39¾ in.
    Washington, D.C., National Gallery of Art

374 JUNO
    Colorplate, page 133
    Canvas. 50 x 42⅜ in.
    New York, Metropolitan Museum of Art (on loan from
    Mr. J. William Middendorf, II)
 a HOMER DICTATING TO A SCRIBE
    Pen and brush drawing. 14.5 x 16.7 cm. (5¾ x 6½ in.)
    Stockholm, Nationalmuseum

372

373

374

375

375 TITUS
   Canvas. 72 x 56 cm. (28¼ x 22 in.)
   Paris, Louvre
376 SELF-PORTRAIT. 1659
   Canvas. 33¼ x 26 in.
   Washington, D.C., National Gallery of Art
377 TITUS IN A MONK'S HABIT. 166(0)
   Colorplate, page 151
   Canvas. 79.5 x 67.7 cm. (31¼ x 26¾ in.)
   Amsterdam, Rijksmuseum

378 CHRIST
   Panel. 24½ x 19¼ in.
   Formerly Milwaukee, Wisconsin, Collection of Mr. Harry
   John
379 AN OLD MAN. 1659
   Panel. 37.5 x 26.5 cm. (14¾ x 10½ in.)
   Birmingham, England, Collection of Mr. D. Cotton

376

377

378

379

433

380

380 SELF-PORTRAIT
   Colorplate, page 145
   Canvas. 45 x 37½ in.
   London, Kenwood House, The Iveagh Bequest
381 SELF-PORTRAIT. 1660
   Canvas. 31⅝ x 26½ in.
   New York, Metropolitan Museum of Art
382 HENDRICKJE. 1660
   Canvas. 30⅞ x 27⅛ in.
   New York, Metropolitan Museum of Art

383 THE DORDRECHT MERCHANT JACOB TRIP
   Canvas. 51¾ x 38¼ in.
   London, National Gallery
384 MARGARETHA DE GEER, WIFE OF JACOB TRIP
   Canvas. 51¾ x 38⅜ in.
   London, National Gallery

381

382

383

384

385

386

388

387

385 MARGARETHA DE GEER. 1661
Canvas. $29\frac{5}{8}$ x $25\frac{1}{8}$ in.
London, National Gallery

386 A CAPUCHIN MONK READING. 1661
Canvas. 82 x 66 cm. ($32\frac{1}{4}$ x 26 in.)
Helsinki, Ateneum

387 HEAD OF AN OLD MAN
Panel. 24.5 x 20 cm. ($9\frac{3}{4}$ x $7\frac{3}{4}$ in.)
Great Britain, Private Collection

388 PORTRAIT OF AN OLD WOMAN. 1661
Canvas. 77 x 64 cm. ($30\frac{1}{4}$ x $25\frac{1}{4}$ in.)
New York, Collection of Mrs. R. W. Straus

389 SELF-PORTRAIT. 1660
Canvas. 111 x 85 cm. ($43\frac{3}{4}$ x $33\frac{1}{2}$ in.)
Paris, Louvre

389

390

390 TWO NEGROES. 1661
   Colorplate, page 147
   Canvas. 77.8 x 64.4 cm. (30½ x 25¼ in.)
   The Hague, Mauritshuis

391 AN OLD MAN IN AN ARMCHAIR
   Canvas. 104.7 x 86 cm. (41¼ x 34 in.)
   Florence, Uffizi

392 PORTRAIT OF A YOUNG JEW. 1661
   Canvas. 64 x 57 cm. (25¼ x 22½ in.)
   Montreal, Collection of Mrs. William Van Horne

393 A MAN SEATED BEFORE A STOVE
   Panel. 48 x 41 cm. (19 x 16 in.)
   Winterthur, Switzerland, Oskar Reinhart Collection

394 PORTRAIT OF A YOUNG MAN. 1660
   Canvas. 36½ x 32½ in.
   Rochester, New York, University, George Eastman
   Collection

391

392

393

394

395

396

397

398

395 STUDY OF AN OLD MAN
   Panel. 9½ x 7½ in.
   New York, Collection of Mr. John Hay Whitney

396 HENDRICKJE IN A FUR COAT
   Canvas. 100 x 83.5 cm. (39½ x 32¾ in.)
   Great Britain, Private Collection

397 PORTRAIT OF A YOUNG MAN. 1662 (?)
   Canvas. 35⅜ x 27⅞ in.
   St. Louis, Missouri, City Art Museum

398 WOMAN WITH A LAP DOG
   Canvas. 32 x 25¼ in.
   Toronto, Art Gallery of Ontario

399 SELF-PORTRAIT
   Canvas. 85 x 61 cm. (33½ x 24 in.)
   Florence, Uffizi

399

400

401

400 DIRK VAN OS
Canvas. 40¾ x 34 in.
Omaha, Nebraska, Joslyn Art Museum
401 MAN IN A TALL HAT
Canvas. 47¾ x 37 in.
Washington, D.C., National Gallery of Art
402 A BEARDED MAN. 1661
Canvas. 71 x 61 cm. (28 x 24 cm.)
Leningrad, Hermitage

402

403

403 SELF-PORTRAIT AS THE APOSTLE PAUL. 1661
Colorplate, page 149
Canvas. 91 x 77 cm. (35¾ x 30¼ in.)
Amsterdam, Rijksmuseum

404 THE SAMPLING OFFICIALS OF THE DRAPERS' GUILD.
1662
Colorplate, page 131
Canvas. 191 x 279 cm. (75¼ x 110 in.)
Amsterdam, Rijksmuseum

a THREE OFFICIALS OF THE DRAPERS' GUILD
Pen and wash drawing. 17.3 x 20.5 cm. (6¾ x 8 in.)
Berlin-Dahlem, Kupferstichkabinett

b AN OFFICIAL OF THE DRAPERS' GUILD
Pen, brush, and wash drawing. 22.5 x 17.5 cm. (8¾ x 7 in.)
Rotterdam, Museum Boymans-van Beuningen

Emmens dismisses the 19th-century notion of Rembrandt as a
man torn between the inner world and the outer as unhistorical.
But what are we then to make of Rembrandt's explicit identification of himself as the apostle Paul (Saul), a figure clearly
representative of just that division of allegiance (see the sword
and book) to Rembrandt and his age?

404

a

b

405

406

405 PORTRAIT OF A YOUNG MAN. 1663
    Colorplate, page 153
    Canvas. $43\frac{1}{4}$ x $35\frac{1}{4}$ in.
    Washington, D.C., National Gallery of Art
406 PORTRAIT OF A YOUNG MAN (TITUS?)
    Colorplate, page 155
    Canvas. $32\frac{1}{2}$ x $26\frac{1}{2}$ in.
    London, Dulwich College Gallery
407 THE PAINTER GERARD DE LAIRESSE. 1665
    Canvas. 112 x 87 cm. (44 x $34\frac{1}{4}$ in.)
    New York, The Lehman Collection

408 PORTRAIT OF A YOUTH. 1666
    Canvas. $31\frac{3}{4}$ x $25\frac{1}{2}$ in.
    Kansas City, Missouri, William Rockhill Nelson Gallery of Art

Rembrandt's portrait of GERARD DE LAIRESSE forms a fascinating link between the two opposed tendencies of Dutch 17th-century painting. As Emmens has shown, Rembrandt was seen as the foremost representative of an "archaic" tradition of painting, rejected after 1660 by the classicistic critics, of whom de Lairesse was the most intelligent and interesting.

446

407

408

409

409 PORTRAIT OF AN OLD MAN. 1667
    Canvas. 32¼ x 26½ in.
    Cowdray Park, Sussex, Collection of Lord Cowdray
410 FREDERICK RIHEL ON HORSEBACK. 1663 (?)
    Colorplate, page 157
    Canvas. 116 x 95 in.
    London, National Gallery

These two canvases represent the two poles of Rembrandt's portrait art of the last decade of his life. The simple directness of the old man with the open collar is underlined by his pose and the quick, unpretentious execution. "Unpretentious" is the last adjective one would use to describe FREDERICK RIHEL ON HORSEBACK, Rembrandt's only equestrian portrait. The splendid airs affected by the sitter are complemented by the painter's surrender to color and ostentation. The extravagance of the whole thing is tempered only by a finicky touch in the details of the costume, no doubt prescribed by the sitter. The poles stand apart in these two works, but Rembrandt knew how to unite them, in such works as A FAMILY GROUP [416; Colorplate, p. 165], where color absconds the function of line. The resulting image, built of color, is the perfect union of intimacy and monumentality, qualities pertaining to these two portraits, respectively, but unmixed, to the detriment of both works.

410

411

412

411 A MAN HOLDING GLOVES
Colorplate, page 158
Canvas. $39\frac{1}{8}$ x $32\frac{1}{2}$ in.
Washington, D.C., National Gallery of Art

412 A WOMAN HOLDING AN OSTRICH-FEATHER FAN
Colorplate, page 159
Canvas. $39\frac{1}{4}$ x $32\frac{5}{8}$ in.
Washington, D.C., National Gallery of Art

413 THE POET JEREMIAS DE DEKKER. 1666
Panel. 71 x 56 cm. (28 x 22 in.)
Leningrad, Hermitage

414 PORTRAIT OF A FAIR-HAIRED MAN. 1667
Colorplate, page 163
Canvas. 43 x $36\frac{3}{4}$ in.
Melbourne, National Gallery of Victoria

JEREMIAS DE DEKKER was one of the most gifted Dutch poets of
the 17th century. He seems to have had an especially insightful
appreciation of Rembrandt's art. He wrote a number of sensitive
laudatory poems on Rembrandt paintings and etchings.

413

414

415

415 SELF-PORTRAIT. 1669
Colorplate, page 167
Canvas. $33\frac{7}{8}$ x $27\frac{3}{4}$ in.
London, National Gallery

416 A FAMILY GROUP
Colorplate, page 165
Canvas. 126 x 167 cm. ($49\frac{1}{2}$ x $65\frac{3}{4}$ in.)
Brunswick, Herzog Anton Ulrich Museum

417 A MAN WITH A MAGNIFYING GLASS
Canvas. 36 x $29\frac{1}{4}$ in.
New York, Metropolitan Museum of Art

418 A WOMAN WITH A CARNATION
Canvas. $36\frac{1}{4}$ x $29\frac{3}{8}$ in.
New York, Metropolitan Museum of Art

The same models seem to have sat for A FAMILY GROUP, THE JEWISH BRIDE, and A MAN WITH A MAGNIFYING GLASS and A WOMAN WITH A CARNATION. This itself is enough to cast fatal doubt on the recurring theory that Titus and his wife, Magdalena van Loo, sat for one or another of these pictures. The couple was 27 years old when they married, and lived together for only seven months before Titus died.

416

417

418

419

419 SELF-PORTRAIT
Canvas. 82 x 63 cm. (32¼ x 24¾ in.)
Cologne, Wallraf-Richartz Museum
420 SELF-PORTRAIT. 1669
Canvas. 59 x 51 cm. (23¼ x 20 in.)
The Hague, Mauritshuis

420

Around Rembrandt

a

b

Any selection of Rembrandt's own words or of what has been said about him, his work, and his surroundings, must be, by definition, incomplete and rather random. Anyone who maintains that this is not so, greatly underestimates the extent of the judgments over Rembrandt that in the course of centuries have been committed to paper, spoken from lecterns and spotlighted by exhibitions. This selection does not pretend to be anything more than such a random collection, the by-product of a catalogue of Rembrandt's paintings.

It contains passages embodying original recognitions of aspects of Rembrandt as well as some that set earlier assessments into sharp relief. These passages brought some of Rembrandt's graphic works to mind and led further to a search for illustrations that breathe the same atmosphere as the citations or that reinforce the picture that had been evoked.

D.W.Bloemena

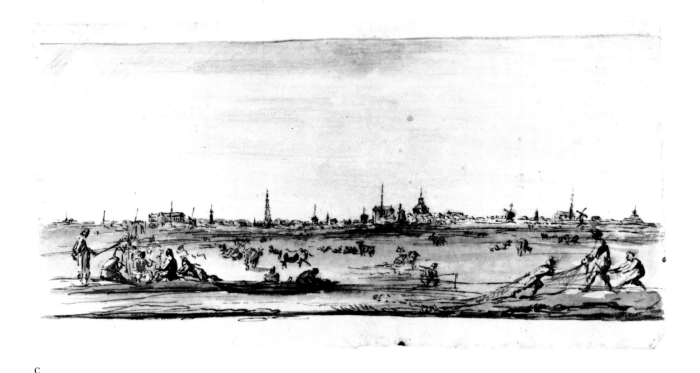

c

[Rembrandt van Rijn], the son of Harmen Gerritsz. van Rijn and Neeltgen Willems van Suydtbrouck, was born in the city of Leyden on July 15, in the year 1606. His parents sent him to school to learn Latin, so that in the course of time he could attend the Leyden Academy. They had hoped that he would grow up equipped to serve and promote the interests of the city and the general good. But he had no inclination whatever in this direction: on the contrary, his natural instincts led him toward painting and drawing only. So his parents had to remove him from school. Falling in with his wishes, they apprenticed him to a painter from whom he should learn the basic principles of art.

Accordingly they brought him to the accomplished Mr. Jacob Isaacsz. van Swanenburgh for instruction. Rembrandt stayed with him about three years, during which time he improved to such an extent that art-lovers were highly astounded. It was clear that he would eventually become an exceptional painter. His father then decided to send him to the renowned painter P. Las(t)man, who lived in Amsterdam, for further and better instruction. After about six months with Lastman, Rembrandt resolved to practice painting independently. His fortune made him one of the most famous painters of our age. And because his art and work has been most enthusiastically received by the Amsterdamers, and because he was frequently requested to do portraits and other works there, he saw fit to move from Leyden to Amsterdam, which he did around 1630; he still lives there now.
J. Orlers, 1641

The countryside of the Netherlands plays but a passive roll— it follows. This nation is essentially urban, the province of Holland even more so than the others. Leyden, where the young Rembrandt used to play in the streets, numbered more than 40,000 souls. Amsterdam, seven leagues to the north, where, dazed, one fine day in 1624, he stepped off the passenger barge, numbers some 110,000...

A few towers, a belfry, pointed roofs create a frieze where below the evermoving sky—the town lies flat. The approaching traveller can soon make out the remains of the ramparts, brick walls or earth dikes, half-ruined or turned into promenades.
Paul Zumthor, 1965

It is a rich life that Amsterdam in the seventeenth century reveals. Wherever we look everything tells of powerful development, flourishing growth and abundant prosperity.

Amsterdam was certainly the most powerful city in the Republic and it was well aware of this power. Amsterdam society forms one fused unit; in everything there is the definite feeling of belonging to a strong community, a community that leads the way in the nation's life and expects to be recognized as such.

The Lord mayors of Amsterdam, not without some right, regard themselves as the kings of the land. And even the Amsterdam resident thinks highly of himself by virtue of his citizenship; he is a part—an indispensable part—of a powerful organism, and he is proud of it. Hear what the poets say! How proudly they exalt themselves as Amsterdamers! How enraptured they are with their ever-growing town! With what feelings of pleasure they stare at the great forest of masts on the waters of the Y. How joyfully they consider their town hall, their Exchange, their churches and their canals! Amsterdam is considered by its citizens as the metropolis of the world, and no other town is to be compared with it. A happy awareness of standing for much in the eyes of the world imparts to all the citizens power and courage, sometimes in excess, but it puts them in a position to do great things.
H. Brugmans, 1944

d

e

f

g

h

a The life of Rembrandt, from the second edition of J. Orlers'
Beschrijvinge der Stadt Leyden, 1641
b Studies with Rembrandt's head, etching, 111 x 93 mm., 1651
Amsterdam, Rijksprentenkabinet
[a and b on preceding page]
c Leyden, about 1670, Leyden, Gemeente Archief
d Type of windmill Rembrandt's father owned, drawing, 1586
e Leyden in Rembrandt's day, fishmarket and town hall,
drawing by Jan van Goyen, 1654
Leyden, Prentenkabinet der Rijksuniversiteit
f Battle in Leyden between two religious sects, contemporary
engraving

g Leyden University today
h Leyden University in 1614, engraving from J. Orlers'
Beschrijvinge der Stadt Leyden, 1641

a

As For the art off Painting and the affection off the people to Pictures, I thincke none other goe beeyond them, there having bin in this Country Many excellent Men in thatt Facullty, some att presentt, as Rimbrantt, etts, All in generall striving to adorne their houses, especially the outer or street roome, with costly peeces. Butchers and bakers not much inferiour in their shoppes, which are Fairely sett Forth, yea many tymes blacksmithes, Coblers, etts., will have some picture or other by their Forge and in their stalle. Such is the generall Notion, enclination and delight that these Countrie Native(s) have to Paintings....
Peter Mundy, 1640

Journeying through every country of the world, where would you find the equal of our Amsterdam in mercantile shipping? Consider Germany, Italy, Spain, France and England, or to the north Norway, Denmark and Sweden, or other regions of the world. If you were to mention Rome, Naples, Paris, Venice or London, the greatest trading-center on that island, I would say and truthfully maintain that in extensive trading and shipping all over the world, Amsterdam can easily outwit them all. This town, having wrested herself from the violent and forceful tyranny of the Spanish kings, thrown off her yoke of slavery and cleansed her churches and religion, will, for as long as she can shelter under such an unobtrusive government, hold her head up high; for now we are experiencing such a state of order and control as has never before been known to any people.
Melchior Fokkens, 1662

The demand for paintings grew steadily. The rising bourgeoisie was pleased to have its naïve and simple self-consciousness depicted once in a while in some newly mastered role or higher level, and the need for paintings increased in proportion to the space available in the middle-class house. And there was another reason too: we said earlier that at the end of the Middle Ages in Holland, so poorly endowed with land and so richly with wealth, a great need for securities had grown which, among other things, led to the reclaiming of lands. Art was found also to be a good investment.

John Evelyn, an Englishman who visited the Rotterdam fair in 1641, writes in his diary (on the 13th of August, citation completed, *Bl.*): "We arrived late at Roterdam, where was at that time their annual Mart or Faire, so furnish'd with pictures (es-

pecially Landscips, and Drolleries, as they call those clownish representations) as I was amazed: some of these I bought and sent into England. The reason of this store of pictures and their cheapnesse proceede from their want of Land, to employ their stock; so as 'tis an ordinary thing to find, a common Farmer lay out two, or 3000 pounds in this Commodity, their houses are full of them, and they vend them at their Kermas'es to very great gains."
Jan Romein

Why did Rembrandt show such an untiring interest in his own features? It is true that in the beginning his face often served as a convenient model for studies in expression. Thus he may have come into the habit of looking at himself with a painter's eye. But this reason alone cannot explain the tremendous quantity and the deep significance of his self-portrait production, for which there was no demand on the part of the public. Rembrandt seems to have felt that he had to know himself if he wished to penetrate the problem of man's inner life. The phenomenon of the soul attracted him as strongly in his own personality as it did in that of others, and such profound self-realization was, it seems, indispensable for his access to the spiritual and the transcendental.

The objectivity which Rembrandt displayed in his self-characterizations does not permit interpreting them as products of an egocentric disposition. In this constant and penetrating exploration of his own self, his range went far beyond an egotistic perspective to one of the universal significance. In fact, this rare accumulation of so many self-portraits offers a key to Rembrandt's whole approach to the world: the search for the spiritual through the channel of his innermost personality.
Jakob Rosenberg, 1948

kers/ Braders en veel Broot-bakkers/ veel
Krupbeniers/en allerlep neringe wort hier ge-
daan; hier swiert het bp dupsenden van men-
schen/ daar is ook de Pieter Jacobs straat, daar
veel Pastep-bakkers wonen: daar aan volgt de

HAL-STEEGH,

hier zijn de groote Winkeliers met allerhande
slach van Schoenen/ en alle andere kostelijke
waren: hier deur komt men in de

Oude Doele-straat.

en so recht upt de Oude Hoogstraat deur/ voor-
bp het Oost-Indisch Huys tot in de Nieuwe
Hooghstraat, deze vier straten zijn recht op elk-
ander/ beginnende van den Dam tot in de

BREE-STRAAT,

deze Bredestraat begint van de Nieuwe Marskt/
over de St. Teunis sluys, is een schoone breede
straat met groote hooge Huysen/ hier woonen
veel rijke Joden/ over de St. Teunis-sluys tot de
Poort woonen al meest Joden/ als ook achter
deze straat ten Oosten in de groote Hout-tuy-
nen/ hier woont niet als Hout-koopers een
lange rp/ soo lank als deze straat/ gelijk ook
noch aen de West-zijde achter deze straat wonen
veel Hout-koopers; en hier is de Joden Kerk,
hier is 't steeds vol van dat volk/ op deze Breestraat staet de Zuyder-Kerk. Nu komt wp op de

ZEE-DYK.

ook een der voornaamste straten der Stad/ en

b

c

d

e

f

a Amsterdam in 1663, seen from the north, from M. Fokkens'
  Beschrijvinge der wydt-vermaerde koopstadt Amstelredam, 1663
b Page from the same book, which describes the street in which
  Rembrandt lived
c Tower of the Westerkerk at Amsterdam, drawing attributed
  to Rembrandt, 190 x 148 mm., Amsterdam, Museum Fodor
d The same tower, today
e Rembrandt's house in the Breestraat as it is today
f View over the Amstel from the Blauwbrug in Amsterdam,
  drawing, 132 x 232 mm., about 1648–1650, Amsterdam,
  Rijksprentenkabinet

a

b

c

Rembrandt depicted himself, in oil paintings, etchings, and drawings, close on to one hundred times, and each time we learn something more about Rembrandt. To some degree, therefore, Rembrandt fulfils Jung's requirement and exhibits the personality as a developing phenomenon. Technically, the progress is towards an increased subtlety of texture, the psyche seeming to penetrate the painted mask and make of it a vibrating register of the inner life of the artist. But Rembrandt evidently felt that even this degree of revelation was inadequate, and the *persona* gradually disintegrated under the stress of the inner reality. The surface lost its smoothness, its conventional symmetry and coherence.
Herbert Read, 1955

Rembrandt did not believe in immortality; perhaps if it existed for him as the object of a religious faith, it did not become for being that a human certitude, active and consoling. It was the origin of his anguish. And as he couldn't transcend the feeling of mortality, as he couldn't project in a superhuman life hereafter the continuity of what stops here below, he remained prisoner of his immense dreams and of his mortal, insatiable, irreconcilable flesh. Thus space and time became for him "dimensions" of a cell. He did not cease to measure with a bitter enjoyment the oppression, as if the foreboding of the infinite was nothing but a more sorrowful consciousness of our end.
Marcel Brion, 1946

d

The effectiveness of the composition of Rembrandt depends on light, a light with no relation to geometric form. His compositions seem still more free than those of Titian. No one has ever been able to separate a figure in the totality of a Rembrandt painting, because it accents the totality of the composition; or its totality is called light. If one follows the rhythm of the light, one understands the radiation of the light going from the setting to the figures. This is the secret of the composition of Rembrandt....
Movement in the painting of Rembrandt is a cosmic vibration of half-lighted nuances, which puts figures into movement but stays independent of them: even more, it exists everywhere, even when the things represented are completely stable, as the wall in the background. The movements of Titian are more decisive and more evident, those of Rembrandt more contained and more intense.
Lionello Venturi, 1950

e

f

g

a Rembrandt with big nose, etching, 71 x 59 mm., 1628
 Amsterdam, Rijksprentenkabinet

b Studies of Rembrandt's head and of beggars, etching,
 101 x 110 mm., 1632. Amsterdam, Rijksprentenkabinet

c Rembrandt with bonnet on forehead, etching, 53 x 46 mm.,
 1630. Amsterdam, Rijksprentenkabinet

d Rembrandt with fur cap, etching, 92 x 70 mm., 1630
 Amsterdam, Rijksprentenkabinet

e Rembrandt with bonnet, etching, 46 x 40 mm., 1634
 Amsterdam, Rijksprentenkabinet

f Rembrandt with bonnet, etching, 93 x 62 mm., 1639
 Amsterdam, Rijksprentenkabinet

g Rembrandt drawing at the window, etching, 158 x 130 mm.,
 1648. Amsterdam, Rijksprentenkabinet

a

Rembrandt, more than just a great artist, took the Bible stories as the subject of his paintings, etchings and drawings; their total number exceeds the thousand. A Bible by Rembrandt reveals his vision on almost every event; but his Bible is not "illustrated" and cannot be, because Rembrandt was no illustrator; to show this, the story is told of how the assignment to depict Christ's sufferings systematically in six scenes gave him apparently the greatest difficulties. Rembrandt does something else; when moved by a Bible story, he tries to imagine the course of events, the attitude and the feeling of the interacting persons. In his early period, in which he brought into practice what he had learned with his master Lastman, he chose stories dear to artistic tradition since the Middle Ages, and sometimes in creating he even followed a standard pattern—a woodcut of Dürer or Lucas among others—but mostly it was his own fantasy which guided his composition and before long, the way in which he would depict the interacting persons. Then he rid himself of the Catholic traditions; painting for a public who knew the Holy Writings through personal reading allowed him to make his own conception of the readings speak. The Bible itself is the base of Rembrandt's work but he has his own conception of it, which is entirely different from that of Italian and Flemish artists. In that sense his religious work is completely Protestant. It is perhaps said too strongly, but there lies still a great truth in the contention that Rembrandt is the most religious artist not only from his time but from all times, because he himself lived his creations.
H. E. van Gelder

It is singular that the dialogue with God of one lone soul responds so powerfully to the great call of men to communion: Rembrandt, as a painter, reveals it. At the time of the birth of secular painting, it was Rembrandt's feverish hands which seized again the cloak of the apparition at Emmaus, and which alone seemed capable of holding it on earth. His art, which had no predecessors, will have no successors: Lastman, Elsheimer, like Bol and Aert de Gelder, have much of his manner, and nothing of his indivisible genius. How much one finds of the picturesque Jew in his professor, Lastman; how much one compares the "Flight into Egypt" by Elsheimer to that of Rembrandt! What more than a revelation separates them? But this Michelangelo doesn't have a Julius II; his trembling praise of God doesn't spread to a praise of the world, still less of the powers. His biblical figures no longer be-

long in the temple which rejects images; the heroic times of Protestantism ended in a country where one was a Protestant by right of birth, and not because one resolved to be so before God; and his paintings, isolated, weighed less imperiously on his contemporaries than the mass of his work weighs on us now. To continue his work, like to continue Dostoevski's, not only a great painter was needed, but another soul related to his and who, like his, establishes alone the language for his dialogue with the Christ.
André Malraux, 1951

We know nothing of Rembrandt's literary interests: his inventory does not point to the possession of many books; there are, though, indications in his art that he visited the theater. His very trusted Bible gave him an abundance of material for enlarging upon such themes. It is debatable whether he knew the work of Shakespeare. But there is not just a casual spiritual relationship with the English poet, who died when Rembrandt was ten years old. No artist before Rembrandt has researched and understood the human soul and so movingly and convincingly attested to it as Shakespeare. But next to the difference in personal character, there is also clearly a difference in the spirit of the age. Shakespeare sees—just as Breughel—people on stage. He guides their fate and their actions. He establishes like Velasquez their reactions. But he seems himself to remain aloof. He never reveals his own face. Fate runs its course. Fate is enacted on the small man. Trumpets sound and life goes on. Life is merciless, knows no compassion; and that's the way it is—there is nothing of Christ in the work of Shakespeare.

Christ is the all controlling power in the life and the creation of Rembrandt. Therefore Rembrandt adds something more to the inexorable tragedy which Shakespeare delineates. He adds the element of mercy, the element of grace. Not Shakespeare, but Rembrandt ends his life's work with the return of the Prodigal Son. Also in this, the seventeenth century which finally came to spiritual peace and harmony, and to deep absorption is another world from the turbulent, armored age of the fierce religious wars in the sixteenth century.

We can say therefore that this Prodigal Son under the radiance of Eternity, who in the sixteenth century strayed in bewilderment and callousness has returned to the safe harbor of inner certitude and faith in mankind in the seventeenth century.
G. Knuttel Wzn., 1956

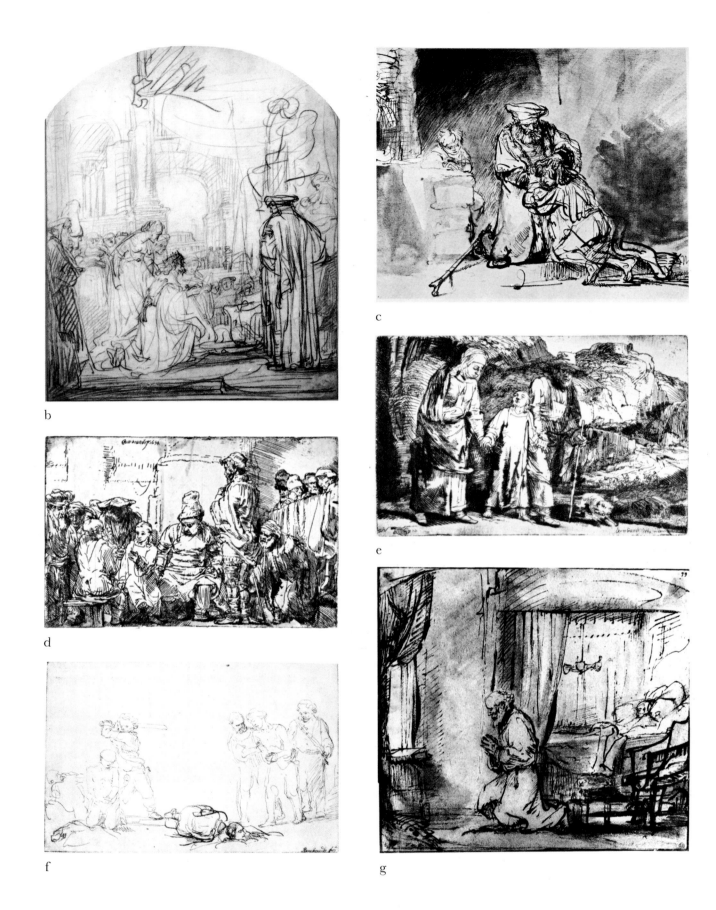

a Study after Leonardo's Last Supper, drawing, 128 x 385 mm.,
  1635. Berlin-Dahlem, Kupferstichkabinett
b The idolatry of Solomon, drawing, 485 x 376 mm., Paris, Louvre
c The return of the prodigal son, drawing, 190 x 227 mm.
  Haarlem, Teyler Museum
d Jesus with the doctors, etching, 94 x 143 mm., 1654
  Paris, Bibliothèque Nationale
e Jesus with his parents, returning from the temple, etching,
  91 x 142 mm., 1654. Berlin-Dahlem, Kupferstichkabinett
f Studies for the beheading of St. John the Baptist, drawing,
  154 x 225 mm. London, British Museum

g St. Peter's prayer before the raising of Tabitha, drawing,
  190 x 200 mm., Bayonne, Musée Bonnat

a   b

Rembrandt ... did not want to conform to the rules of others and still less follow even the most illustrious examples of those who had brought everlasting fame upon themselves as followers of the Beautiful; he was satisfied with following life as it presented itself to him without making any further selections. This is why the good poet Andries Pels says so wittily of him, in his "Use and Abuse of the Stage," page 36, that he

would take no Greek Venus as his model whenever he had to paint a naked woman, but rather a washerwoman or a peattreader from some barn; calling his error the imitation of Nature and everything else but idle decoration.

Hanging bosoms, distorted hands, even the frayed ends of the bodice-laces over the stomach or the garters round the leg, it all had to be followed if Nature was to be satisfied. He wouldn't listen to rules or reasons of moderation in showing parts of the body.

I prize this honesty in Pels highly, and beg the reader to interpret my outspoken judgment in the best possible way, not as coming from hatred of the man's work but for comparing the different concepts and distinct processes of Art and of spurring on those desirous of learning to follow the most worth-while. Apart from this I have to say with the same poet:

What loss it was for Art that so fine a hand didn't put the gifts thrust into it to better use! Who would then have surpassed him? But oh! the greater the genius the further he can stray when he confines himself to no foundation and with no customary bonds and finds that he can discover everything in himself!
A. Houbraken, 1719

Everywhere in a whole series of drawings of nudes made circa 1654–58, there is a charm and a lightness which contrasts with the heaviness of the female body in many other paintings. Do not those which we reproduce (in the book cited *Bl.*) seem to foreshadow the French painters of the female form of the 18th century, perhaps a Fragonard or Watteau?
Claude-Roger Marx, 1960

If Christ had not been, Rembrandt would have found other legends to tell of the human drama, from cradle to tomb, that he lived, or else he would have passed the legends by and then not have put the unnecessary titles under his paintings. In the birth of no matter whom, in the meal of no matter whom, in the death of no matter whom he is found. His humanity is truly formidable, it is fatal like lament, love; change continues, indif-ferent and dramatic, between all which is born and all that dies. He follows our steps to death in the traces of blood which mark them. He does not pity us, he does not comfort us, because he is with us, because he is us. He is there when the cradle lights up. He is there when the young girl appears to us leaning out the window with her eyes which do not know and a pearl between her breasts. He is there when we have undressed her, when her firm torso trembles to the beat of our fever. He is there when the woman opens her thighs to us with the same maternal emotion as when she opens her arms to the child. He is there when the fruit falls from her, ten or fifteen times in her life. He is there when she has matured, when her belly is furrowed, her breasts hanging, her legs heavy. He is there when she has aged, when her wrinkled face is encircled with a bonnet and when her dried hands cross at the waist to say that she wants nothing of life that means pain. He is there when we are old, when we look fixedly at the side of the night that comes, he is there when we are dead and our cadaver drapes the shroud round the arms of our sons.
Elie Faure, 1909

c

d

e

f

g

a Female nude, etching, 178 x 159 mm., 1631
  Amsterdam, Rijksprentenkabinet
b Study for Susanna, drawing, 203 x 164 mm.,
  Berlin-Dahlem, Kupferstichkabinett
c Female nude, asleep, drawing, 135 x 283 mm.,
  Amsterdam, Rijksprentenkabinet
d Female nude seated on a chair, drawing, 222 x 185 mm.,
  Munich, Staatliche Graphische Sammlung
e Female nude, drawing, 286 x 160 mm.,
  London, British Museum
f Female nude before a curtain, drawing, 285 x 190 mm.,
  Rotterdam, Museum Boymans-van Beuningen

g Female nude with arms in a sling, drawing, 292 x 155 mm.
  Amsterdam, Rijksprentenkabinet

a

b

c

Let us look, to be instructed, at the drawings, which are a personal testimony, like a diary, a monologue, and at the etchings which enable a freer flowing of the spirit than could the laborious brushwork of painting. We find then relatively little that can strictly be called "genre." The master found in the people of the lower levels, dressed in ragged and torn clothing, something worth painting: lonely figures, freaks, persons marked by need and grief; outcasts too, with their unkempt hair, undistinguished heads. Scenes seldom conveying particular significance, seldom telling a story, if not Bible illustrations. The Holy Writings, as Rembrandt felt them, were more than abundant with characteristics of pure humanity. His fantasy saw in the figures and events of the Bible the spiritual relationship between man and woman, mother and child, father and son, ruler and subject, teacher and pupil. His subject matter is religious, inspired by compassion; his religious images are secular, as they are non-historical, and non-ecclesiastical. Beggars seen in the slums of Amsterdam were brought into the sacred realm. Rembrandt is a pessimistic Christian, as Rubens who created powerfully spiritual altarpieces is an optimistic heathen. The church of Rome was heathen, compared to the puritanical church of the Reformed. Rembrandt raises the commonplace to the level of the religious, without idealizing Form.
Max J. Friedländer, 1947

Just how great his attraction was to the solitary figure and its characteristic, compelling impact is not only evident in the numerous pages of model studies, but also in the fact that he often takes one of the models as the only subject of a finished work. The fact that he was attracted from the first to these strange and unique, crumpled figures, who live their lives in the depths and that he turned them into common motifs, places him in the tradition of the Low countries, which recalls Pieter Bruegel, Hieronymus Bosch and further back, but his eyes saw this world in a new and fresh way. Beggars, peddlers, quacks and all sorts of tramps and rabble held a certain attraction for him—not only by the way they looked, but also by the spiritual behind them. Their tattered, ragged and worn-out clothing, their grotesqueness and eccentricity—all such creatures have by their very nature— offered to the need to be decorative, which was part of his fantasy, especially favorable possibilities for creation. Until circa 1635 this kind of subjects dominated his production.

During this period most of his beggars came into being. It could be that Callot's famous etchings of beggars inspired him, but those of Callot were created from a different psycho-spiritual condition. To Callot the poor and the ragged offered reason for humor, like the comedians he drew. He was considering the uppercrust of society and courtly circles being his public and he contrived his figures with the intention to stimulate laughter through the strange and grotesque. His close relation with theater and his tendency toward drama lead him to stress and emphasize this. Like a director he instructs his actors to please the public and he communicates with them through his mood, his esprit, his wit and his gracious manner. Rembrandt's beggars are somewhat related, but free of this conception of the comic. He omits the satire that is in the blood of Callot, who invites looking with playful wit from above at people and things. He catches them in caricature; Rembrandt has not the intention to caricaturize. He confronts his figures without criticism and feels only stimulated by their individual characteristics. His naturalistic view of the world includes the ugly as given by nature and seeks to exploit it even in his artistic style.
Werner Weisbach, 1926

a Beggar, leaning on a stick, etching, 156 x 118 mm., 1629
  Amsterdam, Rijksprentenkabinet
b Beggar, "It is very cold," etching, 112 x 43 mm., 1634
  Amsterdam, Rijksprentenkabinet
c Pissing man, etching, 82 x 48 mm., 1631
  Amsterdam, Rijksprentenkabinet
d Two studies of a begging woman with two children, drawing,
  175 x 140 mm. Paris, Louvre
e Two Jews and people on the street, drawing, 175 x 237 mm.
  Haarlem, Teyler Museum
f The couple and the sleeping shepherd, etching, 77 x 57 mm.,
  1644. Amsterdam, Rijksprentenkabinet

g Joseph and Potiphar's wife, etching, 90 x 114 mm., 1634
  Amsterdam, Rijksprentenkabinet
h The monk in the cornfield, etching, 47 x 63 mm., 1645
  Amsterdam, Rijksprentenkabinet

a   b

It is surprising that Rembrandt concerned himself so with reflections. Yes, it seems that reflection of light was his true element, but if he had only understood more of the basic principles; because one who trusts only in his eye and the imagined experience often makes mistakes; they earn the ridicule of their students, not to mention the masters: and even more, this knowledge, for those who take the opportunity, is so easy to come by.
S. van Hoogstraten, 1678

All the great problems of art were resolved in the 16th century. The perfection of drawing, of grace, of composition in Raphael. Of color, of chiaroscuro in Correggio, Titian, Paolo Veronese. Then came Rubens, who had already forgotten traditions of grace and simplicity. Through his genius he remade the Ideal. It comes from his very nature. It is the force, the striking effect, the expression pushed to its own terms. Does Rembrandt find this in the vagueness of the dream and his relation to life?
Eugène Delacroix, 1847

To his extraordinary powers of hand and eye and "rightly judging human heart," Rembrandt added certain unexpected qualities that long passed unrecognized: a deep sympathy for all that was greatest in European art; an excavator's instinct which could lead him back through the stylistic accretions of over a century and an intellectual understanding of the means by which the masters of the classical tradition had achieved their effects. All great artists have studied the work of their predecessors and borrowed from it, if they have felt the need; but few have ranged so widely, or shown such powers of assimilation as Rembrandt. He is the supreme self-educator.
Kenneth Clark, 1966

In our Northern school there is Rembrandt, master of the school, since his influence makes itself felt in no matter who approaches him. We see, for example, Paul Potter painting animals in season and passionate in scenes equally passionate, under storm, under sun, in the melancholy of autumn, while before knowing Rembrandt, this same Paul Potter was rather dry and meticulous. Those are the people who stand together like brothers: the Rembrandt, and the Potter; and even though Rembrandt has never touched his brush to a painting of Potter, do not ignore the fact that Potter and Ruisdael owe to him what they have of the good,

that something which distresses us when we know how to look through their temperament, to a corner of old Holland.
    Now, what is Rembrandt?

The same thing, absolutely; a painter of portraits.
That, first of all, before going further into subject matter, is the great, sensible and clear idea which one must have of these two Dutch summits of equal stature (Rembrandt and Hals, *Bl.*). Once that is understood, there is still ample room for all the landscapes, interiors, animals and philosophical subjects of our glorious republic, represented by these two fruitful portraitists broadly re-established. I implore you still to follow well this line of reason which I undertake to present to you in a very very simple way.

Put yourself in the shoes of this master Frans Hals, painter of diverse portraits, of a whole bold, lively and immortal republic. Put yourself in the shoes of the no less great and universal master painter of portraits of the Dutch republic: Rembrandt Harmensz. van Rijn, a large and natural man, and as sane as Hals himself. And in the stream of Rembrandt flow students direct and true: Vermeer of Delft, Fabritius, Nicolas Maes, Pieter de Hooch, Bol and those influenced by him, Potter, Ruisdael, Ostade, Terborch.
Vincent van Gogh, 1888

But you can of course say that if you paint something... then you paint not only the subject, but also yourself, just as you try to capture the object, because painting is a double and dualistic process. Because for example if you look at a painting of Rembrandt, then I feel as though I know much more about Rembrandt than about his model.
Francis Bacon

c

d

e

f

g

a Drawing by Rembrandt's first teacher Jacob Swanenburgh,
  Festival,
  Leyden, Prentenkabinet der Rijksuniversiteit
b Drawing by Rembrandt's teacher Pieter Lastman,
  David with Goliath's head (detail),
  Leyden, Prentenkabinet der Rijksuniversiteit
c Drawing by an unidentified pupil of Rembrandt,
  Master and pupils in the artist's studio,
  Paris, Collection Frits Lugt
d Drawing by Rembrandt's pupil Nicolaas Maes,
  Study of two figures (detail)
  Leyden, Prentenkabinet der Rijksuniversiteit

e Drawing by Rembrandt's pupil Philips Koninck,
  Landscape,
  London, British Museum
f Drawing by Rembrandt's pupil Govaert Flinck,
  A child, sleeping,
  Paris, Collection Frits Lugt
g Drawing by Rembrandt's pupil G. v. d. Eeckhout,
  Jacob's dream,
  Vienna, Albertina

a

b

c

d

About the time Rembrandt moved into his new house in the Breestraat, he began to look at the city around him, as well as the country and small villages in the vicinity of Amsterdam. Landscape was not an entirely new departure for him. He had already done a few paintings and some drawings. But quite apart from being few in number, they lacked a sense of locality. To judge by these works Rembrandt might have lived almost anywhere in Holland. It was as if he suddenly woke up to the beauty and character of his surroundings, and for approximately the next fifteen years he threw himself into a passionate study, in drawing and etching with an occasional painting, of not just impersonalized landscape but of a definite locality. He analysed the city and its environs in a way that has been equalled in intensity only by Cézanne in Aix-en-Provence. To follow him in his walks even today, when so much has been destroyed or built over, is one of the pleasures of Rembrandt "at home."
Christopher White, 1962

In landscape as in everything else that he did, Rembrandt stands apart and above his contemporaries. His pictures are so different from all the others, so startling in their effect, that it is difficult to realize, as we must from his many drawings, that he constantly studied nature as much if not more than they. But he used his studies to create a complete and peculiarly personal vision of nature. He did this by arbitrarily emphasizing certain elements, subordinating others and using light for the main effect. Each landscape strikes a single poetic note, and there is always a strong feeling of unity. He limits his color range almost to a single tone and rarely uses even an accent that resembles what is to be seen in nature.
Theodore Rousseau, Jr., 1954

e

f

a A road through a wood, drawing, 156 x 200 mm.,
   Chatsworth, Devonshire Collection
b View of Rhenen, drawing, 210 x 324 mm.,
   The Hague, Bredius Museum
c Farmstead with hayrack and weirs, drawing, 120 x 226 mm.,
   Paris, Frits Lugt Collection
d A cottage among trees, drawing, 172 x 271 mm.,
   New York, Metropolitan Museum of Art
e River with trees at dusk, drawing, 136 x 187 mm.,
   Paris, Louvre
f Cottages amongst trees, drawing, 195 x 310 mm.,
   Berlin-Dahlem, Kupferstichkabinett

a

b

How did he differ from all other painters in the world who preceded him?

By his subordination of any object whatsoever to two of the elementary powers: air and light. These became for him real rulers of the world; they became the Ideal. Rembrandt is indifferent to the actual shape of things; their outward appearance is everything to him. Art in general as well as the Ideal can pretend to be indifferent to actual shape and that it is only appearance that counts. It depends on who says it, and how, and in what sense. Events, figures, objects of nature exist for Rembrandt insofar as air and light play upon them in a marvelous way. And the beholder often becomes completely caught up in the game and forgets like Rembrandt the subject represented—because of the method of representation. What happens in the open landscape is impermeated with soft beams of the warmest sunlight; but Rembrandt also knows how to extract an unforeseen magic from nearly cold daylight; and even in an enclosed space he overindulges himself with delight in all possible permutations of natural or artificial light and its reflections. The deepest dark is not yet black, but all relative chiaroscuro. And what's more Rembrandt does not even need color; the etchings he has skilfully executed create an effect similar to that of his paintings. Whether he is to be counted at all among the great colorists as Titian or Rubens, is still a debatable question, he may well remain the greatest chiaroscuro painter of all times, as this he is exactly all he wanted to be. In addition to this particular strength, there was yet another one living in Rembrandt: he is one of the truly great Dutch portraitists, as painter of universal figures. During his earlier life as a painter, he wanted with all his power and will to be essentially only this. Later the persons are no longer painted for their own sake, but only in order that air and light can come to life.

The great painter of light, Rembrandt, used to refer to nature and reality as being in contrast to the idealism in art of his time. As a matter of fact he was unable not only to render even a moderately normal, average likeness of the human figure, but he also committed the most extreme distortions and mistakes in perspective; his forms are often not only ugly as by chance reality offered them to him, but they are often false, even with the highest, magical truths of Air and Light.

It is not true that light, air, harmony and grace cannot be united within the limited execution of a painting. Ruisdael's view of Haarlem contains each quality to the highest degree; it is in execution a miniature. It is not true, that the painting of light can do away with the beauty and truth of the human body. The aging master must have discovered this in the lack of approval and even the desertion of his pupils, that he has incensed his times. It is not true that a single unessential quality may play a game with the total subject. And whenever the master should be forgiven these faults, still may we then build no theories on his doings. It is consoling that those who make a guiding light of him must face the inevitable fate of never reaching him; they remain essentially on the secondary level.
Jakob Burckhardt, 1877

The relative reticence of both artist and patron in 17th century Holland is the main cause for the difficulty of arriving at definitive conclusions about what Rembrandt's contemporaries thought of his work.

One might ask: does it matter to us what Rembrandt's contemporaries thought of him? Is not the important question: what does Rembrandt mean to us today? After all we have his works and it is through the study of them that we must find the formal qualities which are the basis for our understanding of any work of art as an esthetic object. The conditions under which an art object came to be, its history, its effect upon the generation for which it was produced or upon succeeding generations are outside of the work of art *qua* work of art. Agreed. However, even the formal qualities which are distilled out of a work of art must be interpreted and an analysis of what Rembrandt's contemporaries saw in his work will help us see it against the organic whole of the culture in which it was produced. Without attempting this task we run the danger of not seeing the work of art at all.
Seymour Slive, 1953

d

e

f

g

a Frederick Henry, the Dutch Stadholder, to whom Rembrandt
  paintings were sold, engraving after A. van de Venne, 1619
b Constantijn Huygens, secretary of the Stadholder, who bought
  for the latter, drawing by Rembrandt's colleague Jan Lievens
c Rembrandt's 4th letter to Huygens, dated January 1639:
  My Lord,
  It is then with your permission that I send your lordship these
  2 pieces which I think will be considered of such quality that
  His Highness will now even pay me not less than a thousand
  guilders each. But should His Highness consider that they are
  not worth this, he shall pay me less according to his own
  pleasure. Relying on His Highness' knowledge and discretion,

I shall gratefully be satisfied with what he pays. And with my
regards I remain his   Humble and devoted servant
What I have advanced for the frames   Rembrandt
and crate is 44 guilders in all.

d Hendrik de Keyser, Town mason of Amsterdam, an older
  contemporary of Rembrandt, Amsterdam, Rijksmuseum
e Bust of the physician Dr. Tulp, by Artus Quellinus (1609–68),
  Amsterdam, Rijksmuseum
f Head of admiral Michiel de Ruyter by Rombout Verhulst,
  Amsterdam, Rijksmuseum
g Façade with "Fortuna" by Hendrik de Keyser (see d),
  Amsterdam, Rijksmuseum

a   b

In the etching "The Good Samaritan" one sees a horse from the side view; a squire holds the reins. Behind the horse a servant carries the wounded man into the house by the stairs which lead to a balcony. Below the door one sees the well-dressed Samaritan who has given the landlord some money and commends the poor seriously wounded man to him. Toward the left side one sees a young man, whose hat is decorated with a feather, looking outside through a window. To the right in the ordered background one sees a well from which a woman draws water...

This is one of Rembrandt's most beautiful sheets. It seems to be engraved with the greatest care, and notwithstanding all the care, the burin has been lightly carried. The old man below the door especially drew the attention of the esteemed Longhi, saying: "I cannot pass by the page of the Samaritan in silence. There Rembrandt has drawn the good old man under the door in a position that is natural to one who normally trembles, so that to our visual memory he really seems to tremble, which no other painter before or after Rembrandt could obtain through his art."

Johann Wolfgang von Goethe, 1832

He loved great contrasts of lights and darks, and he pushed them far beyond intelligence. His studio, though quite somber was arranged in such a way that it did not receive much light except through a hole, like a dark-room; this lively ray hit, at the will of the artist, the place that he wanted to brighten. When he wanted clear backgrounds he put behind his model a dropcloth of the color of the background which he found suitable, and this canvas receiving the same ray of light that falls on the head, indicated the sensitive gradation, which the painter augmented according to his principles.

Rembrandt's technique is a sort of magic. No one knew more than he about the effects of different colors on each other, and no one distinguished better those which were friends, with those which were not suitable. He put each tone in its place with so much justness and harmony that he assured them their freshness, which mixture could not help injuring. To achieve a tie between the light and dark passages, and to soften the harsh and too brilliant colors, he used transparant tones which he applied with the greatest skill. All is warm in his work, and through an admirable understanding of chiaroscuro he almost always knew how to produce startling effects in his paintings.

Adam Bartsch, 1797

What good comes of running the roads of the world. Even Dürer went knocking on the doors of Italian studios to watch for the secrets of "divine proportion"; he came back up to the Lowlands to catch the formulas used in the studios where one found strange spoils being brought back from the East Indies. Rembrandt scorned to follow, even with his eyes, the directions which flowed from the rose of the winds, the center in which he was situated. He had discovered that in this heart itself, there where he was, opened a profound and unfathomable well; he had only to lean over it to catch with an acclimated and penetrating eye, the darkness where the reflections from the sky, the black depth of water, and the clear image of he who looks, mix; he had only to throw in a daily object to make everything move and animate into facinating mirages, to launch in there a single word to make a sentence roll and rumble in echo.

Réné Huyghe, 1965

Among the most beautiful etchings of Rembrandt are those which give the impression that they have been made with a wooden scrap or the point of a nail. Could you say that Rembrandt didn't know his trade? Quite the contrary, it is because he completely possessed it and he knew the value of hand work found not by interposing between the artist's thoughts and the execution thereof those tools which make the studio of a modern engraver look like a dentist's office.

Pierre-Auguste Renoir

476

c

d

e

f

a Etching of The good Samaritan of which Goethe speaks (on this
   page), 259 x 201 mm., 1633, Amsterdam, Rijksprentenkabinet
b The good Samaritan, drawing attributed to Rembrandt,
   209 x 310 mm., Rotterdam, Museum Boymans- van Beuningen
c Entombment in the cavern, etching, 211 x 158 mm., 1654,
   Amsterdam, Rijksprentenkabinet
d Two studies of a child pulling off the cap of an old man,
   drawing, 189 x 158 mm., London, British Museum
e A recumbent lion, drawing, 119 x 212 mm.,
   Amsterdam, Rijksprentenkabinet
f Mars and Venus caught in a net and exposed by Vulcan to
   the gods, drawing, 210 x 288 mm., Amsterdam, Museum Fodor

a   b

The life of Rembrandt is, like his painting, full of half-tints and
dark corners. Whereas Rubens shows himself as he was in the full
light of his works and of his public and private life, clearly outlined, bright and sparkling with wit, good-tempered, full of lofty
grace and grandeur, Rembrandt seems to steal away and to be
always hiding either something he has painted or something he
has lived through—we see no palace, no grandee's style of living,
no galleries after the Italian fashion. His dwelling is the mediocre,
dark-looking home of a little shopkeeper with all the confusion
of a collector of books, prints, and curiosities. No public business
takes him out of his studio and makes him take part in the politics
of his time, no great favor attaches him to any prince. No official
honors, no orders, no titles, no badges, nothing to connect him
closely or remotely with any deed or person that would have
saved him from oblivion—for history in speaking of them would
incidentally have mentioned him. Rembrandt was of the third
estate—hardly even the third—as they would have said in France
in 1789. He belonged to the crowd in which individuals are lost,
whose behavior is commonplace, whose habits have no stamp
that takes them out of the common; and even in this country of
so-called social equality—Protestant, republican—without aristocratic prejudices, the distinction of his genius did not prevent
the social mediocrity of the man from keeping him down in the
obscure strata and from concealing him in it.
Eugène Fromentin, 1876

I was in England during World War I, moneyless and miserable.
My wife, who is younger and more courageous than I am, said:
"Let's go to a museum for relief." There was destruction in the
whole world. Not only were bombs being dropped on London—
that was of little importance—but every day we heard of another
city destroyed. Devastation, ruins, the annihilation of a world
becoming poorer and sadder. That was bitter. I looked at Rembrandt's last self-portrait: so hideous and broken; so horrible and
hopeless; and so wonderfully painted. All at once it came to me:
to be able to look at one's fading self in the mirror—see nothing—
and paint oneself as the *néant*, the nothingness of man! What a
miracle, what an image! In that I found courage and new youth.
"Holy Rembrandt," I said. Indeed, I owe my life only to the artists.
Oskar Kokoschka

c

d

e

f

a Rembrandt's mother, etching, 150 x 130 mm., 1631
  Amsterdam, Rijksprentenkabinet
b Rembrandt's father (?), etching, 152 x 124 mm., 1635
  Amsterdam, Rijksprentenkabinet
c Saskia, etching, 124 x 102 mm., 1637
  Amsterdam, Rijksprentenkabinet
d Saskia in childbed, drawing, 177 x 240 mm.,
  Amsterdam, Rijksprentenkabinet
e Wedding act of Rembrandt and Saskia,
  Amsterdam, Municipal archives
f Saskia ill in bed, on sheet of studies, etching, 153 x 130 mm.,
  1638. Amsterdam, Rijksprentenkabinet

a   b

Rembrandt is the last eminent painter of seventeenth-century Europe. He is the last man of the Renaissance and ends the line of great universalists. It is true that after him the art of painting knew still many geniuses, but they covered a limited realm and none of them had meaning in such a way for Europe. For Rembrandt helped save Renaissance Europe from her Baroque stage in which she was suffocating. A part of his work would not have been possible without the great Italians before him, but their work would have been of a lesser scope without the conclusions that Rembrandt drew from it. Even if Rembrandt's art has thus an international meaning, it is still just as typical Dutch, as for example, the art of Raphael can be called fully Italian.
Rembrandt's artistry is unthinkable outside our polderland and one cannot really imagine it without our bourgeois Dutch milieu. He works out Dutch problems and with his work sets the crown on the development of our national art.

The essence of Rembrandt is a mirroring of the best of what lives in our people: profound religious conviction, self-consciousness and a spirit of liberty, insatiable and indomitable desire to act. This powerful worker, purposeful and persevering even when affliction and adversity struck him, was a courageous pirate. "If I want to give my spirit relief, then I look not for honour but for freedom" is a known saying by Rembrandt. All along he fought for freedom of the artist and for the right of our sober searching realism to exist freely of emotion and observation.
W. Martin, 1936

In his last creative period Rembrandt is almost exclusively a painter. Among the etchings there were only two from his later period. The few drawings show that color was the only medium in which the elder Rembrandt could completely realize his artistic intentions. The painting takes on the functions of drawing and etching, remaining accordingly "drawinglike" in its structure, perhaps to a greater degree than ever before. Although Rembrandt created his greatest historical painting, history disappeared into the background. There were no longer events that naturally or spiritually prevailed over mankind—the landscape vanished too—it is his conception of human beings that became the essential of his art. Therefore the greater quantity of portraits; there was no longer a difference between commission and free choice. History fades away into the monologue or dialogue, shown in these portraits (The Jewish Bride, Lucretia). Each of

the persons he painted is enclosed in his silent, private world.
Otto Benesch, 1935

... Logic alone does not suffice in explaining genius, above all that of Rembrandt, perhaps the most personal genius ever. One will go astray following it, and one would not be wise to use it as a model. Also we should not dare to assume that he was quite a safe guide for his students, and that the influence which he had on them was quite favorable to their education. His originality was too powerful not to dominate them, and in spite of the physical precautions which he took to isolate his students and to maintain their independence, their characteristics do not differ at all. All submitted to his controlling influence to the point of losing their own personality. The better ones in their better works, succeed in resembling him, and their supreme honor is to be mistaken for Rembrandt. But more often, they imitate him only superficially, his way of composing or his idiosyncracies. As for subject matter they borrow his costumes; they borrow his process of achieving particular effects; they copy him, they confront him, but his proud originality makes the docility of their submission even more obvious.

Indeed, Rembrandt belonged to that race of artists which cannot have descendance, the race of Michelangelo and of Beethoven. Like these Prometheus' of art, he wanted to ravish the celestial fire, set the palpitations of life in inert forms, express in perceptible ways that which by nature is immaterial and unattainable. The infinite attracts these audacious men and the dreamed-of ideal escapes at each moment before their eyes. Yet they set out in search of the sublime and because the feeling which pushes them exists in essence at the base of every human soul, these men evoke in us thoughts which they at the same time fulfill.
Emile Michel, 1896

c

d

e

f

a Titus (?) drawing at a desk, drawing, 182 x 140 mm.
   Dresden, Kupferstichkabinett
b Titus and his nurse Geertje Dircx (?), drawing, 220 x 150 mm.
   Haarlem, Teyler Museum
c Hendrickje Stoffels (?) sleeping, drawing, 245 x 203 mm.
   London, British Museum
d Hendrickje (?) looking out of a window, drawing,
   292 x 162 mm., Paris, Louvre
e Ransdorp, the North Holland village where
   Hendrickje Stoffels came from
f Signature of Hendrickje Stoffels

481

a   b

Rembrandt was not, like Veronese or Ribera, Rubens or Frans Hals, an artist made of one thing and who walks the self chosen sometimes easy, sometimes steep, way. One meets Rembrandt simultaneously in many ways. In him bristles contradiction, enchantingly contracted in one personality. Instincts and powers reveal themselves, and in turn get the better of each other without destroying each other; their union in all that he produces creates a riddle of hidden dynamics. This life work trills like a scale in whose arms unconscious impulse and reasonable will look for balance.

The history of creative art knows some who have something in common with this, but it knows only one figure who possesses these characteristics in the same intense proportion: Shakespeare. Like Rembrandt, Shakespeare also looks at us with so many different faces; both bring about the sibylline wonder of one person speaking at one time and many mouths sounding.

In the development of Rembrandt a series of negations links together his earlier achievements. Over and over again he sets out in battle against this or that former or temporary silent self. In that way he acts like the presumptuous prophet of a sudden creation—who afterwards must search for a slow rhythm and lingering tone, in order to stretch time to a time span.

He seems not to be bound by law or rule. Even that dangerous unconscious law of ritual or routine doesn't exist for him. Every work method he dared to try and in his old days, as from caprice, he exchanged the brush for the palette knife. His etchings and drawings called their own humanity to life—when past forty he chose creatures of more compact builds and from that time on he built them, as if it were child's play, according to another criterion. Light and shadow—at times it is a physical means for plastic effect, at other times an infallible magic for psychic renderings. A colorist? No, say some, because his principal work, drawings and etchings, all that that is personal and self-chosen, is black and white and only chance pushes him to color. Others think that his life long he led up to the open colors of his last works, that he played even in his *grisailles* with color, and his etchings suggest colors. And so, Rembrandt escaped all formula, or better still: is not every formula applicable only to its proteus?

Yet what gathered on all sides of his personality, like clouds, were the unsolvable of the more weighing problems. One carefully looks at all his work—and then comes to assure us that he was predominately—realist, says one, idealist, says the other. Was he a rationalist or a man of intuition? Did he find in the biblical passages a fruitful field for his artistic calling or did his artistic calling serve primarily Christianity? Here begins the indication of Rembrandt's contradictions.

No one, whoever he may be, exists outside of his time, and we question whether the inner discord was not explainable, or at least illuminated through Rembrandt's own century. His creative arts were the down-beat to European development, as well as a pulling to and fro of inner contradictions. Superficially all the reason of the Renaissance, the rhetoric of the new studied manner of speech, the conscious worshipping of the classic hung on. But the later Baroque, outwardly a confirmation of the Renaissance, indicated a disguised rebirth of the Gothic—and there among the many things reborn was the Gothic vision of Christianity in art.

With Rembrandt the pre-Renaissance Christianity returns as though carried by a tidal wave, and with that the Gothic recovers her legal rights—in a weaker fashion this happened also in Italy. Rembrandt's striving toward the dramatic chooses again biblical stories, according to the old manner of expression. Again Christianity becomes something universal, something European as if there had never been a sectarian division.

Rembrandt's depiction of the holy history follows mainly principles of the late Middle Ages. The repulsed Christianity gains back its Gothic customs. Expression in Rembrandt will go beyond the dualistic subject matter of the Renaissance: historical probability and classic beauty of proportions.

Rembrandt stood thus in the discord of his time: the neo-Baroque carried further the form-study of the Renaissance—and Rembrandt participated passionately in that—with these reasonable considerations struggles however an unconscious urge toward deeper value: the revived tradition of the Middle Ages gave the means to that.

F. Schmidt-Degener

c

d

e

a Rembrandt in studio attire, drawing, 203 x 134 mm.
  Text on the attached strip (added later):
  by Rembrandt van Rijn after himself as he was dressed in
  his studio. Amsterdam, Rembrandt-huis
b The inn, De Keizerskroon, in Amsterdam, where in 1657 and
  1658 the sale of Rembrandt's art collection took place,
  18th-century drawing, Amsterdam, Municipal archives
c Corner in the Westerkerk in Amsterdam where Rembrandt
  probably was buried in 1669
d Amsterdam's "homage" to Rembrandt: his statue on the
  Rembrandtplein
e Act of Rembrandt's burial in the register of the Westerkerk,
  Amsterdam, Municipal archives

The passages around and about Rembrandt are taken from the following sources:

p. 458: J. Orlers, *Beschrijvinge der Stadt Leyden*, 2d ed., Leyden 1641.

— : Paul Zumthor, *La Hollande de Rembrandt* in *Rembrandt*, Collection Génies et Réalités, Paris 1965.

— : H. Brugmans, *Opkomst en bloei van Amsterdam*, Amsterdam 1944.

p. 460: *The travels of Peter Mundy in Europe and Asia: 1608–1667*, quoted from Seymour Slive, *Rembrandt and his critics, 1630–1730*, The Hague 1953.

— : Melchior Fokkens, *Beschrijvinge der wijdt-vermaerde Koopstadt Amstelredam*, Amsterdam 1662.

— : Jan Romein, *De lage landen bij de zee*, Utrecht.

— : Jakob Rosenberg, *Rembrandt, Life and Work*, London 1964.

p. 462: Herbert Read, *Icon and Idea*, London 1955.

— : Marcel Brion, *Rembrandt*, Paris 1946.

— : Lionello Venturi, *Pour comprendre la Peinture de Giotto à Chagall*, Paris 1950.

p. 464: H. E. van Gelder, *Rembrandt en de Heilige Schrift*, Amsterdam.

— : André Malraux, *Les voix du silence*, Paris 1951.

— : G. Knuttel Wzn., *Rembrandt, de meester en zijn werk*, Amsterdam 1956.

p. 466: A. Houbraken, *De groote Schouburgh der nederlantsche konstschilders en schilderessen*, Amsterdam 1718–1721.

— : Claude Roger Marx, *Rembrandt*, Paris 1960.

— : Elie Faure, *Histoire de l'Art*, Paris 1909.

p. 468: Max J. Friedländer, *Essays über die Landschaftsmalerei und andere Bildgattungen*, The Hague 1947.

— : Werner Weisbach, *Rembrandt*, Berlin and Leipzig 1926.

p. 470: S. van Hoogstraten, *Inleyding tot de hooge School der Schilderkonst*, Rotterdam 1678.

— : Eugène Delacroix, *Journal, 1822–1863*, (found in the diary of 1847, without date), Geneva 1943.

— : Kenneth Clark, *Rembrandt and the Italian Renaissance*, London [1966].

— : Vincent van Gogh, *Letters to Emile Bernard*, July, 1888, *Collected letters*, Amsterdam 1955.

— : Francis Bacon in an interview on BBC television with Dick Sylvester.

p. 472: Christopher White, *Rembrandt and his world*, London 1962.

— : Theodore Rousseau, Jr., Preface to the catalogue of the exhibition *Dutch Painting in the Golden Century* in The Metropolitan Museum of Art, New York 1954.

p. 474: Jakob Burckhardt, Lecture on Rembrandt on the 6th of November 1877 in the Museum of Basle.

— : Seymour Slive, *Rembrandt and his critics, 1630–1730*, The Hague 1953.

p. 476: Johann Wolfgang von Goethe, *Rembrandt der Denker*, published in 1832, found in *Rembrandt und die Nachwelt* by Suzanne Heiland and Heinz Lüdeke, Leipzig 1960.

— : Adam Bartsch, *Catalogue raisonné de toutes les estampes, qui forment l'œuvre de Rembrandt et ceux de ses principaux imitateurs*, Vienna 1797.

— : Réné Huyghe, *Singularité et grandeur de Rembrandt* in *Rembrandt*, Collection Génies et Réalités, Paris 1965.

— : Ambroise Vollard, *La Vie et l'Œuvre de Pierre-Auguste Renoir*, Paris 1919.

p. 478: Eugène Fromentin, *Les maîtres d'autrefois, Belgique-Hollande*, Paris 1876. English translation by Andrew Boyle, taken from the Phaidon edition of 1948.

— : Oskar Kokoschka in an interview on West-German television.

p. 480: W. Martin, *De hollandsche schilderkunst in de 17e eeuw, 2, Rembrandt en zijn tijd*, Amsterdam 1936.

— : Otto Benesch, *Rembrandt, Werk und Forschung*, Vienna 1935.

— : Emile Michel, *Les artistes célèbres, Rembrandt*, Paris 1896.

p. 482: F. Schmidt-Degener, *Verzamelde studiën en essays, 2, Rembrandt*, Amsterdam 1950.

Translations by Evelyn Burkhardt, D. W. Bloemena, and others.

Notes

NOTES TO PP. 7–8.

1. H. van de Waal, "Rembrandt 1956," *Museum: Tijdschrift voor filologie en geschiedenis*, 61, 1956, p. 193.

2. Van de Waal (see note 1) praises the descriptive texts in the catalogue of drawings while criticizing the superficial notes in the catalogue of paintings. I share his attitude on both counts.

3. For an objective survey, see J. Bialostocki, "Ikonographische Forschungen zu Rembrandts Werk," *Münchner Jahrbuch der bildenden Kunst*, 3/8, 1957, pp. 195–210.

4. J. G. van Gelder, "The Rembrandt exhibition at Edinburgh," *Burlington magazine*, 92, 1950, p. 327; J. A. Emmens, *Rembrandt en de regels van de kunst*, diss. Utrecht 1964.

5. W. Martin, "Rembrandt en de critiek, 1638–1850," *Elsevier's geïllustreerd maandschrift*, 94, 1937, pp. 225–39; G. Brom, "Rembrandt in de literatuur," *Neophilologus*, 21, 1936, pp. 161–91; —, *Hollandse schilders en schrijvers in de vorige eeuw*, Rotterdam 1927; S. Slive, *Rembrandt and his critics, 1630–1730*, The Hague 1953; S. Heiland and H. Lüdecke, *Rembrandt und die Nachwelt*, Leipzig 1960; R. W. Scheller, "Rembrandt's reputatie van Houbraken tot Scheltema," *Nederlands kunsthistorisch jaarboek*, 12, 1961, pp. 81–118.

6. A. B. de Vries, *Rembrandt*, Baarn [1956], p. 86.

7. A. B. de Vries, exhibition catalogue *In the light of Vermeer*, The Hague 1966, and its reviews, e.g. E. de Jongh, *Vrij Nederland*, August 6, 1966. See also P. J. Vinken and E. de Jongh, "De boosaardigheid van Hals' regenten en regentessen," *Oud Holland*, 78, 1963, pp. 1–24.

8. For the monument, see H. E. van Gelder, "Nederlands Rembrandt waardering," *Maatstaf*, 4, 1956, p. 196.

NOTES TO PP. 10–16: DUTCH PAINTING IN THE EARLY 17TH CENTURY

1. K. Freise, *Pieter Lastman, sein Leben und seine Kunst*, Leipzig 1911; C. Müller, "Studien zu Lastman und Rembrandt," *Jahrbuch der preussischen Kunstsammlungen*, 50, 1929, pp. 45–83; K. Bauch, "Frühwerke Pieter Lastmans," *Münchner Jahrbuch der bildenden Kunst*, 3/2, 1951, pp. 225–37.

2. [J. G. van Gelder], exhibition catalogue *Caravaggio en de Nederlanden*, Utrecht-Antwerp 1952; B. Nicolson, *Hendrick Terbrugghen*, London 1958.

3. K. Clark, *Landscape into art*, London 1949; W. Stechow, *Dutch landscape painting of the 17th century*, London 1966.

4. A. H. Kan, *De jeugd van Constantijn Huygens door hemzelf beschreven*, Rotterdam-Antwerp 1946; S. Slive, *Rembrandt and his critics, 1630–1730*, The Hague 1953, pp. 8ff.; —, *Burlington magazine*, 94, 1952, p. 261; A. van Buchell's brief note (*Res pictoriae*, ed. G. J. van Hoogewerff and J. Q. van Regteren Altena, The Hague 1928) is probably older.

5. A. H. Kan, *De jeugd van Constantijn Huygens*, p. 74.

6. P. Geyl, "De kunsthistorie onder de ban van de moderne staat," in *Eenheid en tweeheid in de Nederlanden*, 1946, p. 182. G. J. Hoogewerff, *Mededeelingen der koninklijke akademie van wetenschappen, afd. letterkunde*. ser. B, 4, 42, 1926, p. 124.

NOTES TO PP. 18–32: THE LEYDEN YEARS

1. C. White, *Rembrandt and his world*, London 1964; Dutch translation with notes by H. F. Wijnman, The Hague 1964; see this last, p. 140, note 5.

2. Apart from the difficulties of identifying Rembrandt's father, there is the perennial struggle to find the features of his brother and sister in the surviving portraits and studies. See Catalogue, note [29]. See also H. F. Wijnman, "Rembrandt en Hendrick Uylenburgh te Amsterdam," *Maandblad Amstelodamum*, 43, 1956, pp. 94–103.

3. C. Hofstede de Groot, *Die Urkunden über Rembrandt*, The Hague 1906, no. 11. The document is illustrated in C. White, *Rembrandt and his world*, p. 5.

4. J. J. Orlers, *Beschrijvinge der stadt Leyden*, 2d ed., Leyden 1641, p. 375 (*Urkunden*, no. 86); S. van Leeuwen, *Korte beschrijving van het Lugdunum Batavorum*, Leyden 1672, p. 188 (*Urkunden*, no. 324); A. Houbraken, *De groote schouburgh der nederlantsche schilders en schilderessen*, 1, Amsterdam 1718, pp. 214, 254 (*Urkunden*, nos. 406, 407); C. Hofstede de Groot, *Arnold Houbraken und seine "Groote schouburgh,"* The Hague 1893, p. 396.

5. For the various attributions of this picture, see A. Bredius, *The paintings of Rembrandt*, 3d English edition, ed. H. Gerson, London 1968, no. 485B.

6. A. H. Kan, *De jeugd van Constantijn Huygens*, p. 79.

7. H. Gerson, *Seven letters by Rembrandt*, The Hague 1961, p. 34; H. van de Waal (*Konsthistorisk tidskrift*, 25, 1956, p. 23) speaks of Rembrandt's "scientific bent. Rembrandt was of studious nature... not a genius-by-the-grace-of-God."

8. Philips Angel, *Lof der schilderkonst*, Leyden 1642, p. 47 (*Urkunden*, no. 91).

9. A. H. Kan, *De jeugd van Constantijn Huygens*, p. 79.

10. A. H. Kan, *De jeugd van Constantijn Huygens*, p. 79.

11. J. Huizinga, *Nederland's beschaving in de 17de eeuw*, Haarlem 1941; German edition, Jena 1933. *Verzamelde werken*, 2, Haarlem 1948, p. 491.

NOTES TO PP. 34–40: THE LEYDEN SCHOOL OF PAINTING

1. [E. Pelinck], Catalogue of Stedelijk Museum "De Lakenhal," Leyden 1949, p. 247; J. Bruyn, "David Bailly," *Oud Holland*, 66, 1951, p. 162.

2. J. J. Orlers, *Beschrijvinge der stadt Leyden*, 1641, p. 375.

3. C. Brière-Misme, "Un portrait retrouvé de Constantin Huygens," *Oud Holland*, 53, 1936, pp. 193–201; A. van Schendel, "Het portret van Constantijn Huygens door Jan Lievens," *Bulletin van het Rijksmuseum*, 11, 1963, pp. 5–10; K. Bauch, "Zum Werk des Jan Lievens," *Pantheon*, 25, 1967, p. 264. Lievens was also to make a number of portrait drawings of Huygens (Amsterdam, Rijksprentenkabinet; London, British Museum). See H. Schneider, *Jan Lievens*, Haarlem 1932, p. 196.

4. F. Saxl, "Rembrandt und Italien," *Oud Holland*, 41, 1923/4, pp. 145–60; O. Benesch, "'Caravaggism' in the drawings of Rembrandt," *Actes du 17ème congrès international d'histoire de l'art, Amsterdam 1952*, The Hague 1955, pp. 385–404.

5. C. White, "Did Rembrandt ever visit England?" *Apollo*, 76, 1962, pp. 177–84.

6. H. Schneider, *Jan Lievens*, nos. 169, 221; A. Bredius, *The paintings of Rembrandt*, ed. H. Gerson, 1968, nos. 147, 154, 542, 603.

7. J. J. Orlers, *Beschrijvinge der stadt Leyden*, 1641, pp. 375, 377 (*Urkunden*, nos. 86, 87).

8. J. von Sandrart, *Teutsche Akademie*, 2, Leipzig 1679, p. 320b (*Urkunden*, no. 328); cf. A. R. Peltzer's ed. of Sandrart, Munich 1925, p. 195.

9. R. de Piles, *Abregé de la vie des peintres*, Paris 1699, p. 147.

10. E. Michel, "Un portrait du père de Rembrandt au Brésil," *Gazette des beaux-arts*, 49, 1907, pp. 147–52.

NOTES TO PP. 42–60: REMBRANDT IN AMSTERDAM

1. A. Houbraken, *De groote schouburgh*, 1, 1718, p. 256 (*Urkunden*, no. 407).

2. C. White, "Did Rembrandt ever visit England?" *Apollo*, 76, 1962, p. 177.

3. *Urkunden*, no. 25. Wijnman (in White, *Rembrandt*, The Hague 1964), p. 141.

4. H. Gerson, *Seven letters by Rembrandt*, The Hague 1961, p. 18 (*Urkunden*, no. 47).

5. H. Gerson, *Seven letters by Rembrandt*, p. 34; J. Rosenberg, S. Slive, and E. H. ter Kuile, *Dutch art and architecture, 1600–1800*, Harmandsworth 1966, p. 56.

6. J. A. Emmens, review of *Seven letters by Rembrandt*, *Oud Holland*, 78, 1963, p. 80.

7. A. H. Kan, *De jeugd van Constantijn Huygens*, p. 79.

8. A. Houbraken, *De groote schouburgh*, 1, 1718, p. 260 (*Urkunden*, no. 407).

9. *Urkunden*, no. 54. On October 8, 1637 Rembrandt redeemed this picture, which he had deposited as security with a certain Troyanus de Magistris. There are two replicas (Dresden, Gemaeldegalerie; New Haven, Yale University Gallery). See M. Jaffé, "Rubens in Italy: Rediscovered works," *Burlington magazine*, 100, 1958, p. 419.

10. *Urkunden*, no. 389.

11. In more than one pair of Rembrandt "pendants" the female portrait is by another hand, commissioned (or fabricated) to match a real Rembrandt male portrait.

12. *Urkunden*, no. 67. H. Gerson, *Seven letters by Rembrandt*, and the important emendation of I. H. van Eeghen, *Maandblad Amstelodamum*, 49, 1962, p. 71.

13. A. H. Kan, *De jeugd van Constantijn Huygens*, p. 74.

14. H. G. Evers, *Peter Paul Rubens*, Munich 1942, p. 108.

15. As a result, it is difficult to distinguish Saskia from other young sitters on the basis of facial features alone.

16. *Urkunden*, no. 169, items 17, 40, 70, 93, 104, 124.

17. [E. Haverkamp Begemann], Exhibition catalogue *Hercules Seghers*, Rotterdam 1954, no. 4.

NOTES TO PP. 62–70: REMBRANDT AS A TEACHER

1. *Urkunden*, no. 39. Benesch 448.

2. *Urkunden*, no. 329. Sandrart, *Teutsche Akademie*, ed. Peltzer, 1925, p. 203.

3. G. Falck, "Über einige von Rembrandt übergegangene Schülerzeichnungen," *Jahrbuch der preussischen Kunstsammlungen*, 45, 1924, p. 191–200; O. Benesch, "Neuentdeckte Zeichnungen von Rembrandt," *Jahrbuch der berliner Museen*, 6, 1964, p. 130; cf. drawings Benesch 475–6, 835–7, 1370–84.

4. Copies after Italian works of art are too often attributed directly to Rembrandt, though many of them may well be the work of pupils. K. Clark (*Rembrandt and the Italian Renaissance*, London 1966, p. 151, ill. 156) and Benesch consider the copies after Lattanzio da Rimini (Benesch A104) and one after a Gentile Bellini drawing (HdG 1429) the work of a pupil. I agree with Benesch that his no. A1050a, a copy after Mantegna's ENTOMBMENT, is from the studio, but Rosenberg (*Art quarterly*, 19, 1956, p. 153) and Clark (*Rembrandt and the Italian Renaissance*, fig. 141) claim it for Rembrandt.

5. A. Houbraken, *De groote schouburgh*, 1, 1718, p. 257 (*Urkunden*, no. 407).

6. Mainly in the early study heads (cf. K. Bauch, *Jakob Adriaensz. Backer*, Berlin 1926, p. 84, no. 86; and Oxford, Ashmolean Museum, cat. 1961, no. 62 as F. Bol). A series of the four evangelists in Bamberg Bauch now ascribes to Lievens himself (*Pantheon*, 25, 1967, p. 259).

7. A. Bredius, *The paintings of Rembrandt*, ed. H. Gerson, 1968, nos. 15, 16, 35, 106.

8. A. Houbraken, *De groote schouburgh*, 2, 1719, p. 20 (*Urkunden*, no. 412).

9. A. Bredius, *The paintings of Rembrandt*, ed. H. Gerson, 1968, nos. 223, 224, 363, 364.

10. *Urkunden*, no. 169, items 25, 27, 28, 33, 89, 92, 120, 123.

11. A. Bredius, *The paintings of Rembrandt*, ed. H. Gerson, 1968, nos. 137, 138, 192, 225, 228, 230, 513, 606.

12. J. G. van Gelder, "Rembrandt's vroegste ontwikkeling," *Mededelingen der koninklijke nederlandse akademie van wetenschappen, afd. letterkunde*, n.s. 16/5, 1953, pp. 278, 299.

13. H. Gerson, *Ausbreitung und Nachwirkung der holländischen Malerei*, Haarlem 1942, p. 71.

14. A. Bredius, *The paintings of Rembrandt*, ed. H. Gerson, 1968, no. 238.

15. J. W. von Moltke, *Govaert Flinck*, Amsterdam 1965, p. 96, no. 139.

16. R. de Piles, *Abregé de la vie des peintres*, 2d ed., 1715, p. 426; *Cours de peinture par principe*, Paris 1708, p. 8.

NOTES TO PP. 72–80: THE NIGHT WATCH

1. *Urkunden*, nos. 205–6.

2. M. Kok ("Rembrandts NACHTWACHT: van feeststoet tot schuttersstuk," *Bulletin van het Rijksmuseum*, 15, 1967, pp. 116–21) has now shown that there is no evidence for bringing the NIGHT WATCH into conjunction with the visit of Maria de Medici.

3. Caspar van Baerle, *Blijde inkomste der... Koninginne Maria de Medicis, 1639*; Dutch translation of the Latin, Amsterdam 1639, p. 32; W. Martin, "NACHTWACHT overdenkingen," *Oud Holland*, 66, 1951, pp. 1–9.

4. K. Clark, *Rembrandt and the Italian Renaissance*, London 1966, p. 85.

5. W. Gs. Hellinga, *Rembrandt fecit 1642*, Amsterdam 1956.

6. J. Rosenberg and S. Slive, *Dutch art and architecture*, 1966, p. 268.

7. "Frans Hals als voortzetter van een emblematische traditie," *Oud Holland*, 76, 1961, pp. 117–52.

8. J. Bialostocki, "Ikonographische Forschungen zu Rembrandts Werk," *Münchner Jahrbuch der bildenden Kunst*, 3/8, 1957, pp. 204ff.

9. J. Q. van Regteren Altena, "Quelques remarques sur Rembrandt et LA RONDE DE NUIT," *Actes du 17ème congrès d'histoire de l'art, Amsterdam 1952*, The Hague 1955, pp. 405–420.

10. J. Q. van Regteren Altena, "Rembrandt und die Amsterdamer Bühne," *Kunstchronik*, 10, 1957, p. 135.

11. S. van Hoogstraten, *Inleyding tot de hooge schoole der schilderkonst*, Rotterdam 1678, p. 176 (*Urkunden*, no. 338).

12. A. van Schendel and H. H. Mertens, "De restauraties van Rembrandt's NACHTWACHT," *Oud Holland*, 62, 1947, p. 16.

13. H. Gerson, *Ausbreitung und Nachwirkung der holländischen Malerei*, p. 97.

NOTES TO PP. 84–100: THE 1640'S

1. *Urkunden*, no. 117 (see also 113, 118, 120–3). Two scholars returned to the Geertje Dircx affair at the same moment, to lay before us the harsh facts their predecessors had spared us: H. F. Wijnman, in his note 40 (p. 147) in C. White, *Rembrandt*, The Hague 1964; and D. Vis, *Rembrandt en Geertje Dircx*, Haarlem 1965. The latter places his valuable reading of the archival finds, unfortunately, at the service of a completely corrupt reading of the paintings.

2. J. Gantner, *Rembrandt und die Verwandlung klassischer Formen*, Bern etc. [1964]. See the justly harsh critique of W. Stechow in *Erasmus*, 18, 1966, p. 548. Benesch 443.

3. M. Imdahl ("Raphaels Castiglionebildnis im Louvre," *Pantheon*, 20, 1962, pp. 38–45) believes that Rembrandt drew the Italian models from memory.

4. "Ay Rembrandt maal Cornelis stem," *Nederlands kunsthistorisch jaarboek*, 7, 1956, p. 133.

5. H. Gerson, *Seven letters by Rembrandt*, p. 11.

6. I am greatly indebted to C. Tümpel of Hamburg for letting me consult the manuscript (1966) of his *Studien zur Ikonographie der Historien Rembrandts*; diss. Hamburg 1968; his conclusions are drawn upon frequently in the Catalogue.

NOTES TO PP. 101–120: THE LATER WORKS

1. *Urkunden*, nos. 82–5, 202.

2. Münz 167. W. R. Valentiner ("Rembrandt's LANDSCAPE WITH A COUNTRY HOUSE," *Art quarterly*, 14, 1951, pp. 341–7) has published a landscape painting that corresponds to this etching. J. Q. van Regteren Altena ("Het landschap van de goudweger," *Oud Holland*, 69, 1954, pp. 1–17) recognizes the location as the country house of Christopher Thijs. The attribution of the painting, which neither I nor Bauch have seen, is insecure.

3. J. G. van Dillen, in *Algemene geschiedenis der Nederlanden*, 7, Utrecht 1954, p. 277.

4. *Urkunden*, nos. 169, 176.

5. *Urkunden*, nos. 205–6, 212.

6. *Urkunden*, nos. 233–5.

7. R. de Piles, *Cours de peinture par principe*, 2d ed., 1715, p. 8; *Abregé de la vie des peintres*, 2d ed., 1715, p. 423.

8. *Urkunden*, no. 169, item 203. See Benesch 1187; K. Clark, *Rembrandt and the Italian Renaissance*, London 1966, p. 217, note 10; O. Benesch, "Neuentdeckte Zeichnungen von Rembrandt," *Jahrbuch der berliner Museen*, 6, 1964, p. 135.

9. Benesch 1123.

10. K. Clark, *Rembrandt and the Italian Renaissance*, p. 168.

11. *Urkunden*, no. 169, item 109; no. 201.

12. W. Stechow "Rembrandt's etching of St. Francis," *Allen Memorial Art Museum bulletin*, 10, 1952, pp. 2–12.

13. Münz 158, 249.

14. Benesch 1123.

15. H. M. Rotermund, "Wandlungen des Christus-Typus bei Rembrandt," *Wallraf-Richartz Jahrbuch*, 18, 1956, pp. 197–237; L. Münz, "Rembrandts Vorstellung vom Antlitz Christi," *Festschrift Kurt Bauch*, [1962], pp. 205–26; S. Slive, "An unpublished HEAD OF CHRIST by Rembrandt," *Art bulletin*, 47, 1965, pp. 407–17.

16. F. Baldinucci, *Cominciamento e progresso dell'arte dell'intagliare in rame*, Florence 1686, p. 79 (*Urkunden*, no. 360).

17. J. G. van Gelder, "Two aspects of the Dutch Baroque. Reason and emotion," *De artibus opuscula XL: Essays in honor of Erwin Panofsky*, New York

1961, pp. 451–2.

18. *Urkunden,* no. 169, items 162–4.

19. S. van Hoogstraten, *Inleyding tot de hooge schoole der schilderkonst,* Rotterdam 1678, p. 13 (*Urkunden,* no. 337a).

20. J. A. Emmens, review of Gerson, *Seven letters by Rembrandt, Oud Holland,* 78, 1963, p. 69; H. van de Waal, "Rembrandt 1956," *Museum: Tijdschrift voor filologie en geschiedenis,* 61, 1956, p. 197.

21. A. Bredius, *The paintings of Rembrandt,* ed. H. Gerson, 1968, nos. 40, 271; [H. Miles], *Dutch and Flemish paintings,* Glasgow 1961, no. 599.

22. A. Bredius, *The paintings of Rembrandt,* ed. H. Gerson, 1968, no. 233; exhibition catalogue *Rembrandt als leermeester,* Leyden 1956, no. 72.

23. A. Bredius, *The paintings of Rembrandt,* ed. H. Gerson, 1968, no. 361.

NOTES TO PP. 122–144: THE FINAL YEARS

1. F. Baldinucci, *Cominciamento e progresso dell'arte dell'intagliare in rame,* 1686, p. 79 (*Urkunden,* no. 360).

2. W. v[on] S[eidlitz], "Bericht eines Zeitgenossen über einen Besuch bei Rubens," *Repertorium für Kunstwissenschaft,* 10, 1887, p. 111.

3. Sandrart, *Teutsche Akademie,* ed. Peltzer, 1925, p. 8; Hofstede de Groot, *Arnold Houbraken und seine "Groote schouburgh,"* pp. 37, 206.

4. "Rembrandt and his circle," *Burlington magazine,* 95, 1953, pp. 34–9; "Rembrandt's vroegste ontwikkeling," *Mededelingen der koninklijke nederlandse akademie van wetenschappen, afd. letterkunde,* n.s. 16/5, 1953, pp. 291–2.

5. *Urkunden,* no. 154.

6. G. J. Hoogewerff, *De twee reizen van Cosimo de Medici (Werken van het historisch genootschap,* 3), 1919, p. 67.

7. *Urkunden,* no. 430. A. Houbraken, *De groote schouburgh,* 3, 1721, p. 358.

8. Benesch 1220.

9. A. Bredius, *Oud Holland,* 10, 1892, p. 31 (*Urkunden,* no. 350).

10. Sandrart, *Teutsche Akademie,* ed. Peltzer, 1925, p. 202; R. de Piles, *Abregé de la vie des peintres,* 1699, p. 422 (*Urkunden,* no. 381); S. van Hoogstraten, *Inleyding tot de hooge schoole der schilderkonst,* 1678, p. 257 (*Urkunden,* no. 341).

11. Reported by Houbraken, *De groote schouburgh,* 1, p. 1718, 295.

12. *Urkunden,* nos. 213, 253, 278, 209; I. H. van Eeghen, *Maandblad Amstelodamum,* 43, 1956, p. 113.

13. *Urkunden,* nos. 213, 253, 278, 300.

14. H. van de Waal, "Rembrandt 1956," *Museum: Tijdschrift voor filologie en geschiedenis,* 61, 1956, p. 206. Benesch 1210.

15. W. R. Valentiner, "Die vier Evangelisten Rembrandts," *Kunstchronik und Kunstmarkt,* n.s. 32, 1920/1, pp. 219–22; —, "The Rembrandt exhibitions in Holland, 1956," *Art quarterly,* 19, 1956, pp. 390–404; O. Benesch, "Worldly and religious portraits in Rembrandt's late art," *Art quarterly,* 19, 1956, p. 338.

16. C. White, *Rembrandt,* p. 78; Benesch 1278, 1309, 1334. The Westerkerk drawing (Benesch A62) is probably by a student (J. Q. van Regteren Altena, "Rembrandt's Westertoren," *Maandblad voor beeldende kunst,* 2, 1925, pp. 170–3.

17. "Een 'Rembrandt' op 't stadhuis," *Oud Holland,* 9, 1891, pp. 297–306; 10, 1892, pp. 137–46.

18. *Urkunden,* no. 253.

19. K. Clark, *Rembrandt and the Italian Renaissance,* p. 138.

20. V. Ruffo, "Galleria Ruffo nel secolo XVII in Messina," *Bolletino d'arte,* 10, 1916, p. 100.

21. V. Ruffo, "Galleria Ruffo," pp. 120, 174.

22. O. Benesch, "Worldly and religious portraits in Rembrandt's late art," *Art quarterly,* 19, 1956, pp. 335–54.

NOTES TO PP. 146–156: REMBRANDT AND HIS CENTURY

1. J. F. Backer, "Les tracas judiciaires de Rembrandt," *Gazette des beaux-arts,* 66/1, 1924, pp. 237–48; 66/2, 1924, pp. 219–40, 361–8; 67/1, 1925, pp. 50–60; H. E. van Gelder, "Rembrandts financiële moeilijkheden," *De groene Amsterdammer,* August 25, 1956, p. 10.

2. Letter of January 14, 1611, to Jan Faber; M. Rooses and C. Ruelens, *Correspondance de Rubens,* 6, Antwerp 1909, p. 327.

3. "Dagboek van Constantijn Huygens," ed. J. H. W. Unger, *Oud Holland,* 3, 1885, supplement.

4. Sandrart, *Teutsche Akademie,* ed. Peltzer, 1925, p. 202–3 (*Urkunden,* no. 329). Baldinucci, *Cominciamento e progresso dell'arte dell'intagliare in rame,* 1686 (*Urkunden,* no. 360). French translation in *Oud Holland,* 8, 1890, p. 161.

5. A. Houbraken, *De groote schouburgh,* 1, 1718, pp. 256, 273; J. A. Emmens, *Rembrandt en de regels van de kunst,* diss. Utrecht 1964, p. 83.

6. C. Commelin, *Beschryvinge van Amsterdam,* Amsterdam 1694, p. 651 (*Urkunden,* no. 369).

7. *Urkunden,* nos. 389, 393.

8. I. H. van Eeghen, *Maandblad Amstelodamum,* 43, 1956, p. 113.

9. Even in pictures as late as 1677, as can be seen in the official portrait of Cornelis Tromp at Althorp (Hofstede de Groot 276); H. Gerson, *Het tijdperk*

van Rembrandt en Vermeer, Amsterdam [1952], fig. 60.

10. A. Houbraken, *De groote schouburgh,* 1, 1718, p. 174 (*Urkunden,* no. 405); 2, 1719, p. 100 (*Urkunden,* no. 416).

11. H. van de Waal, "Rembrandt 1956," *Museum: Tijdschrift voor filologie en geschiedenis,* 61, 1956, p. 196.

12. W. A. Visser 't Hooft, *Rembrandts Weg zum Evangelium,* Zurich 1955; see the thorough review of G. Kamphuis, in *Critisch bulletin,* 23, 1956, p. 269); H. van de Waal, "Rembrandt 1956," p. 196; —, "Rembrandt's Faust etching," *Oud Holland,* 79, 1964, p. 17.

13. This is basic to the arguments of both Bruyn (*Rembrandts keuze van bijbelse onderwerpen,* Utrecht 1959) and Tümpel (*Studien zur Ikonographie der Historien Rembrandts,* diss. Hamburg 1968).

14. W. A. Visser 't Hooft, *Rembrandts Weg zum Evangelium,* p. 49.

15. J. Burckhardt, "Vortrag über Rembrandt, 1877," in *Gesamtausgabe,* 14, 1933, p. 178; J. Huizinga, *Nederland's beschaving in de 17de eeuw,* p. 146 (*Verzamelde werken,* 2, p. 490).

16. J. Bruyn, *Rembrandts keuze van bijbelse onderwerpen,* p. 18.

17. G. Kamphuis, *Critisch bulletin,* 23, 1956, p. 274.

18. J. G. van Gelder, *Openbaar kunstbezit,* 8, 1964, no. 11.

19. F. Schmidt-Degener, "Rembrandt en Vondel," 1919 (*Verzamelde studiën en essays,* 2, 1950, p. 27); W. Asselberg, "Vondel en de schilders van zijn tijd," *Pen en penseel, critisch bulletin,* 1947, p. 212; J. A. Emmens, *Rembrandt en de regels van de kunst,* diss. Utrecht 1964, p. 9.

NOTES TO PP. 160–168: REMBRANDT AND POSTERITY: THE BROKEN TRADITION

1. "Men kan de geschiedenis opvatten als een discussie zonder eind," P. Geyl, *Napoleon,* 1946. For the principle of historical uncertainty, see A. E. Cohen's review of Geyl in *Critisch bulletin,* 23, 1956, pp. 377, 380.

2. G. Ritter, "Leistungen, Probleme und Aufgaben der internationalen Geschichtsschreibung zur neueren Geschichte," *Relazioni del X congresso internazionale di scienze storichi,* Rome, 6, 1955, p. 289. T. Lessing, *Geschichte als Sinngebung des Sinnlosen oder die Geburt der Geschichte aus dem Mythos,* 1962.

3. E. Haverkamp Begemann, *Yale review,* 56, 1966/7, p. 308.

4. Models of cautious attributionism in recent literature are: M. Davies, *Burlington magazine,* 70, 1937, p. 88 (Geertgen); J. Folie, *Gazette des beaux-arts,* 6/38, 1951, p. 77 and E. Haverkamp Begemann, *Master drawings,* 3, 1965, p. 403 (Gossaert drawings); and K. Bauch, "Die Wirkung von Rembrandts Frühstil," in *Der frühe Rembrandt und seine Zeit,* 1960, p. 208.

5. J. Emmens, *Oud Holland,* 78, 1963, p. 79, stressing Rembrandt's use of standard art terminology. H. van de Waal, *Museum: Tijdschrift voor filologie en geschiedenis,* 61, 1956, p. 197.

6. J. G. van Gelder, "Rubens in Holland in de zeventiende eeuw," *Nederlands kunsthistorisch jaarboek,* 1950/1, p. 103.

7. When the fragment reached Sweden in the 17th century, its original title had been forgotten. It was called "Ziska's Oath."

8. Copies after Rembrandt are mentioned frequently in 17th-century inventories; cf. *Urkunden,* nos. 46, 58, 72, 81, 111, 169, 175, 180, 211, 227, 294, 321, 332; A. Bredius, *Künstler-Inventare,* vol. 1, 1915, pp. 151, 152, 251, 252, 295, 314; vol. 2, 1916, pp. 314, 503, 510, 713; vol. 4, 1917, p. 1251; vol. 6, 1919, p. 1999.

9. For the adding of signatures to paintings, see E. W. Moes and E. van Biema, *De Nationale Konst-Galery,* 1909, p. 185; W. Martin, "Rembrandt-Rätsel," *Der Kunstwanderer,* 3, 1921/2, p. 30; A. Burroughs, *Art criticism from a laboratory,* Boston 1938, pp. 32–3. There are a number of paintings by Lievens with Rembrandt signatures: SAMSON BETRAYED BY DELILAH (Amsterdam, Rijksmuseum, no. 1458), THE APOSTLE PETER (Bremen, Kunsthalle).

10. The old disposition of the Vienna Gallery is illustrated in F. von Stam, part and A. von Prenner, *Prodomus,* 1735; reproduced by H. Zimmerman-*Jahrbuch der kunsthistorischen Sammlungen,* 7, 1888, p. VIII. A similar arrangement is still preserved in the Garden Pavilion of Schloss Peterhof near Leningrad.

11. H. Gerson, *Ausbreitung und Nachwirkung der holländischen Malerei,* 1942, p. 97; A. van Schendel and H. H. Mertens, "De restauraties van Rembrandt's NACHTWACHT," *Oud Holland,* 62, 1947, p. 17.

12. A. von Wurzbach, *Niederländisches Künstler-Lexikon,* 3, 1911, p. 134; W. Martin, *Der Kunstwanderer,* 3, 1921/2, pp. 6, 30. According to Martin only 500 of Valentiner's 700 Rembrandts are genuine. Another skeptic was P. G. Konody; see *Apollo,* 9, 1929, p. 207. Valentiner's standpoint was defended by C. Hofstede de Groot, *Die holländische Kritik der jetzigen Rembrandt-forschung,* 1922, and J. Rosenberg, *Zeitschrift für Kunstgeschichte,* 1, 1932, p. 83.

13. A. Bredius, *The paintings of Rembrandt,* ed. H. Gerson, 1968. A. Burroughs, *Art criticism from a laboratory,* p. 153, called the first edition of Bredius, *The paintings of Rembrandt,* 1935, "almost as inclusive as Valentiner, Bode, and Hofstede de Groot."

Catalogue

The numbers in parentheses refer to the Bibliography, pp. 505–9.

[1] CONSUL CERIALIS AND THE GERMAN LEGIONS (?) *R f 16(2)6*. First published by C. Hofstede de Groot (*Burlington magazine*, 44, 1924, p. 126). The identification of the subject is still a problem. Some of the earlier suggestions were: The justice of Consul L. Junius Brutus (W. L. Schuylenburg; W. Stechow (95), p. 134; C. Müller (94), p. 78; O. Benesch (136), p. 310); The judgment of Manlius Torquatus' son (W. R. Valentiner, *Rembrandt Handzeichnungen*, 2 [1934], no. 577; —, (318), p. 404); The clemency of Emperor Titus (F. Schmidt-Degener (102), p. 106; G. Knuttel (105), p. 46; J. Rosenberg (29), p. 13, fig. 9). A new proposal has been advanced by K. Bauch (108), p. 99: Consul Cerialis pardoning the legions who had taken sides with the rebels. This scene had been illustrated earlier by Otto van Veen (engraved by Antonio Tempesta). The story is told by Tacitus (*Histories*, 4, 72). Bauch is the first to admit, however, that his explanation is not very much more satisfying than the rest. W. Sumowski (326), p. 23, interprets the painting as an Old Testament subject: Saul sentencing Jonathan (1 Samuel 14:44). I am impressed by the fact that the painting has the same dimensions as the newly discovered STONING OF SAINT STEPHEN [2], and I believe the two paintings to be thematically related, though I have not been able so far to pinpoint the subject of [1].

Even after its recent cleaning, the painting lacks the bravura of design and impetuosity of execution of [2]. Some scholars suggest that it is the product of collaboration with Lievens; others see the traces of reworking by Rembrandt himself. Knuttel (105) elaborates the latter theory unconvincingly. As the background, especially to the right, shows something of the fluent manner of Lastman, I wonder whether this panel may not be a Rembrandt reworking of an (unfinished?) history painting by Lastman. A self-portrait of Rembrandt hides behind the scepter.

[2] THE STONING OF SAINT STEPHEN. *R f 1625*. Acts 7:58–60. The painting was first published by me in 1962 (110). The attribution to Rembrandt is accepted by Slive (112), p. 127, and Bauch (15), no. 41. I have checked the signature since the publication of 1962. The correct version is given here; cf. (110), p. 127, note 4. The picture is the earliest dated Rembrandt we know. F. Erpel (285), p. 138, has observed that the head to the right of the martyr may be that of Lievens. Rembrandt himself appears above Stephen's head. An important forerunner of this painting, not known to me in 1962, is THE STONING OF SAINT STEPHEN by Adam Elsheimer in the National Gallery of Scotland, Edinburgh, published by I. Jost (*Burlington magazine*, 108, 1966, p. 3; see also the exhibition catalogue *Adam Elsheimer*, Frankfurt 1967, no. 21).

[3] DAVID PRESENTING THE HEAD OF GOLIATH TO SAUL. *R H 1627*(?) 1 Samuel 17:57. W. Martin (99), p. 62, note 2, reported the date, before cleaning, as 1625, which fits the stylistic facts much better than the (restored?) date one reads now. However, the same authority is known to have quoted the reading of the date as 1626 on other occasions: (9), p. 34; *Rembrandt en zijn tijd*, 1936, p. 500).

[4] ANNA ACCUSED BY TOBIT OF STEALING THE KID. *R H 1626*. Tobit 2:20–3. First published by Bode (86). Martin (117) and Sumowski (122) have shown that the composition is based on models by W. Buytewech and M. v. Heemskerck. J. Bruyn (137), p. 24, disputes Sumowski's theory.

[5] CHRIST DRIVING THE MONEY-CHANGERS FROM THE TEMPLE. *R f 1626*. John 2:14–16. Published by W. Stschawinsky in *Starij Gody*, 1916, p. 108, as School of Rembrandt. This attribution was corrected by K. Bauch (90) in 1924. Republished by V. Bloch (97), who first mentions the signature, which came to light during a cleaning outside the museum, around 1930, when the picture was in the Dutch art market. I. Grabar (*A newly discovered Rembrandt*, Moscow 1956, p. 4 [in Russian; for an English summary, see J. Białostocki, *Burlington magazine*, 99, 1957, p. 422]) vigorously attacks Bauch and Bloch and declares both the signature and the picture to be a fake. The signature is in all respects comparable to the earliest type of Rembrandt monogram (cf. [2] and [4]), and the picture itself accords perfectly in color and technique with the other small works of 1626. The picture had to be enlarged on all sides (not an uncommon fate of early Rembrandts). G. Knuttel (27), p. 240; (107), takes the side of the skeptics, while Bloch (106); *Apollo*, no. 80, 1964, p. 293, continues to defend the attribution to Rembrandt.

[6] THE ASS OF BALAAM BALKING BEFORE THE ANGEL. *R f 1626*. Numbers 22:27. In all probability identical to the painting referred to by Claude Vignon in a letter of November 1641 from Paris: "Please tell [Rembrandt] that yesterday I appraised his painting of the prophet Balaam, which Sr. Lopez bought from him…" (*Urkunden* (43), no. 90). The composition derives from a drawing by D. Vellert (HdG 26). Lastman drew on the same source for his depiction of the scene (Illustration b, p. 22). I. Grabar (*A newly discovered Rembrandt*, Moscow 1956) thinks that the picture is a modern fake, but as far as I know no one agrees with him.

[7] THE APOSTLE PETER DENYING CHRIST (?) Signed with monogram and dated 1628. Luke 22:55ff. The new identification of the subject is proposed by Bauch (140), p. 143. Verse 55 describes the moment before Peter is accused by "a certain maid." "And when they had kindled a fire in the midst of the hall, and were set down together, Peter sat down among them." I have never seen the painting.

[8] THE FLIGHT OF THE HOLY FAMILY INTO EGYPT. *R H 1627*. Matthew 2:14. The picture was recognized as a Rembrandt by B. Lossky and first published by O. Benesch (104). The date has been recorded, incorrectly, as 1625 (28), p. 14.

[9] SAMSON BETRAYED BY DELILAH. *R HL van Rijn 1628*. Judges 16:19–20. The signature is uncommon for this period; it is painted very thinly in blue-gray. Its dramatic composition and rich color have earned the painting its well-deserved reputation as one of the most expressive works of the Leyden period. Compare especially its subtle draftsmanship and sensitive colors with the raw productions of the preceding years. Kenneth Clark (128), p. 20, praises it rightly as Rembrandt's first Baroque work. Constantijn Huygens may have had this painting in mind when he compared Rembrandt to Lievens, who painted the same theme during this period (Illustration b, p. 26): "Rembrandt likes to pack into the limited scope of small paintings effects one can look for in vain in even the hugest works of others.… Lievens, in the spirit of youth, aims only for vastness and splendor, painting his subjects in life size or even larger." W. Sumowski (122), p. 112, suggests that the poses of Rembrandt's figures derive from Honthorst's GRANIDA AND DAIFILO of 1625. The differences between this classicistic composition and Rembrandt's dramatic new style in the SAMSON are more striking, however, than the similarities. The

strange resemblance of the main group to the single figure of the Virgin in Michelangelo's HOLY FAMILY (the "Doni tondo"; Florence, Uffizi) deserves further investigation.

[10] THE PRESENTATION OF CHRIST IN THE TEMPLE. *Rembrandt f.* Luke 2:25ff. The yellowed varnish weakens the originally powerful contrasts of yellow and blue, and the whitish gray of the background. Except for Mary's face, the picture is in good condition. Perhaps identical with the painting described in the 1632 inventory of Frederick Henry's collections: "Simeon in the temple, holding Christ in his arms, done by Rembrandt or Jan Lievensz" (*Oud Holland*, 47, 1930, p.205). Painted around 1627/8.

[11] TWO SCHOLARS DISPUTING. *RHL 1628.* Also known as ELIJAH PREDICTING HIS DEATH, on the basis of the title Pietro Monaco gave to his engraving of the subject. There is no serious basis for the title, though the picture is surely a history painting, not a genre scene. Benesch (104) calls the subject Democritus and Heraclitus, but Tümpel (139), p. 129, connects the picture with Lucas van Leyden's representation of the apostle Peter and St. Paul. Rembrandt's treatment of the theme is a re-interpretation of what were formerly static cult figures; he gives the holy figures animation and involvement in their dispute. See also Hoff (335), p. 454; —, *Catalogue of the National Gallery of Victoria*, 1961, p. 100.

Probably identical with the "two old men disputing" mentioned in the 1641 inventory of Jacob de Gheyn III (49), p. 127. Rediscovered in 1934 by the Amsterdam art dealer D.A. Hoogendijk.

[12] JUDAS RETURNING THE THIRTY PIECES OF SILVER. Signed with monogram and dated 1629. This is the dramatic picture praised by Constantijn Huygens (32); see p. 28. See also S. Slive (77), pp. 9ff. The composition had been known in various copies (see HdG 123) before the present version was published in 1939 by C. H. Collins Baker (101). Bauch opens his *Der frühe Rembrandt und seine Zeit* (1960) with the words: "Rembrandt's JUDAS has come to light again. This book intends to trace the significance of the art that brought this work forth." L. Münz is more reserved (266), p. 182: "Notwithstanding its poor preservation in some areas, this version has the best claim to be considered the original one." Münz's remarks about the painting's condition are well taken. The drawing Benesch 8 is a sketch for the picture. Benesch 6 verso and 9 are studies for details.

[13] DAVID PLAYING THE HARP BEFORE SAUL. The painting has suffered through the disintegration of the blue pigment, but it surely is a Rembrandt from the Leyden period. Previously attributed to Salomon Koninck, an opinion upheld by J.C. van Dyke, *Rembrandt and his school*, 1923, p. 112. A copy after the picture is reproduced in Catalogue no. 39 of the Amsterdam dealer J.Goudstikker (no. 59, bought in Brussels, May 8, 1929, lot 98). A copy at P. de Boer, Amsterdam, in 1967 (the same painting?) is attributed by Bauch to Lievens (114), p. 166.

[14] THE RISEN CHRIST AT EMMAUS. *RHL.* Luke 24:30-1. Painted about 1628. Bauch dates it 1629 in his book of 1960 (108), and "around 1630" in that of 1966 (15). The Amsterdam exhibition catalogue of 1956 (315) also dates the painting around 1630. I prefer the earlier dating. The drawing Benesch 11, the same composition in reverse, is of the same period. It is generally believed that the composition is based on Elsheimer's PHILEMON AND BAUCIS (Dresden, Gemaeldegalerie), which Rembrandt knew through the engraving of H.Goudt. The traditional nimbus of Christ is replaced by exaggerated natural light.

[15] THE TRIBUTE MONEY. Signed with monogram and dated 1629. Matthew 22:15-22; Mark 12:13-17; Luke 20:20-26. The drawing Benesch 10 is a study for one of the figures. I have not seen the picture, but there seems no reason to doubt it.

[16] THE RAISING OF LAZARUS. John 11:38-44. Bredius (7) seems to be the only scholar to consider the small version (Bredius 537) the original, and this one the copy. The relation of Lievens' painting of 1631 (Brighton), his etching (Bartsch 3), and Rembrandt's drawing of 1630 to this undated composition seems to me more complex than drawn by Bauch (114), p. 166.

[17] THE PRESENTATION OF CHRIST IN THE TEMPLE. *RHL 1631* (redrawn). The semi-circular arch at the top was cut in order to make of the picture a pendant to Dou's YOUNG MOTHER when both were in the collection of the Stadholder. A recent cleaning has revealed the delicacy of color and design that make this moving scene a landmark of the Leyden period. There has been some disagreement as to whether the figure seen from behind is Hannah or the high priest. Stechow (*Print collectors' quarterly*, 27, 1940, p. 371, note 7) first advanced the Hannah theory; H.Schulte Nordholt (167) identifies the figure descending the stair as Hannah. Tümpel (139), p. 207, has pinpointed the moment depicted as the encounter of Simeon and Hannah not before the altar but in the midst of the temple. There are several copies. The one in Dresden is by Willem de Poorter; a copy in the collection of A. Soós is claimed by its owner to be the original, while the Mauritshuis painting would be a work of K. van der Pluym! (A. Soós, *Rembrandt, Simeon in the temple*, London 1965).

[18] THE MUSIC-MAKERS. *RHL 1626.* The picture is recorded for the first time in the F. Cripps sale, London (Christie), November 16, 1936, lot 155 (2100 gns to Speelman). The signature came to light after cleaning. First published by V. Bloch in 1937 (100). Accepted as a Rembrandt by Benesch (*Art*

quarterly, 3, 1940, p. 13), Bauch (108), p. 138, J.G. van Gelder (103), p. 284, and others. Rejected by Knuttel (105), p. 46; (27), p. 240; see also Bloch's rejoinder (106). Bauch insists on an interpretation of the painting as an allegory of Music or the Sense of Hearing, with the members of Rembrandt's family serving as models. I agree that the picture is not a genre scene or a group portrait.

[19] THE MONEY-CHANGER. *RH(L) 1627.* An X-ray photograph is reproduced by Burroughs (294), p. 4. Bauch (108), p. 139; (15), no. 110, considers this picture—as well as other, similar compositions of the Utrecht school—a representation of Avarice.

[20] AN ARTIST IN THE STUDIO ("THE EASEL"). The picture first came to light in the Princess Royal sale, London (Christie), June 26, 1925, lot 14. It was published at the time by C.Hofstede de Groot (91) and W.R.Valentiner (93). C.H. Collins Baker (92) attributed it to Gerard Dou. The attribution to Rembrandt of this vigorously executed, powerfully designed picture does not seem to me to be open to serious doubt. It remains uncertain, however, if it is a self-portrait (Bauch, Benesch, Erpel, Slive, Valentiner, exhib. cat. *De schilder en zijn wereld* (282), no. 94) or a portrait of Gerard Dou, who entered Rembrandt's studio as an apprentice in 1628 (J.G. van Gelder (103), p. 291; C.White, (67), p. 16). A strip 7 cm. high has been removed from the top of the painting; it was originally a vertical rather than a horizontal oblong. Hofstede de Groot thought that the strip—now lost—had been added by another hand, but Slive (113) claims that it was part of the original picture; I am not perfectly convinced. Photographs of the panel in its former state are in the Courtauld Institute (Witt Library), London, and the Frick Art Reference Library, New York. A replica was reproduced in *Art in America*, 6, 1918, p. 118.

[21] A SCHOLAR IN A LOFTY ROOM. *Rem(b)randt (?)* Published by C.J. Holmes (87) in 1917. An excellent oil sketch in gray, painted around 1628.

[22] THE APOSTLE PAUL IN PRISON. *R f 1627* and, in the open book, *Rembrandt fecit.* This and some of the following pictures of holy figures belong to the category which Bauch calls "one-figure history paintings." The painting bears comparison with [11] as concrete depictions of the biblical characters in their actual activities.

[23] THE APOSTLE PAUL AT HIS DESK (REMBRANDT'S FATHER). Painted around 1630.

[24] THE PROPHET JEREMIAH LAMENTING THE DESTRUCTION OF JERUSALEM (REMBRANDT'S FATHER). *RHL 1630.* It is not at all certain that the figure is actually Jeremiah, as was lately proposed by F.Landsberger (70), p. 109. There are other possible causes for the old man's melancholy than the destruction of Jerusalem; see also J.G. van Gelder (153).

[25] THE APOSTLE PETER IN PRISON. *RHL 1631.* Several replicas exist. Having seen this painting lately, I am convinced that it is the original.

[26] A SCHOLAR IN A LOFTY ROOM ("SAINT ANASTASIUS"). *Rembrandt fc 1631.* This type of signature is unusual for the period around 1631. I suspect that the genuine signature is covered by this one. The picture itself is of excellent quality.

[27] THE PROPHETESS HANNAH (REMBRANDT'S MOTHER). *RHL 1631.* In the same delicately drawn style as the figures in [17].

[28] SOLDIER IN A PLUMED CAP. First introduced into the Rembrandt literature by Bredius (14), no. 132. There is a signature, *R H van Rijn*, though it is hard to make out. Valentiner (318) does not accept it as a Rembrandt, and others have expressed doubts as well. Another version was sold in London (Christie), April 25, 1952, lot 148 (as de Poorter). Reproduced in color in *The connoisseur*, 133, 1954, p. 120. Lingering doubts remain.

[29] REMBRANDT'S FATHER. L. Münz (266) has carefully studied the problems concerning the so-called portraits of Rembrandt's parents, and has come to the conclusion that "there is for the moment no picture that can reasonably be considered an authentic portrait of Rembrandt's father." The basis for the identification of Rembrandt's parents has long been the pair of portraits by Dou (Cassel, Gemaeldegalerie, cat.nos. 257-8); but that parentage is far from watertight. The type of old woman shown by Dou seems to be different from that which Rembrandt painted in his youth. There is, however, a drawing in Oxford (Illustration c, p. 188) that bears an old inscription: *Harman Gerrits van de Rhijn* (Benesch 56r; first published by A.M. Hind (256)). If one accepts drawing and inscription as authentic (which Münz does not), we have another type for Rembrandt's father, which occurs in the present portrait and in two holy figures of 1630 [23, 24] as well as in the Rembrandt/Dou TOBIT AND ANNA in the National Gallery, London (no. 4189). See also J.Rosenberg (29), p. 345, note 1A, and Bauch (15), no. 343.

[30] SELF-PORTRAIT. Bauch (109) has published another version, in the Cevat Collection (currently on loan to the Rijksmuseum), as the original (see also (108), p. 178, and (15), no. 287). The Cevat copy is exhibited as a Rembrandt in the Rijksmuseum, as it was in the exhibition *Rondom Rembrandt*, Leyden 1968, no. 35. According to Bauch, van Vliet's etching after Rembrandt (Bartsch 19) was done from the Cevat version; the Cassel picture should be attributed to Jan Lievens. Having seen both versions side by side at the exhibition *De schilder en zijn wereld* (282), nos. 92-3, I am convinced that the Cassel picture is an autograph work by Rembrandt. Rosenberg and Slive (30), pp. 50, 267, are also of this opinion. A copy was formerly in the Matsvansky Collection in Vienna (Frimmel, *Blätter für Gemäldekunde*, 3, 1907,

p. 165 with reproduction); another belongs to Sir John Heathcoat Amory, Bt.

[31] HEAD OF A MAN. Often called "Rembrandt's Father," though it is not likely that the model was either Harman Gerritsz. or the so-called Rembrandt's father. J. Veth (85), p. 136, suggested Rembrandt's brother Gerrit, Bauch (15) Rembrandt's brother Adriaen. The same model is portrayed in the etching Münz 46.

[32] SELF-PORTRAIT. Signed with monogram and dated 1629. Additional strips have been added to the panel, at the left (8 mm.) and at the top (7 mm.). Formerly in the Gotha Museum; acquired from the Duke of Sachsen-Coburg-Gotha in 1953 (Münchner Jahrbuch der bildenden Kunst, 3/5, 1954, p. 218).

[33] SELF-PORTRAIT. Signed with an unusual monogram. G. Glück (278), p. 298, saw this picture as a study in expression rather than a self-portrait. A copy, formerly in the Heugel Collection, was sold at auction in Brussels (Trussart), November 19, 1956, lot 28. A certain amount of confusion over the respective versions was created by Bode and Hofstede de Groot who, in the German edition of their Rembrandt (2), no. 15, reproduced the present version (then in the Stoop Collection) as the original, while in the English edition of the same year they published the Heugel copy.

[34] REMBRANDT'S MOTHER READING. The attribution to Rembrandt has been rejected by Bauch (108), p. 283 and note 127, "work of pupil copying Bredius 67 [which I reject: H.G.] in reverse"; (15), p. 47, "Schulwerk"; J.G. van Gelder (311), p. 328; and Münz (266), p. 146: "close to Lievens." There are certainly weak areas in the picture—the washed out pages of the book, for example, and the empty body of the woman—but on the other hand the picture is strongly constructed and the brushwork of the face of superior quality, so a collaboration with Rembrandt must still be considered a possibility.

[35] REMBRANDT'S MOTHER. Generally connected with the etching Münz 83, of 1628, but to my mind the picture can be dated earlier, considering its powerful execution. Bauch doubts whether Rembrandt's mother was the model for this study.

[36] AN OLD MAN IN A CAP. The cap seems to have been added, though by Rembrandt himself, perhaps to make the painting conform to the etching of 1630 (Münz 39), which is related to it. The painting may be a little earlier. A.B. de Vries has drawn my attention to the fierce colors of the head, which may be—according to him—reflections of a fire at the figure's right shoulder.

[37] REMBRANDT'S MOTHER. Along with the SELF-PORTRAIT in Liverpool [41], one of the pictures given to King Charles I by Robert Kerr, Earl of Ancram, sometime before 1633. The King's inventory of about 1640 lists it only as "an old woman" (see O. Millar, Walpole society, 37, 1958/60, p. 60). There is a label on the back: "Given to the King by Sir Robert Kerr." Kerr (Lord Ancram) probably bought these pictures during his stay in Holland in 1629. See also White (66), p. 177; J.G. van Gelder (313), p. 37. X-ray has revealed a man's head upside down beneath the present painting, also Rembrandt's work, in all likelihood.

[38] SELF-PORTRAIT. Said to be signed with monogram and dated 1629, though the signature is barely legible today, and the date totally invisible. The character of this work, as Slive (112), p. 148, has rightly stressed, is rather formal, and is closer to that of a commissioned portrait than a self-portrait. The state of the picture's preservation is rather poor.

[39] SELF-PORTRAIT.

[40] SELF-PORTRAIT. The condition of the painting seems poor. As it has not been available for inspection for the last 20 years, it would seem wiser not to offer any final comments on the autograph character of the picture. A copy, of smaller size, was sold in London (Sotheby), June 21, 1950, lot 76.

[41] SELF-PORTRAIT. Rembrandt f. The genuineness of the signature is questioned in the Liverpool catalogue. The portrait can be identified as one of the two Rembrandts that Lord Ancram bought in Holland in 1629. The other is REMBRANDT'S MOTHER [37]. These were, in all probability, the first works by Rembrandt to reach England. The SELF-PORTRAIT had been given by Ancram to Charles I by 1633. See Hoff (55); J.G. van Gelder (313), p. 37; Millar, Walpole society, 37, 1958/60, p. 57.

[42] AN OLD MAN IN A FUR HAT. Signed with monogram and dated 1630. Bauch (108), note 129: "after cleaning to be considered a Rembrandt, not a copy." Having seen the painting again recently, I agree with Bauch, though I must add that the painting is not one of the artist's best. Copied by the etcher J.G. van Vliet (Bartsch 24, dated 1633). That copy was in turn adapted by F. Langlois Ciartres in a print he entitled "PHILON LE JUIF."

[43] "THE REPENTANT SAINT PETER." May have been intended as a study for a figure of the repentant apostle. The execution is weak, the drawing unsteady (e.g. the ear). Could it be an old copy? Perhaps by Dou?

[44] SELF-PORTRAIT. Indistinctly signed and dated (1630?). The delicacy of the handling is reminiscent of an etching on copper.

[45] SELF-PORTRAIT. RL 1630. The criticism of F. Winkler (327), p. 143, over the restoration of this painting seems to me to be too severe.

[46] OFFICER WITH A GOLD CHAIN. Signed with monogram. Burroughs (294), p. 4, published a good X-ray photograph. A copy was displayed in the London exhibition Dutch art (312), no. 36 (see J.G. van Gelder (313), p. 37; E. Plietzsch (314), p. 123).

[47] AN OFFICER. A modern signature covers the remains of an old one.

From X-rays it can be seen that there was originally another head to the right of the present one, seen full face.

[48] OLD MAN WITH A GOLD CHAIN. Signed with monogram and dated 1631. Lately cleaned, in good condition. The date of 1631 disputes the identification of the sitter as Rembrandt's father, who died in 1630. The same sitter painted before 1630 is no more likely to be the father, then. According to Bauch, perhaps brother Adriaen. The apparent age of the sitter speaks against this identification.

[49] OFFICER WITH A GOLD CHAIN. RHL. In excellent condition.

[50] OLD MAN WITH A JEWELED CROSS. RHL 1630. One of the most powerful and at the same time most delicately painted studies of the Leyden period. In good condition. Recorded in a Cassel inventory as early as 1731.

[51] YOUNG OFFICER. Signed with monogram and dated 1631. Not known to me in the original.

[52] YOUNG MAN IN A PLUMED HAT. Signed with monogram and dated 1631.

[53] THE AMSTERDAM MERCHANT NICOLAES RUTS. Signed with monogram and dated 1631. (The monogram is no longer legible.) The identity of the sitter as Nicolaes Ruts (1573–1638) is rather well documented: the picture was copied by an 18th-century artist, A. Delfos, with the sitter's name (and the date 1633; it was then in the collection of descendants of Ruts). When Ruts' daughter Suzanna married Pieter van der Hagen in 1636 she owned "'t Contrefeytsel van Nicolaes Ruts by Rembrant gedaen" (Urkunden (43), no. 49). This portrait must have been among the first Amsterdam commissions that Rembrandt received; the portrait type shows the influence of Flemish models.

[54] YOUNG MAN AT A DESK. Signed with monogram and dated 1631. Certainly an important commissioned portrait, though the identity of the sitter has so far eluded scholars. The portrait type is again derived from a Flemish model.

[55] ANDROMEDA CHAINED TO THE ROCK. I would date this study early, about 1627/8. Sumowski (122), p. 111, refers to a drawing by A. Bloklandt as one source for the composition. An Andromeda without her dragon is an iconographical rarity.

[56] CHRIST ON THE CROSS. RHL 1631 (redrawn?). The picture was recognized as a Rembrandt when it was cleaned in the Louvre. It was published by Bauch (168) in 1962. It is obvious that this Crucifixion has some connection with the Passion series that Rembrandt later made for Prince Frederick Henry [64, 65, 80, 87, 88]. Perhaps it was a kind of trial piece, not itself destined for the Stadholder's collection. I rather think that Rembrandt designed the piece as the central scene of three, to be flanked by THE RAISING OF THE CROSS [64] and THE DESCENT FROM THE CROSS [65], the whole an attempt to outdo Rubens, especially the great Antwerp altar. Huygens saw these pieces in the making, to round out the theory, and his interest led to a purchase of the canvases and a commission for more scenes from the Passion. The similarities of CHRIST ON THE CROSS with the Lievens composition in Nancy (Illustration a, p. 44) make it appear likely that both pieces were done in Leyden when the two men were working side by side.

[57] THE ABDUCTION OF PROSERPINA. Iconographically there is a certain connection with antique models, directly or through the Soutman print after Rubens. Clark (128), p. 8, wittily analyzes the difference between Rembrandt's and Rubens' attitudes toward the antique. Frankl (197) has pointed out the less obvious relation of the PROSERPINA to a composition by L. Sustris. The picture was described in the 1632 inventory of the Stadholder's collection as "a great piece, where Pluto abducts Proserpina, made by Jan Lievensz. of Leyden" (Oud Holland, 47, 1930, p. 203), but there can be no doubt that it is a Rembrandt (and not a very large one). There is some disagreement as to its dating. J.Q. van Regteren Altena (Kunstchronik, 10, 1957, p. 135) dates it as late as 1634, but I agree with Winkler (327), p. 137, that it belongs to the Leyden period, perhaps as early as 1628/9.

[58] ESTHER PREPARING TO INTERCEDE WITH AHASUERUS. Signed Rembrant f. 163(.) The subject (Esther 5:1) was identified by M. Kahr (157), taking up a suggestion by W.S. Heckscher (207), pp. 118, 176. Mrs. Kahr says of the signature and date: "It is possible that Rembrandt signed the painting in 1633 and painted a 7 over the final 3 in 1637." I am not very convinced of the originality of the signature, and I still think the picture belongs to the period 1632/3. This difference in dating does not interfere with Mrs. Kahr's convincing re-interpretation of the painting and the etching Münz 90 (Illustration b, p. 249).

[59] DANIEL AND CYRUS BEFORE THE IDOL OF BEL. Rembrandt 1633. The date 1633 (previously read as 1631) came to light after a cleaning in 1959. G. Knuttel (27), p. 249, had already doubted the signature and date of 1631. The subject was identified by H. van de Waal. It is taken from the apocryphal book of Daniel, chap. 14; see J.G. van Gelder (150). K. Bauch (140), p. 125, discusses the iconographical treatment. Cyrus is trying to convince Daniel that his idol of Bel is a living creature, pointing out that it consumed its offerings with great regularity. Daniel eventually disqualified the argument by sprinkling the floor of the chamber with flour one night, and showing Cyrus in the morning the footsteps of the priests who had themselves been feasting on Bel's supper.

[60] CHRIST IN THE STORM ON THE SEA OF GALILEE. *Rembrandt f. 1633.*
The composition is partly derived from an engraving by Maerten de Vos
(K. E. Maison, *Themes and variations*, London 1960, p. 99). The upper surface
of the painting has suffered from abrasion, so that the blues and pinks look
like modern undamped colors. The strong light blue is Rembrandt's, however
(cf. [76]).

[61] THE GODDESS DIANA BATHING, WITH THE STORIES OF ACTAEON
AND CALLISTO. *Rembrandt fe. 1635,* but the last digit is painted over. The date
is probably 1633 or 1632. Stylistically the picture is closely related to [62].
Rembrandt combines two episodes from Ovid (*Metamorphoses*, 2, 409 and 3,
138).

[62] THE ABDUCTION OF EUROPA. *RHL van Rijn 1632.* Ovid, *Metamor-*
phoses, 2, 870. The composition is derived from Elsheimer rather than Lastman
(J. Rosenberg (29), p. 15, fig. 12). Not seen by Bauch or me, but all evidence
points to a good early Rembrandt.

[63] THE HOLY FAMILY. *Rembrandt 163(.)* The picture was formerly thought
to be dated 1631, which to my mind does not match its Baroque style of about
1635. On my request, Dr. Brochhagen has gone into the matter further, and
reports that the last digit is painted on a strip added later. The original shape
of the painting was ⌂. G. Knuttel (27), p. 249, had already doubted the date,
and Rosenberg (29), p. 196, stressed the fact that "in character it is closer to
the Amsterdam period." The X-ray reveals an underpainting of powerful
design deserving of comparison with the proud structure of a Rubens.

[64] THE RAISING OF THE CROSS. This and the following number were the
first pictures of the Passion series bought for Frederick Henry by Constantijn
Huygens (see [56]). We are rather well informed about this affair by seven
letters (the only Rembrandt letters in existence) the artist wrote to Huygens;
see H. Gerson (63). In the first letter, to which the date 1636 has been added
(by Huygens?), Rembrandt writes that he is "very diligently engaged in completing as quickly as possible the three Passion pictures, which His Excellency
himself commissioned me to do: an ENTOMBMENT, a RESURRECTION, and
an ASCENSION OF CHRIST. These are companion pictures to CHRIST'S
ELEVATION and DESCENT FROM THE CROSS." From the wording it can be
deduced that THE RAISING OF THE CROSS and THE DESCENT FROM THE
CROSS were not actually ordered by Huygens, but bought from Rembrandt,
who had begun painting them on his own account. E. Brochhagen (336), p.
58; —, *Kunsthistorische Studien für Hans Kauffmann zum 70. Geburtstag* (in preparation), has carefully studied the drawings connected with the commission and
the pentimenti revealed by X-ray. The most interesting observation is that
the position of Christ's head was originally closer to that in CHRIST ON THE
CROSS of 1631. I. Bergström has plumbed the significance of the self-portrait
that Rembrandt lent to the features of the man helping to raise the cross.

[65] THE DESCENT FROM THE CROSS. *C Rhmbrant* (false). The composition
is etched (in reverse) by Rembrandt himself (Münz 197; Illustration a, p. 46).
The etching is signed and dated 1633. A second version (Münz 198) is in-
scribed *Rembrandt f. cum pryvl°:1633.* Rembrandt used this formula, after the
Flemish pattern, to protect his etchings from copying and selling by others.
Brochhagen (336) reports pentimenti that accord with the details of the etching,
and which have subsequently been changed in the painted version, though by
Rembrandt himself. The face of the man on the ladder bears the features of
Rembrandt, in the style of the earliest self-portraits (see G. Lengl, *Das Münster,*
20, 1967, p. 52).

[66] THE DESCENT FROM THE CROSS. Signed *Rembrandt f. 1634.* An excellent reworking of the 1633 composition, entirely by Rembrandt himself.

[67] THE RISEN CHRIST SHOWING HIS WOUND TO THE APOSTLE
THOMAS. *Rembrandt f. 1634.* John 20:27. In an excellent state of conservation,
with a genuine signature.

[68] THE FLIGHT OF THE HOLY FAMILY INTO EGYPT. *Rembrandt f. 1634 (?)*
Matthew 2:14. The date is difficult to read. The picture appeared for the first
time at the Clinton sale, London (Sotheby), July 19, 1950, lot 114. With the
exception of Knuttel (27), p. 240, all those who saw it at the Royal Academy
exhibition of 1952/3 (312), no. 35, accept it—rightly, it seems to me. For other
favorable comment, see J. G. van Gelder (313), p. 37; E. Plietzsch (314),
p. 122.

[69] SOPHONISBA RECEIVING THE POISONED CUP (?) *Rembrant f. 1634.*
The story of Sophoni(s)ba is told by Livy (Book 30, 12, 15). She was the wife
of Syphax Massinissa, who sent her a cup of poison when she fell prisoner to
Scipio and he asked her to remain with him. The subject has also been interpreted as Artemisia drinking her cup of wine with the ashes of her husband,
King Mausolos (Aulus Gellius, *Noctes Attica*, 10, 18, 3). The iconographic
traditions of the two subjects are so similar that it remains impossible to
decide which story is being depicted. The Prado catalogue (1963, no. 2132)
prefers Artemisia, as does J. I. Kusnetzow (*Publications of the Hermitage, Dept.
of Western European art*, 3, 1964, p. 197; in Russian), who argues that Rembrandt was inspired by the Rubens painting of this theme ("de historie van
Artemise") listed in the collection of Amalia van Solms in 1632 (*Oud Holland*,
47, 1930, p. 227). J. G. van Gelder (*Nederlands kunsthistorisch jaarboek*, 3,
1950/1, p. 113) had already shown that the "Artemise" of the inventory is
Artemisia, not Artemis. The Rubens painting is now in Potsdam, Sanssouci
Gallery, cat. 1930, no. 94. I have not seen the painting for a long time, and

cannot answer the serious charges that have been raised challenging its
authenticity (E. Kieser (119), p. 157).

[70] KING UZZIAH STRICKEN WITH LEPROSY. *Rembrandt f. 1635.* I have
not been able to check the signature or date, which Benesch reads as 1633.
Robert Eisler has identified the subject (communication of T. E. Wragg) as
the sinful king (2 Chronicles 26:19). G. Schwartz points out that the details of
Rembrandt's painting accord better with the account in Flavius Josephus,
Jewish antiquities, 9, 222. See p. 222. There are a number of copies of this
powerful painting.

[71] SAINT JOHN THE BAPTIST PREACHING. Luke 3. This grisaille painting
(originally intended as a study for an etching?) was originally smaller, but it
was enlarged on all sides with strips of about 10 cm. by Rembrandt himself,
perhaps in the fifties (326), p. 228. The sketch itself dates from around 1635/6.
According to Benesch (17), his No. Add 10 is a preparatory study for the
composition (see Benesch's exhaustive comments and J. Rosenberg's criticism
in *Art bulletin*, 41, 1959, p. 118). There are several studies for staffage figures
(Benesch 140-2, 336) and one for the Baptist ([A. Seilern], *Paintings and drawings
of continental schools other than Flemish and Italian*, London 1961, no. 182). There
is also a late drawing of the whole composition with frame, done around 1650.
C. Neumann (*Aus der Werkstatt Rembrandts*, 1918, p. 83) was the first to ob-
serve that the drawing was expressly done for the frame. F. Lugt (*Inventaire
général des dessins, Musée du Louvre*, 1933, no. 1131) believes that the drawing
was done in connection with the transfer of the painting to Jan Six in 1658
(*Urkunden*, (43), no. 195). At the feet of the Baptist Rembrandt places a self-
portrait and a portrait of his mother.

[72] CHRIST BEFORE PILATE AND THE PEOPLE. *Rembrandt f. 1634.* John
19:6. Painted in brown monochrome. A preparatory sketch for the etching
Münz 204 (Illustration b, p. 225), dated 1635.

[73] THE ABDUCTION OF GANYMEDE. *Rembrandt ft 1635.* The signature
(on the boy's shirt) is genuine; the picture itself has suffered somewhat. There
is a preliminary sketch in Dresden (Benesch 92; Illustration b, p. 226), and
the so-called NAUGHTY CHILD (Benesch 401) is also connected with the
composition. For Rembrandt's vision of antique and Renaissance mythological subjects, see Saxl (116, 124), Kieser (119), and Clark (128). V. Bloch
(130), p. 715, remarks: "The rape of Ganymede looks like a grotesque parody
of the Michelangelesque idea known to us through the engraving of Barbizet."

[74] THE ANGEL STOPPING ABRAHAM FROM SACRIFICING ISAAC TO
GOD. *Rembrandt f. 1635.* Genesis 22:10-12. Another version, in the Alte Pinakothek, Munich (no. 438), bears the unusual signature *Rembrandt verandert en
overgeschildert. 1636* (Rembrandt modified and overpainted), which can only
mean that Rembrandt corrected and finished some student's work. The
apprentice who began the job is usually identified as Govaert Flinck (Gerson
(304), p. 122; Sumowski (326), p. 237; von Moltke (305), p. 66, no. 6; and
others), though van Wessem (302), p. 6, sees in it the hand of Lievens, and
Valentiner (318), p. 404, that of Bol. The connection of the work with drawings by Rembrandt and Lastman is discussed by C. Müller (94), p. 66. Brochhagen (336), p. 73, very rightly observes that the painting is reworked so
thoroughly over its whole surface that it is no longer possible to identify the
hand of the pupil in it. Other copies exist.

[75] TOBIAS HEALING HIS FATHER'S BLINDNESS. *Rembrandt f. 1636.* Tobit
11:13-6. The composition has been cut down to the right. The original shape
is recorded in a copy in Brunswick. Related drawings are Benesch 131 and 621
(Illustration a, p. 228). For the medical aspect see Greef (141); for the
humane and art historical, Held (155).

[76] THE BLINDING OF SAMSON BY THE PHILISTINES. *Rembrandt f. 1636.*
Judges 16:20-21. From (rather poor) copies it can be deduced that the picture was originally still larger. The copy in Cassel was lost in World War II.
The drawings of this theme (Benesch 93, 127) are related to another version,
apparently never executed in paint. The painting in Frankfurt is certainly
the gift Rembrandt sent to Constantijn Huygens along with the letter of
January 27, 1639 (*Urkunden* (43), no. 67; Gerson (63), p. 50; and the important emendation of I. H. van Eeghen (64)). H. E. van Gelder (33), p. 177,
has traced the picture's later vicissitudes.

[77] BELSHAZZAR SEES THE WRITING ON THE WALL. *Rembrandt fecit 163(.)*
Daniel 5:5-6. The excellent condition of the painting, its signature, date, and
inscription are discussed in the *61st Annual Report of the National Art Collectors'
Fund*, 1964, no. 2149 and in (334), p. 41. R. Hausherr (154) points out that
the form of the Hebrew inscription is derived from Manasseh ben Israel's
book *De termino vitae* (1639). He interprets this as evidence that the painting
dates from the same year, in support of the theory of W. Sumowski, *Oud
Holland*, 71, 1956, p. 233. I tend to agree with the National Gallery report and
with J. G. van Gelder (313), p. 38, that the painting dates from around the
middle of the thirties. I cannot understand the grounds for K. Clark's very
early dating (128), p. 107: "considerably earlier than Dr. Tulp's Anatomy
Lesson," which has also been rejected by E. Haverkamp Begemann (129),
p. 305. An X-ray report is published in *Speculum artis*, 16, 1964, p. 5. I do not
agree that the pentimenti revealed by the X-ray constitute grounds for sup-
posing that Rembrandt painted the picture twice on the same canvas.

[78] SAMSON THREATENING HIS FATHER-IN-LAW. *Rembrandt ft 163(5).*
Elaborated from Judges 15:1-2. The picture is cut down, but the original

shape is known from an old copy (formerly Goudstikker, Amsterdam), possibly the work of Flinck (Gerson (304), p. 122; von Moltke (305), p. 69, no. 22).

[79] THE PRODIGAL SON IN THE TAVERN. *Rembrandt f.* Luke 15:13. Modern scholars have tended to reject the identification of the painting as a portrait of the artist in a boisterous mood, preferring to see in it a moralizing subject. Emmens (83), pp. 164f., brings it into connection with a verse in the Epistle to Titus (2:12), the only place in the New Testament where the word "worldly" occurs (there opposed to "soberly, righteously, and godly"). Bergström (173) and Tümpel (139), p. 90, see in the painting a representation of the Prodigal Son in the tavern, a theme with an established tradition in northern painting. Tümpel rejects the self-portrait character of the main figure, however, while Bergström underlines it and its moral implications: "Rembrandt and Saskia confess that everyone is a prodigal son." Both point to the influence, in the composition and character of the painting, of the Utrecht school of Caravaggists. The ties of the painting with former depictions of The Prodigal Son in the Tavern did not prevent Rembrandt from investing his version with a compact composition and distinctly portrait-like figures. For further literature, see Bergström's article and the exhib. cat. *De schilder en zijn wereld* (282), no. 95.

[80] THE ASCENSION OF CHRIST. *Rembrandt f. 1636.* Luke 24:50–1; Acts 1:9. See note [64]. The letter quoted there goes on to read: "Of these three aforementioned pictures, one has been completed, namely Christ ascending to Heaven, and the other two are more than half done..." The signature and date of the picture agree with the presumed date of the letter, 1636. E. Brochhagen has published X-rays of the piece, where a figure of God the Father can be seen above the head of Christ. This scheme as well as the angels supporting the clouds pertain to the iconography of the Assumption of the Virgin, which Rembrandt may have had in mind when composing (and modifying) his ASCENSION. The model could well have been Titian's *Assuntà* in the Frari Church or one of the Rubens Assumptions derived from the type.

[81] THE ANGEL LEAVING TOBIAS AND HIS FAMILY. *Rembrandt f. 1637* (redrawn). Tobit 12:21–2. With its brownish tones and strong whites, and with the color of the priming showing through, this painting has the character of an oil sketch. It is in excellent condition, and a cleaning would show off its power of construction (revealed in the X-rays published by M. Hours (301)). Many copies survive. Rembrandt borrowed the basic compositional idea from an engraving by Maerten van Heemskerck. The mutual relations of the painting with the various drawings of the subject and the etching Münz 179 have been discussed most recently by Benesch (152).

[82] THE RISEN CHRIST APPEARING TO MARY MAGDALEN. *Rembrandt f. 1638.* John 20:14–5. This excellent painting is one of those bought for the collections in Cassel from Valerius Roever, who owned it as early as 1721! On the back of the picture is pasted a written copy of the poem of Jeremias de Dekker "On the Painting of the Risen Christ and Mary Magdalene painted by the outstanding Mr. Rembrandt van Rijn, for H. F. Waterloos," which was first published in 1660. Notwithstanding the objections of Hofstede de Groot (*Urkunden* (43), no. 221), the poem is plainly written in praise of this picture; see de Raaf (257). Benesch (nos. 537–8) denies that these drawings are studies for the present painting, but in any case his dating of the drawings is too late.

[83] THE PARABLE OF THE WORKERS IN THE VINEYARD. *Rembrandt f. 1637.* The powerful design accords perfectly with the drawings of this period (e.g. Benesch 329–35).

[84] SUSANNA SURPRISED BY THE ELDERS. *Rembrandt f. 1637.* The latter part of the inscription, after the letters *Rembr*, is painted on a strip added to the painting later, though it probably replaced an original strip. The date is accurate, however, and the painting fits in well with other works of this period [81–2]. It served as a "modello" for the SUSANNA of 1647 [221; q.v.].

[85] SAMSON POSING THE RIDDLE TO THE WEDDING GUESTS. *Rembrandt f. 1638.* This picture has a sketchy quality, but there can be no doubt that it is an independent picture and not a design for some projected composition. Only three years after the painting was completed it was singled out for praise by Philips Angel in a speech given before the painter's guild in Leyden, on the Day of St. Luke (October 18), 1641. He describes it in detail (see an extract on p. 238), concluding: "This blossom of independent, realistic illustration resulted from a careful reading and serious consideration of the story (*Urkunden* (43), no. 91). Nordenfalk (183), p. 78, points to a painting by Otto van Veen as a model for the composition; J. Bruyn (1959), p. 17, to a print by P. Galle after Heemskerck; and de Vries (28), p. 34, and Clark (128), p. 57, to Leonardo da Vinci's LAST SUPPER. The two men in the background give the impression of being actual portraits. Hofstede de Groot called the figure with the feathered beret a self-portrait, while Erpel (285), no. 69, and Scheidegg (328), p. 23, see Rembrandt's features in the man with the flute. The X-ray (by Dr. M. Meier-Siem) is indistinct, possibly because Rembrandt did much correcting and repainting before the final solution was reached.

[86] JOSEPH RELATING HIS DREAMS. *Rembrandt 163(.)* Genesis 37:10. A preparatory sketch for the etching Münz 175, dated 1638 (Illustration b, p. 240). Figure studies go back as far as 1631 (Benesch 20; Illustration a, p. 240). For the inner relation of drawings, painting, and print see Benesch, nos. 127, 455; Münz, no. 175.

[87] THE ENTOMBMENT OF CHRIST. Matthew 27:60–1; Mark 15:46–7; Luke 23:53–5; John 23:53. With the following number, the last pictures in the Passion series. The painting has suffered considerably. Several copies exist. Of the two at Dresden, no. 1566 seems to be from Rembrandt's studio. It bears a (redrawn) Rembrandt signature and the date 1653 (Bauch (15), no. AII).

[88] THE RESURRECTION OF CHRIST. *Rembr(and)t 163(.)* Not described in the Bible. See note to [64]. The restorer of the painting added an unusual inscription on the back: *Rimbrand Creavit me P. H. Brinkmann resuscitavit Te, 1755.* The court painter P. H. Brinkmann apparently restored the painting, then, in 1755; he probably also transferred it from canvas to panel. A number of scholars assume that Brinkmann is also responsible for the figure in the tomb, supposedly derived from a Lazarus (L. van Puyvelde, *Dutch drawings at Windsor*, 1944, no. 117; Sumowski (326), p. 225; Bauch (15), no. 67). There is a drawing by Lambert Doomer in Windsor and an old copy of the RESURRECTION in Munich (no. 4894) that repeat the composition without the figure in the tomb. Brochhagen (336), pp. 68f., refutes this theory. X-rays show that Rembrandt himself brought about the changes in the composition in the course of the four or five years he worked on it. The combination of the Resurrection with the Angel moving the Stone is very rare. See the discussion by Kauffmann (131), p. 74, Tümpel (139), p. 196, and Bauch (140), p. 129.

[89] THE LAMENTATION OVER THE DEAD CHRIST. Not a strictly scriptural subject. Sketch in brown and gray, probably intended as a "modello" for an etching. Benesch (17), no. 63, and, with the utmost care, MacLaren (332), p. 304, have studied the condition of the painting and discussed its dating. The composition, which was "altered drastically several times," was in the making from 1637/8 onwards for quite some time. A drawing for the lower part of the composition (Benesch 154; British Museum) was also cut up and reworked by Rembrandt. For the later history of the painting, see F. Robinson (84). For the iconography, see Stechow (160).

[90] MINERVA. Said to be monogrammed, but I have not been able to make out any traces of one. Probably identical with the "Melancholy, being a woman sitting in a chair near a table with books, a lute, and other instruments, by Jan Lievens," described in a 1632 inventory of the Stadholder's collection (*Oud Holland*, 47, 1930, p. 204). For the iconography, see J. G. van Gelder (103) p. 295.

[91] SCHOLAR IN A ROOM WITH A WINDING STAIR. *RHL van Rijn 163(.)* The date has always been reported as 1633, but the last digit may just as well be read as a one or a two, which accords better with the style of this tender painting (cf. [17, 26]). An early drawing in Copenhagen (Benesch 392) is related in style and composition. Slive (112), p. 125, refers to the drawing and also points out a connection with an engraved perspective interior by Vredeman de Vries. The painting has a "companion piece" also in the Louvre, a Salomon Koninck formerly given to Rembrandt (Valentiner (5), p. 111 top). This is a telling example of the misleading use made of school pictures by later collectors and dealers. The Koninck is now catalogued in the Louvre (no. 1741) as "school of Rembrandt." M. Hours (301), points to the "notable differences" in the X-ray photographs of the two works. Curiously enough, Rosenberg (29), p. 371, upholds the attribution of this "companion picture" to Rembrandt.

[92] SASKIA AS FLORA. *Rembrandt f. 1634.* I lean to the interpretation of this type of portrait as Saskia in the guise of a shepherdess (Kieser (119), p. 155), but Held (201) insists on the Flora connotations.

[93] A SCHOLAR IN HIS STUDY. *Rembrandt f. 1634.* Bauch (15), no. 162, suggests convincingly that the painting depicts an Old Testament personage.

[94] MINERVA. *Rembrandt f. 1635.* The picture was published for the first time, after its appearance in the L. H. Somerville sale, by Valentiner (*Zeitschrift für bildende Kunst*, n.s. 59, 1925/6, p. 267). There is a drawing of the same figure by Bol (formerly in the Amsterdam art market), done after the painting, according to Bauch (15), no. 259. Criticism on the painting varies. J. G. van Gelder (103), p. 297, and Sumowski (326), p. 224, call it Rembrandt and Bol, while Müller Hofstede praises the picture and its cleaning (323), p. 91. I have doubts as to its authenticity. J. G. van Gelder sees in the subject a variant of melancholy [cf. 90], while Bauch, who recognizes the features of Saskia in the model, calls it Melancholy or the prophetess Deborah.

[95] THE STANDARD BEARER. *Rembrandt f. 1636.* Since the recent cleaning, the date can be read as 1636. Valentiner (5), p. 147, Pinder (281), p. 61, and Müller Hofstede (283), p. 89, consider the painting a kind of self-portrait, though they propose it diffidently. The suggestion seems to me (and to others) most unlikely.

[96] SASKIA AS FLORA. *Rem(br)a(.) 1635.* The signature is false, probably copied roughly after the lost original signature. Several copies exist, some in the style of Flinck (von Moltke (305), p. 85, no. 95). See note to [92].

[97] SAINT FRANCIS AT PRAYER. *Rembrandt f. 1637.* There are several other versions of this picture. I have not seen any of them, nor the present painting.

[98] CHILD WITH DEAD PEACOCKS. *Rembrandt (?)* In agreement with Benesch, Bauch, and Rosenberg (29), p. 264, I date the picture in the latter part of the 1630's. There is a drawing for the bird in Berlin (Benesch 456).

[99] SELF-PORTRAIT. *RHL van Rijn 1632.* The first self-portrait in the

more polished style that Rembrandt developed after his move to Amsterdam. Many copies exist.

[100] DOCTOR NICOLAAS TULP DEMONSTRATING THE ANATOMY OF THE ARM. *Rembrant f. 1632.* Dr. Nicolaas Pietersz. Tulp (1593–1674) was an important Amsterdam anatomist who was hailed by contemporaries as "the Vesalius of Amsterdam." He had been a pupil of Pieter Pauw in Leyden, who in turn had studied with the famous Vesalius, and who republished his teacher's works in 1616. From 1628 to 1653 Tulp held the office of Praelector anatomiae of the Amsterdam Guild of Surgeons. He was a city councillor, served eight terms as city treasurer, and four as a Burgomaster of Amsterdam.

This great group portrait was Rembrandt's first important commission after he moved to Amsterdam. The recent cleaning has freed the picture from much of its yellow varnish; it also revealed the slight damage to the head and left hand of Tulp, though this and the other damage suffered by the painting is not as widespread as was feared before the cleaning (A.B. de Vries, *150 jaer Koninklijk Kabinet voor Schilderijen*, The Hague 1967, p. 76). The background has gained translucence. The present signature was revealed by the cleaning, but there seem to be traces of yet another one beneath it (see facsimile in the Mauritshuis catalogue, 1935, p. 277; also Heckscher (207), p. 11, whose reading of the signature cannot be confirmed with the naked eye). The paper one of them holds in his hand originally bore an anatomical drawing; only later were the names of the sitters—not one of whom held a medical degree!—inscribed on it, with numbers corresponding to the ciphers above the head of each. Whether or not the figure at the left and the one furthest in the rear were added by a pupil (Backer?), as Heckscher suggests, was not indicated by the cleaning. My own view is that the figure at the left was added as an afterthought by Rembrandt or Backer.

After a long article by Schrade (204), William Heckscher's book, *Rembrandt's* ANATOMY OF DOCTOR NICOLAAS TULP, 1958, has stimulated fresh discussion around this picture. Heckscher's book is a splendid history of the anatomy through the ages and of anatomical theatres as a source of public entertainment as well as a serious art historical contribution. Heckscher analyzes the painting's perfect balance between lifelike realism and the idealization of the models, individually and corporately (p. 65). The cadaver is depicted realistically, but the anatomical details of the hand under dissection are probably copied from the woodcut in the anatomy text at the feet of the corpse. Heckscher does not stop at tracing the pictorial tradition of anatomies and related scenes—entombments, martyrdoms, vivisections, etc. He insists that the "history of anatomies must be seen in the light of man's attitude toward death." According to this interpretation, the vital energies of the guild members triumph over the lifeless criminal, Tulp triumphs through science over the ignorance of sin (p. 120), and—if we are willing to follow Heckscher's view of the magical meaning of executions—over the enemies of Amsterdam (p. 115).

Critics of Heckscher's book have argued, rightly, I believe, that the anatomy session depicted is not a public but a private one. The public anatomy—whose scientific value in this period was insignificant—invariably began with the dissection of the abdominal cavity, while Tulp has started on the left arm, apparently comparing his original observations with the woodcut in the anatomy handbook of Adriaen van der Spiegel (1627). See the review of Heckscher's book by Kellett (208). Judson (209) accepts this interpretation, and relates it to the setting of the painting. We do not see the actual night-time public demonstration in the anatomy theater, as Heckscher would have us believe; the use of light and fantastic architecture points to a "highly imaginative and original commemoration" rather than a record of an actual moment in January 1632. Heckscher's suggestions, then, that we ought to "try to visualize the presence of a large audience in Rembrandt's painting" and that Tulp "clearly addresses himself to persons outside his inner circle" (p. 5) are misleading, and result from a misinterpretation of the inner logic of the group portrait's structure. Rembrandt's Baroque art can easily deceive the modern critic. A comparable misunderstanding (introduced by Schmidt-Degener) has been uncovered by van de Waal in regard to THE SAMPLING OFFICIALS OF THE DRAPERS' GUILD [404; q.v.]. Notwithstanding all criticism (see also Rosenberg and Slive (30), p. 267), Heckscher's book remains a major attempt to unearth the different layers of meaning that can be concealed in a great work of art.

Medical men still disagree as to whether the dissected left arm was painted from an actual limb or after a woodcut in an anatomical text. See Wolf-Heidegger and A.M. Cetto (211), p. 308, no. 257; and A. Querido (210).

[101] YOUNG MAN WITH A GOLD CHAIN. *RHL van Rijn 1632.* In 18th-century sales catalogues considered a companion piece to SASKIA [174], implying that the present painting is a self-portrait, which is not very likely. What must have happened is that some 18th-century collector or dealer put into matching frames two Rembrandts that happened to be in his possession at the time, and declared them to be "pendants." Bauch (15), no. 142, thinks it possible that the sitter is Ferdinand Bol, who was Rembrandt's pupil in 1632. The painting is of excellent quality and in good condition.

[102] SAINT JOHN THE BAPTIST. *Rembrandt ft 1632.* This kind of signature is unusual for 1632; it may replace the original one (lost when the panel was cut down?); the picture itself is one of the best examples of Rembrandt's early

Amsterdam style in the Rubens manner.

[103] MAN IN FANCIFUL COSTUME ("THE NOBLE SLAV"). *RHL van Rijn 1632.* Rosenberg (29), p. 345, note 1A, observes rightly that the model is the same man who is sometimes called Rembrandt's father, though the painting is dated two years after the death of Harman Gerritsz. But Rosenberg does not disqualify the identification on those grounds.

[104] MAURITS HUYGENS, SECRETARY OF THE STATE COUNCIL OF HOLLAND. *RHL van Rijn 1632.* Maurits Huygens (1595–1642) was the elder brother of Constantijn Huygens. He assisted his father, who was the former Secretary of the State Council, until 1632, when he took over the office, which he held until his early death. The painting is inscribed on the back: *M. Huygens, secretaris van den Raad van Staten in den Hage.* See following number.

[105] THE PAINTER JACOB DE GHEYN III. *RHL van Rijn 1632.* Jacob de Gheyn was a canon of the Utrecht Mariakerk, a kind of sinecure (held a century earlier by Jan van Scorel). He was a close friend of Maurits Huygens. The painting was recognized as a pendant to [104] even before the identity of the sitter was established by H.E. van Gelder (242). Some years after his article appeared, the inscription on the back of the painting was deciphered to read: *JACOBUS GEINIUS IUNr / H[UYGE]NI IPSIUS/EFFIGI-E[M] EXTREMUM MUNUS MORIENTIS ...*; see H.E. van Gelder (244). The inscription proves that this portrait is indeed the very one Jacob de Gheyn left in his will to Maurits Huygens; see Bredius (49), p. 127. The commission was intended from the start as companion pictures of the two friends. They were still together in the A.R. van Waay sale, Utrecht, February 27, 1764: "two original portraits of the Huygens family, by Rembrandt." Jacob de Gheyn's name was already forgotten.

[106] YOUNG MAN IN A TURBAN. Signed with monogram and dated 1631. A portrait of the late Leyden period in a style influenced by Lievens' broad technique. Several copies exist. One of them, in the Museum in Bern, has been attributed to Flinck by von Moltke (305), p. 117, no. 247, though without substantial grounds.

[107] BALD-HEADED OLD MAN. Signed with monogram and dated 1632. I agree with Bauch's comment (15), no. 143, on the poor condition of the picture and its thin paint (in parts). The signature is painted over a grayish color, and it may be false. A careful cleaning, however, may well reveal qualities in the picture that are at present concealed under later restorations.

[108] YOUNG MAN WITH A WIDE COLLAR. *RHL van Rijn 1632.* Reflects the Amsterdam portrait tradition of Thomas de Keyser rather than the Leyden tradition.

[109] BEARDED OLD MAN WITH A GOLD CHAIN. *RHL van Rijn 1632.* Powerfully painted and in a good state of preservation. The X-ray shows underpainting as rich and expressive as the surface handling. The picture can be traced back to the collection of Valerius Roever's father (1693).

[110] THE AMSTERDAM MERCHANT MARTEN LOOTEN. *RHL.* On the letter a few lines of writing beginning *Marten Looten XL January 1632.* The sitter was a well-to-do merchant. He spent his youth in Leyden, and Rembrandt may have known him from there. Attempts to decipher the writing on the letter have led to fantastic interpretations, which are described in J. Paul Getty's memoirs (*The joys of collecting*, 1966, p. 116). See the studies of J.G. van Dillen (*Tijdschrift voor geschiedenis*, 54, 1939, p. 181) and P. van Eeghen (268).

[111] YOUNG MAN SHARPENING A QUILL. *RHL van Rijn* (on the letter). On the basis of an 18th-century sale catalogue, identified as a portrait of Lieven Willemsz. van Coppenol, a "half-witted, conceited calligrapher" who ran a school on the Singel in Amsterdam (H.F. Wijnman, *Jaarboek Amstelodamum*, 30, 1933, p. 150; —, (68), p. 154). His appearance is known to us from two etchings by Rembrandt, one of 1658 (Münz 78) and an undated one from the same decade (Münz 80). The similarity between the sitters is not sufficiently close to warrant an identification of [111] as a portrait of Coppenol. Bauch (15), no. 351, doubts the identification; Münz (19), p. 69, accepts it. The picture is covered with discolored varnish. X-rays reveal a powerful and varied underpainting.

[112] AMALIA VAN SOLMS. *RHL van Rijn 1632.* When this painting was cleaned, in The Hague in 1965, it was seen to have a painted decorative frame similar to the one in Honthorst's portrait of the Stadholder, Frederick Henry (Huis ten Bosch, The Hague). Both pictures are painted on canvas and have the same dimensions, so that the present painting, previously called "Saskia" or "Rembrandt's Sister," can now be identified with some certainty as a portrait of Amalia van Solms, the Stadholder's wife. This is supported by two entries in the 1632 inventory of Frederick Henry's collections, which mention a profile portrait of Amalia van Solms by Rembrandt and one of Frederick Henry by Honthorst (*Oud Holland*, 47, 1930, pp. 213, 210). The Honthorst is signed and dated 1631. The present painting may well be the first commission Rembrandt received from the court. Rembrandt's portrait was removed, probably in the 17th century, and replaced by another Honthorst portrait (on panel!), supposedly the companion portrait of Amalia van Solms (reproduced in A. Staring (245), p. 12, figs. 1, 2).

[113] YOUNG MAN WITH A BROAD COLLAR. Neither Bauch nor I have seen the picture. To judge from reproductions, a masterly portrait by Jan Lievens, of the Leyden period. Bauch seems to endorse the attribution to Rembrandt

(15), no. 350, but draws attention to the fact that the same model was painted by Lievens (Los Angeles).

[114] YOUNG WOMAN IN A PEARL-TRIMMED BERET. *RHL van Rijn 1632.* Bauch (15), no. 451, calls it a portrait of Saskia. The picture is unknown to me in the original.

[115] YOUNG WOMAN WITH AN EMBROIDERED ROBE. *RHL van Rijn 1632.* An excellent picture, whose great beauty would be revealed by a good cleaning.

[116] YOUNG WOMAN WITH A GOLDEN NECKLACE. *RHL van Rijn 1632.* Often called a portrait of Rembrandt's sister, along with many other of the paintings of young women of this period. Pendant to [99]? Not known to me in the original.

[117] YOUNG WOMAN WITH AN EMBROIDERED ROBE. *RHL van Rijn 1632.* Covered by thick varnish; of good quality.

[118] YOUNG WOMAN WITH A FAN. *RHL van Rijn 1632.* The face has suffered somewhat, but the delicate design still makes a considerable impact.

[119] YOUNG MAN WITH A POINTED BEARD. The original signature, *RHL van Rijn* [163]2, is covered by a false *Rembrandt f* (Illustration b, p. 162). In an excellent state. Only the background (and the signature) are retouched. The X-ray confirms the lively underpainting, which is smoothed out on the surface. The portrait of a woman that hangs beside it in Brunswick (Bredius 338) is too poor in quality to be accepted as a Rembrandt.

[120] PORTRAIT OF A MAN. *RHL van Rijn 1632.* Formerly called a portrait of a man of the Beresteijn-Vucht family, on the basis of the picture's provenance. The genealogist of the family, however, insists that none of the 17th-century members of the family could be portrayed here (Jhr. E. A. van Beresteijn, *Genealogie van het geslacht van Beresteijn*, The Hague 1941, p. 135). Although covered by a thick varnish, a painting of extraordinary richness of nuance in color and design.

[121] PORTRAIT OF A WOMAN. *RHL van Rijn 1632* (?) Companion portrait to preceding number; the remarks there concerning the identity of the sitter apply here as well. In technique and expression it is totally dissimilar to the male portrait. The signature seems to be copied from that on the male portrait. The obvious conclusion is that this painting was made to match the Rembrandt painting of the spouse, but by a far weaker hand. A. Burroughs (*Art criticism from a laboratory*, Boston 1938) gives this painting to Backer—to whom he also attributes the male pendant.

[122] A FORTY-YEAR-OLD MAN. *RHL van Rijn 1632.* Also inscribed *AET 40*. An excellent portrait in good condition. Probably the companion piece to the following number.

[123] PORTRAIT OF A WOMAN. *Rembrandt f. 1633.* The execution is weaker than in the male portrait [122]. The attribution to Rembrandt is not wholly convincing.

[124] JORIS DE CAULLERY. *RHL van Rijn 1632.* Joris de Caullery (c. 1600–61) was a ship's captain in Amsterdam, later a wine merchant and innkeeper in The Hague. When he set off on a voyage in 1654, he gave family portraits to his children in order to protect them from seizure by his creditors. His daughter Josyna got: "the portrait of himself with *het roer* in his hand, done by Mr. Rembrandt" (*Urkunden* (43), no. 156). "Roer" can mean either rifle or helm. A rifle in the hand of a sea captain would be strange; the helm makes more sense, but I do not know of any other examples of helm-holding captains. The object held by the sitter in this portrait may be a helm—and on this ground the painting is called JORIS DE CAULLERY—but it has not yet been shown to be one. The painting is in excellent condition.

[125] AELBERT CUYPER. *Rembrant ft 1632.* Also inscribed *AE 47*. The signature may replace an older one; its position in the picture is rather uncommon and the spelling not typical for that year. It may have been retouched when the companion picture [126] was painted the following year. Bauch (15), no. 356, calls the painting poorly conserved, an assertion with which I cannot agree. The X-ray, moreover (M. Hours (301)), reveals a solid pictorial structure (and a number of pentimenti). The sitter was identified by I. H. van Eeghen (247).

[126] CORNELIA PRONCK, WIFE OF AELBERT CUYPER. *Rembrandt ft 1633.* Also inscribed *AET 33*. Companion portrait to [125]. The female portrait is somewhat inferior in quality and, according to Hours (see preceding number), reveals a different technique in the underpainting. Possibly commissioned from another painter to match [125].

[127] OLD WOMAN IN A WHITE CAP. *RHL van Rijn 1632.* Seen by neither Bauch nor me lately, but the attribution to Rembrandt seems correct.

[128] PORTRAIT OF A YOUNG WOMAN. *RHL van Rijn 1632.* The surface of the picture as well as the underpainting, revealed by X-ray, are somewhat more carefully and deliberately painted than is usual in this period.

[129] SELF-PORTRAIT. *Rembrandt f. 1633.* One of the most sensitive and well preserved of the early self-portraits.

[130] PORTRAIT OF A FASHIONABLE COUPLE. *Rembrandt f. 1633* (somewhat redrawn). Although painted only one year later than the TULP [100], this double portrait is less expressively designed, composition and technique being reminiscent of the portrait style of Thomas de Keyser (cf. Illustration a, p. 28). The face of the man is modeled in a richer range of tones than the somewhat flat surface of the woman's face. Most of the early Amsterdam companion portraits show this same characteristic differentiation.

[131] RICHLY DRESSED YOUNG BOY. The same model appears in several other pictures of the first years in Amsterdam. Wijnman suggests that he could be the 8-year-old Gerrit van Uylenburgh, the son of Hendrick (62), p. 102. I am charmed by the idea that the sitter may be Gerrit, but I am not so sure that the artist who painted it was Rembrandt; most of the pictures of the boy are very much in the style of Flinck. W. Martin (9), p. 30, also expressed strong doubts; of the whole group of "children with calf eyes," he says only one is wholly by Rembrandt. All the rest are overpainted (by Jouderville?).

[132] SASKIA WITH A VEIL. *Rembrandt ft 1633.* After the recent cleaning, the delicate handling and the sensitive coloring—to which the warm ground shining through the pigment contributes—have come into their own.

[133] SELF-PORTRAIT. As can be seen from the X-ray (reproduced by Sumowski (326), figs. 92–3), Rembrandt originally painted himself without the cap. Although unsigned, a vigorously painted work of high quality. G. Schwartz suggests (see p. 272) that it was converted by Rembrandt into a companion piece to the following number. The hat would then have been added to accentuate the similarity between the pieces, while the signature may have been cut off at the same time.

[134] SASKIA. *Rembrandt ft 1633.* In excellent condition.

[135] BEARDED OLD MAN WITH A CAP. *Rembrandt f. 1633* (now illegible). I have been able to study the painting since the Catalogue Illustrations were printed. I am now of the opinion that it is the work of a follower of Rembrandt.

[136] OLD MAN. *Rembrandt 1633* (date in a 17th-century hand; signature spurious). The smallest known painting by Rembrandt. Perhaps a fragment of a grisaille sketch. Compare such contemporary drawings as Benesch 89.

[137] JOHANNES UYTTENBOGAERT. *Rembrandt f. 1633.* Also inscribed *AET 76*. The features of Uyttenbogaert (1557–1646) are known from an etching by Rembrandt of 1635 (Münz 50) and a painting by Backer of the same year, still in the possession of the Wardens of the Remonstrant Church in Amsterdam (on loan to the Rijksmuseum; Illustration b, p. 66). Several copies of the head alone are known. See B. Tideman (255).

[138] THE POET JAN HARMENSZ. KRUL. *Rembrandt f. 1633.* The sitter (1602–1644/6) was a poet and owner of a smithy in Amsterdam. The recent cleaning has restored the picture's original beauty and strength.

[139] "THE SHIPBUILDER AND HIS WIFE." *Rembrandt f. 1633* (on the paper in the woman's hand). The cleaning revealed a picture in excellent condition. Münz (243) has shown that it has been cut down somewhat, especially at the top. In 1800 it was engraved by J. de Frey, who reproduced the picture in a format quite different from its present shape.

[140] MAN RISING FROM A CHAIR. *Rembrandt f. 1633.* J. Q. van Regteren Altena (in Jan Veth (21), p. 73) wishes to see Constantijn Huygens in the sitter; H. E. van Gelder (*Ikonografie van Constantijn Huygens*, The Hague 1957, p. 36) rejects this identification. Companion piece to the following number. Not known to me in the original, but the attribution to Rembrandt seems to be fully justified.

[141] YOUNG WOMAN WITH A FAN. *Rembrandt* (f.) *1633.* See [140]. The picture is covered by a thick varnish, which conceals the delicate design of face and head.

[142] SELF-PORTRAIT. *Rembrandt f. 163(3).* The last digit could well be read as a 4.

[143] YOUNG WOMAN WITH A GOLD CHAIN. *Rembrandt f. 1633.* Also called "Rembrandt's Sister." Neither Bauch nor I have seen the picture; to judge from the photograph, not of impressive quality.

[144] SELF-PORTRAIT. Difficult to judge in its present condition. The cloak was overpainted, perhaps in the 18th century, and there are some alterations in the cap. The picture has been cut down, and then a strip of 9 cm. added to the bottom. Weaker than the undoubted self-portraits of the period.

[145] RICHLY DRESSED CHILD. *Rembrandt 1633.* See remarks at [131]. Neither Bauch nor I have seen the original.

[146] WOMAN WITH A LACE COLLAR. *Rembrandt f. 1633.* Not seen by either Bauch or me.

[147] THE ROTTERDAM MERCHANT WILLEM BURCHGRAEFF. *Rembrandt f. 1633.* The sitter (1604–47) was a master baker and wheat dealer. The portrait is mentioned for the first time in the Dresden inventory of 1722, though not by the name of the sitter. Superior in quality to the pendant.

[148] MARGARETHA VAN BILDERBEECQ, WIFE OF WILLEM BURCHGRAEFF. *Rembrandt f. 1633.* Inscribed on the back with the name of the sitter. Although less powerful than the male portrait, it has, to a lesser degree, the vivacious brushwork one expects from a Rembrandt of the early thirties.

[149] BEARDED MAN IN A WIDE-BRIMMED HAT. *Rembrandt f. 1633.* Companion piece to [150]. The pair was still together at the W. H. Moore sale, London (Sotheby), March 23, 1960, lots 67–8.

[150] PORTRAIT OF A YOUNG WOMAN. *Rembrandt f. 1634.* See [149].

[151] BEARDED MAN WITH A FLAT BROAD COLLAR. *Rembrandt fec. 1633.* Published for the first time by Valentiner (11), p. 260, as companion piece to [155]. Not seen by Bauch or me.

[152] MAN IN ORIENTAL COSTUME. *Rembrandt f. 1633.* Possibly a study for a biblical subject.

[153] PORTRAIT OF A SEATED MAN. Companion picture to [154]. The X-rays by Dr. Meier-Siem reveal an underpainting as rich as the surface.

[154] PORTRAIT OF A SEATED WOMAN. Although neither painting is signed, they both conform, in their vigorous execution and the perfect matching of the couple, to Rembrandt's better companion pictures of the early thirties. The inter-relationship between the two pieces comes out even more strongly in the underpainting revealed in the X-rays by Dr. Meier-Siem.

[155] PORTRAIT OF A YOUNG WOMAN. *Rembrandt f. 1633.* First published by Valentiner (6), p. 28. Possibly a companion to [151]. Not known to either Bauch or me, but the attribution to Rembrandt is convincing.

[156] PORTRAIT OF AN 83-YEAR-OLD WOMAN. *Rembrandt f. 1634.* Also inscribed *AE SUE 83.* A drawing by J. Stolker after this portrait (or better: after a lost drawing by Hendrik van Limborch after this portrait) gives the name of the sitter as Françoise van Wassenhoven. Stolker's identifications usually prove to be unreliable; moreover, his own mezzotint after the drawing omits all mention of the name. One of the most powerful and best preserved portraits of this period.

[157] SELF-PORTRAIT. *Rembrandt f. 1634.* The placing of the signature and the calligraphy are both unusual. An attribution to Govaert Flinck should be considered. Difficult to judge through the thick varnish, but the X-ray has a rich design.

[158] SELF-PORTRAIT. *Rembrandt f. 1634.* The last digit is not very clear.

[159] BEARDED MAN WITH A WIDE-BRIMMED HAT. *Rembrant f. 1634.* I am not wholly convinced of the correctness of the signature (with its wrong spelling). Though close to the borderline Rembrandt-Flinck, surely a work by Rembrandt himself.

[160] YOUNG WOMAN WITH A GOLD CHAIN. *Rembrandt f. 1634*(?) Although the signature in the female portrait is written in an odd way, the picture itself is as well constructed and powerful in execution as the companion piece.

[161] BOY WITH LONG HAIR. *Rembrandt f. 1634.* Not seen by Bauch or me. To judge from the photograph, the best version of this type.

[162] THE PREACHER JOHANNES ELISON. *Rembrandt ft 1634.* Companion portrait to [163]. The sitter (c. 1581–1639) was a preacher in Norwich, England. While he and his wife were staying with their son in Amsterdam in 1634, the younger Elison had these portraits of his parents painted. In his will, of 1635, Jan Elison the younger left both portraits (the name of the painter is not mentioned) to his brother-in-law in Norwich. They remained there, in the family of the descendants, until the middle of the last century. See H. F. Wijnman (252, 262); J. Rosenberg, *Bulletin of the Museum of Fine Arts* (Boston), 55, 1957, pp. 3–9.

[163] MARIA BOCKENOLLE, WIFE OF JOHANNES ELISON. *Rembrandt f. 1634.* Companion picture to [162], and in every respect its equal.

[164] MAERTEN SOOLMANS. *Rembrandt f. 1634.* The portraits of the couple Soolmans-Coppit [165] are among the most impressive "official" portraits that Rembrandt painted in the 1630's. It was in 1633 that Maerten Soolmans (1613–41) married Oopjen Coppit, who was two years his senior. The widow remarried, sometime after 1646, with Maerten Daey (d. 1659). In the inventory of the goods of Maerten Daey made at the time of his death, the pictures were still described as "portraits of Maerten Soolmans and Oopie Coppit" (the name of the artist is not mentioned!). The paintings remained with the Daey family, and came to be regarded as family portraits, i.e. portraits of Oopjen Coppit and Maerten Daey. Miss I. H. van Eeghen (246) has reconstructed the history of the paintings and identified the sitters correctly. R. van Luttervelt (251) draws attention to the fact that the female portrait is not dated, and may have been done later than the male portrait, when Oopjen Coppit was a widow. The artistic coherence of the two portraits is so strong, however, that I cannot imagine they were painted at different periods.

[165] OOPJEN COPPIT, WIFE OF MAERTEN SOOLMANS. See [164].

[166] YOUNG MAN WITH MOUSTACHE. *Rembrandt f. 1634.* Said to be a companion piece to the following number.

[167] A YOUNG WOMAN WITH FLOWERS IN HER HAIR. *Rembrandt f. 1634.* Weaker in execution than the probable companion piece [166].

[168] MAN OF THE RAMAN FAMILY. *Rembrandt ft 1634.* Inscribed *AET 47.* Although the signature is retouched, there is no reason to doubt the attribution to Rembrandt. The painting is said to have been in the Raman family collections, hence the title. Like the supposed companion piece [169], originally ten-sided.

[169] WOMAN OF THE RAMAN FAMILY. *Rembrandt f. 1636.* See [168]. J. G. van Gelder (311), p. 328, has doubts about the attribution. Unknown to me in the original.

[170] MAN IN ORIENTAL COSTUME. *Rembrandt f. 1635.* A study for an Old Testament figure?

[171] SELF-PORTRAIT. *Rembrandt f. 1635.* Close, in quality and character, to YOUNG MAN WITH A SWORD in the North Carolina Museum of Art, Raleigh (once dated 1636; reproduced in the museum catalogue, 1960, p. 139), a work probably to be attributed to Flinck, though von Moltke denies this (305), p. 248, no. 108. A copy of the painting was in the Cook sale, London (Sotheby), June 25, 1958, lot 113 (as Rembrandt, signed and dated 1638).

[172] MAN IN FANCIFUL COSTUME. *Rembrandt f. 1635* (?) The last digit could also be a 6. The dark areas are covered with strange cracks. The panel, of imported wood, seems to have been used originally for some utilitarian purpose (see key(?) hole on the back). The brushwork is gross and inarticulate. I doubt the attribution to Rembrandt.

[173] MAN WITH DISHEVELED HAIR. *Rembrandt 1635*(?) Neither Bauch nor I have seen the painting in the original.

[174] SASKIA. The X-ray photograph shows powerful underpainting and a solid structure; the surface is covered by thick varnish. A cleaning would probably have the same dramatic results as in the case of [132].

[175] SASKIA. Like the related drawing (Benesch 431), done around 1633/4. One of the most carefully executed portraits of Saskia (with regard both to the surface and the underpainting. According to K. Wehlte (296), p. 18, the fur was added only shortly before the completion of the painting. New X-rays (taken by Dr. Meier-Siem), reveal other alterations, which deserve careful study. The present appearance of the panel is disfigured by dirty varnish. The history of the painting can be followed without a break from the time it left Rembrandt's hands to go to Jan Six, through the Six sales (1702, 1734), the Valerius Roever Collection, to the collection of Landgraf Wilhelm VIII van Hessen-Kassel, where it came in 1750.

[176] JAN PELLICORNE AND HIS SON, CASPAR. *Rembran(dt) ft* (there may be traces of a date under the signature). Companion portrait to [407]. The identity of the sitters rests on a family tradition which cannot be controlled; the names of the sitters were not identified at the J. van der Poll sale, November 14, 1842 nor at the King William II of Holland sale, August 12, 1850 (lots 84–5). The marriage of the Amsterdam merchant Jan Pellicorne (b. 1567) with Susanna van Collen took place on June 11, 1626. The daughter was born in 1627, the son was baptized on June 11, 1628. In accordance with the age of the children and the stylistic characteristics, I would date the paintings in the early thirties. These large canvases are covered with a heavy varnish and glass, a combination that makes it impossible to appreciate their true character.

[177] SUSANNA VAN COLLEN, WIFE OF JAN PELLICORNE, AND HER DAUGHTER, EVA SUSANNA. *Rembrandt ft 16(..)* See [176].

[178] PHILIPS LUCASZ., COUNCILLOR OF THE DUTCH EAST INDIA COMPANY. *Rembrandt 1635.* I think the date should be read as 1633. Philips Lucasz. (born towards the end of the 16th century, died 1641) was a merchant in the Dutch East Indies, from 1628 to 1631 Governor and in 1633 Commander of the mercantile fleet returning to Holland. The paintings of him and his wife [179] were made for his wife's sister, who was married to Jacques Specx, a Governor-General of the Dutch East Indies. The National Gallery Catalogue mentions the fact that the picture was reduced in size (by Rembrandt himself?). That might have occurred in connection with the commission for a companion piece. The hand of the sitter is overpainted; it is clearly seen in the X-rays, and can even be made out by the naked eye. The identification of the sitters is due to Hofstede de Groot (236) and I. H. van Eeghen (248).

[179] PETRONELLA BUYS, WIFE OF PHILIPS LUCASZ. *Rembrandt f. 1635.* The name of the sitter is inscribed on back of the panel. She was first married to Philips Lucasz., then, after his death, to Jean Cardon (1646). See [178].

[180] MAN IN A WIDE-BRIMMED HAT. *Rembrandt fec. 1635.* Probably the companion piece to [181]. Neither Bauch nor I have seen the original, but judging from photographs there is no reason to doubt the attribution.

[181] PORTRAIT OF A YOUNG WOMAN. *Rembrandt f. 1635.* Probably a companion piece to [180], and quite as powerful in execution.

[182] MAN IN ORIENTAL COSTUME. *Rembrandt ft.* Of the same powerful construction as [103].

[183] THE DIPLOMAT ANTHONIS COOPAL. *Rembrandt f. 1635.* Coopal (1606–72) was a secret agent of the Stadholder; his name and titles are inscribed on the back of the panel. His brother François was married to Saskia's sister Titia. The execution is less vigorous than in other portraits of this period.

[184] SASKIA. *Rembrandt f. 1638* (according to the report of a restorer). Hofstede de Groot (4), no. 613, and Bauch (15), no. 490, give the date as 1635, which would be understandable, as in 1636 Flinck based his portraits of Rembrandt and Saskia as shepherd and shepherdess (Illustrations a, b, p. 134) on this type of idealized portrait. The original is not known to either Bauch or me.

[185] A 70-YEAR-OLD WOMAN SEATED IN AN ARMCHAIR. *Rembrandt f. 1635* (?) Inscribed *AET SUE 70.* Perhaps the companion portrait to Bredius 212, which I do not accept. The attribution to Rembrandt is not convincing. The painting is from the Amsterdam circle of the master.

[186] A MAN IN POLISH COSTUME. *Rembrandt f. 1637.* According to Bauch, perhaps a portrait of Rembrandt's brother Adriaen. A powerfully constructed portrait of a type that served as a model for pupils such as Flinck.

[187] A MAN SEATED IN AN ARMCHAIR. *Rembrandt f. 1637* (?) J. G. van Gelder (311), p. 328: "flattened by relining; once, no doubt, a Rembrandt." Its style is so close to Bredius 213, which I reject, that I doubt the attribution to Rembrandt.

[188] YOUNG MAN WITH A GOLD CHAIN. *Rembrandt* (?) Sometimes called a self-portrait. Neither that nor its attribution to Rembrandt is very convincing. C. Müller Hofstede (*Kunstchronik*, 10, 1957, p. 124): "Reminds one somewhat of Flinck," an opinion in which Benesch concurred, according to a note in

his archives. A copy of the head was recently on the Amsterdam art market.

[189] SELF-PORTRAIT (?) *Rembrandt f.* Glück (278), p. 296, questions the status of this painting as a self-portrait, as does Bauch (15), no. 311.

[190] REMBRANDT'S MOTHER. *Rembrandt f. 1639.* The only portrait of Rembrandt's mother in the Amsterdam period. Bauch (15), no. 262, sees it as a portrait of the mother in the guise of the prophetess Hannah.

[191] SELF-PORTRAIT WITH A DEAD BITTERN. *Rembrandt fc 1639.* In an excellent state of preservation, with a perfect signature.

[192] MAN STANDING IN FRONT OF A DOORWAY. *Rembrandt f. 1639.* Hofstede de Groot (4), no. 535, calls it a self-portrait. F. Schmidt-Degener (*Oud Holland*, 32, 1914, p. 219) identifies the sitter as Frans Banning Cocq. Although this identification is unjustified, stylistically the portrait is closely related to those in THE NIGHT WATCH. The analogy would be more obvious were the dirty varnish removed. The pose is based on a van Dyck formula; this may account for the inexpressive gesture of the hand, which is not as well modeled as one expects of Rembrandts from these years.

[193] ALOTTE ADRIAENSDR. *Rembrandt 1639* (?) I agree with F. Winkler's remarks about this picture's poor state of preservation (327), p. 143, which makes a final attribution difficult. After another cleaning in 1947 the hand and table (?) were brought to light. Alotte Adriaensdr. (1589–1656) was married in 1609 to Elias Trip, whose brother Jacob and his wife were also painted by Rembrandt [383–5]. See also following number.

[194] MARIA TRIP, DAUGHTER OF ALOTTE ADRIAENSDR. *Rembrandt f. 1639.* The signature is very thin. J. Q. van Regteren Altena's suggestion (165), p. 24, that the sitter is Saskia has been replaced by Miss van Eeghen's theory (267) that we have here a portrait of Maria Trip, one of the ancestors of the van Weede family. The portrait is painted—like [235]—on Indonesian djati panel, which may help to account for the unusually careful, somewhat heavy, even impersonal technique, which extends to the underpainting as seen in the X-ray. The preparatory drawing (Illustration a, p. 304) is vigorous and straightforward in character. It covers a larger field than the painting, suggesting that the latter has been cut down on all four sides.

[195] LANDSCAPE WITH THE BAPTISM OF THE EUNUCH. *Rembrandt ft 1636* (?) The picture came to light at the Ravensworth Castle sale, London (Christie), June 15, 1920, lot 113, and was published for the first time by Valentiner (6), p. 37. It has suffered somewhat from relining and pressing; the sky is heavily restored.

[196] LANDSCAPE WITH A STONE BRIDGE. Cleaning would probably result in stronger, more "Baroque" contrast between the light and dark areas. A sensitive appreciation by van de Waal (291).

[197] STORMY LANDSCAPE WITH AN ARCHED BRIDGE. The underpainting revealed by the X-ray is as beautiful and differentiated as the surface. Stylistically closest to [196]; it probably dates before 1638.

[198] LANDSCAPE WITH AN OBELISK. Illegible remains of a questionable signature. In older publications the date was given as 1638. Hofstede de Groot already had doubts about the signature (4), no. 941. Stylistically close to [199]. In good condition, except for the slight alteration in tone of the blue-greens.

[199] LANDSCAPE WITH THE GOOD SAMARITAN. *Rembrandt f. 1638.* "The best work by Rembrandt in Poland" (J. Bialostocki and M. Walicki, *Europäische Malerei in polnischen Sammlungen*, 1957, no. 236); acquired at the beginning of the 19th century by the Czartoryski's; see Załuski (290). Also praised by Benesch (325), p. 190. This sketch in oils is in excellent condition, except for some repainting in the left part of the sky.

[200] STORMY LANDSCAPE. *Rembrandt f.* A beautiful landscape study from the same period as the picture in Cracow [199]. The brushwork in the group of trees is reminiscent of the parts of the Seghers landscape in the Uffizi (Illustration b, p. 58) that are supposed to have been added by Rembrandt (E. Haverkamp Begemann (289), no. 4).

[201] WOODY LANDSCAPE WITH RUINS. Remains of a signature.

[202] THE DEPARTURE OF THE SHUNAMITE WIFE. *Rembrandt f. 1640.* 2 Kings 4:24. A strip of 4 cm. has been added at the top. The new interpretation of the subject (previously called THE CASTING OUT OF HAGAR) is due to Tümpel (138), p. 302; the design and execution are of the utmost delicacy.

[203] THE MEETING OF MARY AND ELIZABETH (THE VISITATION). *Rembrandt* (f.) *1640.* Luke 1:39–56. Bruyn (137), p. 9, notes that the subject is unique in Rembrandt's work. His inspiration is probably the Duerer print, while the setting is derived from Lastman.

[204] THE ANGEL ASCENDING IN THE FLAMES OF MANOAH'S SACRIFICE. *Rembrandt f. 1641.* Judges 13:20. The first careful study of the drawings connected with the painting is that of Saxl (144). The drawings all seem to be the work of students, some of them reworked by Rembrandt. Some were later than the painting (Benesch (152), p. 81). As to the painting itself, I agree with Sumowski (326), p. 227, that it was executed by Jan Victors and retouched by Rembrandt in parts. The date of 1641 is not unlikely, though I doubt that the present signature is original. It remains quite possible that there was another version of this theme (now lost, or perhaps never completed) in working by Rembrandt at the same time. There seem to be traces of another such work in later drawings. Bauch, Benesch Clark (128), p. 156,

Tümpel, and de Vries (28), p. 51, consider the Dresden painting the work of Rembrandt pupil(s), perhaps executed in the fifties. Bruyn (137), p. 18, Rosenberg (29), p. 194, and Rosenberg and Slive (30), p. 63, uphold the attribution to Rembrandt very emphatically.

[205] THE HOLY FAMILY. *Rembrandt f. 1640.* The X-ray photograph published by M. Hours (301), shows an unusual light near the window.

[206] "DE EENDRAGT VAN 'T LANT" (THE CONCORD OF THE STATE). *Rembrandt f. 1641.* Painted in brown monochrome except for the dark blue sky. The sketchy technique makes it appear likely that the picture was meant as a project either for an etching (J. Q. van Regteren Altena (193), p. 59, considers it the design for an etched composition later reworked on the plate into THE HUNDRED-GUILDER PRINT) or a larger painting (F. Schmidt-Degener (188, 189), thinks of it as an allegorical composition destined for the mantlepiece of the civic guard hall in Amsterdam). The sketch was still in Rembrandt's possession in 1656, and is described in his inventory (*Urkunden* (43), no. 169, item 106). The subject is interpreted convincingly in the catalogue of the Boymans-van Beuningen Museum: "Rembrandt probably wished to symbolize the unification of all the Netherlandish forces to fight the common enemy—Spain." Concord is based on political union (the column to the left), religious union (the inscription *Deo soli gloria*), military union (the mounted troop), and justice (the blindfolded figure to the left). The dominance of Amsterdam in the union is reflected in the prominent position given in the composition to the arms of Amsterdam. The allegory is vague, and recent discussion has sought, without total success, to clarify such points as Rembrandt's allegiance in the political situation of his own day (did he take sides with Amsterdam, the States General, or the Prince?), the more general relevance of later developments to Rembrandt's view of the Netherlandish struggle for independence, and the meaning of particular details, e.g. the chained lion, the display of arrows, the empty throne, the broken tree, the action of the troops (are they setting out or returning victorious?), etc. See Bibliography (188–94).

[207] THE RECONCILIATION OF DAVID AND ABSALOM. *Rembrandt f. 1642.* 2 Samuel 14:33 (?) Loevinson Lessing (149) is followed by most art historians in naming the painting THE PARTING OF DAVID AND JONATHAN (1 Samuel 20:41); for an English summary, see *Burlington magazine*, 99, 1957, p. 422. Cf. exhib. cat. *Rembrandt paintings* (315), no. 46; Bauch (15), no. 24; J. G. van Gelder, *Kunstchronik*, 10, 1957, p. 146; C. Tümpel (139), p. 138; Valentiner (318), p. 395; and de Vries (28), p. 47. J. Q. van Regteren Altena (*Kunstchronik*, 9, 1956, p. 347) and Rosenberg (316), p. 383, still prefer the older title as we give it. Not only is the golden hair of the youth so important in the painting, but the quiver of arrows on the ground militates against the Jonathan theory, since Jonathan had just sent his servant back to the city with his arrows. Neither identification is altogether satisfactory.

[208] CHRIST AND THE WOMAN TAKEN IN ADULTERY. *Rembrandt f. 1644.* John 8:7. MacLaren (332), p. 308, rightly observes that "to a limited extent the picture harks back to a much earlier phase of Rembrandt's evolution, namely in the finish and elaboration of detail, and in the construction of the background." Moreover, MacLaren has corrected the history of the picture, and traces it back well into the 17th century. There are some preparatory drawings (Benesch 531–42, Add C5, A42; some are copies).

[209] ANNA ACCUSED BY TOBIT OF STEALING THE KID. *Rembrandt f. 1645.* Tobit 2:20–3. As far as size, date, and mahogony support, a companion picture to [210], but there seems to be no thematic connection. The drawing Benesch 572 shows the strongly built forms that went into this sensitively executed picture.

[210] JOSEPH'S DREAM IN THE STABLE AT BETHLEHEM. *Rembrandt f. 1645* (thin and redrawn). Matthew 2:13. See note to [209]. The X-ray photographs published by C. Wolters (297), p. 60, repr. 96/7, show that there were important changes made around the figure of the angel.

[211] THE HOLY FAMILY WITH ANGELS. *Rembrandt f. 1645.* The drawing Benesch 567 is a preparatory study, and nos. 569 and 570 are also probably connected with it. Benesch rightly stresses that his no. 567 is "one of Rembrandt's most brilliant projects for the lay-out of a painting."

[212] THE HOLY FAMILY (WITH PAINTED FRAME AND CURTAIN). *Rembrandt fc 1646.* The X-ray reveals an underpainting as delicate as the surface, though the strong white of the pot shines out in the X-ray.

[213] BATHSHEBA AT HER TOILET SEEN BY KING DAVID. *Rembrandt ft 1643.* The style of the work is not uniform over the whole surface; the old servant, for example, is in the "Leyden manner." I would imagine that it is a reworking by Rembrandt of some earlier painting by a student.

[214] ABRAHAM SERVING THE THREE ANGELS. *Rembrandt f. 1646.* Not seen by me. The drawings connected with it (Benesch 576–7) are school products. According to Rosenberg and Valentiner (*Rembrandt Handzeichnungen*, 1, 1925, nos. 12–3) they are done after the picture, but Benesch insists they were done before it, as preparatory studies.

[215] THE ADORATION OF THE SHEPHERDS. Signed indistinctly and dated 1646. Luke 2:16. See p. 92.

[216] THE ADORATION OF THE SHEPHERDS. *Rembrandt f. 1646.* Luke 2:16. The composition of this sketchy picture is more or less the reverse of [215]. Its underpainting is as vigorous and varied as the surface. There are

several pentimenti. See X-ray (Illustration b, p. 92).

[217] THE ENTOMBMENT OF CHRIST. Matthew 27:60-1; Mark 15:46-7; Luke 23:53-5; John 23:53. I agree with Bauch (15), no. 74, that this wonderful sketch must have been intended for an (unexecuted) etching. I cannot agree with him, however, that the picture should be dated later than [87]. I think the powerful brushwork is completely in accordance with the energetic drawings of the thirties. J. G. van Gelder (311), p. 328, and Valentiner (318), p. 404 also date [217] in the forties.

[218] THE RISEN CHRIST AT EMMAUS. *Rembrandt f. 1648* (redrawn but genuine). Luke 24:13-31. Bauch (108), p. 187, gives a sensitive interpretation of the light. Clark (128), p. 60, and others have remarked on the Leonardesque type of Christ, which Rembrandt derived through Duerer's woodcut in the Small Passion series. On the other hand, one should not overlook the Venetian heritage in the niche behind the harmonious composition. The X-rays published by M. Hours (301) accentuate the solid construction of the picture. The yellow varnish weakens the rich nuances of tone and line. For the iconography of this and the following number, see W. Stechow (162).

[219] THE RISEN CHRIST AT EMMAUS. *Rembrandt f. 1648* (signature genuine; the date is thin). One of the three paintings not in Bauch (15) that I restore to Rembrandt (the other two are [34] and [352]). I agree with J. Q. van Regteren Altena (16), p. 70, that the picture is a genuine Rembrandt. Altena (165) had earlier given an iconographic and stylistic history of the theme and its relation to the Last Supper. He also drew attention to the unorthodox lighting from the right which Rembrandt had employed earlier, in THE HUNDRED-GUILDER PRINT (Illustration a, p. 358). A cleaning would probably restore to the curtain its proper function in the balance of colors.

[220] THE REST ON THE FLIGHT INTO EGYPT. *Rembrandt f. 1647*. One of the most sensitively painted "landscapes with figures" in the Elsheimer tradition. Some landscape details recall the trees of the Paris landscape [268].

[221] SUSANNA SURPRISED BY THE ELDERS. *Rembrandt f. 1647* (redrawn). H. Kauffmann (142) was the first to demonstrate that the picture consists of two different layers: the first was done around 1635, the second, the one visible today, in 1647. Preparatory drawings for both stages exist (Benesch 155-9, 536, 592). Kauffmann's theory has been disputed by K. von Baudissin (*Repertorium für Kunstwissenschaft*, 46, 1925, pp. 190, 204), but A. Burroughs's X-ray report confirms that important changes took place in the design of the figures. In the final version the excitement of the first lively draft was reduced. There is a beautiful detail study (Benesch 590) and the painted study in The Hague [84], but the most important inspiration for the reworking of 1647 was Lastman's painting of the same theme (Illustration, p. 94), drawn by Rembrandt at this time (Illustration a, p. 327).

[222] BIBLICAL FIGURE. *Rembrandt f. 1643*. Bauch (15), no. 177, records the date as 1642.

[223] HANNAH IN THE TEMPLE AT JERUSALEM. *Rembrandt f. 16[50]*. 1 Samuel 2:24ff. (?) The date is difficult to read, but on the evidence of infrared photography it "can hardly be anything except 1650" (Colin Thompson, keeper of paintings, National Gallery of Scotland). The subject is also interpreted as TIMOTHY AND LOIS (2 Timothy 1:5). Tümpel (139), p. 162, goes into the problem of the picture's iconography, deciding that it represents the New Testament prophetess Hannah, while the figure in the background is Simeon offering his song of praise. The close linking of the prophetess with a child, who appears in the neighborhood of Hannah in some of the biblical etchings, is said by Tümpel to mark the painting as a school work, corrected by Rembrandt, a conclusion that answers to the doubts as to authenticity previously expressed by Bredius and Bauch (15), no. 81. The particular pupil involved could be van Hoogstraten or perhaps Abraham van Dijck.

[224] YOUNG GIRL. *Rembrandt f. 1641* (?) Companion to following number, although the relative proportions of the figures differ somewhat. The whereabouts of the two paintings have not been known since the Second World War. To judge from photographs, the attribution to Rembrandt is not sound.

[225] SCHOLAR AT HIS DESK. *Rembrandt f. 1641*. See [224].

[226] SASKIA WITH A FLOWER. Indistinctly signed and dated 1641. The connection with Titian's FLORA, which was in Amsterdam during Rembrandt's lifetime, has often been noted. See F. Lugt, *Oud Holland*, 53, 1936, p. 127; Stechow (120); E. M. Bloch, (57); Held (201).

[227] HENDRICKJE IN BED. *Rembra(ndt) f. 164(.)* In the 18th century the date was read as 1641 (N. Trivas (263)), but the picture must date from the late forties; stylistically it is close to the biblical scenes of the early fifties. It is probably a fragment of a picture depicting the wedding night of Sarah and Tobias. Tümpel (139), p. 117, stresses its importance as a painting where the individual portrayed (Hendrickje) serves a function in the narrative and symbolic sense of the story without losing her own identity. The identity of the model as Hendrickje, however, is not beyond dispute.

[228] YOUNG GIRL LEANING IN A WINDOWSILL. *Rembrandt ft 1645*. This beautiful, seemingly delicately drawn portrait is built up by forceful strokes in the face and dress. The background too has a powerful tectonic structure. The X-ray confirms this observation, and reveals moreover the original shape of the picture (the top was squared off at the corners, with a semi-circular projection in the middle) and some restorations in the girl's left sleeve. There is a study for it in the Seilern Collection (no. 192). Several 18th-century

copies exist: Leningrad, no. 5848, as J. Reynolds; Collection of Lord Polwarth, a crayon copy by A. Grenville Scott (see exhib. cat. (310), no. 2).

[229] SELF-PORTRAIT. *Rembrandt f. 163(.)* Probably dates from around 1638. J. G. van Gelder (311), p. 328, dates it 1638/9, pointing at the same time to an engraving by J. B. le Sueur, said to be done after a portrait by Flinck of 1636.

[230] THE FRAMEMAKER HERMAN DOOMER. *Rembrandt f. 1640*. Companion picture to [231]. The sitter (before 1600-1654) was the father of Rembrandt's pupil Lambert Doomer. His widow bequeathed the portraits in 1662 to her son on condition that he have them copied for each of his five brothers and sisters. Several copies are known to exist. The pair at Chatsworth is signed (*Doomer*) and the female portrait is dated as well (*1654*). See *Urkunden*, 1st supplement (44), no. 251a; I. H. van Eeghen (249); W. Martin (235).

[231] BAARTJEN MARTENS, WIFE OF HERMAN DOOMER. *Rembrandt f.* See [230].

[232] NICOLAAS VAN BAMBEECK. *Rembrandt f. 1641*. Inscribed *AE 44* Companion to [233]. The identity of the pair was established by I. H. van Eeghen (253). Nicolaes van Bambeeck was a merchant with a house in the St. Anthonisbreestraat; in 1640 he furnished some money to the art dealer Hendrick van Uylenburgh (as Rembrandt had done earlier). The inventory of the younger van Bambeeck (d. 1671) includes portraits of his parents by Flinck, which can no longer be traced.

[233] AGATHA BAS, WIFE OF NICOLAAS VAN BAMBEECK. *Rembrandt f. 1641*. Inscribed *AET 29*. See note to [232]. The cleaning of the painting in the early 1950's has not only revealed the original beauty and delicacy of the portrait, but also uncovered the inscription with the sitter's age, which made the identification of the sitter (and her spouse) possible, disqualifying the earlier identification of the woman as Titia van Uylenburgh; see J. G. van Gelder (311, 313). There is a copy of the female portrait (drawing) in the Rijksprentenkabinet with the inscription: *Fine portrait by Rembrandt, seen at Mr. Cocler's (at Amsterdam), May 1805*.

[234] THE MENNONITE MINISTER CORNELIS CLAESZ. ANSLO IN CONVERSATION WITH A WOMAN. *Rembrandt f. 1641*. Anslo lived from 1592 to 1646. There is an etched portrait of Anslo also dated 1641 (Illustration b, p. 335), and two drawings for the etching and the painting (Benesch 758-9; Illustration a, p. 334), both dated 1640. The poet Joost van den Vondel wrote a poem on the etched portrait: "Rembrandt, why don't you paint Cornelis' voice?/his looks are not his forte./But what can't be seen can at least be heard:/To see Anslo at all you have to hear him." Emmens (250) has gone carefully into the literary tradition of epigrams contrasting the body and the spirit, picture and word, sight and hearing. Daring the artist to depict the voice was already a commonplace in antiquity, and appears in modern literature from Petrarch on. The poem has a special bearing on Rembrandt's art, if we accept the proposition that it was written in praise (or criticism) of the etching, and that the painting is Rembrandt's reply—a portrait of Anslo in mid-conversation, open-mouthed and gesticulating. The woman who listens so attentively might be one of the domestic servants who lived at the "Anslohofje," a home for retired domestics, where the painting may have hung. Hamann (25), p. 167, thinks the servant was added by a pupil. As a matter of fact, her head is painted rather thinly (see Burroughs (294), p. 9, and reproduction). But its construction is solid and the underpainting is comparable to that of Anslo's head, which itself lacks the vigor of many other portrait heads of the time. Hamann's remark may be accepted, with this modification: the woman may have been added as an afterthought (her position in the painting is rather awkward), but by Rembrandt himself, to give "Cornelis' voice" even greater visibility. Sumowski (326), p. 236, also stresses the similarities of the X-ray photographs of the two heads.

[235] ANNA WIJMER (?) *Rembrandt f. 1641*. Anna Wijmer (1584-1654) married Jan Six in 1606; their son, Jan Six, Jr. (1618-1700), was painted by Rembrandt in 1654 [309]. Both the identity of the sitter and the attribution to Rembrandt have been questioned. Bauch (15), no. 500, has rightly observed that the lady looks rather young for a woman of 57, which age she would have reached in 1641. There is a poem by Vondel "On the Picture of Mrs. Anna Wijmer" (published for the first in 1660), but there is no hint that the portrait was painted by Rembrandt (or by J. Backer: a portrait of Anna of Wijmer by "the old Backer" is described in the 1704 inventory of a grandson the sitter; information kindly supplied by Miss I. H. van Eeghen). White (319), p. 322, and Winkler (327), p. 144, Rosenberg (317), p. 349, and Sumowski (326), p. 225, defend the attribution to Rembrandt more or less reluctantly. On djati panel.

[236] SELF-PORTRAIT. *Rembra* (the rest is cut off). Two versions of this portrait exist. The other one is in Woburn Abbey, Collection of the Duke of Bedford; it was bought for Woburn Abbey in the Bragge sale in 1748 (lot 56) for less than £20. The Ottawa version (cat. 1957, p. 88) comes from the collection of the Earl of Listowel. Rosenberg (29) accepts the Bedford version; J. G. van Gelder (313), p. 33, the Ottawa one, which Winkler (327), p. 143 calls an "overpainted copy." Bauch (15), no. 314, quotes Blunt and Wilde (in the Ottawa catalogue) to the effect that the Ottawa version is the superior one, and concludes with them that both versions were done in the studio, after a lost original. I have only seen the Bedford version, which seems to me too weak to be an original Rembrandt.

[237] SELF-PORTRAIT. *Rembrandt* (?) Originally, the top was squared off at the corners, with a semi-circular projection in the center. This portrait is close to Flinck, but despite its weak features (rather dull in execution, with short strokes) probably Rembrandt.

[238] SELF-PORTRAIT. *Rembrandt f. 1640 Conterfeycel* (according to Mac-Laren (332), p. 321, the last word is by another hand). The original shape—the same as that of [237]—could not be restored during the last treatment of the painting in 1964/5, but a lot of overpainted details (not mentioned in the catalogue of 1960) were removed at that time. X-ray photographs reveal that more of the shirt was visible at the bottom and that the left hand originally rested on the parapet. See p. 86 for the derivation of the portrait type.

[239] THE MILITIA COMPANY OF CAPTAIN FRANS BANNING COCQ ("THE NIGHT WATCH"). *Rembrandt f. 1642.* See text, pp. 72–80, and Bibliography (212–26).

[240] SELF-PORTRAIT. Although a pendant (according to S. Gudlaugsson) to [241], which appears to be autograph, there are many strange features which make me doubt the attribution to artist and period.

[241] SASKIA (POSTHUMOUS PORTRAIT). *Rembrandt f. 1643.* (the date is not very clear). See [240]. An X-ray is reproduced by Wolters (297), pl. 1. The X-ray and the painted surface show an uncommon technique: very careful, rather dry, without the usual accents that Rembrandt created with the brushstrokes.

[242] OLD MAN WITH A BERET. False monogram, but genuine Rembrandt. A copy was in the collection of the Earl of Brownlow, wrongly signed and dated 1632.

[243] AN OLD MAN IN RICH COSTUME. *Rembrandt f. 1643.* Neither Bauch nor I have seen the picture, which is especially highly praised by J. G. van Gelder (311), p. 328.

[244] YOUNG MAN HOLDING A SWORD. *Rembrandt ft 1644.* Not known to me in the original. To judge from the photograph, the attribution to Rembrandt is not very convincing.

[245] MAN HOLDING A GLOVE. *Rembran*(dt) *f. 164*(.) I would date the picture in the second half of the forties. There are some pentimenti in the hat and areas of restorations in the coat and collar. The execution of the portrait is rather weak.

[246] MAN STANDING IN A DOORWAY. *Rem*(brandt) *f. 164*(.) Through the dark varnish some pentimenti (ear, hat) can be discerned.

[247] OLD MAN WITH A STICK. Signed and dated 1645. A picture of excellent quality that can serve as a standard against which several doubtful attributions of this period can be measured.

[248] YOUNG WOMAN AT A DOOR. [*Rembrandt f. 16*]*45.* The part of the inscription in brackets appears on the painting, but in another hand. Although accepted as a Rembrandt in the recent literature (de Vries (28), p. 54; Rosenberg (29), p. 91; Clark (128), p. 64; Rosenberg and Slive (30), p. 97), the painting is much stiffer and less sensitive than similar subjects of that year [e.g. 228]. This might be due to the patching work of later restorers, but then again it may be the original work of a pupil (Jan Victors?), basing himself on a Rembrandt design.

[249] WOMAN SEATED IN AN ARMCHAIR. *Rembrandt f. 1644.* Possibly a pendant to the portrait of Jan C. Sylvius in Cologne (Bredius 237), which I do not accept as a Rembrandt. In that case the sitter would be Aaltje van Uylenburgh, the preacher's widow (in 1644). A drawing in Frankfurt (Benesch 765) could be a study for a portrait of this type, after another sitter or model.

[250] THE ART DEALER CLEMENT DE JONGHE (?) *Rembrandt f.* The identification of the sitter as the art dealer de Jonghe (d. 1679) was first put forward by Schmidt-Degener (308), no. 25; it is based on the resemblance between the painting and Rembrandt's etched portrait of de Jonghe (Illustration a, p. 381) but the argument is not perfectly convincing. Clement de Jonghe's inventory compiled after his death included 73 etchings by Rembrandt mentioned by title (*Urkunden* (43), no. 346). It is the first "catalogue" of Rembrandt etchings. Linked in the Faringdon Collection with a female portrait not by Rembrandt and not originally the companion piece to this portrait.

[251] THE PAINTER HENDRICK MARTENSZ. SORGH. *Rembrandt f. 164*(7). The date could also be read as 1644. Companion picture to [252], though of distinctly higher quality than the female portrait. The identity of the pair was established by comparison with Sorgh's self-portrait and his portrait of his wife, which were formerly on loan to the Museum Boymans, Rotterdam (F. Schmidt-Degener, *Oud Holland*, 32, 1914, p. 223). Konody thought that "Rembrandt's hand had no part in the pictures"; he attributes the female portrait to van den Eeckhout. He calls attention to the unusual support (Honduras mahogany?).

[252] ARIAENTJE HOLLAER, WIFE OF HENDRICK MARTENSZ. SORGH. *Rembrandt 1647* (?) See [251].

[253] SELF-PORTRAIT. *Rembrandt f. 164*(.) Probably painted around 1642. The picture has suffered somewhat from Rembrandt's own alterations—the beret has been changed more than once—and later restorations, but Winkler's drastic charge (327), p. 143: "a totally overpainted original," seems too strong.

[254] OLD MAN IN A FUR-LINED COAT. *Rembrandt f. 1645* (a false signature, covering a possibly good one). Face and hands are good, but the rest has suffered from pressing by relining.

[255] CHRIST. The heads of Christ or studies of a young Jew have received attention recently from a number of scholars. See Rotermund (166); Münz (169); and Slive (172). Most studies belong to the second half of the forties, when Rembrandt painted the Emmaus pictures and etched the HUNDRED-GUILDER PRINT. The condition of the bust is not good, but the lighter parts of the face are well preserved.

[256] CHRIST. First published by Valentiner in 1930 (161). Probably one of the last of the series of heads of Christ of the forties. J. Rosenberg (29), p. 117, has described the character of the painting with great sensitivity: It "moves a step farther from reality toward a more idealized expression of mildness and humility. But Rembrandt's transition from the realistic to the imaginary is so subtle that it is almost impossible to draw a borderline between the two." The picture is not known to me.

[257] CHRIST. *Rembrandt f.* (?) Published by Valentiner in 1930 (161). This study is especially close to the Christ in the Louvre Emmaus [218], and should probably also be dated around 1648.

[258] CHRIST. For the condition, see J. L. Allen (337). Notwithstanding some weak details (the ear) and its blackish color, a genuine picture which has suffered. Not listed by Slive (172). I would date it later than Bauch does (around 1648).

[259] AN OLD MAN WEARING A FUR CAP. *Rembrandt f. 1647* (redrawn).

[260] A YOUNG JEW. Although not signed, one of the best studies from the latter half of the forties.

[261] "THE MAN WITH THE GOLDEN HELMET." Bode suggested that the model is Rembrandt's brother Adriaen (*Oud Holland*, 9, 1891, p. 4); but the brother, a modest cobbler, remained in Leyden, where he died in 1652; the model occurs in a study of 1654 [302] and other paintings of the years in Amsterdam, including studio works. The contrast between the thickly painted helmet (cf. the uniform of the lieutenant in THE NIGHT WATCH) and the thinly painted face adds to the richness and variety of the conception.

[262] SELF-PORTRAIT. Some remains of a signature. By the 18th century (or earlier) the picture was enlarged to a rectangular shape. Some of these additions, on the left, have survived the modern restorations. The portrait is painted over another, of an elderly man with a beard, probably also by Rembrandt. The X-ray shows the old man clearly, but even with the naked eye he obtrudes in parts (see the double ear). A work of the first half of the forties.

[263] THE JEWISH PHYSICIAN EPHRAIM BUENO. An oil sketch for the etching of 1647, of excellent quality. See Illustration a, p. 349. Dr. Ephraim Bueno (1594–1665) was a well-known physician and publisher of Jewish works in Amsterdam.

[264] AN OLD WOMAN WITH A BOOK. *Rembrandt f. 164*(7). Rosenberg (29), p. 77, compares this portrait to a female portrait by Frans Hals, stressing the stylistic difference between the two artists. The comparison has a positive side, however: there are elements here that derive from the late Frans Hals. There are some weaknesses in the portrait: the hands are without expression, the collar has no sense of design. I am undecided whether to attribute this to the ravages of time or the efforts of a student like van den Eeckhout.

[265] LANDSCAPE WITH A CHURCH. I share the opinion of those who think that the picture is nearer to Seghers than Rembrandt. See the report of a discussion in *Kunstchronik*, 10, 1957, pp. 142, 145.

[266] LANDSCAPE WITH A COACH. Probably painted around 1640–1. Comparable with landscape details in [206].

[267] WINTER LANDSCAPE. *Rembrandt f. 1646.* Painted fluently and quickly, as a sketch; the signature is so pressed into the wet paint that it can even be read in the X-rays—a very rare case!

[268] LANDSCAPE WITH A CASTLE. This important addition to the corpus of Rembrandt landscapes was first published by M. Conway (286) in 1925. Formerly in the Stroganoff Collection in Leningrad. I would date it in the very early 1640's.

[269] THE RISEN CHRIST APPEARING TO MARY MAGDALENE. *Rembrandt 165*(1). John 20: 16–7. There seem to be traces of letters before the signature. The painting is so dark and thin that it is really difficult to judge the painterly qualities of the surface, which may have suffered from abrasion. But I do see some connection with the work of Samuel van Hoogstraten.

[270] DANAE. *Rembrandt f. 16*(3)6. With Panofsky's demonstration (195) that the subject of the painting is Danae receiving Jupiter in a golden blaze the older interpretations of Weisbach (Venus awaiting Mars), Rosenthal (Rachel awaiting Jacob), and Niemeijer (Sarah awaiting Abraham) were abandoned. There has been a subsequent attempt to return to a biblical heroine, however: C. Brière Misme (199) proposes Leah expecting Laban, an interpretation followed by A. B. de Vries (28), p. 28. Observations by Agafonova (Publications of the Hermitage, *Dept. of European art*, 1940, p. 23) and Tümpel (139), p. 191 tend to support Panofsky's thesis, which is also accepted here.

J. I. Kusnetzow (202) has demonstrated that the painting, which was first executed in the thirties—the difficult-to-read date may be 1636—was reworked by the artist in a later period (this had already been guessed by a.o. Julius Held). Kusnetzow puts the date of the reworking around 1645. I would go further to "around 1650." The later reworking touched mainly the figure of Danae herself who, to my mind, can be compared in softness of surface texture and "classical" structure to BATHSHEBA of 1654 [271]. X-rays showing the extensive reworking of such details as the arm confirm this. Once we perceive the monumental style of the figure (as contrasted to the Baroque design of curtains and bed) we can better appreciate Clark's hymn (128), p. 108, to the Venetian mood of DANAE. In this light, too, we can weigh Hofstede de Groot's previously discredited assumption that the drawing in Munich (Benesch 1124) is a study for the figure of Danae.

[271] BATHSHEBA WITH KING DAVID'S LETTER. *Rembrandt ft 1654* (?) 2 Samuel 11:4. Although covered by heavy varnish and probably damaged severely in the shadows, one of Rembrandt's great biblical creations. Hendrik Bramsen (121) has demonstrated that an engraving by Fr. Perrier after an antique relief inspired the composition. X-rays published by M. Hours (301) reveal that the head of Bathsheba was originally raised and her gaze directed upwards. The model is surely Hendrickje. The Oriental hat worn by the servant appears on a contemporary nude drawing (Illustration a, p. 361) which is not, however, directly connected with the composition.

[272] CHRIST AND THE WOMAN OF SAMARIA. *Rembrandt f. 1655.* John 4:7–26. The subject appears in two other paintings of the fifties [273, 349] as well as in drawings and etchings, and always with a strong Venetian flavor. I see powerful emotional interpretations in all the painted treatments of the subject, related yet independent works of art.

[273] CHRIST AND THE WOMAN OF SAMARIA. *Rembrandt f. 1655.* See note to [272]. I cannot accept Sumowski's judgment (326), p. 231: "compilation by a pupil."

[274] JOSEPH ACCUSED BY POTIPHAR'S WIFE. *Rembran(dt) f. 1655* (?) Genesis 39:17–8. The recent cleaning has disclosed earlier damage to the pigments closest to the surface, so that the balance of colors is now slightly off. But I nevertheless agree with Rosenberg (29), p. 222, and others (see following number) that this version is superior to the Washington one: the drama is more concentrated; and the pentimenti around Potiphar's wife expose the actual process of artistic invention. The underpainting is especially beautiful in its powerful cubic construction and "impressionistic" execution. In an earlier stage Joseph covered his face with his hand. For a poor reproduction of the excellent Berlin X-ray, see Sumowski (326), p. 237. A rather poor copy was sold in London (Christie), on December 8, 1961 (lot 84).

[275] JOSEPH ACCUSED BY POTIPHAR'S WIFE. *Rembrandt f. 165* (5). See [274]. According to Benesch's interpretation of the drawing Benesch 958 one may conclude that this version is the earlier of the two JOSEPHS. The quality of the painting is difficult to ascertain through the heavy varnish and the curious *craquelé*. The X-ray photograph of Potiphar's wife makes rather a good impression, though. Bauch has analyzed the differences between [274] and [275] very well (109), p. 321; (15), nos. 32–3. His final conclusion has much merit: were the two versions to be placed side by side, he believes the Berlin painting would prove the better, though Rembrandt surely had something to do with the Washington version as well, perhaps correcting a pupil's work. The connection with the drawing, Benesch 623, is not convincing.

[276] THE TRIBUTE MONEY. *Rembrandt f. 1655.* Matthew 22:15–22; Mark 12:13–17; Luke 20:20–26. Schmidt-Degener (*de Gids*, 1919, p. 32) launched the theory that this is a sketch for the painting that hung over the mantle of the Treasury Room in the Amsterdam Town Hall. The painting itself does not survive, but it was praised in a poem by Vondel which does not mention the name of the artist. Nordenfalk (183), p. 81, supports the idea and the attribution to Rembrandt, both of which are questioned by Hamann (25), p. 281, and Schneider (reported by van de Waal (176) p. 217). The alternative attribution proposed is Gerbrand van den Eeckhout. I have not seen the picture.

[277] JACOB BLESSING THE SONS OF JOSEPH. *Rembran(dt) f. 1656* (false; copied from the good signature?) Genesis 48:17–20. Although the picture has suffered from relining and pressing and was perhaps never completely finished, it is a work of enormous power, inner emotion, and painterly richness. Notwithstanding the date (not inscribed by Rembrandt in any case) I could imagine that parts of the picture were reworked by the master in the sixties. The X-rays (taken by Dr. Meier-Siem and others), though difficult to read on account of the layer of paint on the back of the picture, show small compositional changes—the elder boy was originally seen more in profile. Stechow (145), p. 193, and von Einem (146) have carefully traced, in different ways, the iconographic tradition of the subject, its connection with the biblical text and secondary sources, showing how these are reflected—or not—in Rembrandt's version. Important features of the interpretation that are unique to Rembrandt are the presence of Asnath, Joseph's wife, and the diminished emphasis on the motif of the crossed hands. Interesting observations have been made by Manke (151), Held (155), p. 32, note 23, Rosenberg (29), p. 223, and Rosenberg and Slive (30), p. 79. The text makes it clear that the blond child, larger in the picture, is the younger of the brothers, Ephraim, blessed with the right hand, while Manasseh is shown as a small, dark child.

[278] JUPITER AND MERCURY VISITING PHILEMON AND BAUCIS. *Rembrandt f. 1658.* The signature is difficult to read through the varnish. The picture is beautifully painted and sensitively drawn. The drawings formerly connected with it (Benesch A 76 and 940) belong to another period and another composition. Kieser (119), p. 147, has rightly observed the inner connection with the early Emmaus picture [14].

[279] A YOUNG WOMAN AT HER MIRROR. *Rembrandt f. 165* (4) (indistinct). W. Martin suggested that the picture is a fragment (9), p. 33, but Glück (278), p. 301, rightly denies this, pointing out that the picture could well be identical with no. 39 of Rembrandt's inventory (*Urkunden* (43), no. 169): "one courtesan doing her hair." (See also Clark (128), p. 195). Strips have been added to the top and bottom of the original panel.

[280] A MAN IN FANCIFUL COSTUME. *Rembrandt f. 1650.* Companion picture to [281]. Although I listed this picture in the Fitzwilliam Museum catalogue (1960, p. 102) as a Rembrandt, I am now doubtful about the attribution, especially since the companion piece only accentuates the "theatrical conception and composition, unusual for Rembrandt" (Bauch (15), no. 510). The many surface cracks (especially over the hat and the feather) make a judgment of the painterly qualities difficult.

[281] A WOMAN IN FANCIFUL COSTUME. See [280]. Shown for the first time at the Rembrandt exhibition in Detroit (1930, no. 4). Although neither Bauch nor I have seen the picture, I doubt it as well as its companion.

[282] KING DAVID. *Rembrandt f. 1651.* If Bauch (15), no. 202, is right about the style: "end of the fifties," the signature is not good. Neither Bauch nor I have seen the picture.

[283] OLD MAN IN AN ARMCHAIR (THE PATRIARCH JACOB?). The surmise that Jacob is represented is Bauch's (15), no. 203. In any case, the work clearly belongs to the series of studies for history paintings and has nothing to do with any portrait commission. A copy was recently sold in the Cook sale, London (Sotheby), June 25, 1958, lot 112.

[284] YOUNG GIRL HOLDING A BROOM. *Rembrandt f. 1651* (?) The date is not very clear. X-rays reveal that the position of the hands was originally higher, the sort of change that usually reflects an artist's changing conception in the course of work and not a copyist's correction. On the other hand, neither the structure of the surface pigments nor the underpainting is as powerful and decisive as that of [285]. The surface is made up of small particles of paint standing upright, which one observes on paintings exposed to immoderate heat—and on pictures of the 18th century. The latter possibility should not be excluded at this stage of research.

[285] YOUNG GIRL AT A WINDOW. *Rembrandt f. 1651.* A small drawing in Dresden (Benesch 1170) is the preparatory study for this most powerful picture. See p. 70 for de Piles' remarks on his Rembrandt (40), p. 423.

[286] ARISTOTLE CONTEMPLATING A BUST OF HOMER. *Rembrandt f. 1653.* For the circumstances of the commission, see p. 114. See also Ruffo (50); Hoogewerff (51); C. Ricci, *Rembrandt in Italia*, 1918; Schneider (52); von Einem (200); and Rousseau (186).

We know that Rembrandt owned busts of Socrates, Homer, and Aristotle (*Urkunden* (43), no. 169, items 162–4), though we cannot know if they were antique or Renaissance originals or copies. In the Ruffo commission, Rembrandt followed a Hellenistic type, "adapted faithfully and respectfully" (Kieser (119), p. 135). Emmens (83), pp. 173–4, remarking that Aristotle was the "official" philosopher of Dutch Calvinism, goes on to show that the combination of Homer, Aristotle, and Alexander (the philosopher wears a medallion with the bust of his old pupil on it, according to Emmens) reflects the three sources of artistic creation in 17th-century theory: invention (the poet), science (the philosopher), and discipline (the ruler). It must have been Rembrandt, not Ruffo, who worked out the details of this program. However, Kraft (187) argues that the medallion shows Athena, not Alexander.

From the Ruffo documents we learn that all the pictures that went to Sicily were originally larger; some have suffered from fire and other damage. Yet they remain among the most impressive examples of Rembrandt's rich evocations of historical characters.

[287] "THE POLISH RIDER." *Re...* The picture has been cut at the right edge, so that only part of the signature can be read. A strip had been added to replace a strip removed from the original canvas; this has been removed and replaced in its turn. The basic interpretation of the subject is due to Held (264); it is not a real portrait but a poetic composition with allegorical meaning, connected with the concept of the "Christian soldier." To Valentiner (133) the painting remains a historical portrait, of Gysbrecht van Amstel, the mythical founder of Amsterdam. A Polish historian has recently shown, however, that the title of the painting—which was in Poland as early as the 18th century (Ciechanowiecki (274))—is in fact justified. The elements of dress and military equipment are indeed Polish; see Zygulski (276). J. Białostocki (277) has suggested that the idea of creating a symbol (and a kind of ideal portrait) of a "Polish Knight" may have been suggested by the struggle for liberty of conscience led in Holland by the Polish Socinian Jonasz Szlichtyng. His *Apologia* was published in Amsterdam in 1654; it attacked the States General edict of the previous year, which banned the preaching of the Socinian doctrine. The Polish Socinians in Holland (called the Polish Brethren there) found a good deal of support for their belief in the circles of Dutch dissidents, among them the Mennonites, with whom Rembrandt was connected through the van Uylenburgh family.

[288] HENDRICKJE AS FLORA. See Held's instructive demonstration of how the erotic aspect of Flora has been reduced in this later picture (201), p. 218. Kieser's assertion (119), p. 155, that the work is Rembrandt's answer to the condemnation of Hendrickje's "fornication" by the church council is not

supported by the visual evidence. See also Stechow (120).

[289] HENDRICKJE BATHING IN A STREAM. *Rembrandt f. 1654* (*1655*?). MacLaren (332), p. 312, reads the date as 1655, but the last digit still looks like a 4. The cleaning of the picture in 1946 started a long controversy between proponents of radical cleaning of paintings and the more conservative party, who argued that HENDRICKJE had suffered irreparable damage in the laboratories of the National Gallery. See exhib. cat. *Cleaned pictures* (299), no. 68. I think the cleaning was done well, and that the ground shining through some thinly painted areas is an important element of the artistic expression of this oil sketch, which is in good condition except for a vertical crack. The X-ray shows a powerful underpainting (Burroughs (294), p. 9).

[290] THE SLAUGHTERED OX. *Rembrandt f. 16(..)* (inscribed on a band of dark paint along the bottom of the picture—added later?). I share the opinion of the cataloguer of the Glasgow collection, H. Miles (329), no. 600: acceptable as an autograph work, despite some evident weaknesses of execution. If autograph, painted in the late thirties; formerly dated around 1650. Bredius (ms. note) had doubts, which were shared by Schneider.

[291] THE SLAUGHTERED OX. *Rembrandt f. 1655*. The picture has enjoyed rather a special reputation since it was acquired by the Louvre in 1857. There are copies by Delacroix, Bonvin, and Soutine; the motif was used once by Daumier. B. Lemann, *Bulletin of the Fogg Art Museum*, 6, 1936, p. 13. J. Emmens (293).

[292] AN OLD WOMAN READING. *Rembrandt f. 1655*. Praised by J. G. van Gelder (311), p. 329, when exhibited in Edinburgh in 1950 (no. 29). According to Emmens an allegory of Faith.

[293] ALEXANDER THE GREAT. The Ruffo documents (50) make it clear that Rembrandt painted two versions of ALEXANDER for Don Antonio Ruffo. The first was sent off in July 1661, by Ruffo's agent in Amsterdam, with a bill: "a picture called the Great Alexander done by the painter Rembrandt van Rijn, as per agreement with the painter, in the sum of 500 guilders." Costs for materials—and for a picture of HOMER—appear in the same document. ALEXANDER, Rembrandt had proposed, should be hung between ARISTOTLE and HOMER. After more than a year Ruffo wrote to Amsterdam complaining about this ALEXANDER: the canvas was originally just a head, and the painter had pieced it out to a half-length figure with four pieces of canvas. Rembrandt replied, through the agent, that he was quite willing to paint a second ALEXANDER. The question remains: Are the two surviving versions of ALEXANDER THE GREAT [293, 294] the same paintings discussed in the Ruffo papers? Until now art historians have been reluctant to grant that the additions sewn onto the Glasgow version could have been painted as late as 1661. The painting bore a date of 1655; moreover, the figure seemed to be a female, whose owl would make her an ATHENA or BELLONA. The latest numismatic and art historical evidence seems to make it possible to accept these two paintings as Ruffo's ALEXANDERS, however. In the Renaissance there was a confusion between the iconography of Alexander and Athena, so that the type of Alexander was derived from ancient coins showing Athena (Kraft (187), p. 7). As a result, the so-called special attributes of Athena displayed by the Rembrandt figures (owl, hairlocks, shield of Medusa) came to appear on representations of Alexander. The armor worn by the figure, moreover, makes no allowance for the female breasts (cf. Bredius 467), while the lance is an attribute of Alexander that does not belong to the iconography of Athena. The stylistic relation between the two paintings does not present any difficulties in accepting this theory. The date of 1655 formerly read on the Glasgow painting can no longer be made out—but even if the original canvas was painted and dated in 1655, there is no reason why Rembrandt could not have converted an earlier profile (of Titus?) into a figure of a warrior. In fact, it is more than likely that Rembrandt used an earlier composition of his to meet the first Ruffo commission for an ALEXANDER: if he had painted a new composition, there would never have arisen the need to piece out a canvas. The additional pieces of canvas presently sewn onto the Glasgow picture are recent, but they may replace Rembrandt's additions. The style of [293] is later than that of [294], to my mind, and I am quite prepared to accept it as the second ALEXANDER that Rembrandt painted for Ruffo in 1662. R. van Luttervelt (*Gazette des beaux-arts*, 6/37, 1950, p. 99) also dates [293] about five years later than [294], but I do not agree with the arguments which help him to this conclusion.

[294] ALEXANDER THE GREAT. See [293]. For a drawing connected with this painting, see K. A. Agafonova, *Burlington magazine*, 107, 1965, p. 404.

[295] THE APOSTLE PAUL AT HIS DESK. *Rembrandt f.* The picture has suffered from pressing, but it remains splendid. Probably to be dated 1657, as [296].

[296] THE APOSTLE BARTHOLOMEW. *Rembrandt f. 1657*. Cleaned in 1951; in especially good condition. The hand and face, for example, show clearly the broad, powerful brushwork of the late style of figure painting. [295], [296], and [298] may have been painted in the same year without necessarily being companion pieces or part of a series; their dimensions differ.

[297] A BEARDED MAN. Published by Bode (*Jahrbuch der preussischen Kunstsammlungen*, 38, 1917, p. 107). Although it has suffered somewhat from relining, still one of the most expressive studies of the period. Related to [297]. Bode's suggestion that the model is a Russian is not very convincing.

[298] THE APOSTLE PAUL. *Rembrandt 165(9)*. Valentiner (159) discusses the dual aspect of the picture as a portrait and a member of the series of apostles [359 ff.]. There are weak features (the modeling of the hands, the unbalanced color scheme) that may be due to heavy wear, but also suggest the possibility that the piece is an old copy.

[299] AN OLD MAN IN FANCIFUL COSTUME. *Rembrandt f. 1651*.

[300] A FRANCISCAN MONK. *Rembrandt f. 165(..)* If the date of this "badly worn and cracked" picture (MacLaren (332), p. 315) is rightly read as 1655 (or 1656), it must be earlier than [377] and [386]. Though less sensitively painted than these, the attribution to Rembrandt seems to be correct.

[301] MAN LEANING IN A WINDOWSILL. *Rembrandt f. 1650*. First published by Hofstede de Groot (8), p. 43. Sometimes called a self-portrait, though this was doubted by Bredius (14), no. 41, Glück (278), p. 296, and Bauch (15), no. 399, who calls it "perhaps the portrait of an artist." Judging from a photograph, I am not convinced that the attribution to Rembrandt is correct.

[302] AN OLD MAN WITH A BERET. *Rembrandt f. 1654* (?) The thick varnish conceals a powerful composition. The hand seems to have suffered. Companion to [303].

[303] AN OLD WOMAN WITH A HOOD. *Rembrandt f. 1654* (?) One of the finest of Rembrandt's studies of old women. See [302].

[304] PORTRAIT OF A MAN. *Rembrandt f. 1650*. It was this painting Bode originally introduced as the portrait of brother Adriaen (*Oud Holland*, 9, 1891, pp. 1–6). The brushwork is very close to that of Carel Fabritius. The canvas must have been folded once; creases are clearly visible on the painted surface.

[305] AN OLD MAN IN AN ARMCHAIR. *Rembrandt f. 1652* (?) The Venetian mood of this portrait has often been stressed (most recently by Clark (128), p. 130). As imposing as the rich mood is, however, the overall structure of the picture—in particular the painterly execution of the beard and fur coat, as well as the right hand—is very weak, and even inconsistent. The left hand and the sleeve above it, for example, are conceived in a superficially impressionistic style that is out of tune with the rest of the painting, the sort of contradiction that does not occur in the good portraits of the period [cf. 307].

[306] AN OLD MAN IN A LINEN HEADBAND. *Rembrandt f. 1651*. A picture of excellent quality, too often dismissed for the faults of its shabby reproduction in the first edition of Bredius.

[307] NICOLAES BRUYNINGH. *Rembrandt f. 1652*. The sitter was a distant relative of Frans Jansz. Bruyningh, who was in charge of Rembrandt's *cessio bonorum* of 1657–8 (W. F. H. Oldewelt (56), p. 158). The picture was in the possession of Bruyningh's sister, Hildegonda Graeswinkel, whose daughter exchanged it in 1728 with the well-known collector and dealer Valerius Roever of Delft, who sold it with many other items to the Landgraf Wilhelm VIII of Cassel in 1750.

[308] SELF-PORTRAIT... *dt f. 1652*. Glück (278), p. 308, reported on the cleaning, noting that a strip of 7–8 cm. had been cut from the left side. Several copies exist, one of the bust being exhibited at Bregenz in 1966 (no. 79) as the "preparatory study for the Vienna portrait." See the pose of the full-length self-portrait drawing in the Rembrandt-huis (Illustration a, p. 482).

[309] JAN SIX. Painted in 1654, as appears from a poem composed by Six himself: *AonIDas tenerIs qUI sUM VeneratUs ab annIs/TaLIs ego JanUs SIXIUs ora tULI.* (Such a face had I, Jan Six, who since childhood have worshipped the Muses; *Urkunden* (43), no. 151). The capital letters (except for the A, T, and S), read as Roman numerals, add up to 1654. Jan Six was a merchant of Amsterdam who had rather close ties with Rembrandt from the middle of the forties. He was married to Margareta Tulp, a daughter of Nicolaas Tulp, and served later in the century (1691) as Burgomaster of Amsterdam. An anecdote in Gersaint (see p. 100) links Rembrandt with Six. In 1647 Rembrandt did an etched portrait of the poet (Illustration a, p. 90), and in 1648 he made an etching to serve as title-page of a drama Six had written and was having published (Illustration a, p. 318). There are several drawings of him as well, among others two in the family album of Six (Benesch 913–4; Illustration b, p. 90). Contact between the two men seems to have ceased after 1654, when Rembrandt made good on all his debts to Six. See White (67), p. 93 and M. G. de Boer (*Jaarboek Amstelodamum*, 42, 1948, pp. 10–34). See also [235].

[310] SELF-PORTRAIT. *Rembrandt f. 165(4)*. Companion to [311]? Painted over a female portrait in the style of the thirties. The X-ray showing the underlying image is reproduced by Wehlte (296), p. 13. The picture is difficult to judge in its present thickly varnished state. Although it belonged to the Roever collection in 1709, a provenance distinguished enough to dispel minor doubts, the attribution is not wholly convincing.

[311] HENDRICKJE STOFFELS. Covered by thick varnish. The surface has suffered a great deal; in its present state impossible to decide whether an original or a copy. M. Hours (301), reports that the picture "seems to have been signed below, but in the present state of the painting nothing can be read." Companion to [310]?

[312] AN OLD WOMAN IN AN ARMCHAIR. *Rembrandt f. 1654* (?) Companion to the following number, both of which have been enlarged from 35 x 30 in. The respective positions of the pendants (the man is almost invariably on the left side) as well as the weaker execution of this piece leave doubts as to its authenticity.

[313] AN OLD MAN IN AN ARMCHAIR. *Rembrandt f. 1654*. See [312].

[314] AN OLD MAN IN AN ARMCHAIR. *Rembrandt f.* Distinctly inferior to other old men of the period [e.g. 313].

[315] AN OLD WOMAN SEATED. *Rembrandt f. 16 (..)* (signed thinly). Parts of the costume have suffered, and are less expressive than the powerful hands, head, and headdress.

[316] A MAN IN A FUR-LINED COAT. *Rembrandt f.* followed by an indistinct date, formerly read as 1655, and accepted as such by Bauch (15), no. 409. Valentiner (11), p. 266, read the date as 1665 and later (254), p. 233, as 1666, in accordance with Heil (307), p. 383. Valentiner sees the features of Titus in this great portrait. I prefer a date in the late fifties.

[317] THE STANDARD BEARER. *Rembrandt f. 1654.*

[318] HENDRICKJE.

[319] CHILD IN FANCIFUL COSTUME. Considering that the painting cannot date from the forties, the model can hardly be Titus (b. 1641) as is often claimed.

[320] SELF-PORTRAIT. *Rembrandt f. 1655.* The condition is not as bad as F. Winkler believes (327), p. 143: "a beautiful ruin."

[321] CHRIST. The signature comes on a part of the painting added later, not by Rembrandt. See Slive (172), p. 413. It is not absolutely certain that this is the painting in the van Loo sale, Paris 1772, sketched by Saint-Aubin in his copy of the sales catalogue, as Langton Douglas believes (*Art in America*, 36, 1948, p. 69).

[322] CHRIST. First published by Slive (172). Came to America (art dealer A. E. Silberman) in 1939 from Poland. Slive rightly dates the painting with the rest of this series of Christ heads in the late forties, stressing the relations to THE HUNDRED-GUILDER PRINT.

[323] CHRIST. This head has more the character of a study from life than any of the others, and Slive quite rightly places it first in the series. Bauch's dating of around 1656 seems too late.

[324] SELF-PORTRAIT. *Rembrandt f.* Painted around the same time as [329]. Hofstede de Groot's dating of c. 1665 is much too late.

[325] TITUS AT HIS DESK. *Rembrandt f. 1655.* Probably the earliest portrait of Rembrandt's son. A sensitive interpretation is given by van de Waal (275).

[326] THE ANATOMY LESSON OF DOCTOR JOAN DEYMAN. *Rembrandt f. 1656.* Doctor Deyman (1620–66) was the successor to Nicolaes Tulp as Praelector Anatomiae of the Amsterdam Guild of Surgeons, from 1653. To his left is the college master Gysbrecht Matthijsz. Calcoen, with the crown of the skull in his hand. Representations of dissections of the brain are very rare in Dutch art (see A. M. Cetto, *CIBA Symposium*, 6, 1958, p. 122). The records of the anatomy theater book show that "on January 28, 1656 there was punished with the rope Joris Fonteyn of Diest, who was granted us by the Worshipful Lords of the Lawcourt as anatomical object. On the 29th Dr. Johan Deyman made his first demonstration on him in the theater of the Anatomy, three lessons altogether." See I. H. van Eeghen (205), p. 34; White (67), p. 105; Heckscher (207), p. 191. The picture hung (like [100]) in the Anatomy Theater of Amsterdam; it was partially destroyed by a fire in 1723. The surviving area also suffered. The drawing in the Rijksmuseum (Illustration a, p. 398) is not a preparatory study, but a sketch done after the painting was completed, for the frame and hanging (Held (264), p. 259; J. Q. van Regteren Altena (206), p. 171), *pace* Benesch (*Drawings* (17), no. 1175). It is generally believed that the eloquent foreshortening of the corpse stems from an Italian model, esp. Mantegna's DEAD CHRIST (Illustration, p. 128; Clark (128), p. 93), but Haverkamp Begemann and others point to the DEAD CHRIST of Orazio Borgianni (Rome, Galleria Spada; also engraved) as the more likely source, while other works of art and anatomical illustrations seem to have served as intermediate visual stimuli (Wolf-Heidegger and Cetto (211), p. 313, no. 261).

[327] THE AMSTERDAM PHYSICIAN ARNOUT THOLINX. *Rembrandt f. 1656.* The sitter was an inspector of the Amsterdam medical colleges from 1643 to 1653, when he was succeeded by Joan Deyman. Tholinx was related to both Nicolaes Tulp and Jan Six. His portrait is identified on the basis of the etching Münz 73. The picture is covered by thick varnish, which makes it hard to verify the signature and estimate the real quality of the execution.

[328] A YOUNG MAN WITH A BERET. *Rembrandt f.* Bredius and Bauch rightly reject the often expressed opinion that this is a portrait of Titus. The picturesque mood is similar, though, to the intimate portraits of Titus of the late fifties [375, 377].

[329] SELF-PORTRAIT. *Rembrandt f. 1657.* Later additions were removed during restoration. But it seems to me that the painting must have been larger originally.

[330] TITUS. *R...* The initial was the first letter of the full signature, which was cut off. It must have been painted in the later fifties. The present appearance of the painting is disfigured by thick varnish.

[331] A YOUNG WOMAN WITH A CARNATION. *Rembrandt f. 1656* (false). Enlarged with strips on the bottom and left to make it match the dimensions of the pseudo-pendant, Bredius 287. The attribution to Rembrandt is not wholly convincing, but the uneven quality may be due to faulty restorations.

[332] AN OLD MAN WITH A GOLD CHAIN. *Rembrandt f. 1657.* Also called PORTRAIT OF A RABBI. Published by Rosenberg (265) as the original of Bredius 259, which I have never seen. I am not convinced that either painting is by Rembrandt.

[333] AN OLD MAN IN A CAPE. Not seen by either Bauch or me.

[334] A BEARDED MAN IN A CAP. *Rembrandt f. 165(.)* The same model as in [286], [332], and [402]. See Benesch (134).

[335] TITUS READING. After restoration in 1938 a strip previously bent back over the stretcher was exposed, with the result that the picture has become 2 cm. broader. See Münz (243), p. 253.

[336] CATRINA HOOGHSAET. *Rembrandt f. 1657.* Inscribed *CATRINA HOOGH/SAET. Out 50/jaer.* The sitter (1607–after 1657) and her husband Hendrick Jacobsz. Rooleeuw belonged to the Mennonite church. Rembrandt may have painted the (lost) husband's portrait (H. F. Wijnman (262), p. 81).

[337] A YOUNG WOMAN. Bauch (15), no. 520, identifies the sitter as Hendrickje, and dates the painting ca. 1659. I prefer a later date, ca. 1665 (cf. exhib. cat. *The age of Rembrandt*, San Francisco etc. 1966/7, no. 75) and no name.

[338] PORTRAIT OF A MAN. The picture has gained allure through its recent cleaning. I agree with Bauch's dating "around 1660."

[339] HENDRICKJE AT AN OPEN DOOR. Possibly a companion to a lost self-portrait. Clark (128), p. 132, rightly stresses the connection with Venetian art, in this case with a type created by Palma Vecchio. X-rays show heavy reworking by Rembrandt: Hendrickje was first seen in full face, with her hands together.

[340] A MAN HOLDING A MANUSCRIPT. *Rembrandt f. 1658.* A particularly sensitive appreciation of this beautiful portrait has been written by Benesch (134), p. 340.

[341] A MAN HOLDING A LETTER. *Rembrandt f. 1658.* Probably a most impressive late portrait; unknown to Bauch or me in the original.

[342] A MAN WITH ARMS AKIMBO. *Rembrandt f. 1658.* Published by Borenius (261) and Valentiner (11). The picture came to light in the George Folliott of Chester sale, London (Sotheby), May 14, 1930, lot 51.

[343] SELF-PORTRAIT. *Rembrandt f. 1658* (repainted; the date may also be read as 1655). One of the most powerful and regal self-portraits in the Venetian vein. See Clark (128), p. 130.

[344] RIVER LANDSCAPE WITH RUINS. *Rembrandt f.* There are many pentimenti, showing either that Rembrandt changed the composition while working on it or that he remodeled a somewhat earlier project, which was more sketchlike. The powerful picture as we see it today must date from the early fifties. Bauch (15), no. 554 and de Vries (28), p. 62, agree, but Benesch (17), vol. 4, p. 210, dates it around 1642/3. There is some damage in the foreground and in the sky; the barge and mill are the best preserved parts, an observation confirmed by the X-rays.

[345] EVENING LANDSCAPE WITH COTTAGES. *Rembrandt f. 1654.* The same spot appears repeatedly in drawings and etchings by Rembrandt and his pupils. See Lugt, *Mit Rembrandt in Amsterdam*, p. 120; *Jahrbuch der preussischen Kunstsammlungen*, 52, 1931, p. 60. Bredius once wrote (in a note to the compiler of the first edition of *Rembrandt paintings*): "Probably all right, but it has something that alarms me." I have the same feeling of uneasiness.

[346] JACOB WRESTLING WITH THE ANGEL. *Rembrandt f.* (the signature appears on a separate piece of canvas inserted on the lower right of the painting). Genesis 33:24f. The canvas was cut down at one time. It may have been painted for the Amsterdam Town Hall, according to Heppner. M. M. van Dantzig (*Het vrije volk*, June 27, 1956) declares it to be a fake but the claim cannot really be sustained. Rosenberg calls it a perplexing painting. The X-rays (not seen by me) are praised by Sumowski (326), p. 236.

[347] MOSES WITH THE TABLES OF THE LAW. *Rembrandt f. 1659* (on a damaged area of the canvas). Exodus 32:15–19 or Exodus 35:29. Related to the preceding number, and probably part of a larger series, with it, whether or not they were designed for the Amsterdam Town Hall (Heppner (143), p. 241). Heppner interprets the subject as Moses showing the second tables of the Law to the people, while Tümpel (139), p. 107, argues in favor of Moses breaking the first tables. Sumowski (326), p. 237, praises the X-rays, which I have not seen.

[348] OLD TOBIT AND ANNA WAITING FOR THEIR SON. *Rembrandt f. 1659.* Tobit 10:1–4. The drawing Benesch 597 is the first idea for this composition. In 1947 cleaning revealed the date 1659 (previously read as 1650); the later date is easier to reconcile with Rembrandt's stylistic development, especially in view of the painting's violet-red color scheme and loose structure, both elements taken over by Aert de Gelder, who became Rembrandt's pupil later in the fifties. Bauch, however, (15), no. 30, defends the date of 1650. There was originally a still life painted on the right side of the picture, traces of which still interfere with the harmony of the painting in its present state. Held (155), p. 30, points out the similarity of the composition to Emblem XLIV of Johan de Brune's *Emblemata of zinne-werk* (Amsterdam 1624), illustrating a text in praise of humble industry.

[349] CHRIST AND THE WOMAN OF SAMARIA. *Rembrandt f. 1659* (redrawn, but genuine). John 4:7–26. Bredius' notes (ms.): "rather questionable." I do not agree. Although the painting has suffered, and was painted rather thinly to begin with, it fits perfectly with the monumental compositions in the Venetian mood of the fifties. It is the last, beautiful example of this series.

[350] THE CIRCUMCISION OF CHRIST. *Rembrandt f. 1661.* Luke 2:21. Violates the iconographical tradition, which places the Circumcision in the

temple, not in the manger. Tümpel (139), p. 201, defends Rembrandt, showing that he read the biblical text more accurately than his predecessors, and that the scene ought to take place outside of the temple. A superb example of the late style with its avoidance of emphatic structural lines and its vibrant picturesque evocation of the scene.

[351] HAMAN AND AHASUERUS AT THE FEAST OF ESTHER. *Rembrandt f. 1660.* Esther 7:1-6. Although darkened by varnish, the beauty of the original yellow-golds and reds can still be imagined.

[352] THE RISEN CHRIST AT EMMAUS. Luke 24:13-31. The attribution to Rembrandt has always been uncertain (see provenance in Hofstede de Groot (4), no. 146), and the painting is generally rejected by modern scholars (Benesch (17), no. A66; Martin (9), p. 33; Bauch (15), p. 49; Sumowski (326), p. 226; Rosenberg (29), p. 371). J. Q. van Regteren Altena had discussed it in his essay on Rembrandt's Emmaus pictures (165), p. 24, notes 43-4, as had Stechow in his (162), p. 329, relating it to drawings. The picture is in very poor condition, but what remains points to an original by Rembrandt, not—as Lilienfeld (*Arent de Gelder*, The Hague 1914, p. 166, no. 98) had suggested hesitantly—Aert de Gelder. The evidence of the X-ray published by M. Hours (301) is inconclusive, although she interprets it negatively.

[353] THE APOSTLE PETER DENYING CHRIST. *Rembrandt 1660.* Luke 22:55ff. The model has been sought in works by Gerard Seghers (Henkel, *Pantheon,* 12, 1933, p. 292; *Burlington magazine,* 64, 1934, p. 153; 65, 1935, p. 187), and Jacob Pynas (Judson (171), p. 141). Henkel also treats the Rembrandt drawings connected with the composition (Benesch 1050 and Valentiner 465), concerning which opinion is divided. Von Einem (200), pp. 202-5, relates it to the Homer theme in the weakness and "blindness" of the hero. An affectionate appreciation of this powerful picture was written by H. E. van Gelder, *Rembrandt:* SAUL EN DAVID, PETRUS VERLOOCHENT CHRISTUS, The Hague 1948.

[354] THE CONSPIRACY OF JULIUS CIVILIS: THE OATH. See p. 136f. Van de Waal (176), vol. 1, p. 233, has analyzed the reasons for the refusal of Rembrandt's work, going into the whole tradition of this sort of history painting in the Netherlands. The revolt against the Romans under Julius (Claudius) Civilis was plainly understood by Dutchmen of the 17th century as a typological predecessor of the revolt against the Spaniards under William of Orange. The reader can compare his own experiences of official representations of The Father of his (own) Country to get an idea of what the Amsterdam city government expected from Rembrandt. It was Rembrandt's refusal to submit to the standards of decorousness, his insistence on a dramatic—and archaeologically responsible—reconstruction of the original scene that led to the rejection of his work.

To picture the original design, one must turn to the preparatory drawing or drawings. According to Benesch, there are four surviving studies (all in Munich), though many other scholars, myself included, accept only one of them as genuine (Benesch 1279; Illustration a, p. 419). The sketch is drawn on back of the funeral announcement of Rebecca de Vos, to take place on October 25, 1661. The sketch cannot have been made long after (or before; cf. Benesch) that date. It shows just how important the architectural features of the great hall were to the composition. The (repainted) fragment, which suffered slightly from pressing, is still "the supreme example of Rembrandt's work [in the] Venetian mood... Light becomes the means of revealing [the] expressive possibilities [of the forms]" (Clark (128), p. 98).

A double number of the *Konsthistorisk tidskrift* was devoted to the painting at the time of the Rembrandt exhibition in Stockholm in 1956, with valuable contributions by many authors (Bibliography, nos. 176-82). Further contributions have been made by Sumowski (326), p. 233, Clara Bille, *Oud Holland,* 71, 1956, p. 54, C. Müller Hofstede, *Kunstchronik,* 10, 1957, p. 129, and A. J. Moes-Veth (225), p. 143. See also the controversy between Noach and van de Waal, *Oud Holland,* 56, 1939, pp. 49, 145 and the critical summary by Bruyn (184).

[355] THE RETURN OF THE PRODIGAL SON. *R v Rijn f.* (this unusual signature may not be genuine). Luke 15:20-1. Strips of 10 cm. have been added to the right and below. One of the great miracles of Rembrandt's art. Lately praised anew by Clark ("Motives," *Studies in western art,* 4, New York 1963, pp. 189-205).

[356] ISAAC AND REBECCA ("THE JEWISH BRIDE"). *Rembrandt f. 16(..)* Sumowski claims that the date can be read as 1666. There is a drawing in the Kramarsky Collection (Illustration a, p. 421) that probably formed the basis for the composition. The drawing represents the biblical love story of Isaac and Rebecca (Genesis 26:8). Opinion is divided over whether the painting is primarily a double portrait (Benesch (134), p. 352) or a history painting at a personal emotional level (Tümpel (139), p. 302). The X-ray shows that the figures were originally seated, which makes the connection with the drawing stronger. I am inclined to see the biblical incident as the main source of inspiration. Rosenberg (29), p. 128, and Rosenberg and Slive (30), p. 269, however, see in it a portrait commission of "an actual couple alluding to a biblical pair." Portraits in biblical guise are by no means rare in Dutch art.

None of the attempts to identify the couple are very convincing (J. Zwarts (240): Miguel de Barrios and Abigaël de Pina; Valentiner (254): Titus and

Magdalena van Loo, whom he also sees in [417] and [418]). Haverkamp Begemann also considers it a double portrait in disguise. The Italian (Venetian) influence is stressed by Clark (128), p. 142, while Begemann sees no need for "influence" in accounting for similar solutions to a formal problem like love, which is bound to elicit "somewhat similar expressions of similar human experiences."

[357] THE DISGRACE OF HAMAN. *Rembrandt f.* (?) Kahr (156) and Tümpel arrived independently of each other (and with different arguments) at the conclusion that the subject is Haman departing to lead Mordecai on his triumphal tour of the capital (Esther 6:10). J. Nieuwstraten (158) rejects this explanation, but it seems basically sound to me. The alternative suggestion, based on a hint of Valentiner (6), p. 128, and elaborated by J. Linnik (148), is Uriah sent by David to the front lines (2 Samuel 11:14-15). De Vries (28), p. 80, asks whether Rembrandt might have been responsible only for the chief figure, quoting Knuttel (27), p. 266, to the effect that Jhr. D. C. Roëll and Schmidt-Degener also had their doubts. I do not share any of these reservations about the painting. See also J. Linnik, *Iskusstvo,* 7, 1956, pp. 46-50 (in Russian; English summary by J. Białostocki in *Burlington magazine,* 99, 1957, p. 422).

[358] SIMEON WITH THE CHRIST CHILD IN THE TEMPLE. Luke 3:25-32. First published by Valentiner (6), p. 99. The painting is unfinished and in very bad condition, but what remains is impressive. The woman is by another hand. It is quite possible that this fragment is identical with the SIMEON in the collection of Dirck van Cattenburgh in Amsterdam, in 1671, which he had commissioned from Rembrandt but which was reported as being unfinished a few months before the death of the painter (Bredius (47), p. 239).

[359] THE EVANGELIST MATTHEW INSPIRED BY THE ANGEL. *Rembrandt f. 1661.* Valentiner's suggestion that Rembrandt painted a regular series of holy figures in 1661 does not answer to the facts (see p. 134). This does not take anything away from the appreciations of Valentiner and Benesch. This is one of the best preserved and carefully executed of the group. The underpainting shown by the X-rays is as thoroughly modeled as the surface.

[360] THE RISEN CHRIST. *Rembrandt f. 1661.* The iconographic "function" of this piece is not clear. Valentiner (159) combines it with the paintings of apostles and evangelists as part of a series, while Knuttel (27), p. 195, sees it as part of an Ecce Homo and Lengl (*Das Münster,* 20, 1967, p. 55) as part of an Emmaus. There seem to have been important changes made during the execution of the work: one X-ray (Munich 601) shows Christ with a book (?) in his hands. In the new catalogue of Dutch paintings in Munich (336), however, Brochhagen does not mention this X-ray. Whatever its original meaning and original shape, the painting is one of the most sincere and carefully executed works of the group.

[361] THE APOSTLE JAMES. *Rembrandt f. 1661.*

[362] THE APOSTLE SIMON. *Rembrandt f. 1661* (on the blade of the saw). Published by Münz (164) in 1948. Fits in well with the other half-figures of 1661.

[363] AN EVANGELIST WRITING. This "man with the red cap" does not fit very well with the other evangelists, but the discrepancy in style is probably due to the impression created by the abraded upper surface, with the blocks of color isolated and robbed of expressive interplay.

[364] AN EVANGELIST WRITING. *Rembrandt f. 166(.)* Cleaning has brought out the scarf and removed the beard; cf. reproduction in the first edition of Bredius (14), no. 618; see also C. C. Cunningham (163). The state of the picture has always been deplored (Rosenberg (317), p. 350, Winkler (327), p. 143)), but in many parts the original delicate modeling can still be grasped.

[365] AN APOSTLE PRAYING. *Rembran(t) f. 166(.)* (?) The remains of another signature on the upper edge of the book? The picture has recently been cleaned; see Sherman F. Lee (174). My reservations about the place of this painting in the late group of apostles and its attribution to Rembrandt in the first place have not altogether vanished with the varnish. There is a kind of looseness of surface execution that I have not observed in other works of Rembrandt.

[366] THE APOSTLE BARTHOLOMEW. *Rembrandt f. 1661.* In contrast to the softly modeled MATTHEW [359], the BARTHOLOMEW is brushed on furiously. Had the painting not been engraved in the 18th century, one could be led to believe that it was painted in the 19th.

[367] THE VIRGIN MARY ("PORTRAIT OF A NUN"). *Rembrandt f. 1661.* Bauch observes that the rosary is added later. The identity of the figure as Mary would have been clearer in the context of the set to which the painting no doubt belonged.

[368] CHRIST. The figure was cut out of the original canvas irregularly. This operation and a rubbing of the surface all over have damaged the painting, but it is still a splendid interpretation of an idealized Christ type, far from the realistic Christ heads of the forties. The angle of the head is similar to that of [256], but as Slive observes (172), p. 415, Rembrandt's "incredible power of invention led him to depict quite another aspect of Christ's character." The work was painted around 1661; Valentiner (318) would join it with his series of the four evangelists.

[369] CHRIST. *Rembrandt f. 1661.* Rotermund (166), p. 230, interprets it as a Jewish pilgrim. Valentiner (318) links it with the apostles; indeed, in its

formal presentation this vision of Christ is the one most likely to have crowned off a traditional series of holy figures.

[370] MAN WITH A FALCON (COUNT FLORIS OF HOLLAND?). First published by Valentiner (6), p. 97a. See also Benesch, *Jahrbuch für Kunstgeschichte*, 3, 1924/5, p. 115, Romdahl, *Göteborg Museums arsstrijck*, 1929, p. 93, Valentiner (133), p. 122, and Gantner (126), p. 177ff. Gantner follows Valentiner's interpretation of the picture as a historical portrait of the Dutch Count Floris V (1254–96). Rembrandt could have become acquainted with the figure of Floris in plays and stories by Vondel, Colevelt, and P. van Zesen. Gantner goes further, presuming a connection between this historical portrait and the Passion of Christ, expressing the view that "this picture also shares the timelessness of all sacred things." Gantner's idea is even more fantastic than Valentiner's, as well as having less relevance to the visual aspect of the painting. See the suggestion of Schwartz, p. 428. The picture is not identical with the "Rembrandt YOUNG MAN" sold at the L.Lesser sale, London (Christie), February 10, 1912, lot 81, *pace* Valentiner and Bredius.

[371] HOMER DICTATING TO A SCRIBE...andt f. 1663. The third of the paintings commissioned by Don Antonio Ruffo [see 286, 293]. In July 1661 Rembrandt was reimbursed for the purchase of canvas, but work on the painting had not yet begun. By November of the following year the painting had been sent to Italy, but at that time it was returned with complaints that it was "half finished" and Rembrandt was requested to finish it. He apparently did so, since the painting bears a genuine signature with the date 1663. It was damaged by fire in the 18th century, and is now only a fragment. The painting was described in the Ruffo inventory of 1737 as a "half-figure, giving instruction to two disciples, life size." The canvas had a rounded top. The original composition can be reconstructed by comparing the Rembrandt drawing in Stockholm (Illustration a, p. 430) and a picture by Aert de Gelder (Illustration, p. 140), who was Rembrandt's pupil when all of this was going on, and whose work may reflect that of his master. For the motif of Homer's blindness in Rembrandt's art, see Panofsky, *Studies in iconology*, New York 1939, p. 109; Held (338); and von Einem (200).

[372] THE SUICIDE OF LUCRETIA. *Rembrandt f. 1666.* Livy, *Histories*, I:57–8. The cord of the curtain to the right might be a theater prop, if Rembrandt's image of the heroine is borrowed, as has been suggested, from a stage performance (Stechow (175); however, see the convincing comparison with Caravaggio's DAVID (Rome, Borghese Gallery) by M.Hirst, *Burlington magazine*, 110, 1968, p. 221). See the following number.

[373] THE SUICIDE OF LUCRETIA. *Rembrandt f. 1664.* This earlier version of the theme shows the moment before Lucretia plunges the knife into her breast, while in [372] she is already dying from her wound. The glorious gold and greenish colors would shine forth to even greater effect after cleaning, while the damage—especially below—would not necessarily disturb the overall impression.

[374] JUNO. First published by Bredius (196) and van Rijckevorsel, *Oud Holland*, 53, 1936, pp. 270ff. See also Kieser (119), p. 141. Rembrandt painted this JUNO for the art collector Harmen Becker, who complained in the spring of 1664 that the picture was still unfinished. Finished or unfinished, it was in his collection in 1678, when the inventory of his goods was taken (Bredius (48), p. 195). In fact there were two JUNOS in his collection: a "Juno, life size" (no name of painter) and a "Juno by Rembrandt van Rijn." The painting was lost after that, but it came to light again at the Wesendonk sale, Cologne, November 27, 1935, lot 87 ("in the manner of Rembrandt"), after having been on loan (but not on exhibition) in the Museum in Bonn. Recent cleaning shows it to be of as great beauty as the Lucretia pictures of the same period [372–3]. Held (203) supposes that the picture was begun before 1660 and finished around 1665. The first idea seems to have been to show the figure with both hands resting on a red table.

[375] TITUS. The last portrait of Titus that can be identified with some certainty.

[376] SELF-PORTRAIT. *Rembrandt f. 1659* (?) Bauch (15), no. 330, believes that the portrait was first painted without the cap. The X-rays do not sustain this claim.

[377] TITUS IN A MONK'S HABIT. *Rembrandt f. 166(0).* There has been some discussion as to whether this is a portrait of Titus as a monk or a picture of Saint Francis. Valentiner (318), p. 400, argues for "a Franciscan monk," Bauch (272) for a representation of Saint Francis with Titus as the model. It is certainly not a portrait of Titus in the ordinary sense, but it was not unusual for Rembrandt to imbue a "historical portrait" with the living likeness of a sitter. This is common 17th-century practice, and need not be suspected as an anachronistic interpretation.

[378] CHRIST. Published for the first time by Hofstede de Groot in 1922 (8), p. 41. Not known to Bauch or me, and not listed by Slive (172).

[379] OLD MAN. Refused by Bredius. I have never seen the painting, but the photographs lead me to believe that the painting is by Rembrandt.

[380] SELF-PORTRAIT. The cleaning of the picture in the late forties emphasized the "rectangular, flat areas of paint" and its "solid framework" (280), but it also revealed damages caused by pressing during relining. The head is in good condition. The circles on the walls have troubled interpreters. They were formerly seen as cabbalistic signs reflecting God's perfection, or were

related to the *rota aristotelis* (J.G. van Gelder (79), pp. 408–9). Emmens (83), p. 174, brings Ripa's emblems of "theory" and "practice" to bear on the imagery, and interprets the painting as Rembrandt as "invention" between the compass of "theory" and the compass and ruler of "practice." To my mind the visual imagery in the portrait is not explicit enough to permit such particular interpretations; I agree with the author of the *Burlington magazine* editorial (280) that the circles serve to stress the geometry of the design.

[381] SELF-PORTRAIT. *Rembrandt f. 1660.* Probably a companion piece to [382]. An impressive X-ray is reproduced by Burroughs (294), p. 10.

[382] HENDRICKJE. *Rembrandt f. 1660.* Companion picture to [381](?) The face is the best preserved part of this damaged painting.

[383] THE DORDRECHT MERCHANT JACOB TRIP. *Rembr*(andt). Companion portrait to [384]. The identification of the sitters in this pair of portraits is due to Hofstede de Groot (238), p. 255. MacLaren's statement (332), p. 328, that the picture is "in very good condition except for the area beneath the seat of the chair" seems over-optimistic; the face is all right, but the dress and, to a lesser degree, the hands have suffered from pressing and relining (as have so many late Rembrandts). The X-ray reveals some pentimenti in the area of the left hand; the stick may have originally been held in an oblique position.

[384] MARGARETHA DE GEER, WIFE OF JACOB TRIP. Companion portrait to [383]. Margaretha de Geer (1583–1672) was a sister of the merchant Louis de Geer. She married Jacob Trip around 1600. In the portrait she wears, as old people often do, a costume no longer in fashion. There are pentimenti in the area of the hands which can be seen in the X-ray.

[385] MARGARETHA DE GEER. *Rembrandt f. 1661* (retouched). The head is in excellent condition. There is a carefully executed portrait drawing in the Museum Boymans-van Beuningen, Rotterdam (Benesch 757; Illustration b, p. 132) that almost certainly portrays the same lady. For stylistic reasons the drawing must date around 1635/40. Did Margaretha de Geer's expression change so little in 20 years? See also [383–4].

[386] A CAPUCHIN MONK READING. *Rembrandt f. 1661.* This may be the same kind of portrait-cum-historical-portrait as [298] and others; as such, it may even belong to the group of holy figures of 1661. The surface of the painting has suffered, but the original delicacy can still be appreciated. There are some pentimenti in the area of the left shoulder.

[387] HEAD OF AN OLD MAN. Enlarged on all four sides. A study for the MATTHEW in the Louvre [359]. While Rosenberg/Slive (30), p. 78, accept Bredius 302–5 as autograph studies for [359], I agree with van Regteren Altena (16), p. 70, that this is the only genuine version, at least to judge from a photograph.

[388] PORTRAIT OF AN OLD WOMAN. *Rembrandt f. 1661.* Not seen by me.

[389] SELF-PORTRAIT. *Rem*(brandt) *f. 1660.* The original signature is restored and cut, and the date added later, but it probably replaces an original date of 1660. The face is the best preserved part; the hands are thin and lack crispness. The X-rays have revealed a pentimento in the cap, which can also be seen with the naked eye; originally there was a bonnet, later to be replaced by the white turban (see repr. in M.Hours (301), p. 39). A replica of the head (probably 19th century) is reproduced by van Ryckevorsel opposite the title page of his *Rembrandt en de traditie* (118).

[390] TWO NEGROES. *Rembrandt f. 1661.* Bredius supposed that "the picture was probably begun earlier, and the date added some years afterwards, when Rembrandt worked on it again." A.B. de Vries puts the origin of the picture about seven years earlier than the inscribed date (*150 jaer Koninklijk Kabinet van Schilderijen*, The Hague 1967, p. 222), a hypothesis also accepted by Bauch (15) no. 539. These efforts seem dedicated to equating [390] with an item in Rembrandt's inventory of 1656: "no. 344. Two Moors in one picture." From a study of the painting itself, I cannot detect anything pointing to a date earlier than that inscribed on the painting. There are two inferior copies, one in the Museum of the Rumanian People's Republic in Bucharest and the other in an English private collection (exhib. Nottingham, September 1945, no. 34).

[391] AN OLD MAN IN AN ARMCHAIR. *Rembrandt f. 166(.)* (?) The actual painted surface is almost invisible, so thick is the yellow varnish. The signature is doubtful, but the painting is good. The catalogue of the Rembrandt exhibition in Amsterdam, 1956 (315), no. 76, dates the picture around 1657, but I would not be surprised if the picture belonged to the half-figure holy men of 1661. The identification of the sitter as Haham Saul Levy Monteyra by J.Zwarts (260) is probably not correct (see (315), no. 76). The picture was probably in the collection of the Medici's before the end of the 17th century. The date 1670, however (315), no. 76, cannot be confirmed. The painting was among the possessions of Prince Ferdinand di Cosimo III Medici, who died in 1713 (information kindly supplied by Dr. Karla Langedijk).

[392] PORTRAIT OF A YOUNG JEW. *Rembrandt f. 1661.* This model served for Rembrandt's late portrayals of Christ.

[393] A MAN SEATED BEFORE A STOVE. Published by Valentiner in 1921, p. 90. Recent re-examination of the picture enabled me to decide that it is a work of the Rembrandt school with much modern restoration.

[394] PORTRAIT OF A YOUNG MAN. *Rembrandt f. 1660.* The portrait has suffered, but the attribution to Rembrandt is correct.

[395] STUDY OF AN OLD MAN. Neither Bauch, who has some doubts about

the attribution (15), no. 245, nor I have seen this small study.

[396] HENDRICKJE IN A FUR COAT. *Rembrandt f. 166(.)* Neither Bauch (15), no. 521, nor I have seen this picture. There seems to be some doubt about the reading of the date. MacLaren (332), p. 313–4, prefers a reading of 1650.

[397] PORTRAIT OF A YOUNG MAN. *Rembrandt f. 1662* (the signature is spurious; besides, the date can also be read as 1661). The picture looks like the portrait of a painter (with the beret that Rembrandt himself liked to wear), but so far the sitter has not been identified. The costume is probably not wholly finished. There are pentimenti to the right.

[398] WOMAN WITH A LAP DOG. Valentiner (12), pl. 158, supposed that this portrait was a companion to [397], but neither the dimensions nor the style of the paintings match very well.

[399] SELF-PORTRAIT. Probably a picture of good quality, but covered by such heavy varnish that it is impossible to judge its true quality. The X-ray (by Dr. Meier-Siem) shows a very powerful underpainting.

[400] DIRK VAN OS. Inscribed near the coat of arms: *D VAN OS (DIJCK-GRA)EF VAN D(E BEEMSTER).* Not seen by either Bauch or me. To judge from the photograph, the attribution to Rembrandt is not at all convincing.

[401] MAN IN A TALL HAT. Bauch rightly stresses (15), no. 437, that the portrait has suffered considerably; I too insist on the poor condition of the hands and costume, but the face may—after cleaning—reveal the quality of an original.

[402] A BEARDED MAN. *Rembrandt f. 1661* (indistinct). As Rosenberg has observed (29), p. 360, and (265), p. 87, probably the same model as [286, 332, 334].

[403] SELF-PORTRAIT AS THE APOSTLE PAUL. *Rembrandt f. 1661.* It has been rightly argued that this painting belongs—as a "disguised" Saint Paul—to the group of apostles of 1661; see Valentiner (159), p. 219; Münz (164), p. 64, and Benesch (134), p. 353.

[404] THE SAMPLING OFFICIALS OF THE DRAPERS' GUILD. *Rembrandt f. 1662* (on the table cloth; the signature on the paneling to the right: *Rembrandt f. 1661,* is apocryphal, probably copied from an etching. See van Schendel, *Kunsthistorisk tidskrift,* 25, 1956, p. 39). The picture was formerly in the *Staalhof,* the cloth makers' office, where four different committees held their meetings. The sitters for this group portrait were probably the "Waerdijns van de Laekenen" (cloth sampling officials), who served for one-year terms beginning on Good Friday. If the sitters are the group of 1661–2, we can identify them all (van Eeghen (229), p. 65; (231), p. 80). The X-ray examination conducted by the Rijksmuseum after the war revealed many important changes during the execution. The position of the servant was changed a few times (van Schendel (228)).

Van de Waal, in a magisterial study (227), has analyzed the history of the interpretations of this picture. He stresses the importance of the placing of the sitters around a table seen in sharp foreshortening. However we reconstruct the meaning of the scene in the 17th century, it remains a fact that modern observers sense tension in the gesture of the figures, and are tempted to suppose that the sitters are involved with an audience on our side of the picture plane (see Rosenberg (29), p. 146; Rosenberg and Slive (30), p. 73; and compare Heckscher's interpretation of the TULP [100]). In that regard Hellinga's reply to van de Waal is sound. The picture is more, to us, than a realistic group portrait of "five gentlemen, all in black, who do nothing but sit to have their portraits painted" (C. S. Roos, Inspector of the "National Art Gallery" of Holland in a report to his superior in 1801 commenting on the refusal of the state to buy the painting. He continued: "you would not have liked it in the long run, and moreover it would have taken up an enormous stretch of wall space.") There must be an inner meaning reflected in the emotionally vivid expression and gestures of the sitters. P. J. J. van Thiel (in a lecture in Amsterdam in 1968) has identified the book—clearly a focus of attention in the composition—as a sample book of the cloth the officials are charged to control, a sort of touchstone of quality. The guildmaster pointing to the book is signaling the beacon of the syndics. The painting became the symbol of good administration for generations of governors to come. For the beacon in the painting—a symbol of good citizenship and good government—see Tolnay (232), van de Waal-(233), and E. de Jongh, *Zinne- en minnebeelden in de schilderkunst van de zeventiende eeuw,* 1967, p. 63.

[405] PORTRAIT OF A YOUNG MAN. *Rembrandt f. 1663* (1662?). One of the most beautiful of the late commissioned portraits. Only the hands have suffered.

[406] PORTRAIT OF A YOUNG MAN (TITUS?). The vindication of this beautiful portrait as a genuine Rembrandt is now accomplished. Valentiner's identification of the sitter as Titus is less generally accepted. There are remains of a date, which have been interpreted as 1663, though stylistically it could be even later. Martin (9), p. 34, calls the attribution to Rembrandt "incomprehensible."

[407] THE PAINTER GERARD DE LAIRESSE. *Rembrandt f. 1665.* The left hand and some other parts have suffered from pressing, but the face is well preserved. Schmidt-Degener's identification of the sitter as de Lairesse (1640–1711) is universally accepted.

[408] PORTRAIT OF A YOUTH. *Rembrandt f. 1666* (retouched). Tentatively

identified as Samuel van Hoogstraten by Bauch (15), no. 443. A late portrait of high quality.

[409] PORTRAIT OF AN OLD MAN. *Rembrandt f. 1667.* Identical with Hofstede de Groot (4), no. 829. Published by Valentiner in 1921 (6), no. 98. Bredius (7), p. 151, attacked the authenticity of the painting vigorously, calling it a Belgian fake of the 19th century. He must be mistaken, however. The portrait, which has been shown at the Royal Academy in London (1938, no. 128; 1952/3, no. 175), in Edinburgh (1950, no. 35), and in Manchester (1957, no. 105), is genuinely signed and dated. It can be traced in English collections in 1758 and 1761. Moreover, it matches in power of characterization and directness of expression the other commissioned portrait of 1667 [414]. As far as I can see, it has received only praise from scholars other than Bredius (J. G. van Gelder (313), p. 39; C. Hofstede de Groot (8), p. 13, and Rosenberg (29), p. 371).

[410] FREDERICK RIHEL ON HORSEBACK. *R(em)brandt 1663* (?) The faint signature and date were detected during the cleaning undertaken after the painting was acquired by the National Gallery in 1961 (333), p. 72. A dating of "around 1665" (as opposed to the former dating of 1649) had already been put forward by Hugh Honour (*Leeds art calendar,* 95, 1959, p. 395). There is some reason to suppose that the rider portrayed belonged to the honorary escort which greeted Prince William III on his entry into Amsterdam. Two candidates have been advanced, though objections have been raised against them both. R. van Luttervelt's man (269) is Jacob de Graeff (who was, however, 18 years old in 1660, the year of the entry); Miss van Eeghen (270) takes up Bredius' suggestion (48), p. 193, that this is the portrait described in the 1681 inventory of Frederick Rihel ("the portrait of the deceased on horseback by Rembrandt"). Valentiner and Bauch also adhere to the Rihel theory.

[411] A MAN HOLDING GLOVES. Said by Bauch to be signed *Rembrandt f. 165(.),* though this is denied by The National Gallery. Companion portrait to [412], which is lighter in tonality. The lower right area of the canvas has suffered badly, and the left hand is repainted. The X-ray confirms, however, that the structure of the painting in the light areas is vigorous.

[412] A WOMAN HOLDING AN OSTRICH-FEATHER FAN. *Rembrandt f. 166(.)* Companion to [411]. A rare exception: a female portrait of higher quality than her companion. In excellent condition.

[413] THE POET JEREMIAS DE DEKKER. *Rembrandt f. 1666.* Painted in the year of the poet's death. The identification is based on resemblance with the engraved portrait in one of the editions of de Dekker's works. In 1667 there appeared a poem of gratitude "to the excellent and world famous Rembrandt van Rijn." Around 1660 Rembrandt had done another (lost or unidentified) portrait of the poet.

[414] PORTRAIT OF A FAIR-HAIRED MAN. *Rembrandt f. 1667.* Ursula Hoff has rightly observed (335), p. 456, that "this is Rembrandt's last commissioned portrait" and one of his most impressive.

[415] SELF-PORTRAIT.... *f. 1669.* The portrait was cleaned in 1966 and the remains of the signature revealed (G. Martin, *Burlington magazine,* 109, 1967, p. 355). A strip of about 3 cm. has been cut from the left side. X-rays reveal that the turban, originally higher, was reduced by Rembrandt himself and that at first the artist showed himself holding brush and maulstick.

[416] A FAMILY GROUP. *Rembrandt f.* (?) C. Müller Hofstede (300) has written a very sensitive appreciation of this late group portrait. It has suffered somewhat from relining and pressing, and it was probably never finished in the usual sense of the word. Some minor changes made during execution are revealed by X-ray. Valentiner (254), p. 234, calls the sitters Magdalena van Loo and her brother-in-law François van Bylert with his children. According to Heckscher (207), p. 93, the composition is based on the Heemskerck FAMILY PORTRAIT in Cassel.

[417] A MAN WITH A MAGNIFYING GLASS. Companion portrait to [418]. There has been much speculation concerning the pair portrayed in these beautiful, late "unofficial" portraits: J. Goekoop-de Jong (237), suggested that Spinoza is represented; J. Zwarts (239) proposes Miguel de Barrios and Abigaël de Pina. Lugt (241) prefers J. Lutma the younger, while Valentiner favors Titus and Magdalena van Loo (5), pp. 482–3; —, in Glück (278), p. 346. There is some resemblance with the pair in ISAAC AND REBECCA [356].

[418] A WOMAN WITH A CARNATION. Companion portrait to [417]. To the left of the woman was originally the head of a child, painted out by the artist himself (Rosenberg (29), p. 348). Although the portrait has suffered from relining (in the area of the hands) it is still—with the pendant—one of the most impressive of the late paintings.

[419] SELF-PORTRAIT. For the convincing interpretation of Białostocki (284), see p. 142 f. The X-rays on which he bases much of his argument were earlier published by C. Müller Hofstede (283), p. 83.

[420] SELF-PORTRAIT. *Rembrandt f. 1669* (redrawn, but correct). An upper strip has been covered (by Rembrandt himself?) with black; it does not show in our reproduction. See also H. E. van Gelder (281a).

Having seen REMBRANDT'S MOTHER (Salzburg, Czernin Collection; Bredius 63) since the setting of the Catalogue, I now consider it an autograph work, deserving of mention here.

Bibliography

The Bibliography is a guide to new research on the paintings of Rembrandt, with some of the more important older publications that have not lost their value. Complete Rembrandt bibliographies are to be found in O. Benesch, *Rembrandt: Werk und Forschung*, Vienna 1935; H. van Hall, *Repertorium voor de geschiedenis der nederlandsche schilder- en graveerkunst*, The Hague 1936 and 1949; and the yearly volumes of the *Bibliography of the Netherlands Institute for Art History*, The Hague 1943–.

CATALOGUES OF REMBRANDT'S PAINTINGS

(1) J. Smith, *A catalogue raisonné of the works of the most eminent Dutch, Flemish and French painters*, 7, Rembrandt van Rhyn, London 1836.
(2) W. Bode and C. Hofstede de Groot, *Rembrandt*, Paris 1897–1905; English version, Paris 1897–1906.
(3) A. von Wurzbach, *Niederländisches Künstler-Lexikon*, Vienna 1906–10; supplement, Vienna 1911.
(4) C. Hofstede de Groot, *Catalogue raisonné of the works of the ... Dutch painters*, 6, Esslingen 1916; German ed., 1915.
(5) W. R. Valentiner, *Rembrandts Gemälde (Klassiker der Kunst)*, 3d ed., Stuttgart-Berlin [1909].
(6) W. R. Valentiner, *Wiedergefundene Gemälde (Klassiker der Kunst)*, Stuttgart-Berlin 1921; 2d ed., 1922. Reviews and reactions: (7) A. Bredius, *Zeitschrift für bildende Kunst*, 56, 1921, pp. 146–52; (8) C. Hofstede de Groot, *Die holländische Kritik der jetzigen Rembrandtforschung*, Stuttgart etc. 1922; (9) W. Martin, *Der Kunstwanderer*, 3, 1921/2, pp. 6–8, 30–4; (10) —, *Der Kunstwanderer*, 4, 1922, pp. 407–10.
(11) W. R. Valentiner, "Rediscovered Rembrandt paintings," *Burlington magazine*, 67, 1930, pp. 259–71.
(12) —, *Rembrandt paintings in America*, New York 1931. Review: (13) J. Rosenberg, *Zeitschrift für Kunstgeschichte*, 1, 1932, pp. 83–5.
(14) A. Bredius, *Rembrandt paintings*, London 1935; 2d ed., 1937; 3d ed., revised by H. Gerson, London 1968.
(15) K. Bauch, *Rembrandt Gemälde*, Berlin 1966. Review: (16) J. Q. van Regteren Altenà, *Oud Holland*, 82, 1967, pp. 69–71.

The standard catalogues of the drawings and etchings are:
(17) O. Benesch, *The drawings of Rembrandt*, London 1954–7; supplemented by (18) —, "Neuentdeckte Zeichnungen von Rembrandt," *Jahrbuch der berliner Museen*, 6, 1964, pp. 104–50.
(19) L. Münz, *Rembrandt's etchings*, London 1952.

MONOGRAPHS AND GENERAL WORKS

(20) J. Burckhardt, "Rembrandt," lecture of Nov. 6, 1877; reprinted in *Burckhardt Gesamtausgabe*, 14, Stuttgart etc. 1933, pp. 178–97.
(21) J. Veth, *Rembrandt's leven en kunst*, Amsterdam 1906; 2d ed., with notes by J. Q. van Regteren Altena, Amsterdam 1941.
(22) C. Neumann, *Rembrandt*, Berlin 1902; 3d, expanded ed., Munich 1922.
(23) W. Weisbach, *Rembrandt*, Berlin 1926.
(24) A. M. Hind, *Rembrandt*, Cambridge 1932; 2d ed., London 1938.
(25) R. Hamann, *Rembrandt*, Berlin [1948].
(26) F. Schmidt-Degener, *Verzamelde studiën en essays*, 2, Rembrandt, Amsterdam 1950.
(27) G. Knuttel Wzn., *Rembrandt*, Amsterdam 1956.
(28) A. B. de Vries, *Rembrandt*, Baarn [1956].
(29) J. Rosenberg, *Rembrandt: Life and work*, Cambridge, Mass. 1948; 2d, revised ed., London 1964. All references in the notes are to the 2d ed.
(30) J. Rosenberg, S. Slive, and E. H. ter Kuile, *Dutch art and architecture 1600–1800*, Harmandsworth 1966, pp. 48–100.

SOURCES

(31) A. van Buchell, *Res pictoriae*, ed. G. J. Hoogewerff and J. Q. van Regteren Altena, The Hague 1928.
(32) C. Huygens, *De jeugd van Constantijn Huygens*, trans. and ed. A. H. Kan, Rotterdam-Antwerp 1946. Full Latin text ed. by J. A. Worp, *Bijdragen en mededeelingen van het historisch genootschap*, 18, 1897, pp. 1–122. (33) H. E. van Gelder, "Constantijn Huygens en Rembrandt," *Oud Holland*, 74, 1959, pp. 174–9.
(34) Ph. Angel, *Lof der schilderkonst*, Leyden 1642. See (43) no. 91.
(35) J. J. Orlers, *Beschrijvinge der stad Leyden*, 2d ed., Leyden 1641.
(36) J. von Sandrart, *Teutsche Akademie ...*, Leipzig 1675–9. The critical edition is (37) —, *Academie ...*, ed. and annotated by A. R. Peltzer, Munich 1925.
(38) S. van Hoogstraten, *Inleyding tot de hooge schoole der schilderkonst*, Rotterdam 1678.
(39) F. Baldinucci, *Cominciamento e progresso dell'arte dell'intagliare in rame*, Florence 1686.
(40) R. de Piles, *Abregé de la vie des peintres*, Paris 1699; 2d ed., Paris 1715.
(41) A. Houbraken, *De groote schouburgh der nederlantsche konstschilders en schilderessen*, Amsterdam 1718–21. Never use it without (42) C. Hofstede de Groot, *Arnold Houbraken und seine "Groote schouburgh,"* The Hague 1893.

DOCUMENTS AND THEIR INTERPRETATION

(43) C. Hofstede de Groot, *Die Urkunden über Rembrandt*, The Hague 1906; (44) 1st supplement, by "M. C. Visser," The Hague 1906, is a hoax. Only nos. 8a, 76a, ad no. 88, nos. 112a, 251a, and 325a are genuine (see review (45) by W. Martin, *De nederlandsche spectator*, 1906, pp. 60–1).
(46) W. R. Valentiner, "Rembrandt auf der Lateinschule," *Jahrbuch der preussischen Kunstsammlungen*, 27, 1906, pp. 118–28.
(47) A. Bredius, "Uit Rembrandt's laatste levensjaar," *Oud Holland*, 27, 1909, pp. 238–40.
(48) —, "Rembrandtiana. I. Rembrandt's zoogenaamde portret van Turenne bij Lord Cowper te Panshanger; II. De nalatenschap van Harmen Becker...," *Oud Holland*, 28, 1910, pp. 193–204.
(49) —, "Rembrandtiana," *Oud Holland*, 33, 1915, pp. 126–8. Inventory of Jacob de Gheyn III.
(50) V. Ruffo, "Galleria Ruffo nel secolo XVII in Messina," *Bolletino d'arte*, 10, 1916, in 6 parts.

(51) G. J. Hoogewerff, "Rembrandt en een italiaansche maecenas," *Oud Holland*, 35, 1917, pp. 129–48.

(52) H. Schneider, "Rembrandt in Italien," *Kunstchronik und Kunstmarkt*, 54, 1918, pp. 69–73.

(53) G. J. Hoogewerff, *De twee reizen van Cosimo de Medici (Werken van het historisch genootschap, 3)*, Amsterdam 1919.

(54) J.-F. Backer, "Les tracas judiciaires de Rembrandt," *Gazette des beaux-arts*, 66/1, 1924, pp. 237–48; 66/2, 1924, pp. 219–40, 361–8; 67/1, 1925, pp. 50–60.

(55) U. Hoff, *Rembrandt und England*, diss. Hamburg 1935.

(56) W. F. H. Oldewelt, *Amsterdamsche archiefvondsten*, Amsterdam 1942.

(57) E. M. Bloch, "Rembrandt and the Lopez collection," *Gazette des beaux-arts*, 88/1, 1946, pp. 175–86.

(58) I. H. van Eeghen, "Rembrandts portret van Salomon Walens," *Maandblad Amstelodamum*, 43, 1956, p. 113.

(59) —, "Toen de Rembrandts nog de amsterdamsche woonkamers sierden," *Maandblad Amstelodamum*, 43, 1956, p. 113.

(60) H. E. van Gelder, "Rembrandts financiële moeilijkheden," *De groene Amsterdammer*, August 25, 1956, p. 10.

(61) J. Goudswaard and I. H. van Eeghen, "Hendrickje Stoffels: jeugd en sterven," *Maandblad Amstelodamum*, 43, 1956, pp. 114–6.

(62) H. F. Wijnman, "Rembrandt en Hendrick Uylenburgh te Amsterdam," *Maandblad Amstelodamum*, 43, 1956, pp. 94–103.

(63) H. Gerson, *Seven letters by Rembrandt*, The Hague 1961. Reviews: (64) I. H. van Eeghen, *Maandblad Amstelodamum*, 49, 1962, p. 71; (65) J. A. Emmens, *Oud Holland*, 78, 1963, pp. 79–82.

(66) C. White, "Did Rembrandt ever visit England?" *Apollo*, 76, 1962, pp. 177–84.

(67) —, *Rembrandt and his world*, London 1964; (68) Dutch translation with notes by H. F. Wijnman, The Hague 1964.

(69) D. Vis, *Rembrandt en Geertje Dircx*, Haarlem 1965.

REMBRANDT AND RELIGION

(70) F. Landsberger, *Rembrandt, the Jews, and the Bible*, Philadelphia 1946.

(71) H. M. Rotermund, "Rembrandt und die religiösen Laienbewegungen in den Niederlanden seiner Zeit," *Nederlandsch kunsthistorisch jaarboek*, 4, 1952/3, pp. 104–92.

(72) W. A. Visser 't Hooft, *Rembrandts Weg zum Evangelium*, Zurich 1955. Review: (73) G. Kamphuis, *Critisch bulletin*, 23, 1956, p. 269.

HISTORY OF REMBRANDT CRITICISM

(74) G. Brom, *Hollandse schilders en schrijvers in de vorige eeuw*, Rotterdam 1927.

(75) —, "Rembrandt in de literatuur," *Neophilologus*, 21, 1936, pp. 161–91.

(76) W. Martin, "Rembrandt en de critiek, 1630–1850," *Elsevier's geïllustreerd maandschrift*, 94, 1937, pp. 225–39.

(77) S. Slive, *Rembrandt and his critics, 1630–1730*, The Hague 1953.

(78) H. E. van Gelder, "Nederlands Rembrandtwaardering," *Maatstaf*, 4, 1956, pp. 186–201.

(79) J. G. van Gelder, "Rembrandt en de zeventiende eeuw," *de Gids*, 119/6, 1956, pp. 397–417.

(80) H. van de Waal, "Rembrandt 1956," *Museum: Tijdschrift voor filologie en geschiedenis*, 61, 1956, pp. 193–209.

(81) S. Heiland and H. Lüdecke, *Rembrandt und die Nachwelt*, Leipzig [1960].

(82) R. W. Scheller, "Rembrandt's reputatie van Houbraken tot Scheltema," *Nederlands kunsthistorisch jaarboek*, 12, 1961, pp. 81–118.

(83) J. A. Emmens, *Rembrandt en de regels van de kunst*, diss. Utrecht 1964.

(84) F. W. Robinson, "Rembrandt's influence in 18th-century Venice," *Nederlands kunsthistorisch jaarboek*, 18, 1967, pp. 167–96.

REMBRANDT'S BEGINNINGS; HIS RELATION TO LASTMAN AND LIEVENS

(85) J. Veth, "Rembrandt's vroegste werk," *Onze kunst*, 4, 1905, pp. 133–48.

(86) W. Bode, "The earliest dated painting by Rembrandt, of the year 1626," *Art in America*, 1, 1913, pp. 3–7.

(87) C. J. Holmes, "An undescribed panel by Rembrandt," *Burlington magazine*, 31, 1917, pp. 171–2.

(88) Anonymous, "Early works by Rembrandt," *Art in America*, 6, 1917/8, pp. 118–23.

(89) C. Hofstede de Groot, "Rembrandt's youthful works," *Burlington magazine*, 44, 1924, p. 126.

(90) K. Bauch, "Zur Kenntnis von Rembrandts Frühwerken," *Jahrbuch der preussischen Kunstsammlungen*, 45, 1924, pp. 277–80.

(91) C. Hofstede de Groot, "Rembrandt's PAINTER IN HIS STUDIO," *Burlington magazine*, 47, 1925, p. 265.

(92) C. H. Collins Baker, "Rembrandt's PAINTER IN HIS STUDIO," *Burlington magazine*, 48, 1926, p. 42.

(93) W. R. Valentiner, "Two early self-portraits by Rembrandt," *Art in America*, 14, 1926, pp. 116–9.

(94) C. Müller, "Studien zu Lastman und Rembrandt," *Jahrbuch der preussischen Kunstsammlungen*, 50, 1929, pp. 45–83.

(95) W. Stechow, "Römische Gerichtsdarstellungen von Rembrandt und Bol," *Oud Holland*, 46, 1929, pp. 134–9.

(96) H. Schneider, *Jan Lievens*, Haarlem 1932.

(97) V. Bloch, "Zum frühen Rembrandt," *Oud Holland*, 50, 1933, pp. 97–102.

(98) C. Brière-Misme, "Un portrait retrouvé de Constantin Huygens," *Oud Holland*, 53, 1936, pp. 193–201.

(99) W. Martin, "Uit Rembrandt's leidsche jaren," *Jaarboek nederlandse maatschappij voor letterkunde*, 1936/7, pp. 51–62.

(100) V. Bloch, "Musik im Hause Rembrandt," *Oud Holland*, 54, 1937, pp. 49–53.

(101) C. H. Collins Baker, "Rembrandt's THIRTY PIECES OF SILVER," *Burlington magazine*, 75, 1939, pp. 179–80, 235.

(102) F. Schmidt-Degener, "Rembrandt's CLEMENTIE VAN KEIZER TITUS," *Oud Holland*, 58, 1941, pp. 106–11.

(103) J. G. van Gelder, "Rembrandt's vroegste ontwikkeling," *Mededelingen der koninklijke nederlandse akademie van wetenschappen, afd. letterkunde*, n.s. 16, 1953, pp. 273–300.

(104) O. Benesch, "An unknown Rembrandt painting of the Leiden period," *Burlington magazine*, 96, 1954, pp. 134–5.

(105) G. Knuttel, "Rembrandt's earliest works," *Burlington magazine*, 97, 1955, pp. 44–9. (106) V. Bloch, letter to *Burlington magazine*, 97, 1955, pp. 259–60. (107) G. Knuttel, letter to *Burlington magazine*, 97, 1955, p. 260.

(108) K. Bauch, *Der frühe Rembrandt und seine Zeit*, Berlin [1960].

(109) —, "Ein Selbstbildnis des frühen Rembrandt," *Wallraf-Richartz Jahrbuch*, 24, 1962, pp. 321–32.

(110) H. Gerson, "LA LAPIDATION DE SAINT ETIENNE peinte par Rembrandt en 1625," *Bulletin des musées et monuments lyonnais*, 3, 1962/6, [1962], n.p.; reprinted in English, *Apollo*, 77, 1963, pp. 371–2.

(111) A. van Schendel, "Het portret van Constantijn Huygens door Jan Lievens," *Bulletin van het Rijksmuseum*, 11, 1963, pp. 5–10.

(112) S. Slive, "The young Rembrandt," *Allen Memorial Art Museum bulletin*, 20, 1963, pp. 120–49.

(113) —, "Rembrandt's SELF-PORTRAIT IN A STUDIO," *Burlington magazine*, 106, 1964, pp. 483–6.

(114) K. Bauch, "Zum Werk des Jan Lievens," *Pantheon*, 25, 1967, pp. 160–70, 259–69.

REMBRANDT AND ARTISTIC TRADITION

(115) J. Veth, "Rembrandt's wijze van adapteeren," *Onze kunst*, 4, 1905, pp. 79–90.

(116) F. Saxl, "Rembrandt und Italien," *Oud Holland*, 41, 1923/4, pp. 145–60.

(117) W. Martin, "Buytewech, Rembrandt en Frans Hals," *Oud Holland*, 42, 1925, pp. 48–51.

(118) J. L. A. A. M. van Ryckevorsel, *Rembrandt en de traditie*, Rotterdam 1932.

(119) E. Kieser, "Über Rembrandts Verhältnis zur Antike," *Zeitschrift für Kunstgeschichte*, 10, 1941/2, pp. 129–62.

(120) W. Stechow, "Rembrandt and Titian," *Art quarterly*, 5, 1942, pp. 135–46.

(121) H. Bramsen, "The classicism of Rembrandt's BATHSHEBA," *Burlington magazine*, 92, 1950, pp. 128–31.

(122) W. Sumowski, "Einige frühe Entlehnungen Rembrandts," *Oud Holland*, 71, 1956, pp. 109–13.

(123) J. Rosenberg, "Rembrandt and Mantegna," *Art quarterly*, 19, 1956, pp. 153–61.

(124) F. Saxl, "Rembrandt and classical antiquity," in *Lectures*, London 1957.

(125) M. Imdahl, "Raphaels Castiglionebildnis im Louvre," *Pantheon*, 20, 1962, pp. 38–45.

(126) J. Gantner, *Rembrandt und die Verwandlung klassischer Formen*, Bern etc. [1964]. Review: (127) W. Stechow, *Erasmus*, 18, 1966, p. 548.

(128) K. Clark, *Rembrandt and the Italian Renaissance*, London 1966. Reviews: (129) E. Haverkamp Begemann, *Yale review*, 56, 1966/7, pp. 301–9; (130) V. Bloch, *Burlington magazine*, 109, 1967, pp. 714–6.

GENERAL ICONOGRAPHIC STUDIES

(131) H. Kauffmann, "Rembrandt und die Humanisten vom Muiderkring," *Jahrbuch der preussischen Kunstsammlungen*, 41, 1920, pp. 46–81.

(132) K. von Baudissin, "Rembrandt und Cats," *Repertorium für Kunstwissenschaft*, 45, 1925, pp. 148–79.

(133) W. R. Valentiner, "Rembrandt's conception of historical portraiture," *Art quarterly*, 11, 1948, pp. 117–35.

(134) O. Benesch, "Worldly and religious portraits in Rembrandt's late art," *Art quarterly*, 19, 1956, pp. 335–54.

(135) J. Białostocki, "Ikonographische Forschungen zu Rembrandts Werk," *Münchner Jahrbuch der bildenden Kunst*, 3/8, 1957, pp. 195–210.

(136) O. Benesch, "Rembrandt and ancient history," *Art quarterly*, 22, 1959, pp. 309–32.

(137) J. Bruyn, *Rembrandts keuze van bijbelse onderwerpen*, Utrecht 1959.

(138) C. Tümpel, "Ikonographische Beiträge zu Rembrandt," *Kunstchronik*, 19, 1966, pp. 300–2.

(139) —, *Studien zur Ikonographie der Historien Rembrandts*, diss. Hamburg 1968. Citations are to the typewritten draft, 1966.

(140) K. Bauch, "'Ikonographischer Stil,'" in *Studien zur Kunstgeschichte*, Berlin, 1967.

OLD TESTAMENT

(141) R. Greeff, *Rembrandt's Darstellungen der Tobiasheilung*, Stuttgart 1907.

(142) H. Kauffmann, "Rembrandts Berliner SUSANNA," *Jahrbuch der preussischen Kunstsammlungen*, 45, 1924, pp. 72–80.

(143) A. Heppner, "MOSES ZEIGT DIE GESETZESTAFELN bei Rembrandt und Bol," *Oud Holland*, 52, 1935, pp. 241–51.

(144) F. Saxl, *Rembrandt's SACRIFICE OF MANOAH*, London 1939.

(145) W. Stechow, "Jacob blessing the sons of Joseph, from Early Christian times to Rembrandt," *Gazette des beaux-arts*, 85/1, 1943, pp. 193–208.

(146) H. von Einem, *Rembrandt: DER SEGEN JAKOBS*, Berlin [1948].

(147) G. Knuttel, "On the BATHSHEBA of Rembrandt in the Metropolitan Museum," *Actes du 17e congrès international d'histoire de l'art, Amsterdam 1952*, The Hague 1955, pp. 421–4.

(148) I. Linnik, "Sur le sujet du tableau de Rembrandt dit LA DISGRACE D'AMAN," *Bulletin du musée de l'Ermitage*, 11, 1957, pp. 8–12 (in Russian; a German summary appears after Białostocki (135), p. 210.

(149) V. Loevinson-Lessing, "Sur l'histoire du tableau de Rembrandt DAVID ET JONATHAN," *Bulletin du musée de l'Ermitage*, 11, 1957, pp. 5–8 (in Russian).

(150) J. G. van Gelder, "Een Rembrandt van 1633," *Oud Holland*, 75, 1960, pp. 73–8.

(151) I. Manke, "Zu Rembrandts JAKOBSEGEN in der Kasseler Galerie," *Zeitschrift für Kunstgeschichte*, 23, 1960, pp. 252–60.

(152) O. Benesch, "Über den Werdegang einer Komposition Rembrandts," *Bulletin du Musée Hongrois des Beaux-Arts*, 22, 1963, pp. 71–87.

(153) J. G. van Gelder, "Rembrandt: JEREMIA, TREURENDE OVER DE VERWOESTING VAN JERUZALEM," *Openbaar kunstbezit*, 7, 1963, no. 15.

(154) R. Hausherr, "Zur Menetekel-Inschrift auf Rembrandts Belsazarbild," *Oud Holland*, 78, 1963, pp. 142–9.

(155) J. Held, *Rembrandt and the book of Tobit*, Northhampton, Mass. 1964.

(156) M. Kahr, "A Rembrandt problem: Haman or Uriah," *Journal of the Warburg and Courtauld Institutes*, 28, 1965, pp. 258–73.

(157) —, "Rembrandt's ESTHER: A painting and an etching newly interpreted and dated," *Oud Holland*, 81, 1966, pp. 228–44.

(158) J. Nieuwstraten, "Haman, Rembrandt and Michelangelo," *Oud Holland*, 82, 1967, pp. 61–3.

NEW TESTAMENT

(159) W. R. Valentiner, "Die vier Evangelisten Rembrandts," *Kunstchronik und Kunstmarkt*, n.s. 32, 1920/21, pp. 219–22.

(160) W. Stechow, "Rembrandts Darstellungen der Kreuzabnahme," *Jahrbuch der preussischen Kunstsammlungen*, 50, 1929, pp. 217–32.

(161) W. R. Valentiner, "A bust of Christ by Rembrandt," *Detroit Institute of Arts bulletin*, 12, 1930, pp. 2–3.

(162) W. Stechow, "Rembrandts Darstellungen des Emmausmahles," *Zeitschrift für Kunstgeschichte*, 3, 1934, pp. 329–41.

(163) C. C. Cunningham, "THE EVANGELIST by Rembrandt van Rijn," *Bulletin of the Museum of Fine Arts* (Boston), 37, 1939, pp. 56–7.

(164) L. Münz, "A newly discovered late Rembrandt," *Burlington magazine*, 90, 1948, pp. 64–7.

(165) J. Q. van Regteren Altena, "Rembrandt's Way to Emmaus," *Kunstmuseets årsskrift*, 35/6, 1948/9, pp. 1–26.

(166) H.-M. Rotermund, "Wandlungen des Christus-Typus bei Rembrandt," *Wallraf-Richartz Jahrbuch*, 18, 1956, pp. 197–237.

(167) H. Schulte Nordholt, "Rembrandt: SIMEON IN DE TEMPEL," *Openbaar kunstbezit*, 4, 1960, no. 40.

(168) K. Bauch, "Rembrandts CHRISTUS AM KREUZ," *Pantheon*, 20, 1962, pp. 137–44.

(169) L. Münz, "Rembrandts Vorstellung vom Antlitz Christi," in *Festschrift Kurt Bauch*, [1962], pp. 205–26.

(170) E. Fechner, *Rembrandt: THE PRODIGAL SON*, Leningrad-Moscow 1964 (in Russian).

(171) J. R. Judson, "Pictorial sources for Rembrandt's DENIAL OF SAINT PETER," *Oud Holland*, 79, 1964, pp. 141–51.

(172) S. Slive, "An unpublished HEAD OF CHRIST by Rembrandt," *Art bulletin*, 47, 1965, pp. 407–17.

(173) I. Bergström, "Rembrandt's double-portrait of himself and Saskia at the Dresden Gallery," *Nederlands kunsthistorisch jaarboek*, 17, 1966, pp. 143–69.

(174) S. F. Lee, "Rembrandt: OLD MAN PRAYING," *Bulletin of the Cleveland Museum of Art*, 54, 1967, pp. 295–301.

HISTORICAL SUBJECTS

(175) W. Stechow, "'Lucretiae statua,'" *Beiträge für Georg Swarzenski*, Berlin 1951, pp. 114–24.

(176) H. van de Waal, *Drie eeuwen vaderlandsche geschied-uitbeelding, 1500–1800*, The Hague 1952.

The special Claudius Civilis issue of the *Konsthistorisk tidskrift*, 25, 1956, included the following articles:

(177) R. van Luttervelt, "Amsterdams Rådhus och dess byggnadshistoria," pp. 3–10.

(178) H. van de Waal, "The iconological background of Rembrandt's CIVILIS," pp. 11–25.

(179) C. Bille, "Rembrandt's CLAUDIUS CIVILIS at Amsterdam in 1734," pp. 25-30.

(180) C. Nordenfalk, "The new X-rays of Rembrandt's CLAUDIUS CIVILIS," pp. 30-8.

(181) C. Müller Hofstede, "Eine Nachlese zu den münchener Civilis-Zeichnungen," pp. 42-55.

(182) I. H. van Eeghen, "Rembrandt's CLAUDIUS CIVILIS and the funeral ticket," pp. 55-7.

(183) C. Nordenfalk, "Some facts about Rembrandt's CLAUDIUS CIVILIS," pp. 71–93.

A critical review of these articles is found in:

(184) J. Bruyn Hzn., "Het Claudius Civilis-nummer van het *Konsthistorisk tidskrift*," *Oud Holland*, 71, 1956, pp. 49–54.

(185) S. Kraft, *En Rembrandt-Tavlas politiska bakgrund*, Stockholm 1959.

(186) T. Rousseau, "ARISTOTLE CONTEMPLATING THE BUST OF HOMER," *Metropolitan Museum of Art bulletin*, 20, 1961/2, pp. 149–56.

(187) K. Kraft, "Der behelmte Alexander …," *Jahrbuch für Numismatik und Geldgeschichte*, 15, 1965, pp. 7–32.

ALLEGORY

(188) F. Schmidt-Degener, "Een voorstudie voor DE NACHTWACHT: DE EENDRACHT VAN HET LAND," *Onze kunst*, 21, 1912, pp. 1–20.

(189) —, "Een meeningsverschil betreffende DE EENDRACHT VAN HET LAND," *Oud Holland*, 31, 1913, pp. 76–80.

(190) J. D. M. Cornelissen, DE EENDRACHT VAN HET LAND, Nijmegen 1941.

(191) F. Schmidt Degener, "Rembrandt's EENDRACHT VAN HET LAND opnieuw beschouwd," *Maandblad voor beeldende kunst*, 18, 1941, pp. 161–72.

(192) J. A. van Hamel, DE EENDRACHT VAN HET LAND, Amsterdam 1945.

(193) J. Q. van Regteren Altena, "… Het genetische probleem van DE EENDRACHT VAN HET LAND," *Oud Holland*, 67, 1952, pp. 30–50, 59–67.

(194) C. Bille, "Rembrandt's EENDRACHT VAN HET LAND en Starters *Wt-treckinge van de borgery van Amsterdam*," *Oud Holland*, 71, 1956, pp. 25–35.

MYTHOLOGY

(195) E. Panofsky, "Der gefesselte Eros? Zur Genealogie von Rembrandts DANAE," *Oud Holland*, 50, 1933, pp. 193–217.

(196) A. Bredius, "Ein wiedergefundener Rembrandt," *Pantheon*, 18, 1936, p. 277. The JUNO [374].

(197) P. Frankl, "Die Persephone-Bilder von Lambert Sustris, Rubens, und Rembrandt," *Oud Holland*, 55, 1938, pp. 156–71.

(198) W. Stechow, "The myth of Philemon and Baucis in art," *Journal of the Warburg and Courtauld Institutes*, 4, 1940/1, pp. 103–13.

(199) C. Brière-Misme, "La DANAE de Rembrandt et son véritable sujet," *Gazette des beaux-arts*, 6/39, 1952, pp. 305–18 et seq.

(200) H. von Einem, "Rembrandt und Homer," *Wallraf-Richartz Jahrbuch*, 14, 1952, pp. 182–205.

(201) J. Held, "Flora, goddess and courtesan," *De artibus opuscula XL: Essays in honor of Erwin Panofsky*, New York 1961, pp. 201–18.

(202) J. I. Kusnetzow, "New data on Rembrandt's DANAE," *Bulletin du musée de l'Ermitage*, 27, 1966, pp. 26–31.

(203) J. Held, *The story of Rembrandt's JUNO*, ms., [1967].

GROUP PORTRAITS

A. The ANATOMIES

(204) H. Schrade, "Rembrandts ANATOMIE DES DR. TULP," *Das Werk des Künstlers*, 1, 1939/40, pp. 60–100.

(205) I. H. van Eeghen, "De anatomische lessen van Rembrandt," *Maandblad Amstelodamum*, 35, 1948, pp. 34–6.

(206) J. Q. van Regteren Altena, "… De zoogenaamde voorstudie voor DE ANATOMISCHE LES VAN DR. DEYMAN," *Oud Holland*, 65, 1950, pp. 171–8.

(207) W. S. Heckscher, *Rembrandt's ANATOMY OF DR. NICOLAAS TULP*, New York 1958. Reviews: (208) C. E. Kellett, *Burlington magazine*, 101, 1959, pp. 150–2; (209) J. R. Judson, *Art bulletin*, 42, 1960, pp. 305–10.

(210) A. Querido, "De anatomie van de ANATOMISCHE LES," *Oud Holland*, 82, 1967, pp. 128–36.

(211) G. Wolf-Heidegger and A. M. Cetto, *Die anatomische Sektion in bildlicher Darstellung*, Basel etc. 1967.

B. THE NIGHT WATCH

(212) F. Schmidt-Degener, "Het genetische probleem van DE NACHT-WACHT," *Onze kunst*, 26, 1914, pp. 1–17; 29, 1916, pp. 61–84; 30, 1916, pp. 29–56; 31, 1917, pp. 1–32.
(213) F. Schmidt-Degener, "De ringkraag van Ruytenburch," *Onze kunst*, 33, 1918, pp. 91–4.
(214) J. G. van Dillen, "De sergeants en schutters van Rembrandt's schuttersoptocht," *Jaarboek Amstelodamum*, 31, 1934, pp. 97–110.
(215) D. Wijnbeek, DE NACHTWACHT, Amsterdam 1944.
(216) T. Koot, *Rembrandt's* NACHTWACHT *in nieuwe luister*, Amsterdam 1947.
(217) W. Martin, *Van nachtwacht tot feeststoet*, Amsterdam etc. 1947.
(218) A. van Schendel and H. H. Mertens, "De restauraties van Rembrandt's NACHTWACHT," *Oud Holland*, 62, 1947, pp. 1–52.
(219) W. Martin, "Een sleutel voor Rembrandt's NACHTWACHT," *Miscellanea Leo van Puyvelde*, Brussels 1949, pp. 225–8.
(220) A. van Schendel, "Some comments on the cleaning of THE NIGHT WATCH," *Museum*, 3, 1950, pp. 220–2.
(221) W. Martin, "NACHTWACHT overdenkingen," *Oud Holland*, 66, 1951, pp. 1–9.
(222) J. Q. van Regteren Altena, "Quelques remarques sur Rembrandt et LA RONDE DE NUIT," *Actes du 17ème congrès international d'histoire de l'art, Amsterdam 1952*, The Hague 1955, pp. 405–20.
(223) W. Gs. Hellinga, *Rembrandt fecit 1642*, Amsterdam 1956.
(224) K. Bauch, *Die Nachtwache*, Stuttgart 1957.
(225) A. J. Moes-Veth, "Rembrandt's CLAUDIUS CIVILIS en DE NACHT-WACHT van ter zijde beschouwd," *Oud Holland*, 75, 1960, pp. 143–56.
(226) M. Kok, "Rembrandts NACHTWACHT: van feeststoet tot schuttersstuk," *Bulletin van het Rijksmuseum*, 15, 1967, pp. 116–21.

C. THE SAMPLING OFFICIALS OF THE DRAPERS' GUILD

(227) H. van de Waal, "DE STAALMEESTERS en hun legende," *Oud Holland*, 71, 1956, pp. 61–107.
(228) A. van Schendel, "De schimmen van DE STAALMEESTERS," *Oud Holland*, 71, 1956, pp. 1–23.
(229) I. H. van Eeghen, "DE STAALMEESTERS," *Jaarboek Amstelodamum*, 49, 1957, pp. 65–80.
(230) W. Gs. Hellinga, "De bewogenheid der STAALMEESTERS," *Nederlands kunsthistorisch jaarboek*, 8, 1957, pp. 151–84.
(231) I. H. van Eeghen, "DE STAALMEESTERS," *Oud Holland*, 73, 1958, pp. 80–4.
(232) C. de Tolnay, "A note on THE STAALMEESTERS," *Oud Holland*, 73, 1958, pp. 85–6.
(233) H. van de Waal, "The mood of THE STAALMEESTERS," *Oud Holland*, 73, 1958, pp. 86–9.
(234) J. G. van Gelder, "Rembrandt: DE STAALMEESTERS," *Openbaar kunstbezit*, 8, 1964, no. 11.

DOUBLE PORTRAITS AND PENDANTS

(235) W. Martin, "Rembrandt's portretten van Herman Doomer en Baartjen Martens," *Bulletin van den nederlandschen oudheidkundigen bond*, 2/2, 1909, pp. 126–9.
(236) C. Hofstede de Groot, "Rembrandts portretten van Philips Lucasse en Petronella Buys," *Oud Holland*, 31, 1913, pp. 236–40.
(237) J. Goekoop-de Jongh, "De man met het vergrootglas door Rembrandt," *Feestbundel Dr. Abraham Bredius*, [1915], pp. 53–60.
(238) C. Hofstede de Groot, "De portretten van het echtpaar Jacob Trip en Margaretha de Geer…," *Oud Holland*, 45, 1928, pp. 255–64.
(239) J. Zwarts, "Het echtpaar van HET JOODSCHE BRUIDJE van Rembrandt," *Onze kunst*, 46, 1929, pp. 11–42.
(240) —, *The significance of Rembrandt's* THE JEWISH BRIDE, Amersfoort 1929.
(241) F. Lugt, "THE MAN WITH THE MAGNIFYING GLASS," *Art in America*, 30, 1942, pp. 174–8.
(242) H. E. van Gelder, "Marginalia bij Rembrandt," *Oud Holland*, 60, 1943, pp. 33–7.
(243) L. Münz, "The original shape of Rembrandt's SHIPBUILDER AND HIS WIFE," *Burlington magazine*, 89, 1947, pp. 253–4.
(244) H. E. van Gelder, "Rembrandt's portretjes van M. Huygens en J. de Gheyn III," *Oud Holland*, 68, 1953, p. 107.
(245) A. Staring, "Vraagstukken der Oranje-Iconographie. III: Conterfeitte Rembrandt Frederik Hendrik en Amalia?" *Oud Holland*, 68, 1953, pp. 12–24.
(246) I. H. van Eeghen, "Marten Soolmans en Oopjen Coppit," *Maandblad Amstelodamum*, 43, 1956, pp. 85–90.
(247) I. H. van Eeghen, "De echtgenoot van Cornelia Pronck," *Maandblad Amstelodamum*, 43, 1956, pp. 111–2.
(248) —, "De portretten van Philips Lucas en Petronella Buys," *Maandblad Amstelodamum*, 43, 1956, p. 116.
(249) —, "Baertjen Martens en Herman Doomer," *Maandblad Amstelodamum*, 43, 1956, pp. 133–7.
(250) J. A. Emmens, "Ay Rembrandt maal Cornelis stem," *Nederlands kunsthistorisch jaarboek*, 7, 1956, pp. 133–65.
(251) R. van Luttervelt, "Bij het portret van Oopje Coppit," *Maandblad Amstelodamum*, 43, 1956, p. 93.
(252) H. F. Wijnman, "Rembrandts portretten van Joannes Elison en zijn vrouw Maria Bockenolle naar Amerika verkocht," *Maandblad Amstelodamum*, 44, 1957, pp. 65–72.
(253) I. H. van Eeghen, *Een amsterdamse burgemeestersdochter van Rembrandt in Buckingham Palace*, Amsterdam 1958.
(254) W. R. Valentiner, "Noch einmal DIE JUDENBRAUT," *Festschrift Kurt Bauch*, [1967], pp. 227–37.

SINGLE PORTRAITS

(255) B. Tideman Jzn., "Portretten van Johannes Wtenbogaert," *Oud Holland*, 21, 1903, pp. 125–8.
(256) A. M. Hind, "The portraits of Rembrandt's father," *Burlington magazine*, 8, 1905/6, pp. 426–31.
(257) K. H. de Raaf, "Rembrandt's portret van Jeremias de Decker," *Oud Holland*, 30, 1912, pp. 1–8.
(258) F. Schmidt-Degener, "Rembrandt's portret van Gerard de Lairesse," *Onze kunst*, 23, 1913, pp. 117–29.
(259) O. Benesch, "Rembrandt's Falkenjäger," *Wiener Jahrbuch für Kunstgeschichte*, 3, 1925, pp. 115–8.
(260) J. Zwarts, "Haham Saul Levy Monteyra en zijn portret door Rembrandt," *Oud Holland*, 43, 1926, pp. 1–17.
(261) T. Borenius, "The new Rembrandt," *Burlington magazine*, 57, 1930, pp. 53–9.
(262) H. F. Wijnman, "Een drietal portretten van Rembrandt," *Jaarboek Amstelodamum*, 31, 1934, pp. 81–96.
(263) N. S. Trivas, "New light on Rembrandt's so-called HENDRICKJE at Edinburgh," *Burlington magazine*, 70, 1937, p. 252.
(264) J. Held, "Rembrandt's 'Polish' rider," *Art bulletin*, 26, 1944, pp. 246–65.
(265) J. Rosenberg, "Rembrandt's PORTRAIT OF A RABBI WITH A RED CAP," *Bulletin of the California Palace of the Legion of Honor Museum*, 6, 1948, pp. 86–91.
(266) L. Münz, "Rembrandts Bild von Mutter und Vater," *Jahrbuch der kunsthistorischen Sammlungen in Wien*, 50, 1953, pp. 141–90.
(267) I. H. van Eeghen, "Maria Trip op een anoniem vrouwsportret van Rembrandt," *Maandblad Amstelodamum*, 43, 1956, pp. 166–9.
(268) P. van Eeghen, "Eensaem was mij Amsterdam," *Maandblad Amstelodamum*, 44, 1957, pp. 150–4.
(269) R. van Luttervelt, "De grote ruiter van Rembrandt," *Nederlands kunsthistorisch jaarboek*, 8, 1957, pp. 185–219.
(270) I. H. van Eeghen, "Frederick Rihel, een 17de eeuwse zakenman en paardenliefhebber," *Maandblad Amstelodamum*, 45, 1958, pp. 73–81.
(271) R. van Luttervelt, "Frederick Rihel of Jacob de Graeff," *Maandblad Amstelodamum*, 45, 1958, pp. 147–50.
(272) K. Bauch, "A portrait of Rembrandt's last period," *Burlington magazine*, 101, 1959, pp. 105–6.
(273) J. Gantner, "Rembrandts FALKENIER in Göteborg," *Festschrift Karl M. Swoboda*, Vienna etc. 1959, pp. 97–102.
(274) A. Ciechanowiecki, "Notes on the ownership of Rembrandt's POLISH RIDER," *Art bulletin*, 42, 1960, pp. 294–6.
(275) H. van de Waal, "Rembrandt: PORTRET VAN ZIJN ZOON TITUS," *Openbaar kunstbezit*, 9, 1965, no. 9.
(276) Z. Żygulski, "Rembrandt's LISOWCZYK: A study of costume and weapons," *Bulletin du musée national de Varsovie*, 6, 1965, pp. 43–67.
(277) J. Białostocki, "Rembrandt's EQUES POLONUS," *Journal of the Warburg and Courtauld Institutes*.

SELF-PORTRAITS

(278) G. Glück, "Rembrandts Selbstbildnis aus dem Jahre 1652," in *Aus drei Jahrhunderten europäischer Malerei*, Vienna 1933, pp. 294–312.
(279) W. Stechow, "Rembrandt-Democritus," *Art quarterly*, 7, 1944, pp. 233–8.
(280) "The Iveagh Bequest at Kenwood," *Burlington magazine*, 92, 1950, p. 183.
(281) W. Pinder, *Rembrandts Selbstbildnisse*, Königstein [1950].
(281a) H. E. van Gelder, "Rembrandt: ZELFPORTRET," *Openbaar kunstbezit*, 1, 1957, no. 28.
(282) *De schilder en zijn wereld*, Delft/Antwerp 1964/5. An exhibition catalogue of interest for some self-portrait problems.
(283) C. Müller Hofstede, "Das Stuttgarter Selbstbildnis von Rembrandt," *Pantheon*, 21, 1963, pp. 65–90.

(284) J. Bialostocki, "Rembrandt's TERMINUS," *Wallraf-Richartz Jahrbuch*, 28, 1966, pp. 49–60.

(285) F. Erpel, *Die Selbstbildnisse Rembrandts*, Vienna etc. 1967.

LANDSCAPES, ETC.

(286) M. Conway, "A Rembrandt landscape in the Hermitage," *Burlington magazine*, 46, 1925, p. 245; cf. letter of E. G. Hawke, p. 322.

(287) W. R. Valentiner, "Rembrandt's LANDSCAPE WITH A COUNTRY HOUSE," *Art quarterly*, 14, 1951, pp. 341–7.

(288) J. Q. van Regteren Altena, "...Het LANDSCHAP VAN DE GOUD-WEGER," *Oud Holland*, 69, 1954, pp. 1–17.

(289) E. Haverkamp Begemann, *Hercules Seghers*, Rotterdam 1954. Exhibition catalogue with discussions of Rembrandt's debt to Seghers.

(290) A. Zaluski, "Le paysage avec le bon samaritain de Rembrandt...," *Biuletyn historii sztuki*, 18, 1956, pp. 370–83 (in Polish, with summary in French).

(291) H. van de Waal, "Rembrandt: LANDSCHAP MET STENEN BRUG," *Openbaar kunstbezit*, 2, 1958, no. 26.

(292) W. Stechow, *Dutch landscape painting of the 17th century*, London 1966.

(293) J. A. Emmens, "Reputation and meaning of Rembrandt's SLAUGH-TERED OX," *Museumjournal*, 12, 1967, p. 112.

TECHNIQUE

(294) A. Burroughs, "New illustrations of Rembrandt's style," *Burlington magazine*, 59, 1931, pp. 3–10.

(295) A. P. Laurie, *The brushwork of Rembrandt and his school*, London 1932.

(296) K. Wehlte, "Gemäldeuntersuchung mit Röntgenstrahlen," *Verhand-lungen der deutschen Röntgengesellschaft*, 25, 1932, pp. 12–18.

(297) C. Wolters, *Die Bedeutung der Gemäldedurchleuchtung mit Röntgenstrahlen für die Kunstgeschichte*, Frankfurt 1938.

(298) J. Rosenberg, "Rembrandt's technical means and their stylistic signi-ficance," *Technical studies in the field of the fine arts*, 8, 1940, pp. 193–206.

(299) *Cleaned pictures*, London 1947. The National Gallery's controversial dis-play of the results of restoration.

(300) C. Müller Hofstede, *Rembrandts Familienbild und seine Restaurierung*, Brunswick 1952.

(301) M. Hours, "Rembrandt: Observations et présentations de radio-graphies...," *Bulletin du laboratoire du musée du Louvre*, 6, 1961, pp. 3–43.

REMBRANDT AND HIS PUPILS

(302) J. van Wessem, *Rembrandt als leermeester*, Leyden 1956. Exhibition cata-logue with literature. The following numbers are the major publications since the show in Leyden.

(303) J. Białostocki, "Rembrandt et ses élèves: trois problèmes," *Biuletyn historii sztuki*, 18, 1956, pp. 349–69.

(304) H. Gerson, "Probleme der Rembrandtschule," *Kunstchronik*, 10, 1957, pp. 121–4.

(305) J. W. von Moltke, *Govaert Flinck*, Amsterdam 1965.

REMBRANDT EXHIBITIONS

(306) 1930: Detroit. Reviewed by (307) W. Heil, *Pantheon*, 6, 1930, pp. 380–3.

(308) 1932: Amsterdam. Catalogue by F. Schmidt-Degener.

(309) 1947: Los Angeles.

(310) 1950: Edinburgh. Review: (311) J. G. van Gelder, *Burlington magazine*, 92, 1950, pp. 327–9.

(312) 1952/3: London. *Dutch art, 1600–1700*, with a generous sprinkling of Rembrandts. Reviews: (313) J. G. van Gelder, *Burlington magazine*, 95, 1953, pp. 34–9, 395; (314) E. Plietzsch, *Kunstchronik*, 6, 1953, pp. 121–32.

(315) 1956: Amsterdam-Rotterdam. Reviews: (316) J. Rosenberg, *Art quar-terly*, 19, 1956, pp. 381–90; (317) —, *Kunstchronik*, 9, 1956, pp. 345–54; (318) W. R. Valentiner, *Art quarterly*, 19, 1956, pp. 390–404; (319) C. White, *Burlington magazine*, 98, 1956, pp. 321–4. (320) Raleigh, North Carolina, *Rembrandt and his pupils*. Review: (321) P. L. Grigaut, *Art quarterly*, 19, 1956, pp. 404–10. (322) Stockholm. Review: (323) C. Müller Hofstede, *Kunst-chronik*, 9, 1956, pp. 89–96. (324) Warsaw. Review: (325) O. Benesch, *Kunstchronik*, 9, 1956, pp. 189–204. Reviews of the Rembrandt year in general: (326) W. Sumowski, "Nachtrage zum Rembrandtjahr 1956," *Wissenschaftliche Zeitschrift der Humboldt-Universität zu Berlin: Gesellschafts- und sprachwissenschaftliche Reihe*, 7, 1957/8, pp. 223–78; (327) F. Winkler, "Echt, falsch, verfälscht," *Kunstchronik*, 10, 1957, pp. 141–7. See also van de Waal (80).

MUSEUM CATALOGUES AND DISCUSSIONS OF THE REMBRANDTS IN PARTICULAR MUSEUMS

(328) Dresden: W. Scheidegg, *Rembrandt und seine Werken in der Dresdener Galerie*, Dresden 1958.

(329) Glasgow, Art Gallery and Museum: H. Miles, *Dutch and Flemish... paintings*, Glasgow 1961.

(330) Leningrad: *Catalogue des peintures, département de l'art occidental, musée de l'Ermitage*, Leningrad-Moscow 1958 (in Russian).

(331) Leningrad and Moscow: E. Fechtner, *Rembrandt*, Leningrad-Moscow 1964 (a fully illustrated treatment of the Russian Rembrandts; in Russian).

(332) London, National Gallery: N. MacLaren, *The Dutch school*, London 1960; (333) *Acquisitions, 1953–62*; (334) *The National Gallery, June 1962–December 1964*.

(335) Melbourne: U. Hoff, "Dutch and Flemish pictures in Melbourne," *Apollo*, 79, 1964, pp. 448–57.

(336) Munich: E. Brochhagen, *Holländische Malerei des 17. Jahrhunderts*, Munich 1967.

(337) New York, Metropolitan Museum of Art: J. L. Allen, "The museum's Rembrandts," *Metropolitan Museum of Art bulletin*, n.s. 5, 1945, pp. 73–7; (338) J. Held, *Paintings by Rembrandt*, New York 1956.

Concordances

In the first column of this concordance are the catalogue numbers of Rembrandt paintings in the present work. The second, third, and fourth columns give the corresponding catalogue numbers in C. Hofstede de Groot, *Catalogue raisonné of the... Dutch painters*, 6, Esslingen 1916; A. Bredius, *The paintings of Rembrandt*, ed. by H. Gerson, London 1968 (first edition, Utrecht 1935); and K. Bauch, *Rembrandt Gemälde*, Berlin 1966.

Ger	HdG	Bre	Bau
1	—	460	96
2	—	531A	41
3	34	488	3
4	64a	486	2
5	—	532	42
6	26	487	1
7	—	533	44
8	—	532A	43
9	32	489	4
10	81	535	46
11	—	423	5
12	—	539A	47
13	35	490	7
14	147	539	49
15	117	536	48
16	107a	538	51
17	80	543	52
18	—	632	97
19	282	420	110
20	—	419	112
21	—	427	119
22	179	601	111
23	177	602	120
24	49	604	127
25	122	607	134
26	186	430	135
27	316	69	252
28	—	132	109
29	—	633	343
30	533	1	288
31	674	78	347
32	542	2	290
33	531	5	298
34	320	68	—
35	685	64	249
36	676	77	116
37	688	70	251
38	529	8	292
39	544	6	295
40	552	7	294
41	552A	12	297
42	677	76	124
43	672	73	123
44	570	11	299
45	530	9	300
46	675	81	129
47	673	79	130
48	679	82	131
49	681	80	117
50	371	141	128
51	375A	144	137
52	577	143	138
53	670	145	348
54	775	146	349
55	195	462	254
56	—	543A	54
57	213	463	99
58	311	494	9
59	50	491	11
60	103	547	58
61	200	472	103
62	201	464	100
63	92	544	53
64	130	548	57
65	134	550	56
66	135	551	59
67	148	552	60
68	—	552A	61
69	223	468	101
70	346	179	164
71	97	555	63
72	128	546	62
73	207	471	102
74	9	498	13
75	69	502	16
76	33	501	15
77	52	497	21
78	31	499	14
79	334	30	535
80	149	557	64
81	70	503	17
82	142	559	66
83	116	558	65
84	57	505	18
85	30	507	20
86	14	504	19
87	140	560	68
88	141	561	67
89	136	565	69
90	209	466	253
91	233	431	156
92	206	102	258
93	236	432	162
94	—	469	259
95	270	433	171
96	205	103	261
97	187	610	175
98	968	456	558
99	573	17	302
100	932	403	530
101	557	156	142
	588		
102	171	608	140
103	349	169	141
104	654	161	352
105	745	162	353
106	354	142	136
107	372	148	143
108	783	155	355
109	373	152	146
110	659	166	358
111	635	164	351
112	612	99	456
113	762	154	350
114	697	84	451
115	699	89	452
116	696	86	453
117	694	87	454
118	698	85	455
119	733	159	354
120	624	167	360
121	625	331	459
122	761	160	357
123	867	335	462
124	633	170	359
125	668	165	356
126	669	336	471
127	877	333	461
128	884	330	460
129	566	18	303
130	930	405	531
131	492	186	151
132	606	94	473
133	525	23	304
134	608	97	474
135	405	181	147
136	369	183	153
137	726	173	361
138	657	171	363
139	933	408	532
140	736	172	366
141	881	341	469
142	567	19	305
143	691	95	468
144	538	20	306
145	490	190	150
146	873	340	475
147	629	175	368
148	630	339	466
149	769	177	365
150	874	344	480
151	—	176	364
152	348	178	155
153	785	163	367
154	883	332	470
155	—	337	472
156	856	343	476
157	534	22	307
158	526	21	308
159	732	197	369
160	848	346	482
161	494	191	159
162	645	200	372
163	646	347	477
164	637	199	373
165	638	342	478
166	777	196	371
167	859	345	479
168	739	194	374
169	882	354	492
170	353	206	163
171	584	25	309
172	387	207	166
173	415	205	167
174	615	96	488
175	607	101	489
176	666	406	533
177	667	407	534
178	660	202	376
179	661	349	486
180	730	201	375
181	846	350	485
182	351	180	170
183	634	203	377
184	613	104	490
185	868	348	491
186	271	211	174
187	744	214	381
188	582	26	172
189	545	24	311
190	511	71	262
191	283	31	312
192	535	216	384
193	619	355	497
194	845	356	498
195	—	439	542
196	939	440	543
197	951	445	544
198	941	443	546
199	109	442	545
200	942	441	547
201	946	444	548
202	5	508	22
203	74	562	70
204	27	509	23
205	93	563	71
206	227	476	105
207	38	511	24
208	104	566	72
209	64	514	26
210	85	569	76
211	94	570	73
212	90	572	77
213	40	513	25
214	1a	515	27
215	78	574	79
216	77	575	78
217	139	554	74
218	145	578	82
219	144	579	—
220	88	576	80
221	55	516	28
222	230	435	177
223	154	577	81
224	331	359	265
225	239	219	176
226	609	108	264
227	305	110	266
228	327	368	268
229	576	32	313
230	642	217	385
231	643	357	499
232	734	218	386
233	860	360	501
234	620	409	536
235	728	358	500
236	—	(33)	314
237	559	27	315
238	550	34	316
239	926	410	537
240	565	36	317
241	605	109	503
242	437	229	183
243	457	185	165
244	746	235	184
245	757	221	387
246	747	222	390
247	438	239	185
248	324	367	507
249	861	369	506
250	735	265	391
251	749	251	394
252	865	370	509
253	555	37	319
254	364	236	190
255	159	620	194
256	—	625	197
257	161	621	195
258	160	626	196
259	362	249	395
260	365	250	396
261	261	128	199
262	547	38	320
263	627	252	397
264	876	362	508
265	949	446	549
266	948	451	550
267	943	452	552
268	960	450	553
269	143	583	83
270	197	474	104
271	41	521	31
272	100	588	86
273	101	589	87
274	17	524	32
275	18	523	33
276	118	586	85
277	22	525	34
278	212	481	106
279	309	387	272
280	532	256	398
281	—	380	510
282	39	611	202
283	363	269	203
284	299	378	270
285	330	377	269
286	413	478	207
287	268	279	211
288	202	114	282
289	306	437	278
290	971	458	561
291	972	457	562
292	315	385	279
293	210	479	281
294	208	480	280
295	178	612	221
296	169	613	217
297	—	284	216
298	291	297	224
299	399	266	204
300	191	308	205
301	593b	41	399
302	442	131	406
303	507	383	275
304	384	130	400
305	292	267	206
306	453	263	402
307	628	268	404
308	580	42	322
309	712	276	405
310	536	43	324
311	721	111	512

Ger	HdG	Bre	Bau	Ger	HdG	Bre	Bau	Ger	HdG	Bre	Bau	Ger	HdG	Bre	Bau	Ger	HdG	Bre	Bau	Ger	HdG	Bre	Bau
312	506	381	274	331	854	389	516	350	82	596	93	369	164	629	241	388	498	396	526	407	658	321	441
313	439	270	210	332	—	259A	219	351	46	530	37	370	—	319	242	389	569	53	333	408	780	322	443
314	440	274	407	333	454	282	220	352	146	597	—	371	217	483	244	390	336	310	539	409	829	323A	444
315	879	371	277	334	392	283	218	353	121	594	92	372	220	485	286	391	380	285	431	410	772	255	440
316	750	278	409	335	238	122	418	354	225	482	108	373	218	484	285	392	407	300	435	411	779	327	446
317	269	275	408	336	652	391	519	355	113	598	94	374	—	485A	285	393	—	298	432	412	880	402	528
318	717	112	513	337	503	400	520	356	929	416	38	375	709	126	427	394	782	299	433	413	776	320	442
319	489	119	410	338	753	277	425	357	48	531	39	376	554	51	330	395	366	261	245	414	743	323	445
320	528	44	325	339	716	116	518	358	—	600	95	377	193	306	227	396	715	113	521	415	551	55	339
321	163	624	212	340	756	294	422	359	173	614	231	378	—	627	228	397	744A	311	438	416	931	417	541
322	—	624A	213	341	774	295	423	360	157	630	240	379	367	295A	225	398	852	398	527	417	755	326	447
323	158	622	215	342	—	290	421	361	170	617	236	380	556	52	331	399	540	60	340	418	869	401	529
324	581	49	326	343	563	50	329	362	—	616A	237	381	562	54	332	400	664	315	428	419	560	61	341
325	702	120	411	344	944	454	554	363	185	618	248	382	720	118	522	401	781	313	437	420	527	62	342
326	927	414	538	345	950	453	555	364	183	619	238	383	393	314	429	402	441	309	239				
327	725	281	415	346	13	528	36	365	194	616	234	384	857	394	523	403	575	59	338				
328	703	293	417	347	25	527	226	366	168	615	235	385	863	395	524	404	928	415	540				
329	553	48	327	348	65	520	30	367	189	397	283	386	190	307	232	405	784	312	439				
330	704	123	419	349	102	592A	91	368	162	628	229	387	175	304	233	406	705	289	434				

To find the corresponding number in the present work of the paintings listed in the catalogues of Hofstede de Groot, Bredius, or Bauch, look up the older catalogue number in the first column. You will find the Gerson number under the appropriate column to the right. (For example: HdG 5 = Ger 202; Bre 5 = Ger 33; Bau 5 = Ger 11.)

	HdG	Bre	Bau		HdG	Bre	Bau		HdG	Bre	Bau		HdG	Bre	Bau		HdG	Bre	Bau		HdG	Bre	Bau
1	—	30	6	64a	4	—	—	130	64	304	47	196	—	166	258	263	—	306	—	330	285	128	376
1a	214	—	—	65	348	—	83	131	—	302	48	197	270	159	256	264	—	—	226	331	224	121	380
2	—	32	4	66	—	—	82	132	—	28	—	199	—	164	261	265	—	250	224	332	—	154	381
3	—	—	3	67	—	—	88	134	65	—	25	200	61	162	—	266	—	299	227	333	—	127	389
4	—	—	9	68	—	34	87	135	66	—	26	201	62	180	—	267	—	305	—	334	79	—	—
5	202	33	11	69	75	27	89	136	89	—	106	202	288	178	282	268	287	307	228	335	—	123	—
6	—	39	—	70	81	37	203	137	—	—	51	203	—	183	283	269	317	283	285	336	390	126	—
7	—	40	13	71	—	190	205	138	—	—	52	204	—	—	299	270	95	313	284	337	—	155	—
8	—	38	—	72	—	—	208	139	217	—	—	205	96	173	300	271	186	—	—	338	—	—	403
9	74	45	58	73	—	43	211	140	87	—	102	206	92	170	305	272	—	—	279	339	—	148	415
11	—	44	59	74	203	—	217	141	88	50	103	207	73	172	286	274	—	314	312	340	—	146	399
12	—	41	—	76	—	42	210	142	82	106	101	208	294	—	—	275	—	317	303	341	—	141	419
13	346	—	74	77	216	36	212	143	269	52	107	209	90	—	—	276	—	309	—	342	—	165	420
14	86	—	78	78	215	31	216	144	219	51	—	210	293	—	313	277	—	338	315	343	—	156	29
15	—	—	76	79	—	47	215	145	218	53	—	211	—	186	287	278	—	316	289	344	—	150	—
16	—	—	75	80	17	49	220	146	352	54	109	212	278	—	321	279	—	287	292	345	—	167	—
17	274	99	81	81	10	46	223	147	14	—	135	213	57	—	322	280	—	—	293	346	70	160	—
18	275	129	84	82	350	48	218	148	67	107	—	214	—	187	—	281	—	327	296	347	—	163	31
19	—	142	86	83	—	—	269	149	80	—	—	215	—	—	323	282	19	333	238	348	152	185	53
20	—	144	85	84	—	114	—	150	—	—	145	216	—	192	297	283	191	334	478	349	103	179	54
21	—	158	77	85	210	118	276	151	—	—	131	217	371	230	296	284	—	297	373	350	—	181	113
22	277	157	202	86	—	116	272	152	—	109	—	218	373	232	334	285	—	391	—	351	182	—	111
23	—	133	204	87	—	117	273	153	—	—	136	219	—	225	332	286	—	—	372	352	—	—	104
24	—	189	207	88	220	—	—	154	223	113	—	220	372	—	333	288	—	—	30	353	170	—	105
25	347	171	213	89	—	115	—	155	—	108	152	221	—	245	295	289	—	406	—	354	106	169	119
26	6	188	209	90	212	—	—	156	—	101	91	222	—	246	—	290	—	342	32	355	—	193	108
27	204	237	214	91	—	—	349	157	360	—	—	223	69	—	—	291	298	—	—	356	—	194	125
28	—	—	221	92	63	—	353	158	323	—	—	224	—	—	298	292	305	—	38	357	—	231	122
30	85	79	348	93	205	—	350	159	255	119	161	225	354	—	379	293	—	328	—	358	—	235	110
31	78	191	271	94	211	132	355	160	258	122	—	226	—	—	347	294	—	340	40	359	—	224	124
32	9	229	274	95	—	143	358	161	257	104	—	227	206	—	377	295	—	341	39	360	—	233	120
33	76	(236)	275	96	—	174	1	162	368	105	93	228	—	—	378	297	—	298	41	361	—	—	137
34	3	238	277	97	71	134	18	163	321	153	170	229	—	242	368	298	—	393	33	362	259	264	—
35	13	—	—	99	—	112	57	164	369	111	70	230	222	—	—	299	284	394	44	363	283	—	138
36	—	240	346	100	272	—	62	165	—	125	243	231	—	—	359	300	—	392	45	364	254	—	151
37	—	253	351	101	273	175	69	166	—	110	172	232	—	—	386	302	—	—	99	365	260	—	149
38	207	262	356	102	349	92	73	167	—	120	173	233	91	—	366	303	—	—	129	366	395	—	140
39	282	—	357	103	60	96	61	168	366	—	—	234	—	—	367	304	227	387	133	367	379	248	153
40	213	—	—	104	208	184	270	169	296	103	—	235	—	424	358	305	289	377	144	368	—	228	147
41	271	301	2	105	—	—	206	170	361	124	182	236	93	254	361	306	—	386	157	369	136	249	159
42	—	308	5	106	—	—	278	171	102	138	95	237	—	—	362	307	—	300	158	370	—	252	—
43	—	310	8	107a	16	—	—	172	—	140	188	238	335	—	364	308	—	390	—	371	50	315	166
44	—	320	7	108	—	226	354	173	359	137	—	239	225	247	402	309	279	402	171	372	107	—	162
46	351	—	10	109	199	241	28	174	—	—	186	240	—	—	360	310	—	390	—	373	109	—	164
47	—	—	12	110	—	227	19	175	387	147	97	241	—	—	369	311	58	397	189	374	—	—	168
48	357	329	15	111	—	311	22	176	—	151	225	242	—	—	370	312	—	405	191	375	—	—	180
49	24	324	14	112	—	318	20	177	23	149	222	244	—	—	371	313	—	401	229	375A	51	—	—
50	59	343	—	113	355	396	—	178	295	152	—	245	—	—	395	314	—	383	236	376	—	—	178
51	—	376	16	114	—	288	—	179	22	70	—	248	—	—	363	315	292	400	237	377	—	285	183
52	77	380	17	116	83	339	36	180	—	182	—	249	—	259	35	316	27	—	238	378	—	284	—
53	—	389	63	117	15	—	49	181	—	135	—	250	—	260	—	317	—	—	240	380	391	281	—
54	—	381	56	118	276	382	—	183	364	136	242	251	—	251	37	319	—	370	253	381	—	312	187
55	221	415	—	119	—	319	21	184	—	—	244	252	—	263	27	320	34	413	262	383	—	303	—
56	—	—	65	120	—	325	23	185	363	243	247	253	—	—	90	321	—	407	—	384	304	—	192
57	84	—	64	121	353	—	—	186	26	131	—	254	—	—	55	322	—	408	308	385	—	292	230
58	—	—	60	122	25	335	—	187	97	—	—	255	—	410	—	323	—	414	—	386	—	—	232
59	—	403	66	123	—	330	43	190	386	145	254	256	—	280	—	323A	—	409	—	387	172	279	245
60	—	399	67	124	—	—	42	191	300	161	—	258	—	—	92	324	248	—	310	389	—	331	—
61	—	419	68	126	—	375	—	193	377	—	—	259	—	—	94	325	—	—	320	390	—	—	246
62	—	420	72	127	—	—	24	194	365	168	255	259A	—	332	—	326	—	417	324	391	—	336	250
63	—	—	71	128	72	261	50	195	55	—	257	261	261	395	96	327	228	411	329	392	334	—	—
64	209	35	80	129	—	—	46					262	—	—	190	329	—	—	343	393	383	—	—

HdG	Bre	Bau
394	—	384	251

Group 1:

	HdG	Bre	Bau
394	—	384	251
395	—	385	259
396	—	388	260
397	—	376	263
398	—	398	280
399	299	—	301
400	—	337	304
401	—	418	—
402	—	412	306
403	—	100	—
404	—	—	307
405	135	130	309
406	—	176	302
407	392	177	314
408	139	—	317
409	—	234	316
410	—	239	319
411	325	—	—
413	286	—	—
414	—	326	—
415	173	404	327
416	—	356	—
417	—	416	328
418	—	—	335
419	—	20	330
420	—	19	—
421	—	—	342
422	—	—	340
423	—	11	341
425	—	—	338
427	—	21	375
428	—	—	400
429	—	—	383
430	—	26	—
431	—	91	391
432	—	93	393
433	—	95	394
434	—	—	406
435	—	222	392
437	242	289	401
438	247	—	397
439	313	195	405
440	314	196	410
441	402	200	407
442	302	199	413
443	—	198	408
444	—	201	409
445	—	197	414
446	—	265	411
447	—	—	417
450	—	268	—
451	—	266	114
452	—	267	115
453	306	345	116
454	333	344	117
455	—	—	118
456	—	98	112
457	243	291	—
458	—	290	—
459	—	—	121

Group 2:

	HdG	Bre	Bau
460	—	1	128
461	—	—	127
462	—	55	123
463	—	57	—
464	—	62	—
466	—	90	148
468	—	69	143
469	—	94	141
470	—	—	154
471	—	73	126
472	—	61	155
473	—	—	132
474	—	270	134
475	—	—	146
476	—	206	156
477	—	—	163
478	—	286	165
479	—	293	167
480	—	294	150
481	—	278	—
482	—	354	160
483	—	371	—
484	—	—	373
485	—	372	181
485A	—	374	—
486	—	4	179
487	—	6	—
488	—	3	174
489	319	9	175
490	145	13	184
491	—	59	185
492	131	—	169
494	161	58	—
497	—	77	193
498	388	74	194
499	—	78	231
500	—	—	235
501	—	76	233
502	—	75	—
503	337	81	241
504	—	86	—
505	—	84	—
506	312	—	249
507	303	85	248
508	—	202	264
509	—	204	252
510	—	—	281
511	190	207	—
512	—	—	311
513	—	213	318
514	—	209	—
515	—	214	—
516	—	221	331
518	—	—	339
519	—	—	336
520	—	348	337
521	—	271	396
522	—	—	382
523	—	275	384
524	—	274	385

Group 3:

	HdG	Bre	Bau
525	133	277	—
526	158	—	388
527	420	347	398
528	320	346	412
529	38	—	418
530	45	351	100
531	33	357	130
531A	—	2	—
532	280	5	139
532A	—	8	—
533	30	7	176
534	157	—	177
535	192	10	79
536	310	15	234
537	—	—	239
538	144	16	326
539	—	14	390
539A	—	12	—
540	399	—	404
541	—	—	416
542	32	—	195
543	—	17	196
543A	—	56	—
544	39	63	197
545	189	—	199
546	—	72	198
547	262	60	200
548	—	64	201
549	—	—	265
550	238	65	266
551	415	66	—
552	40	67	267
552A	41	68	—
553	329	—	268
554	376	217	344
555	253	71	345
556	380	—	—
557	101	80	—
558	—	83	98
559	237	82	—
560	419	87	—
561	—	88	290
562	381	203	291
563	343	205	—
565	240	89	—
566	129	208	—
567	142	—	—
569	389	210	—
570	44	211	—
572	—	212	—
573	99	—	—
574	—	215	—
575	403	216	—
576	229	220	—
577	52	223	—
578	—	218	—
579	—	219	—
580	308	—	—
581	324	—	—
582	188	—	—

Group 4:

	HdG	Bre
583	—	269
584	171	—
586	—	276
588	101	272
589	—	273
592A	—	349
593b	30	—
594	—	353
596	350	—
597	—	352
598	—	355
600	—	358
601	—	22
602	—	23
604	—	24
605	241	—
606	132	—
607	175	25
608	134	102
609	226	—
610	—	97
611	—	282
612	112	295
613	184	296
614	—	359
615	174	366
616	—	365
616A	—	362
617	—	361
618	—	363
619	193	364
620	234	255
621	—	257
622	—	323
624	120	321
624A	—	322
625	121	256
626	—	258
627	263	378
628	307	368
629	147	369
630	148	360
632	—	18
633	124	29
634	183	—
635	111	—
637	164	—
638	165	—
642	230	
643	231	
645	162	
646	163	
652	336	
654	104	
657	138	
658	407	
659	110	
660	178	
661	179	

Group 5:

	HdG
664	400
666	176
667	177
668	125
669	126
670	53
672	43
673	47
674	31
675	46
676	36
677	42
679	48
681	49
685	35
688	37
691	143
694	117
696	116
697	114
698	118
699	115
702	325
703	328
704	330
705	406
709	375
712	309
715	396
716	339
717	318
720	382
721	311
725	327
726	137
728	235
730	180
732	159
733	119
734	232
735	250
736	140
739	168
743	414
744	187
744A	397
745	105
746	244
747	246
749	251
750	316
753	338
755	417
756	340
757	245
761	122
762	113
769	149
772	410

Group 6:

	HdG
774	341
775	54
776	413
777	166
779	411
780	408
781	401
782	394
783	108
784	405
785	153
829	409
845	194
846	181
848	160
852	398
854	331
856	156
857	384
859	167
860	233
861	249
863	385
865	252
867	123
868	185
869	418
873	146
874	150
876	264
877	127
879	315
880	412
881	141
882	169
883	154
884	128
926	239
927	326
928	404
929	356
930	130
931	416
932	100
933	139
939	196
941	198
942	200
943	267
944	344
946	201
948	266
949	265
950	345
951	197
960	268
968	98
971	290
972	291

Locations of Rembrandt Paintings

214 ABRAHAM SERVING THE THREE ANGELS

—, Collection of Mr. and Mrs. Charles S. Payson
328 A YOUNG MAN WITH A BERET

—, Collection of Mrs. R. W. Straus
388 PORTRAIT OF AN OLD WOMAN

—, Collection of Mr. and Mrs. John Hay Whitney
395 STUDY OF AN OLD MAN

—, Private Collection
155 PORTRAIT OF A YOUNG WOMAN

Omaha, Nebraska, Joslyn Art Museum
400 DIRK VAN OS

Philadelphia, Pennsylvania, The John G. Johnson Collection
321 CHRIST

Rochester, New York, University of Rochester
394 PORTRAIT OF A YOUNG MAN (The George Eastman Collection)

St. Louis, Missouri, City Art Museum
397 PORTRAIT OF A YOUNG MAN

San Diego, California, Fine Arts Gallery
51 YOUNG OFFICER (Gift of the Misses Anne R. and Amy Putnam)

—, Timken Art Gallery
296 THE APOSTLE BARTHOLOMEW

San Francisco, California Palace of the Legion of Honor
332 AN OLD MAN WITH A GOLD CHAIN (Mildred Anna Williams Fund
  Purchase)

—, M. H. de Young Memorial Museum
124 JORIS DE CAULLERY (Roscoe and Margaret Oakes Foundation)

Santa Barbara, California, Collection of Mr. C. M. Converse

146 WOMAN WITH A LACE COLLAR

Sarasota, Florida, John and Mable Ringling Museum of Art
281 A WOMAN IN FANCIFUL COSTUME

Toledo, Ohio, Museum of Art
52 YOUNG MAN IN A PLUMED HAT (Gift of Edward Drummond Libbey)

Washington, D.C., National Gallery of Art
174 SASKIA (Widener Collection)
182 MAN IN ORIENTAL COSTUME (Andrew Mellon Collection)
186 MAN IN POLISH COSTUME (Andrew Mellon Collection)
264 AN OLD WOMAN WITH A BOOK (Andrew Mellon Collection)
275 JOSEPH ACCUSED BY POTIPHAR'S WIFE (Andrew Mellon Collection)
278 JUPITER AND MERCURY VISITING PHILEMON AND BAUCIS
  (Widener Collection)
284 YOUNG GIRL HOLDING A BROOM (Andrew Mellon Collection)
295 THE APOSTLE PAUL AT HIS DESK (Widener Collection)
350 THE CIRCUMCISION OF CHRIST (Widener Collection)
373 THE SUICIDE OF LUCRETIA (Andrew Mellon Collection)
376 SELF-PORTRAIT (Andrew Mellon Collection)
401 MAN IN A TALL HAT (Widener Collection)
405 PORTRAIT OF A YOUNG MAN (Andrew Mellon Collection)
411 A MAN HOLDING GLOVES (Widener Collection)
412 A WOMAN HOLDING AN OSTRICH-FEATHER FAN (Widener
  Collection)

WHEREABOUTS UNKNOWN

18 THE MUSIC-MAKERS
28 SOLDIER IN A PLUMED CAP
40 SELF-PORTRAIT
143 YOUNG WOMAN WITH A GOLD CHAIN
150 PORTRAIT OF A YOUNG WOMAN
151 BEARDED MAN WITH A FLAT BROAD COLLAR
171 SELF-PORTRAIT
224 YOUNG GIRL
225 SCHOLAR AT HIS DESK
256 CHRIST

Index of Rembrandt Paintings

Mythology, Allegory, and History (See also Men in costume and Women in costume)

FIGURE PAINTINGS

Self-portraits

Children

Men

a. in costume; historical characters

General Index

524

Photographic acknowledgments

All the color reproductions in this book were made after original ektachromes taken expressly for this edition by André Held of Lausanne, with the following exceptions:
BERLIN-DAHLEM, W. Steinkopf: pp. 115, 125
THE HAGUE, A. Frequin: p. 17
MELBOURNE, Ritter-Jeppesen Pty.: p. 163
MUNICH, J. Remmer: pp. 13, 37, 43, 65, 81, 95, 143
NEW YORK, W. Suhr: p. 133
VIENNA, E. Meyer: p. 91
and the reproductions on pp. 53, 73, 82, 103, 107, 109, 111, 121, 153, 158, and 159, which were provided by the respective museums.

Black-and-white reproductions were made after photographs supplied by the owner, unless otherwise specified below. All photographs of objects in the Gemaeldegalerie and Kupferstichkabinett of the Staatliche Museen, Berlin-Dahlem, come from the atelier of W. Steinkopf. The publisher wishes to acknowledge a special debt of gratitude to Miss B. Stokhuyzen of the Rijksmuseum, Amsterdam, and Miss M. Korpershoek of the Rijksbureau voor Kunsthistorische Dokumentatie, The Hague, for their help in assembling photographic material.

AMSTERDAM, Gemeentemusea: pp. 461 c; 477 f
—, Lichtbeelden Instituut: pp. 30; 138
—, Karel Mayer: pp. 461 d, e; 481 e; 483 c, d
—, Rijksmuseum (and Rijksprentenkabinet): pp. 90 b; 142; 178 [10]; 180; 183 [16]; 203 [48]; 215 [61]; 225 a; 240 a; 247; 258 [104]; 279 [144]; 288 [164-5]; 317; 325 [220]; 335 [235]; 340 [240]; 351 [265]; 387; 389 [312]; 395 [322]; 399 [328]; 403; 427 [366]; 428 [367]; 436 [386]; 439 [391]; 441; 451 [413-4]; 454
—, Amsterdam University Library: p. 457 a
BRUSSELS, Koninklijk Instituut voor het Kunstpatrimonium: pp. 191 [25]; 333 [232]
CAMBRIDGE, ENGLAND, Stearns & Sons: p. 366 [280]
DRESDEN, Deutsche Fotothek: pp. 142; 233
DUBLIN, The Green Studio: p. 12
EDINBURGH, The Ideal Studio: p. 70 a
GENEVA, J. Arlaud: p. 405 [341]
GLASGOW, Annan: pp. 289 [167]; 299 [187]; 327 [223]; 341 [243]
GLENS FALLS, NEW YORK, Richard K. Dean: p. 428 [368]
GRONINGEN, Instituut voor Kunstgeschiedenis: p. 279 [143]
THE HAGUE, Dingjan: pp. 32; 36; 250; 455
—, A. Frequin: pp. 48; 58 b; 152
—, Gemeente museum: pp. 346 [255]; 472 c
—, Rijksbureau voor Kunsthistorische Dokumentatie: pp. 22 b; 24 b; 38 a, b; 40; 50; 54; 60; 68 a; 70 b; 90 b; 106; 124 a, b; 166; 186 [18]; 201 [40]; 215 [62]; 261 [113-4]; 279 [145]; 284 [155]; 289 [169]; 295 [179]; 367 [282]; 401 [333]; 409 b; 421 a; 436 [387]; 439 [392]; 440 [396]
HAMBURG, R. Kleinhempel: p. 14 b
INNSBRUCK, Demanega: p. 201 [42]
LA JOLLA, CALIFORNIA, John F. Waggaman: p. 379 [296]

LAUSANNE, André Held: pp. 162 b; 172; 173 [2]; 174 [4]; 175; 181; 182 [14]; 185; 187; 188 [22]; 189; 190; 192; 193 [27]; 195 [29-31]; 196 [32-3]; 197 [35]; 198 [36]; 200; 202 [44-5]; 205 [50]; 210; 216; 217; 218; 223; 225 [72]; 228 [75]; 230; 235; 236 [81]; 237 [82]; 238; 241; 243; 245; 246 [91]; 248; 251; 253 [98]; 254; 255 [100]; 258 [105]; 259 [106-7, 109]; 261 [111-2]; 262 [117]; 263; 264; 267 [125-6]; 268; 271; 276; 278; 280 [148]; 281 [152]; 284 [156]; 285 [157]; 290; 293; 295 [178]; 300; 303; 304 [193]; 305; 306; 307 [196]; 309 [200]; 312 [202]; 316; 318 [208]; 321 [212]; 322; 323 [216-7]; 324; 330; 331; 333 [233]; 337; 345 [251-2]; 347 [259]; 349 [263]; 352; 354; 358; 364; 369; 373; 374; 375; 377 [294]; 380; 383; 384 [305]; 385; 388 [310-1]; 397; 399 [327]; 400 [329]; 401 [334]; 408; 414; 419 [354]; 421 [356]; 423 [358]; 424; 426; 427 [363]; 430; 433 [377]; 435 [383-4]; 436 [385]; 437; 438; 439 [393]; 445 [404]; 446 [406]; 449; 452; 453 [416]
LEEDS, Pickard: p. 118 a
LEYDEN, N. van der Horst: pp. 458 c; 459 c, d, f, g, h
LIVERPOOL, Elsam, Mann & Cooper: p. 201 [41]
LONDON, Courtauld Institute: p. 213 [59]
—, John R. Freeman: pp. 203 [47]; 363 [276]
—, Leggatt Bros: p. 221 [68]
—, The National Gallery: p. 342
—, Sidney W. Newbery: p. 390
—, Phaidon Press, Ltd.: p. 297 [184]
—, Photo Studios, Ltd.: pp. 198 [37]; 275; 277 [139]; 285 [161]; 291 [172]; 344; 345 [253]; 376; 448
—, Sotheby: pp. 249 [94]; 281 [150]; 433 [379];
LOS ANGELES, D. Hatfield: p. 281 [151]
LUGANO, Brunel: pp. 194; 281 [149]
MELBOURNE, Ritter-Jeppesen Pty.: p. 179
NEW YORK, Guggenheim Museum: p. 436 [388]
—, Metropolitan Museum of Art: p. 274 [136]
—, F. Mont: p. 213 [58]
—, Rosenberg & Stiebel: p. 321 [214]
—, John D. Schiff: pp. 406; 440 [395]
—, Taylor & Dull: pp. 295 [180]; 297 [183]; 433 [378]
PARIS, Bulloz: p. 44 a
—, Caisse nationale des monuments historiques: p. 465 g
—, Laboratoire du musée du Louvre: p. 211
STOCKHOLM, Nationalmuseum: pp. 259 [108]; 384 [306]; 429 [370]
UTRECHT, Kunsthistorisch Instituut: p. 176 [8]
VERSAILLES, Service de la documentation photographique de la réunion des musées nationaux: pp. 188 a; 252 a; 334; 469 d
VIENNA, E. Schwenk: p. 394
—, Kunstverlag Wolfrum: pp. 291 [171]; 299 [188]; 328 [224-5]

COLOPHON: Typesetting: NV Drukkerij Bosch, Utrecht. Lithography: L. van Leer & Co. NV, Amsterdam. Printed by NV Drukkerij Bosch, Utrecht; Jan de Lange NV, Deventer; L. van Leer & Co. NV, Amsterdam. Paper: Leykam, Vienna. Ink: Sinclair & Valentine Co. NV, Soest. Bound by Proost & Brandt NV, Amsterdam.

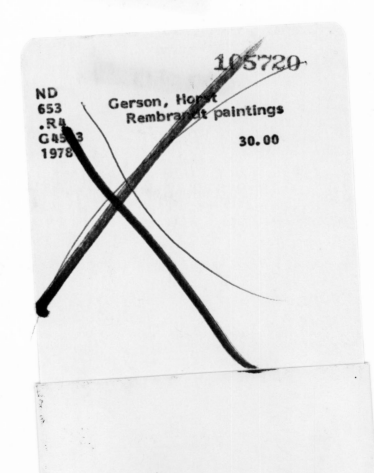